Stories from Medan, Volume 1

"What a lovely book, enhanced as it is by so many rare photographs. The auth should be congratulated. They have produced a fitting tribute to a fine city and cosmopolitan inhabitants both old and new. Filled with the historical detail t will interest scholars, Stories from Medan should also appeal to a broad, gene readership. I look forward to the next two volumes."

—Dr Michael R. Godley, author of *The Mandarin-Capita from Nanyang*, Aust

"The authors have assembled a surprising amount of information about Me history. It is an amazing tale of rapid colonial development and sometimes de in less than a century with Europeans and Chinese as leading figures. I am cert looking forward to the other side of the story and its people."

—Dr Mary Somers Hedhuis, author of *Southeast Chinese Minorities*, Ger

"Budiman Minasny and Dirk Aedsge Buiskool take the highly readable app of presenting Medan through stories of its inhabitants and visitors... The bo be of interest to both specialists in Indonesian or urban Southeast Asian h and general audiences who wish to expand their understanding of Indon will also be of interest to Chinese-background audiences in Southeast Asia, those teaching and researching in the field of the Nanyang or 'Overseas Chi

—Professor Adrian Vickers, The University of Sydney, author of *A of Modern Indonesia*, A

Budiman Minasny • Dirk Aedsge Buiskool

Stories from Medan, Volume 1

History, Society and Business

palgrave
macmillan

Budiman Minasny
Professor of Soil Science
The University of Sydney
Sydney, NSW, Australia

Dirk Aedsge Buiskool
Historian, Founder and co-director
P.T. Deli River Resort
Medan, North Sumatra Indonesia

ISBN 978-981-95-7706-4 ISBN 978-981-95-7707-1 (eBook)
https://doi.org/10.1007/978-981-95-7707-1

The print edition is not for sale in Singapore and Malaysia. Customers from Singapore and Malaysia please order the print book from: GB Gerakbudaya Enterprise Sdn Bhd. [ISBN of the Local Edition]

This Palgrave Macmillan imprint is published by the registered company Springer Nature Singapore Pte Ltd.
The registered company address is: 152 Beach Road, #21-01/04 Gateway East, Singapore 189721, Singapore

Preface

As authors of this book, we, Budiman and Dirk, share a deep connection with Medan, a city rich in history and culture. Budiman was born and raised in Medan, where the city's atmosphere shaped his early life and inspired a long-standing interest in its past. Dirk, a European history lecturer and entrepreneur, has called Medan home since 1990. His fascination with the city's history led him to extensive research in archives across the Netherlands and Indonesia, long before the digital era simplified such efforts.

Our collaboration began in 2020 with a shared passion for uncovering Medan's history, particularly the significant role of the Chinese community. This book represents the culmination of our research and discussions, offering a unique perspective on Medan's people and places that has received comparatively limited attention in English-language scholarship.

Medan, often overshadowed by more documented colonial towns like Batavia and Surabaya, has rich stories waiting to be told. While important scholarly work has been undertaken, particularly Dirk Buiskool's dissertation, much of Medan's past remains scattered across archives and family histories. Our aim is to bring together these fragments and present the lives of individuals who shaped the city and its surroundings. We do not seek to promote or romanticise colonial times, but merely to tell how the city has evolved, who shaped it, and who benefited from it or exploited it.

The digital age has greatly facilitated our research, enabling easy access to online archives in the Netherlands, Indonesia, Singapore, Australia, and elsewhere. We discovered a past life in Medan through historical newspapers, memoirs, and books. Digital tools like Google Translate and Large Language Models simplify translating and summarising historical documents.

This book, the first part of the *Stories from Medan*, explores the city's history, the Chinese quarter, and the businesses that flourished there. We aim to present a balanced account of the city's growth, acknowledging both its achievements and inequalities.

We extend our gratitude to the descendants of Medan's residents and numerous scholars who have generously shared materials, knowledge, and encouragement. Among those who are no more among us, we remember Mrs Lemye Tjong Sze-Yin (daughter of Tjong A Fie), Tan Boen Djin (son of Tan Tang Ho), Hiu Kian Jin (son of Hiu Ngi Fen), Jan de Knegt (son-in-law of Harm Kamerlingh Onnes), and Benjamin Kam (grandson of Jacob Herman Haas).

We are equally grateful to members of the present generation, Rebecca Chandra from the Tjong Yong Hian family; Mimi Tjong from the Tjong A Fie family; Emily Ruth Auw, daughter of Auw Pit Seng; Laura Lee Hüttenbach, Heinrich Hüttenbach's great-granddaughter; Suriadi Lau, Law Ah Yok's great-grandson; Peter Janssen, the great-great-grandson of P.W. Janssen; and Tammo Zijlker, great-grandson of Aeilko Jan Zijlker's brother, Hero Jan Zijlker. Andreas Zangger (University of Bern) provided information about Hermann Küng, and Holger Warnk (University of Frankfurt) provided information about the Hüttenbach family. Sumio Aoki (formerly Chubu University) and Masatoshi Ito (Nihon University) shared information on Japanese in Medan before the war. Ichwan Azhari (Universitas Negeri Medan) and Ulrich Kozok (University of Hawai'i) offered stimulating and, at times, provocative discussions. Suryadi (Universiteit Leiden) and Tom Hoogervorst (KITLV) provided archival materials that enriched this work. We thank Maarten Ryder for his careful proofreading. Thanks to Josh Stenberg (University of Sydney) for encouraging us to get the book published, Adrian Vickers for his support, and Mary Somers Heidhues for the constructive comments.

Finally, we dedicate this book to our families. Budiman dedicates this book to his father Ekoanto Leo, his mother Minasny, and his late brother Krismanlo, who all cherished Medan deeply. Budiman also dedicates this book to his family, Fang, Felix, and Clara. Dirk dedicates this work to his family, Diana, Roderick, and Frederick, for their unwavering support.

Together, we present *The Stories from Medan*, a record of the city's heritage and the many lives that have shaped its society.

Sydney, NSW, Australia Budiman Minasny
Medan, Indonesia Dirk Aedsge Buiskool

Introduction

Medan, the capital of North Sumatra, is a dynamic city renowned for its far-reaching trade networks across Southeast Asia and beyond. Known as the gateway to Sumatra's flourishing oil palm and rubber plantations, Medan conceals a rich and often overlooked history beneath its modern façade of skyscrapers, hotels, cafés, shopping centres, and crowded streets.

The city's transformation began in 1870, when Europeans capitalised on the lucrative Deli tobacco industry, using cheap Chinese and Javanese labour. In the decades that followed, petroleum exploration in North Sumatra, pioneered by Aeilko Zijlker and later developed by the Royal Dutch Petroleum Company, further stimulated economic expansion and attracted merchants eager to profit from new opportunities. By the early twentieth century, Medan had emerged as one of the most important commercial centres in the Dutch East Indies.

This first volume of *Stories from Medan* looks back to a time when the city was still taking shape, a frontier of swamps, estates, and ambition. It begins, quite naturally, with the people who first left written and visual records of its growth: the European and Chinese communities. Their presence dominates this volume not because they were the only actors in Medan's past, but because they built the administrative, commercial, and cultural structures through which early Medan entered recorded history. The tobacco planters, merchants, and entrepreneurs left a paper trail of news, photographs, and correspondence that defines the city's earliest archives.

Yet this is only one layer of a much deeper story. Long before plantations, North Sumatra's Indigenous societies sustained trade routes, kinship networks, and spiritual landscapes. Along the east coast, Malay polities such as Deli, Langkat, and Serdang negotiated land concessions and political arrangements with European entrepreneurs. In the highlands lived diverse Batak groups, including Toba, Karo, Simalungun, Angkola–Mandailing, and Pakpak/Dairi, whose institutions and histories shaped the wider region. Javanese migrants, Minangkabau traders, Mandailing scholars, Arab traders, Indian workers, Japanese settlers, and many others joined merchants, civil servants, clerks, teachers, workers, and craftsmen to form a cosmopolitan society.

Religious life reflected this diversity. Protestant and Catholic missionary networks, including the Rheinische Mission in Toba, Dutch Protestant and Capuchin missions, and American Methodists, operated alongside established Muslim communities from the Malay coast and Minangkabau uplands. Chinese Buddhist–Taoist temples, Indian Hindu congregations, and even a small Japanese Shinto circle formed part of Medan's spiritual landscape. These interactions of communities gave Medan a distinctly cosmopolitan character.

Unlike the well-documented colonial towns of Batavia and Penang, Medan's unique history, particularly its distinctive social and economic fabric born from the plantation industry, remains largely unexplored in historical literature. This opening volume tells how the city began, how a colonial settlement took root on the Deli plain, and how its fortunes were shaped by the ambitions and collisions of European planters, Chinese merchants, and local rulers. It focuses on its residents between 1870 and 1942, through stories drawn from historical records and personal interviews. The chapters that follow are portraits of builders of estates and railways, founders of newspapers and companies, lives whose private wagers helped create a city that would, in time, belong to many more than them. Read as vignettes, these stories also point to wider forces, the Suez Canal, World War I, global depressions, and modernisation in China that pressed upon Medan's streets and shaped its communities.

Digitised historical newspapers, magazines, and books have made it possible to reconstruct parts of history. Key sources include Delpher for Dutch newspapers, books and reports, Perpustakaan Nasional Republik Indonesia for Indonesian newspapers, the National Library of Singapore for Malaya and Singapore newspapers, and Trove for Australian news archives. Visual materials have been drawn from collections of the University of Leiden, the Tropenmuseum and Wereldmuseum, and the Geheugen van Nederland. Recent advances in generative AI and large language models have accelerated the translation of documents and the depiction of past conditions.

This first volume of our book is organised into three parts. The History and Society part narrates the history of Medan and the East Coast of Sumatra, which was developed in the late nineteenth century as a plantation city and plantation belt. It highlights the diverse communities living in the region: Dutch, Swiss, German, French, Indian, and Japanese. We also recount how the opening of the Suez Canal accelerated Sumatra's development. The second section examines the Chinese in Medan, from leaders such as Tjong Yong Hian and Tjong A Fie to rickshaw drivers. The third part relates to the rise and fall of European and Chinese businesses in the region. In the next volume, we will deal with stories of the coolies, the nationalist movement, arts and science, and more.

As a convention in this book, geographical locations in the Dutch or Netherlands Indies and other parts of Asia are referenced using the historical spellings and names of the period discussed. Laboean Deli refers to Labuhan Deli, Atjeh for Acheh, Batavia for Jakarta, etc. The term "Netherlands Indies" refers to the colonial polity that preceded the Republic of Indonesia (established in 1945). The term "Indigenous" is used here to translate the colonial legal category "Inlander", while recognising the limitations and historical specificity of that classification. Chinese personal and organisational names are generally presented in Hokkien spelling, followed where appropriate by Pinyin. Quotations in English or translated from Dutch or other languages are italicised.

Acknowledging that this collection is not exhaustive and may contain omissions or inaccuracies, we welcome comments and suggestions. Feedback can be sent to medan.kesawan@gmail.com, as we are committed to refining Medan's history.

Competing Interests The authors have no competing interests to declare that are relevant to the content of this manuscript.

Contents

List of Figures

List of Tables

PART I

History and Society

The white, fresh city of Medan, with its elegant, pristine buildings and villa districts, lies as if under a shower. This is never dirty, as Western rain can make a city and even nature. It does not turn into filthy city mud; it remains bathed earth. The stately foliage of coconut palms, the needle-like whirling of tamarisks, the broad, satiny paddle leaves of banana trees, all have become an intense green as if gold hides beneath the green. The cicadas in the trees emit their continuous jubilant cry. Lower down, the crickets fiddle on their sharp, happy violins and clatter with their castanets. The flowers—the pink and red hibiscus and waru, the yellow of the fragrant oleanders—are overwhelmed by the power of the water, but as soon as the rain stops, all the new buds will immediately bloom into new splendor, so that there is never death or decay. For it is the life-giving gods who have arranged and govern these moments in this nature, in this world.[1]

[1] Couperus, Louis. *Oostwaarts*, 1924: 36 (original text in Dutch).

CHAPTER 1

Medan, a Plantation City on the East Coast of Sumatra

The city of Medan was established in the 1860s, driven by the rise of large-scale plantations on the east coast of Sumatra. The Deli Maatschappij, a tobacco plantation company, chose to establish its headquarters in this *kampong*, transforming this small village into a colonial city.[1] Chinese and Javanese labourers were recruited to work on the plantations, reshaping the social structure of the region. Infrastructure such as roads, railways, telephone lines, and telegraph connections was built by the plantation group, attracting numerous international companies to settle in the city. While Europeans dominated the plantation economy, Chinese merchants largely managed the daily operations of Medan. Among them, Tjong A Fie, a Mandarin capitalist known as the informal king of Medan, stood out as a prominent figure. The development of Medan was driven by the collaboration of three main groups: European planters who established the plantations, the local Malay community under the Sultan, who owned the land, and Chinese entrepreneurs who managed the trade. A minority of Indian traders also contributed to the city's growth (Fig. 1.1).

[1] *Kampong* (Malay) means village.

B. Minasny, D. A. Buiskool, *Stories from Medan, Volume 1*,
https://doi.org/10.1007/978-981-95-7707-1_1

Fig. 1.1 Medan's post office around 1914 (Kleingrothe, KITLV 101136)

1.1 The Making of Medan

By the time Marco Polo sailed past the coast of Sumatra in 1292, Arab merchants had already brought Islam to its coasts. Three centuries later, the Portuguese arrived in search of pepper and control over the lucrative trade of the Straits of Malacca. They captured Melaka in 1511, connecting it to pepper ports such as Pedir in Atjeh and Indrapura in Siak. When the Dutch took Melaka in 1641, the Vereenigde Oost-Indische Compagnie or Dutch East India Company (VOC) expanded its network to Padang, Jambi, and Palembang, while power along Sumatra's east coast shifted among Atjehnese, Malay, and Minangkabau rulers. During this era, Johor crossed the strait, conquered the Aru kingdom, and established its seat at Deli Tua, just south of present-day Medan. Between 1619 and 1669, Deli, Asahan, and Langkat fell under Atjehnese rule, later gaining independence before being absorbed by Siak in 1780. Atjeh reasserted its claims in 1856, and Siak raised a Tengku Panglima of Deli to the rank of Sultan to strengthen its influence.[2]

[2] Buiskool 2025: 17–21.

Amid these shifting powers, a more local beginning took root. Karo tradition remembers Guru Patimpus Sembiring Pelawi, a leader who descended from the Karo highlands to settle in Kampong Medan Poetri in the late sixteenth century. This riverside settlement served as a bridge market between the Karo upland trade routes and the Malay coastal networks.[3]

By 1822, the Dutch had signed a trade treaty with Siak, forbidding other European powers from opening posts in the region. The British reacted quickly and sent a fact-finding mission in 1823. John Anderson sailed from Penang to Deli and wrote about its abundant natural resources. He noted villages along the Deli River, with Labuhan, a miserable assembly of small huts, and Meidan, a small village of about 200 souls. He also wrote about the remains of an older Chinese settlement near Labuhan Deli, known as Kota China.[4] The following year, the Anglo-Dutch Treaty of 1824 fixed the colonial spheres of influence: Britain retained Singapore, while the Dutch secured Sumatra.

Actual control, however, remained limited. For much of the nineteenth century, the Dutch held only Lampung and a few scattered coastal forts, while the interior remained largely autonomous. European writers still spoke vaguely of a vast lake in the Batak highlands, a region governed by its own institutions and sustained by selective trade with the coast, including the exchange of captives for firearms. In 1858, Dutch official Eliza Netscher brought Asahan, Batu Bara, Serdang, Deli, Langkat, and Tamiang under Siak's nominal authority, though in practice, the Sultan of Deli acknowledged Dutch power but resisted Siak's supremacy.[5]

By 1862, the east coast of Sumatra came under direct Dutch administration, and two years later, the first government representative, *Controleur* Baron J.A.M. Cats de Raet, established residence at Laboean Deli, near the river mouth. In 1876, he undertook a journey to the highland and described Medan as not even a *kampong*:

[3] The historical accuracy of the story is being debated.

[4] Anderson 1826: 273, 294.

[5] The Netherlands Indies territory was organised into three governorates—namely, the Great East, Borneo, and Sumatra—and three provinces within Java. Each province and governorate was further subdivided into residencies. Residencies within the provinces were divided into regencies (*Regentschappen*), while those within the governorates were divided into departments (*afdeelingen*). A Resident, with the assistance of an Assistant Resident, led a residency. A department or *afdeeling* was headed by an Assistant Resident, supported by a *Controleur*. An afdeeling could be further divided into subdivisions, or *onderafdelingen*, each overseen by a *Controleur* or Civil Administrator (Clemens & Lindblad 1989: 68).

> *We left Laboean, the main town of Deli, at 9 a.m., and arrived at Kampong Baroe at 5 p.m. We passed through Kampong Alaij, Gengah, Kampong Besar, Rautoe Blimbing, Mertoeboeng, Rengas Sambilan, Kotta Bangon, Ma Bar, Rengas Sekoepang, Poeloe Brayan, Gloegoer, Medan, Kesawan, and Tebing-Tinggi. Although these settlements bear the name of kampong, they cannot really be considered as such.*[6]

The Sultanate of Deli consisted of three main territorial components. First was the core Deli area around Laboean Deli, which was under the direct authority of the Sultan. Second was the *Soekoe*, comprising four federations of villages and called *oeroeng* in Karo, each ruled by a local leader called *Datoek*, *Orang Kaja*, or *Kejuruan*. The four *soekoes* were Serbanjaman, Sapoeloeh Doewa Kota, Soekapiring, and Senembah. Third was the territory or landscapes such as Pertjoet, Danai, Bedagei, and Padang. Territorial boundaries were defined largely by rivers, including the Deli, Sikambing, Selaijan, Karang, Barboera, and Bahala. Malay communities resided in *kampongs* under the authority of *datoeks* within the *soekoes*, whereas Batak populations lived separately in villages (*doesoens*) and were led by *panghoeloe* or *sebaija*. Medan was under Sapoeloeh Doewa Kota *soekoe*.[7]

In 1870, the Dutch abolished the *cultuurstelsel*, or forced cultivation system, which had compelled peasants to grow crops for the state. That same year, the Dutch Agrarian Law opened colonial lands to European private enterprise, allowing long-term leases. The end of the American Civil War created a surge in global demand for agricultural raw materials, drawing European investors to Sumatra's fertile lands. From these converging forces, colonial policy, global trade, and local initiative, Deli's great plantation era was born.[8]

1.1.1 *The Beginning of the Deli Plantation*

The Sultan of Deli Mahmoed Perkasa Alam Shah sought investors to develop and cultivate the land. In 1863, Said Abdulah Bilsagih, an Arab

[6] DC 08-07-1917.

[7] *Soekoe* (*suku*) or *Oeroeng* (*urung*) is a traditional socio-political unit or a tribal district. The four *sukus* in Malay/Karo are: Sunggal/Serbanaman, Hamparan Perak/Sepuluh Dua Kuta, Kampung Baru/Sukapiring, and Senemba (Uli Kozok, personal communication). Halewijn 1876: 147–152

[8] *Indische Gids* 1921, I: 320.

merchant claiming to be a prince from Deli, approached Java's tobacco trading houses with promises of monopolies from the Sultan of Deli in exchange for rewards and partnership. A couple of companies decided to pursue the venture, sending representatives, along with Jacobus Nienhuys for his tobacco expertise, to Deli.[9] Nienhuys and other Dutch traders arrived in Deli in 1863, but they were disappointed as there were no plantations, only jungle. Nevertheless, Nienhuys decided to stay and received permission from Sultan Mahmoed Perkasa Alam Shah to experiment with tobacco planting just south of Laboean Deli at the mouth of the Deli River. The first harvest was a disappointment, but the second harvest in 1865 proved that the tobacco was high quality and fetched a good price in the European market. As a result, Nienhuys sought ventures in the Netherlands and got the green light for further investments. The tobacco plants grew so well and were such a great success that, in a short time, many Europeans flocked to Deli and tried their luck. Deli tobacco leaves are thin, elastic, yet strong, *fijn als zijde* (fine as silk), excellent as a cigar wrapper, and known as the best in the world. Tobacco flourished so well due to the confluence of several factors, including fertile soil, optimal temperatures, altitude above sea level, rainfall, cloud cover, humidity, and sunshine. Large quantities of tobacco leaves were in demand in Europe and the United States.

Local labour was in short supply on the east coast of Sumatra as the native Malay and Batak populations were not interested in plantation work. The solution was to import the labour force. Nienhuys hired Chinese coolies (workers) from Penang to fill the workforce for tobacco planting. At this time, both China and Java were suffering from high unemployment, with concomitant poverty and hunger, so people from these places were easily swayed to work in the wilds of Sumatra. Eventually, recruitment took place directly from China, and over 300,000 workers were shipped to Sumatra between 1870 and 1930. Coolies began arriving from Java around 1900. Consequently, a substantial Chinese and Javanese population settled along Sumatra's east coast. Banjar people from East Borneo were recruited to build houses and bridges. Plantation workers were also recruited from the Indian coast of Coromandel. Most of these workers never returned to their homeland, and their offspring remained in Sumatra, creating a diverse community.

[9] Schadee 1918, I: 171.

The plantation companies in Deli were entirely export-oriented. They initially focused on tobacco production and later expanded into rubber and palm oil, while also producing tea, coffee, gambier, cacao, and other commodities for export. Investment was not limited to Dutch firms. European entrepreneurs from Switzerland, Germany, France, Britain, Denmark, Belgium, and the United States established plantations in Deli, each seeking opportunity in the rapidly expanding frontier economy. Labour for the plantations was drawn from across Asia. Chinese workers were recruited to clear and cultivate the land and to plant and tend crops. South Indian labourers constructed roads and became skilled cart drivers, while migrants from Bawean built plantation sheds and housing. Sikhs and Afghans were employed as guards and night watchmen. With few exceptions, everyone involved in the plantation economy, European investors, estate managers, and coolies alike, was a newcomer to the region.[10]

The Malay sultanates cooperated closely with the planters. Sultan Mahmoed Al Rasjid Perkasa Alam Sjah of Deli was the first to give concessions to Europeans. From then on, the Malay sultanates received large annual sums from the tobacco planters for their concessions. The three sultanates where the first plantations were established were Deli, Langkat, and Serdang. Starting in 1910, many rubber and oil palm plantations were established in the Asahan district.

In 1870, there were no hospitals, no medicines, no police, and no court of justice. Malaria, typhus, and cholera were rampant, with little or no medical care available. In response to the economic expansion, the Dutch Indies government sent an Assistant Residents to Deli to represent the government in the 1870s. The system mirrored that of the former VOC (Vereenigde Oost-Indische Compagnie or Dutch East India Company), where the Sultan ruled de facto, and the Dutch only represented the Batavia government. The planters negotiated directly with the Sultan, and land contracts between the Sultan and Europeans required approval from the Resident. This arrangement is a blend of local rule under the Sultan and oversight by the colonial government. In 1875, the population in the region of Deli and Serdang was as follows: Europeans 70, Arabs 5, Chinese 3979, Other Foreign Orientals 489, and Malays 11,963, a total of 16,506 people.[11]

[10] *Utrechtsche Courant* 02-07-1927.
[11] Halewijn 1876: 151.

Around 1880, the situation in Deli was comparable to America's Wild West. Outside the few domesticated centres, Medan, Tandjoeng Balei (150 kilometres south of Medan), and Bindjei (25 kilometres west of Medan), the landscape was sparsely populated, with only scattered settlements here and there. Herds of elephants roamed the plantations. When crocodiles caught people, the papers only reported if the crocodile had eaten more than two people.[12] Tigers were regularly reported in the papers. In addition, a war was going on in Atjeh, during which the Atjehnese launched attacks on European settlements both on land and at sea. Further, the Batak from the highlands regularly attacked the people in the lowlands. Chinese coolies, often in gangs, attacked and killed European assistants either due to abuse or due to discontent with payment. Europeans walked around with a revolver or rifle.

As in the American Wild West, heavy drinking was commonplace. Beer was the standard. In America, it was whiskey; in Deli, it was the Dutch liquor jenever. In the early years of the plantation industry, Deli was characterised by unregulated free enterprise. The new town of Medan became the centre of activity, and with the turn of the century, the city expanded rapidly.

1.1.2 Queen City

Medan is the queen city of the island of Sumatra, and is, moreover, the chief trading centre on the east coast, which is the most important and progressive quarter of the island. Until about 48 years ago the site was wild, virgin jungle. Today there exists a charming city, brisk and bustling in its business quarters, surrounded by pretty suburbs, with a sanitary system equal to that of any English town. It has two fine hotels, a railway station of handsome architecture, a racecourse, a palatial club, sports ground for football and lawn tennis, a cinema theatre, and all the modern attributes of an up to date centre. ...The place in its earlier days was known as Medan Poetri, which means, in the Malay tongue, the Square of the Princesses. ... the territory on which Medan now stands was private garden for the use of the daughters of the Sultans of Deli and the recreation ground upon which they played. The square now has its beauties heightened by the fashionable costumes of the ladies of Medan; in the morning equestrians and equestriennes trot or canter round it; at night a band plays cheerful music, and altogether, Medan is a very pleasant place, a joy for ever.[13]

[12] Kam 1995: 26.
[13] Feldwick 1917: 1185.

Fig. 1.2 The early establishment of Medan with the Esplanade and the railway station, A view from Hotel de Vink, taken in 1886. (Stafhell and Kleingrothe, KITLV 111125)

That quote is from Feldwick's *Present Day Impressions of The Far East* in 1917. The same source also mentions that the name Medan was derived from the Hindustani word *Maidan*, which means an open space or park.[14] The backbone of Medan's city structure was established in the 1880s and is still visible today.[15] In the year 1880, the open plain near the Deli company head office was made a central square, surrounded by major roads and named the Esplanade. This was the centre of the town, from which other areas expanded. After Indonesian independence, the square was named Lapangan Merdeka or the Independence Square (Fig. 1.2).

Medan got its first layout around 1870 when Kampong Medan Poetri—the Land of the Princess—and Kampong Kesawan joined. Laboean Deli, at the mouth of the Deli River, where the Sultan of Deli initially resided and where the first tobacco was planted, was a swampy area prone to

[14] Feldwick 1917: 1180.
[15] Passchier 1993: 314.

malaria and unsuitable as the administrative centre for the plantations. Therefore, the planters chose the more inland settlement of Medan as a strategic base for its administration.[16] The institutional foundation had been laid in 1869, when the Deli Maatschappij (Deli Company) was established by G.C. Clemen, P.W. Janssen, and J. Nienhuys with the Netherlands Trading Company as its main shareholder.[17]

In 1871, Jacob Theodoor Cremer from the Netherlands Trading Company succeeded Nienhuys, who was repatriated to Europe. A rudimentary office of the Deli Company was built in Medan Poetri, at the junction of the Baboera and the Deli River. The early years were harsh. In November 1874, Cremer made an announcement in *Bataviaasch Handelsblad* on the birth of his son.[18] Eight months later, he announced the death of his son.[19] The condition was very grim, but slowly, Medan began to develop.

Medan became the seat of the Resident in 1886, and in 1889, the Sultan of Deli chose Medan as his residence and built his new Maimoon Palace on the city's southern border. In the same period, Chinese traders settled in Medan. The wooden office of the Deli Maatschappij was completed in 1898 at the end of Deli-laan. The road was subsequently widened and renamed Deli Maatschappij-weg (now Jl. Tembakau Deli). Later, the complex was expanded with a new main office building and the principal administrator's residence, designed by the company's architect, Colijn.

In its early years, Medan consisted mainly of the Deli Maatschappij settlement, the railway company, and the Kesawan shopping area. The city centre was located in the central square, known as the Esplanade. Urban infrastructure slowly followed. Most of the European population resided on the west side of the Esplanade. Later, the Polonia villa quarter was established there. On the south side of the Esplanade, around Kesawan, the oldest street in the city, a Chinatown was established. Further south, a Malay village was located near the Sultan's palace. Additionally, there was a quarter for the Indian community, known as Kampong Kling or Kampong Madras. The Deli Spoorweg Maatschappij or Deli Railroad Company had its own area as it built its head office and houses for its personnel along the railroad east of the Esplanade.

[16] Naudin ten Cate 1905: 41.

[17] Nederlandsche Handel-Maatschappij, now ABN AMRO, Schadee 1918: 181.

[18] *Bataviaasch Handelsblad* 27-11-1874.

[19] *De Locomotief* 01-12-1874; 09-07-1875.

Coming out of the station building, one sees before one a large esplanade, which, if well maintained, provides a beautiful sight. Around the esplanade are some neat private houses, the White Society, the Medan hotel and the military canteen. The houses here are not built so close together as in the large towns on Java; each house stands alone, and makes a pleasant impression through its order and neatness. The floor of most houses is a little above the ground, the view of the damp terrain, while most have two floors.[20]

From the beginning, Medan was planned as a modern town with parks, a European villa quarter, and separate areas for the Indigenous, Chinese, and Indian populations. This was the result of the so-called quarter system; the colonial government required each population group to reside in its own quarter. If, for instance, a Chinese person wanted to leave their area, a pass was required, which they had to obtain from their headman, i.e. the Chinese *kapitan* or captain. The segregation occurred naturally, as people from the same country tended to settle in the same areas. Over time, they were eventually required to live in those designated areas. Segregation was spontaneous, yet at the same time, it was obligatory. The quarter system made the city a clearly structured place. This system was abolished in 1918; however, the social structure had already been established. [21]

Medan expanded rapidly from 1880, with the development of Malay, Chinese, Indian, and European quarters. Because of the large European villa area, the town became a sort of garden city, called *Parijs van Sumatra* (Paris of Sumatra). Multi-ethnic interactions characterised the city as the different population groups lived side by side. The Indonesians and Europeans bought from Chinese shops, and the Chinese from European importers. There was a small Indian population; some were cloth merchants, others were ox drivers, and others kept cows and sold milk. There were also Chetty moneylenders.

The Dutch East Indies had a plural legal system: Europeans and assimilated foreigners followed Dutch-style civil law; Indigenous and Foreign Orientals (i.e. Chinese, Arabs, Indians) followed *adatrecht* or personal status law. Under *adatrecht*, land was not privately owned but held communally or granted as use rights, with sovereignty typically claimed by local rulers (*Zelfbesturen*).

[20] *De Locomotief* 05-11-1887.
[21] Cator 1936: 33.

The land of Medan was, in principle, owned by the *Zelfbestuurders* (self-government), the Sultan of Deli. The Sultan granted planters rights of use through long-term concessions, while ultimate ownership of the land remained with the sultanate. Under the Agrarian Law of 1870, Europeans and so-called Foreign Orientals (including Chinese and Indians) were not permitted to obtain full landed property rights. In principle, only Indigenous inhabitants could acquire land ownership. Exceptions were limited to small parcels intended for village use or the public interest.

Land in Medan was generally held under grant rights derived from *adatrecht* (customary law). A grant primarily conferred a right of use—most commonly for housing construction—without transferring ownership. It created a *sui generis* legal title for a fixed term, typically 50, 75, or 100 years. Various forms existed, including *controleur* grants (issued by the district officer) and Sultan's grants. These were registered in public records and later administered through the Sultan's office or the local court of justice. There were also sub-grants issued by the Deli Maatschappij. Although the original grants to the company had been issued by the Sultan, they were not transferable to third parties. Because Europeans and Foreign Orientals were officially barred from purchasing grants directly, a legal modification was introduced in 1909: local holders could transfer their grants to the government. The government could then sell this land to private individuals, including Europeans and Chinese. A further legal conversion followed in 1916, allowing land to be held under *opstal* (building and planting rights) or *erfpacht* (long-term leasehold).

There were exceptions, for example, in 1899, Tjong Yong Hian and Tjong A Fie were granted full rights by the Sultan for parcels of land in Kesawan. In 1918, the sultans of Deli and Serdang transferred land free of charge to the municipality of Medan. From that point onwards, substantial portions of Medan's land formally came under municipal control. This enabled urban improvements, including village upgrading, expansion of the Polonia residential quarter, and the development of the industrial area in Gloegoer. Outside Sumatra, this grant system existed only in a few other regions under strong self-governing authority, notably Yogyakarta and Surakarta (Solo). In modified form, elements of this system continue to exist today.

Around the turn of the twentieth century, Medan became a modern city. In 1885, the railway station on the Esplanade was constructed, and in 1887, a clubhouse, the Witte Sociëteit, was built. The first bank in Medan was the Chartered Bank of India, Australia and China, which opened its branch in Medan in 1887. In the years that followed, many more businesses and buildings emerged, including the town hall and Java Bank. In 1897, an electricity company was established, and in 1905, the Ajer Bersih water company began to supply tap water in households. Telephone and telegraph connections, along with a railway, connected Medan to the coast and the interior.

Modernisation was to be seen in all aspects, for example, the luxurious Hotel de Boer. The construction of the Hotel de Boer began in 1898, and very quickly became famous in the Dutch Indies.[22] Madelon Székely Lulofs, wife of the Hungarian author László Székely, published her semi-autobiographical novel *Rubber* in 1935 about plantation life in the 1920s. She wrote:

> *The principal hotel of Medan, Hotel de Boer, was situated at a wide grass field, around which went a broad asphalt promenade. The main building had two stories. Downstairs were the dance hall and the dining room, with a large terrace. Upstairs were bedrooms. On either side of the main building stood a pavilion, two long rows of bedrooms each with its veranda and its bathroom. The annexes were joined to the main building by a roofed cement path. Between the main building and the pavilions lay a strip of garden, a path, and a strip of grass.*[23]

Hotel de Boer also introduced the "mosquito-free room" with wire gauze surrounding the bed, thus creating a bedroom within a bedroom (Fig. 1.3). This was mentioned in Wright's *Twentieth Century Impressions of the Netherlands Indies* published in 1909:

> *These bedrooms are a novelty in Eastern hotel life, quite unlike anything to be found either at Batavia, Singapore or Colombo. The old fashioned mosquito curtains give place to a wire gauze frame, which is perfectly insect proof, and makes sleep the comfort it ought to be.* [24]

The first hotel in Medan, Hotel Medan, was established in 1887 on the opposite side of the Esplanade. Hotel de Boer and Hotel Medan were the settings for festivities with heavy drinking during the *Hari Besar* (day off) twice a month, when the European planters came to town. The Grand Hotel Medan appeared in Ladislao Székely's novel *Tropic Fever*:

[22] Wright 1909: 576.
[23] Székely Lulofs 1932: 31.
[24] Wright 1909: 576.

Fig. 1.3 The room within a room, a feature of the room of Hotel de Boer (Tropenmuseum 10013649)

Briskly we turned in before a curious building: it was the hotel. …In front a hall. No, not really a hall, only a roof built on wooden pillars; the hall had no walls, doors or windows. To right and left of it were two equally incomplete halls. One was the billiard room, the other the dining room. In the centre two semi-circular counters, one of them the bar, behind which a Chinaman with the face of Buddha, sat between countless bottles of various colours and sizes, waiting with mute seriousness for orders. Behind the desk an absolutely identical looking Chinaman was entering the names of the new arrivals in a large book.

This group of buildings was connected by a walk covered with zinc plate, with two others, long and on level ground. In these buildings were the hotel rooms. In front of each room was a veranda and behind each room a bathroom.

…

Nervously we stood in the centre of this strange room. The furniture consisted of a table, a wardrobe and two curious, somewhat alarming objects: enormous frames, a metre wide and two long, and one and a half metre in height, of thin white netting. "What can that be? Mass coffins?… Cautiously, on tiptoe, we approached one of the enigmatic objects. We searched round and felt it, and at

> *last we discovered what it was. Pulling back the flimsy material, we saw a mattress covered with white sheet, while two hard-stuffed little pillows and a large white sausage were lying inside the frame. "A bed", Peter declared. "The white covering is a mosquito-netting, but whatever is that large funny sausage?"*[25]

Székely's novel *Tropic Fever* was set around 1913. Then, many of the buildings surrounding the Esplanade, which give the centre its present character, were already built. The town hall was completed in 1909, followed by the Javasche Bank (Java Bank) in the same year, the new head office of the Deli Company in 1910, and the post office in 1911. Due to the rapid growth of the Dutch Indies' government, many new buildings were needed to accommodate the diverse range of government services, including schools, jails, and post offices. Next to the post office was the building of Witte Sociëteit, the White Club, which was demolished in the 1970s. On the west side of the Esplanade was the Java Bank, designed and built by the Architectural and Engineering Firm Hulswit, Fermont and Cuypers in 1910.

One of the finest buildings on the Esplanade was the office of the British plantation company Harrisons & Crosfield, built in 1911, on the corner of the Kesawan and the Esplanade. The Harrisons & Crosfield office was named the Juliana building after the Dutch princess Juliana, born in 1909. It was the first building in Sumatra to have an elevator. The main buildings of the city were all located on the Esplanade. This was the prestigious centre of the modern town of Medan, reflecting the success of the plantation industry.

Medan became an official municipality on April 1, 1909. At that time, development beyond the railway line was still minimal. Expansion began around 1910 with new streets in the Chinese quarter, followed by asphalted roads, a slaughterhouse, and the Oranje cinema in 1913. In the

[25] Székely 1937: 31–33. The white sausage is a *guling* or Dutch wife. A *guling* is a long pillow or bolster that is placed between the knees to keep one cool. The first report was by medical doctor M.J.E. Muller in Semarang who wrote in 1845 *Tijdschrift van Nederiandsch-Indië*: *The strangest thing about the bed is the "bantal goeling," a long, round, stiff pillow filled with kapok, which the sleeper takes between their legs and embraces with one arm. Indeed, it contributes so much to a cool and comfortable position that it is adopted as a habit by people of all classes, nationalities, and both sexes* (*De Avondpost* 17-07-1935). It is also called a Dutch wife by the English; apparently the first Dutch colonials came without a wife and the *guling* was a kind of substitute.

Table 1.1 Population of Medan from 1892 to 1938

	1892	*1900*	*1905*	*1912*	*1915*	*1920*	*1930*	*1938*
Indigenous	3328	3129	2191	13,257	17,300	23,823	40,096	41,270
Chinese	6261	7745	6397	10,997	13,650	15,916	27,180	27,287
Other Foreign Orientals, incl. Arabs, and Indians	23 + 776	1301	3708	1318	3360	2381	3408	3734
Europeans	334	549	954	1408	1970	3128	4292	4293
Total	12,924	12,724	13,250	26,980	36,280	45,428	74,976	76,584

Source: *Regerings-almanak voor Nederlandsch-Indië* 1894; Reclame 1903–1904, *Verslag Handelsvereeniging Medan*, 1912: 9; *Pinang Gazette and Straits Chronicle* 23-05-1916; *Volkstelling* 1930; *Het nieuws van den dag voor Nederlandsch-Indië* 14-12-1934; DC 29-04-1938

northern part, a new industrial area, Gloegoer, was established in 1915. The Kampong Kling area expanded in 1917.

Between 1922 and 1930, Medan experienced rapid expansion in all directions (Table 1.1). Municipal housing projects improved kampong infrastructure, new road networks were laid out, and key public works such as the sewer system, the Centrale Passar, and the municipal hospital were established. Major development in the Polonia district only began around 1928, transforming former tobacco land into a prestigious residential quarter within a few years. In the 1930s, social housing was realised in Medan Baroe.[26]

1.1.3 Connections and Transportation

From the original capital Laboean Deli, the Deli Company built a road to Medan. The roads were rudimentary, suitable only for ox carts. Other plantations relied on *sampans* (small boats) for transportation along the rivers. The Europeans mostly travelled on horseback. The oxen were imported from British India, and Indian ox drivers were subsequently hired. In 1881, Cremer initiated the establishment of the Deli Spoorweg Maatschappij (Deli Railroad Company) or DSM for the transportation of tobacco from the plantations to the harbour. Construction commenced in October 1883. Three years later, the first line, Laboean–Medan, was

[26] SP 15-08-1938.

opened in July 1886, and in February 1888, the line Laboean–Belawan was finalised. However, the construction environment proved perilous due to its remoteness and the widespread disease. All workers and materials had to be transported from distant locations and Chinese workers were contracted. There were cholera outbreaks in 1884 and 1885, and all the time, malaria claimed many victims. After the Belawan line was completed, the lines extended from Medan far into the districts of Serdang and Langkat. In the years after, narrow-gauge railroads for locomotives were constructed to connect plantations in Deli, Langkat, and Serdang.[27] Today, remnants of the gauge railroads can still be found around Medan, but they are no longer in use; in some areas, houses were even built over them. In 1916, the DSM extended the Tebing Tinggi-Pematang Siantar line, whereby tea from plantations around Siantar could be transported to Belawan.[28] The railroad extension from Kisaran to Rantau Prapat was completed in 1929.

With the construction of the railway, the DSM also installed telephone lines along the railway. In 1887, a government telegraph line was finished from Medan to the west coast. The post office in Medan became the post and telegraph office. As telegraph lines went long distances through the jungle, many elephants living in the area enjoyed uprooting the telegraph poles, causing disturbances in the telegraph connection. In 1891, a telegraph connection was established between Medan and Penang, linking Medan to the world's telegraph traffic.[29]

The first automobile, a steam car of the Tengkoe Besar of Deli, appeared in 1900.[30] In 1907, J.T. Cremer, for the first time, took a ride to Brastagi in the Batak highlands with two Spyker cars over a road that was still under construction.[31]

For shipping tobacco to Europe, the harbours had to be improved. The first harbour was Laboean Deli, but after a few years, the planters chose a new harbour near the island of Belawan, a few kilometres north. In 1923, Belawan was equipped with an ocean harbour, after which steamers could directly enter the harbour.[32]

[27] Naudin 1905: 32; Schadee 1918, II: 228.
[28] *Tabak en Deli* (MvO). Article about Deli and Serdang. KIT 689.
[29] Schadee 1918: II, 231–232.
[30] Schadee 1918: 194, 235, 239.
[31] Cremer, *Eigen Haard*, April 1907, no. 16.
[32] Schadee 1918, II: 239.

1.1.4 Plantations Around Medan

Medan was once surrounded by tobacco plantations, many of which have since been absorbed into the modern city. The names of these estates often reflect the international origins of their founding investors (Fig. 1.4). To the east of the town lay the Medan Estate, a property of the Deli Maatschappij, which dominated plantation ownership in the region. Deli Maatschappij owned Anniedale in Pulo Brayan and Vesuvius (named after the Italian volcano) in Tandjong Sepassei. West of the city, near Soengei Kriauw, stood the Rotterdam plantation—named after the Dutch port where the first batch of tobacco was auctioned but operated by German planters Ritgen and Cramer. Further west in Kampong Lalang was the Enterprise Estate, established by the British planter Thomsen.

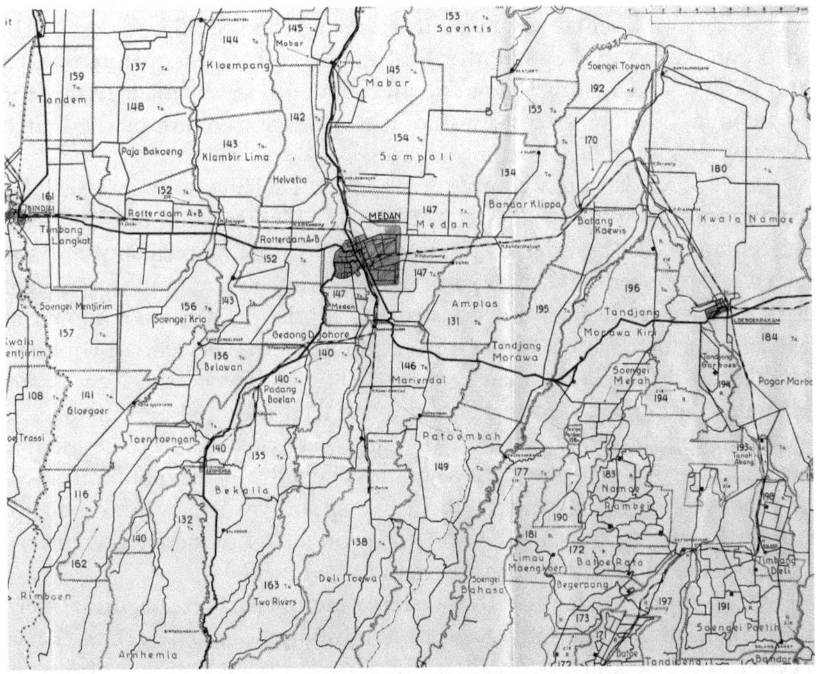

Fig. 1.4 Plantations surrounding Medan around 1940 (Voorlopige overzichtskaart van de cultuur ondernemingen Sumatra's Oostkust naar gegevens v.d. Afd. Ondern. Landbouw Dept. E.Z. en Geografisch Instituut v.d. Top. Dienst - sheet 1, KITLV, KK 066-05-04/05)

In the north, along the Deli River, stood Arendsburg, named after one of the first Dutch planters, Van den Arend, and Persévérance, meaning persistence in French. West of the Deli River were the Mabar and Sampali estates. Sampali (or Sempali), established in 1889 by the Deli Company, occupied the grounds of the former Petersburg estate, established in 1874 and named after the Russian city of Saint Petersburg. As early as 1865, the German planter Von Mach, along with Swiss planters Mots and Breker, settled in Deli. Mots and Breker founded the Königsgrätz plantation east of the Deli River, later renamed Helvetia—the Latin name for Switzerland. Nearby were the Germania estate, named after Germany, and Danemark, founded by the Danish planter Carl Gamborg. Saëntis, named after a mountain in the Swiss Alps, was established by the Swiss planter Hermann Küng. North of Helvetia was Maryland, locally known as Marelan, which was owned by another Swiss, Krüsi, who named the estate after his wife, Mary. Afterwards, Krüsi and Kaufmann established the Bavaria estate. In the same area were the estates of Kloempang by the Swiss planters Peijer and Gülich, and Klambir Lima. Soengei Sikambing was managed by the Frenchman de Guigné, and south of it was Charlottenburg by the Dutch Weduwe (widow). Nederveem Pieterse.[33]

South of Medan's city centre, between the Deli and Baboera rivers, lay the Polonia plantation, founded by the Polish planter Michalsky. In 1919, the Sultan of Deli transferred this concession to the municipality, and the area was developed into a villa park for the European community. Adjacent to the park, an airfield was constructed in the 1920s, later known as Medan's former Polonia Airport. Continuing south was Gedong Djohore, established by the Dutchman Leyssius, who also owned the New Rivers plantation in Stabat. Gedong Djohore was later acquired by Deli-Batavia Maatschappij, but in the 1990s, the land was converted into residential housing. Further south was the plantation Two Rivers, named for its location between the Deli and Baboera rivers, and owned by Baron Band. Locally known as Trepes, it became the ground of Indonesian revolutionary fighters against the British forces in December 1945.

Still south of Medan, on the western side of the Baboera River, were the plantations Soengei Sipoet and Rudolphsburg, founded by the German Pechul. Rudolphsburg was named after Crown Prince Rudolph of Austria (1858–1889) and was later renamed Padang Boelan. In the 1960s, the

[33] Schadee 1918, I: 179.

campus of the University of North Sumatra (Universitas Sumatera Utara, USU) was built on these plantation lands. Continuing south and towards the Karo highland were Bekalla and Arnhemia. J. van der Sluis, former manager of Padang Boelan, founded his own enterprise, Bleckmann & Co., named after his wife. She was from Arnhem, which inspired the name Arnhemia for the plantation. Nearby, van der Sluis also established a plantation called Saint Cyr, named after the French military academy his son attended. Over time, ownership of these plantations changed hands. Arnhemia was eventually acquired by the Rotterdam Deli Company. Today, the area is known by its local name, Pancur Batu, located about 15 kilometres south of Medan on the road to Brastagi.

In the southeast of Medan, in the Serdang district between the Pertjoet and Batang Koewis rivers, the Amplas plantation was developed by the Swiss planter Hüber and later sold to the Amsterdam Deli Company. Adjacent to it was the Mariëndal plantation, established in 1872 and named after an estate near Arnhem in the Netherlands. South of Amplas was Patoembah, established by German Näher and the Swiss Grob. They also owned Tandjong Morawa, which was east of Batang Koewis. The plantations were part of the Senembah Company. Tandjong Morawa was the first tobacco plantation in Serdang and now serves as the headquarters of PTP II (Perseroan Terbatas Perkebunan II), one of Indonesia's state-owned plantation companies. Kuala Namu, now the site of the international airport, was originally the Kwala Namoe tobacco plantation, established in 1888 and incorporated into the Senembah Company in 1920.[34]

By 1872, there were 13 plantations established in Deli, with only one each in Langkat and Serdang. As land in Deli became increasingly occupied, European planters began expanding into Serdang and Langkat. Notably in Serdang, the Scotsman MacIntyre established the Glenorchy estate along the Soengei Galang. In Serdang's Kampong Baroe, McEwen and Johnston founded the Kotozan estate, while Otzen and Thomsen developed the Reliance estate in Oeloe Serdang. The Dutch C. Rodijk established Constantia, Reliance, and Wenholt estates.[35] The German

[34] Janssen and Bool 1939: 47. Initially plantations were given European names; as the Malay and Chinese were often confused by these names, they simply named the plantations after the nearby river or *kampong*, or after a peculiarity in the terrain, and the planters followed suit. Since the 1880s, Malay names were used for plantations (*Opregte Haarlemsche Courant* 14-02-1883).

[35] *Koloniaal Verslag* 1877, 1879.

Hüttenbach company had several plantations in Serdang, including Ludwisburg and Augustburg (named after their founders Ludwig and August) in Stabat, Frankfurt (later called Bobongan) and Bengabing in Perbaoengan. Nearby were Fortuna by Leyssius, and Esperance by Van der Sluijs.

British capital was primarily concentrated in Langkat, making the region notable for its British presence. British Douglas and Polish Nowinski established the Glen-Bervie estate, which later became a rubber plantation and was absorbed by the Anglo-Dutch Estates. Other major firms were the United Langkat Plantations Company, Shanghai Sumatra Tobacco Company, the London Langkat Syndicate, and the British Deli and Langkat Tobacco Company. By 1890, more than 170 plantations were established along Sumatra's east coast, but this number declined following a crash caused by overproduction and market saturation.[36]

1.2 Entrepreneurs

The Chinese played a crucial role in Medan's economy by engaging in intermediate trade, establishing retail businesses, and acting as middlemen between European wholesalers and the local Indigenous population. This was essentially the classic structure throughout the Dutch Indies. Some of the Chinese in Medan were former plantation workers; the majority, however, came directly from China. In due time, their family members came over and settled in Medan. The most famous Chinese of Medan were the Tjong brothers.

A huge labour force was needed for the plantations. For this reason, Chinese from China were recruited to work as plantation workers or coolies. Between 1870 and 1933, about 300,000 Chinese moved to Deli. Key figures in charge of the Chinese population were the brothers Tjong Yong Hian (1850–1911) and Tjong A Fie (1860–1921), originally from Meixian, Guangdong.[37] While the Dutch held dominance over the plantation industry, Tjong A Fie's influence was in land and housing. In 1921, he owned, according to several sources, about 75% of the real estate of the fast-growing city of Medan and practically the whole newly built city of Tebing Tinggi.[38] He had interests in the Parapat and Medan hotels and,

[36] Loderichs et al. 1999: 14; *Koloniaal Verslag* 1887, 1918.
[37] Bool 1918: 6; de Bruin, 1918: 45, 109; Buiskool 1999: 23–28.
[38] Buiskool 1999: 32,68,74,76.

from 1906, was the first Chinese in Sumatra who owned plantations. Their diverse businesses operated under the Chong Lee Company.[39]

The Tjong brothers both served as Chinese officers, the official representatives of the Chinese in Deli. The Dutch government appointed these officers, from the rank of lieutenant to major, selected from successful individuals who enjoyed respect and status in their community. Thanks to the facilities provided by the government and their business acumen, the Tjong brothers managed to build an immense fortune in real estate, hotels, banks, plantations, palm oil and sugar factories, and even the railway line in South China. Together with the appointment as Chinese officers came commercial privileges. They were involved in supplying plantations and mediated in the recruitment of coolies from China. It was not long before they became the official suppliers of crucial products such as sugar and opium. Until 1918, the Dutch government sold monopolies to the highest bidder, mostly to wealthy Chinese traders. Tjong A Fie acquired the opium monopoly over the east coast of Sumatra and made a fortune. As Chinese officers, the brothers knew the city planning of Medan in advance, bought the adjacent land, and built rows of houses in a Chinese-European style.[40] In 1886, they established a meat market, followed by a fish market in 1887 and a vegetable market in 1906. The profits from these markets were used to fund the Chinese hospital Tjie On Djie Jan.[41] After Tjong Yong Hian died in 1911, Tjong A Fie succeeded as the Chinese major and thus became the leading representative of the Chinese on Sumatra's East Coast.[42]

In most of their business ventures—including revenue farming (monopolies), shipping, and banking—they collaborated closely with their uncle, Thio Tiauw Siat, who had strong connections with Singapore and Penang. Their most significant joint enterprise was the Swatow railway project. Well before the abolition of the revenue farm system on Sumatra's east coast in 1918, Tjong A Fie had already begun investing in plantations. He purchased his first estate in 1908, and by 1919, he owned nearly 20. For the management of these estates, Tjong A Fie employed the Dutchman

[39] *Handboek van Cultuur- en Handelsondernemingen in Nederlandsch-Indië* 1916: 1414; *Handboek* 1919: 1699; Wright, 1909: 576.

[40] Li Songyan 1984: 183–202, 1984, *Soerabaiasch Handelsblad* 19-04-1921.

[41] *Memorie van overgave* (MvO), Mayor Mackay of Medan, 1933: 106–109; SP 10-9-1918, 25-9-1918.

[42] SP 13-9-1916; DC: 4-2-1921; Kühr 1921: 3-5; De Bruin 1918: 111.

Dolf Kamerlingh Onnes.[43] After Thio Tiauw Siat's death in 1916, Tjong A Fie established the Batavia Bank together with Batavia Chinese major Khouw Kim An.

Tjong A Fie was also renowned for his philanthropy. He funded the construction of schools, bridges, Chinese temples, mosques, churches, and hospitals across Sumatra, Malaya, and China. Through his vast wealth and charitable contributions, he became a legendary figure in his lifetime. No other individual in Medan's history is known to have contributed as extensively to public welfare initiatives. His generosity earned him widespread respect across ethnic communities, including Indonesians, Indians, Dutch, and Chinese.

To mark the 30th anniversary of his service as a Chinese officer, the city of Medan held three days of celebrations featuring fireworks, processions, and communal feasts. The festivities involved all segments of the population, making it a truly multi-ethnic event. The jubilee highlighted the spirit of inter-ethnic harmony and Tjong A Fie's role as a unifying figure. His influence extended beyond economics; he served as a civic leader who fostered cooperation among Medan's diverse communities.

Another important entrepreneur in real estate was Tjong A Fie's successor as the Chinese major, Khoe Tjin Tek. Although he was not as high-profile as Tjong A Fie, by the time he became a major, he had already amassed a fortune through his wood-trading and construction firms. Khoe Tjin Tek's Chung Hwa Shang Yeh bank became one of the leading banks in the city.[44] Just like the Tjong brothers and other leading Chinese entrepreneurs, Khoe Tjin Tek invested in monopolies such as the gambling farm. Khoe Tjin Tek was the last Chinese major of Medan. His function ended with the Japanese invasion in 1942.

Not only did the Chinese become prominent in real estate, but some Indian entrepreneurs also rose to success. The best example was the brothers Hakam and Gurdit Singh, who started real estate projects in the Indian quarter with the help of the Sultan of Deli. Later on, they cooperated with Tjong A Fie on building housing projects. Hakam and Gurdit Singh also actively promoted Medan to their fellow Indian compatriots. They invited Indian families from Punjab to Deli to settle in Medan, gave them land and some cows, and stimulated the establishment of an Indian community in Medan.[45]

[43] SP 18-10, 21-10 and 26-10-1918.

[44] Vleming 1925: 230; Lim Ren Huan 1964, 146–152; Wright 1909, 581.

[45] Information from Mrs. Miki Singh, Medan. October 2003.

1.2.1 Companies

If we examine Medan's companies, we see a diverse range of enterprises from different nationalities. This reflects the international character of the town. In 1890, the Netherlands Trading Company, the most important Dutch trading company, opened a sub-agency in the city. The German firm Hüttenbach & Co., established in 1875 as the first trading house in Medan, was the oldest European business organisation on Sumatra's east coast. The firm also owned plantations and was actively involved in selling various products, including insurance, textiles, food, and beverages. Hüttenbach & Co. also operated the retail store Medan's Warenhuis.[46] There were Dutch companies, such as Nolte & Haas, which later became the Deli-Atjeh company. There were also companies selling luxury items, including Austrian W. Cornfield and German Goldenberg & Zeitlin and S. Katz & Co. The largest Chinese companies were Soei Tek Bie, owned by the Chinese businessman Wee Swee Boo (Oei Soei Boe); Chong Lee & Co., owned by the Tjong brothers; and Seng Hap, owned by Tan Tang Ho. Dutch company Van Nie & Co., established in 1885, was an agent of the shipping firm the KPM (Koninklijke Paketvaart Maatschappij) or Royal Dutch Package Shipping Company. German F. Kehding was an agent of the Ocean Steamship Company and Güntzel & Schumacher was an agent of the Norddeutsche Lloyd.[47]

In 1915, the commercial and industrial Dutch firm of Lindeteves-Stokvis setup an office on the Kesawan. Soon afterwards, the branch bought a large piece of ground on the Paleisweg, the present Jalan Katamso, with an area of about 14,000 square metres, on which large premises and extensive warehouses were completed in 1921. Sadly, this building was torn down in 2002. Lindeteves-Stokvis was an agent for several large factories in Europe and the United States. The firm even built complete plantation factories.[48] The Chinese trading company Ban Lian was established in 1915 for import and export businesses.[49] The first modern Chinese pharmacy was Hiu Ngi Fen's Poo Tai Foo dispensary, also in the Kesawan.[50]

[46] Schadee 1918 II: 205; Wright 1909: 573; Feldwick 1917: 1185, 1187, 1192.
[47] Feldwick 1917: 1194; Wright 1909: 573.
[48] Feldwick 1917: 1192.
[49] Feldwick 1917: 1185, 1187, 1192, 1194, 1195; Wright 1909: 573.
[50] *Handboek* 1940.

In 1912, the Medan Chamber of Commerce was established for European trades, and in the same year, the Chinese Chamber of Commerce was founded. One of the largest British plantation companies in Sumatra was Harrisons & Crosfield. Later, the Belgian Société Financière des Caoutchoucs (Socfin) owned numerous rubber and oil palm enterprises on the East Coast of Sumatra and Atjeh. The brothers Karl and Julius Schadt of Société Financière des Caoutchoucs initiated the cultivation of oil palms in Sumatra. The well-known American rubber company Goodyear started rubber plantations around 1915. Medan was characterised by an international atmosphere with American, Dutch, Chinese, British, French, Belgian and German companies.

1.2.2 Plantation Industry Fuels Medan's Economy

The three most important plantation products on Sumatra's east coast were initially tobacco, followed later by rubber and palm oil. The economic prosperity generated by these plantations contributed significantly to Medan's growth and affluence. The original tobacco-growing region lay between the Soengei Ular and Soengei Wampu rivers, where optimal conditions made it ideal for cultivation. The profitability of tobacco attracted a steady influx of European planters. In 1880, there were 49 plantations; by 1888, this number had tripled to 149. However, overproduction in Deli led to a crisis in 1890, resulting in land abandonment and a shift towards other crops. Many plantations were converted to rubber, coffee, sisal, palm oil, and tea.[51]

By 1910, a rubber boom had taken hold in England, driven by speculation and the rising demand from the automobile industry. Anticipation of global conflict further spurred investment in rubber cultivation. British rubber plantations managed by Harrisons & Crosfield began to take hold in Serdang and Langkat. Rubber plantations expanded from 21,926 hectares in 1909 to 173,000 hectares by 1924 and 284,213 hectares in 1932. In Asahan, large tracts were occupied by the Hollandsch-Amerikaansche Plantage Maatschappij (Dutch-American Plantation Company), along with other major firms such as the German Marihat Plantagen GmbH and the Belgian Société Financière de Caoutchouc (Socfin).

This plantation boom also led to the rise of new towns such as Pematang Siantar, Tebing Tinggi, Tandjoeng Balei, and Rantau Prapat. Medan

[51] Pelzer 1978: 51–54.

emerged as the principal beneficiary of this economic surge. It became the administrative and commercial hub, with new head offices, infrastructure, and public amenities. The British firm Harrisons & Crosfield, specialising in rubber, established its office at the corner of the Esplanade and Kesawan in November 1914. As prosperity grew, Medan developed into a modern city with elegant shops, warehouses, restaurants, cinemas, and other urban facilities.

1.3 Areas Around Medan

1.3.1 Kota Matsoem

Sultan Mahmoed Al Rasjid Perkasa of Deli became rich as he sold concessions to the plantation companies. In a short time, he obtained a huge fortune and his new *Istana* (palace) Maimoen in Medan was finished in 1887, built by the Dutch architect van Erp. The Sultan chose Medan for his new residence, following the head office of the Deli Company. Close to the palace stood the Sultan's private residence in the Kota Matsoem or the Sultan's village. *Istana* Maimoon, or Maimoon Palace, was a gift from the tobacco companies to the Sultan and was used for official receptions and festivities.

In 1906, the *Mesjid Raja* (Big Mosque) near the Sultan's palace was completed under the architectural supervision of W.H.M. Schadee. The mosque was financed by three parties: the Deli Railroad Company, the sultan of Deli, and Tjong A Fie. It has a copper *mimbar* (pulpit) by Dutch master blacksmith Dingemans.[52] Opposite the great mosque was the Derikanpark. This complex of villas and bungalows was constructed in the 1920s and early 1930s. On the other side of Jalan Radja, now Jalan Sisingamangaraja, stood the wooden palace of the sultan in Kota Matsoem. Also on Jalan Radja was the Medansche Zwembad (Medan swimming pool), one of the largest and most beautiful swimming facilities in the Dutch Indies in the 1930s.[53] Historically, many Malay and Minangkabau from West Sumatra settled in Kota Matsoem. Most of the Minangkabau were small traders. Until today, these two population groups have formed the majority in this area. In colonial times, only a few Batak people were

[52] DC 28-12-1907; SP 14-08-1913.

[53] SP 25-08-1909; 03-09-1918; *Pewarta Deli* 27-07-1917; Feldwick 1917: 1195; Veersema 1939: 40, 41.

living in Medan. A large group arrived in the city after 1950, settling in the Padang Boelan area. Most of the Javanese population lived on the plantations near the city.

1.3.2 Kesawan

> *They say that on the empty ground in front of the Roman Catholic Church, the capitalists intend to build an enormous office that competes with the Harrisons & Crosfield building. If all will be realised, we will see from one end to the other of the Kesawan giant beautiful buildings, the people of Medan will appreciate this.*[54]

The AVROS (Algemeene Vereeniging van Rubber Planters ter Oostkust van Sumatra) (General Association of Rubber Planters of Sumatra's East Coast) building was designed by architect Mulder and was completed in 1919. The building is located on the corner of the Paleisweg (Jalan Katamso), the Soekamulia (Jalan Palang Merah), Kesawan (Jl. A. Yani), and Kerkstraat (Jl. M.T. Hariono). AVROS, established in 1910, was an organisation for all plantation companies except tobacco companies.[55] It was an influential institution with over 300 member plantations, with rubber as the main commodity. The green-roofed building housed a dactyloscopy institute that registered over five hundred thousand fingerprints of contract labourers.

Opposite the AVROS building was Kesawan, the oldest street in Medan and the centre of the Chinese quarter. Kesawan, during colonial times, was the commercial centre of all kinds of firms, banks, and offices. It originated as a Malay *kampong*, but since 1880, many Chinese from Penang and Malacca and later on from China made this street a Chinatown. In 1889, a large fire destroyed 67 wooden houses and shops in Kesawan.[56] Hereafter, brick Chinese shophouses (*ruko or rumah toko*) were built in rows with a gallery below. There were mostly two-storey houses, the shop or atelier below and the living compartments upstairs. Large tablets with Chinese characters displayed the name of the firm and the products they sold. Until the 1960s, Chinese tablets could still be found in front of shops. Following the implementation of Indonesian policies that banned the use of the Chinese language and writing, these tablets had to be removed.

[54] *Pewarta Deli* 29-07-1917.
[55] Volker 1928: 83.
[56] Naudin 1905: 43.

In the Chinese quarter, markets were spread out over several locations. The Tjong family operated all the markets. First, there was De Oude Markt (the Old Market) from 1886, now known as Jalan Perdana. In 1888, the fish market was opened in Spoorstraat (Jalan Kereta Api), while in 1906, the meat market was established at Nieuwe Markt (New Market) (Jalan Perniagaan). For hygienic reasons, the municipality wanted to bring all the markets under one roof and therefore planned to construct a new central market on the former racecourse.[57] This was delayed due to the economic crisis of 1920, and it was not until the 1930s that Medan got its central market, now called Pusat Pasar.

On the other side of the railway, a second Chinese area was constructed with Chinese street names like Canton Street, Hong Kong Street, Hakka Street, Peking Street, Amoy Street, Shanghai Street, and Swatow Street. Row after row, Chinese shophouses were constructed in 1910 by Chinese entrepreneurs like the Tjong brothers, Oen Huat Kim, and Khoe Tjin Tek. The Indian Singh brothers also established houses and shops in this area. In 1934, the Catholic mission established the Dutch Chinese school on Hakka Street (Jalan Nusantara). Next to the school, a Catholic Chinese church was constructed in the Amsterdam School of Architecture by Han Groenewegen and completed in 1937.

An interesting landmark of architecture from the 1920s was the office of the Nederlandsch-Indische Escompto Maatschappij (Dutch Indies Escompto Company). Next to the Escompto building was the office of the firm Varekamp & Co., publishers of *De Sumatra Post*, and next to Varekamp was the mansion of Tjong A Fie. Further in Kesawan were various shops, including Gerzon's clothing store, the fashion house De Zon, and the import-export firm of Geo Wehry. One of the most remarkable buildings still standing at the entrance of Kesawan was the warehouse and trading company Seng Hap, established by Tan Tang Ho in the 1880s. The lunchroom Tip Top, established in 1934, still stands as it was. Kesawan also had the lunchroom Epperlein, the Chartered Bank of India, Australia and China, the oldest bank in town, the furniture shop of Hwa Nam, and the import firm S.D. Kaper, who was an agent of "His Master's Voice" gramophones.[58]

[57] *Gemeenteblad Medan* 12-3-1928: 36.
[58] Veersema 1939: 28,29

1.3.3 Polonia

After the land grant of 1918, the municipality of Medan got possession of a huge former tobacco field named Polonia between the Deli and Baboera rivers. This area became the new villa quarter where most Europeans settled if they could afford the expensive land. In this area, the new Elizabeth Hospital from 1930 and the Princess Beatrix School (nowadays Immanuel School), both in the style of the Amsterdam school of architecture, as well as many private houses, were built by architect Han Groenewegen. The Princess Beatrix School was completed in 1938, the year of the birth of the Dutch Princess Beatrix of the Netherlands.

Nearby, on the borders of the Deli River, in 1924, the impressive office of the Handels Vereeniging Amsterdam (HVA, Amsterdam Trading Company) was completed and designed by Fermont and Cuypers. The HVA owned dozens of plantations, including tobacco, sugarcane, and tea, and part of the substantial profits went into creating this monumental office on Jalan Soeprapto. Another landmark in Polonia was the fine *Deli Proefstation* (research station for tobacco) from 1913 in the Manggalaan, nowadays Jalan Diponegoro. Later, this building became the office of the governor of North Sumatra. Nearby were the exercise fields with the court of justice.[59] The Polonia quarter was traditionally the European quarter in town. From 1918, the area expanded rapidly with many fine buildings when the city received these grounds from the Sultans of Deli and Serdang.

1.3.4 Kampong Madras

All manner of races mingle at Medan. Japanese, Chinese, Cingalese and the various Sumatra types - among which are Battas and a few Mingang - Kabauers - are easily distinguished. The first two form a small shopkeepers' class, and among the Hindus -the so called 'Klings'- you will notice in particular the usurers, the money-lenders, is the Orang Chetti, whose guild - if I may use this word - is old as Time (for Ptolemaeus mentions Chettis in his writings). They are pre-Indian merchants who arrived on battleships to do business and lend money to the Malay rulers. These Chettis or usurers honour their traditions and antique Hindu religion, and have in Medan a separate temple among the three or four other temples which one finds there…[60]

[59] Veersema 1939: 26,29
[60] Couperus 1924: 72-4 in Reid 1995: 287.

Dutch writer Louis Couperus wrote this impression in 1923 when he visited the Indian quarter. Nowadays, not many Indians reside in this quarter; however, there is still an Indian temple. There were northern and southern Indian people who migrated to Deli. The "Kling" came from the Coromandel coast, the south of India, and they spoke Tamil. However, the term *orang Kling* (Kling people) was considered derogatory. There were several Indian communities in Medan. The Dutch also installed an Indian Captain; one of the first was Bawadji, who was a Muslim and a religious head, Nazir, who owned a slaughter shop.[61] There were Sikhs from the northeast of India or Punjab. Some Sikhs worked as guards or raised cows for milk, often called Bengalis, but they were not from Bengal or Bangladesh. Some merchants opened *toko Bombay* selling silk and ladies' clothing. Again, they were not from Bombay, but Sindh in Pakistan.[62] A famous Sindh merchant was Khemchand from Hyderabad, who established the Hoondamall and Sons store in Kesawan in 1885.[63] There were also Chettys from Tamil Nadu who were moneylenders. Another group of Tamils, who were Catholics, originated from French-occupied Pondicherry. A Catholic church was constructed at Daendelstraat (Jalan Hayam Wuruk) for them and completed in 1915.[64]

The Indian quarter used to be an isolated section of town. The Tjong Yong Hian Bridge, considered the most beautiful bridge in Medan, spans the Baboera River and connects Padang Bulan with the Indian quarter. The Tjong Yong Hian Bridge enabled the quarter to be connected with the rest of the city. Numerous Indian households lived on streets such as Bombay Street and Calcutta Street. The Tjong family donated the bridge to the city in 1917 as a tribute to Tjong Yong Hian, the elder brother of Tjong A Fie.[65] The bridge was restored in 2002, after which the text on the marble columns in Chinese and in Latin script became visible again.

[61] DC 07-12-1877; SP 12-07-1939.
[62] Jansen 1934.
[63] DC 11-09-1935.
[64] https://id.wikipedia.org/wiki/Gereja_Santo_Antonius_dari_Padua_Medan.
[65] *Andalas* 1-2-1917.

1.4 Medan in the 1920s and 1930s

Around 1920, Medan experienced another period of rapid development, driven by the expansion of plantations. In the 1920s, the number of villas in the Polonia quarter gradually increased. Another newly built area was the Deli Spoorweg Maatschappij (DSM) or Deli Railroad Company housing quarter, located along the Serdang road, for middle- and higher-level DSM personnel.

South of the Chinese quarter was the so-called *Oranje buurt*. This was the Orange quarter, with street names honouring the Dutch royal family of Orange, such as Julianestraat, Wilhelminestraat, Emmestraat, and Amaliestraat. In the eastern part of the city, several new housing quarters were opened. In 1930, a new municipal hospital was built on Serdang road. In the same year, the Roman Catholic Elisabeth Hospital was completed. The *Hogere Burger School* (HBS) (Higher Secondary School) was established in 1928, and in 1930, two mixed public schools were opened.[66] In 1927, the Su Tung School, Medan's first secondary Chinese school, was opened.[67]

After the First World War, social housing projects were started, such as the village of Sido Dadi. Other housing projects were located in the villages of Sekip, Djatie Oeloe, and Padang Loemba. In 1927, the municipality began constructing new city areas, such as Medan Baru, for lower-income groups. Here, many Indo (Eurasian) and lower-income European employees lived.

In 1920, rubber prices fell sharply, which directly impacted Medan's economy. As a result, new plantation products were tried out in the region, after which the economy rose again in 1924. In the mid-1920s, Medan experienced its second boom, during which the city expanded significantly. This was all possible because of the rise of plantation products. The high prices remained until 1930, when the world economic crisis hit Sumatra's east coast.[68] The economy was extra vulnerable as the plantations were fully export-oriented.

Despite financial hardship, Medan's greatest public work was started in 1930 and finished in 1933, during the height of the economic crisis. It was the construction of the new Central Market at the former racecourse

[66] Franke 1988: 145,146,148; *Gemeenteblad* 20-06-1928; *Gemeente Medan* 1909–1934; Loderichs et al 1997: 28.

[67] Information from Thio Han Cheng, Medan, 2001, 2002, 2003.

[68] De Waard 1934: 221.

site on the Wilhelminestraat, designed by architect van der Valk. After many negotiations, an agreement was reached between the Medan town council and the market exploiters, the Tjong family. The old markets were closed the day the new central market was opened in 1933.[69] In the years after 1930, the Medan municipality had to cut expenses, which remained so until the Japanese invasion in 1942.

1.4.1 Endnote

Medan's development was rooted in the plantation industry, starting with tobacco and later expanding to include rubber and palm oil. As a result of the huge profits, the plantation companies built impressive offices in the city centre, and Medan became a planters' town. During colonial times, each ethnic population group was required to reside in separate quarters, resulting in distinct divisions into European, Chinese, Malay, and Indian quarters. The Sultan had his palace in the *Kota* Matsoem or Sultan's village. Many Malays, as well as many Minangkabau, still live here. Furthermore, there was the Indian area, known as Kampong Madras. From the start, Medan's economic development attracted many Chinese, resulting in a lively Chinatown. This Chinatown remains largely intact today, as most Chinese shops are still located in this part of the city. Remarkably, a limited number of Chinese businessmen controlled a considerable share of the town's economy. The main example was Tjong A Fie, who owned over half of all the houses in town. The different ethnic groups, including Indonesians, Chinese, Europeans, Arabs, and Indians, all contributed to Medan's development. After independence, the city expanded explosively. Nowadays, the city is home to over two and a half million people. Despite the growth, you can still see many remaining colonial houses, offices, and villas. Although Medan is no longer a planters' town, the built heritage that gave the city her unique character is still visible today (Tables 1.2 and 1.3).

[69] *Gemeente Medan* 1909–1934.

Table 1.2 The population of the East Coast of Sumatra[a]

Year	*Indigenous*	*Chinese*	*Other Orientals*	*European*	*Total*
1873	?	5647	574	128	
1880	90,000	25,700	2533	522	118,755
1890	191,000	70,325	4236	1628	267,189
1900	306,035	103,768	9208	2079	421,090
1905	450,941	99,236	15,573	2667	568,417
1913	635,840	119,088	14,198	3980	123,068
1915	681,000	132,000	14,320	5200	832,520
1920	1,042,930	134,750	11,992	7882	1,197,554
1930	1,470,395	192,822	18,904	11,079	1,693,200

Deli Data 1863–1938; *Pinang Gazette and Straits Chronicle* 23-05-1916

Table 1.3 The population of the East Coast of Sumatra according to the government census[a]

	1905			*1920*			*1930*		
	Male	Female	Subtotal	Male	Female	Subtotal	Male	Female	Subtotal
Indigenous	247,873	203,068	450,941	555,426	487,504	1,042,930	769,858	700,537	1,470,395
Chinese	92,646	6950	99,236	108,731	26,019	134,750	134,145	58,677	192,822
Other Foreign Orientals	10,796	4777	15,573	8447	3545	11,992	11,953	6951	18,904
European	1703	964	2667	4890	2992	7882	6300	4779	11,079
Total	353,018	215,759	568,417	677,494	520,060	1,197,554	922,256	770,944	1,693,200

From Volkstelling 1920, 1930, SP 29-01-1908

CHAPTER 2

Swiss Planters in Deli

Switzerland is renowned for its long-standing neutral foreign policy, which has kept it from participating in political or military conflicts involving other nations. This commitment to peace has been upheld since 1515. Although Switzerland never established its own colonies, Swiss individuals played a role in colonisation, particularly during the early phases of tobacco cultivation in Deli, Sumatra. Young Swiss men served as mercenaries in the Dutch army, and Swiss migrants were among the pioneers in cultivating the fertile lands of Deli. Swiss historian Andreas Zangger states that approximately 8000 Swiss private soldiers served in Asia, including those who fought for the Dutch in the Atjeh War. Additionally, between 1870 and 1930, approximately 500 Swiss merchants went to invest in the plantations of the Dutch Indies (Fig. 2.1).[1]

2.1 Helvetia and Polonia

The Swiss were among the first Europeans to venture into Deli and establish Sumatra's plantation economy. One pioneer was Peyer, who arrived in Laboean in 1866 and founded the Persévérance estate, one of the earliest tobacco plantations in the region.[2] He was soon followed by Albert Breker, who partnered with fellow Swiss man Mots to establish the Königsgrätz

[1] Zangger et al. 2020:26.

[2] The plantation's name was later changed to Paya Bakong (SP 01-08-1936).

B. Minasny, D. A. Buiskool, *Stories from Medan, Volume 1*,
https://doi.org/10.1007/978-981-95-7707-1_2

Fig. 2.1 A Swiss planter's house in Deli in the late nineteenth century (H. Ernst, KITLV Or. 27.360)

estate. Demonstrating national pride, Breker later renamed his plantation Helvetia—the Latin name for Switzerland. In 1867, Breker and Peyer joined an expedition, trekking on foot with a Dutch *controleur* (district officer) and an English lieutenant to the Batak land, where they met its chief.

Breker's success in tobacco cultivation led him to expand his ventures. He became an important figure in forming the Deli Planters Vereeniging (Deli Planters Society), which would later shape the region's agricultural policies. Recognising the potential for further growth, he invited his brother-in-law, Michalski, to join him in Deli, marking the beginning of a broader European entrepreneurial network in Sumatra's plantation industry.[3]

Born in 1836 in Kraków as the son of Michael Matyasek and Julie Goderecka, Ludwig Michalsky (sometimes recorded as Michalski) overcame early adversity after losing both parents in his youth. Despite this hardship, he received an excellent education. At age 23, Michalsky began

[3] Broersma 1919: 48.

military service in the Austrian army, seeing deployment in both Italy and Hungary. However, his thoughts stayed with his homeland. When he was granted leave in the spring of 1863, he returned to Kraków, only to find that the uprising in Russian Poland had already been suppressed.

Facing an uncertain future in partitioned Poland, his godfather arranged for his safe passage beyond Austro-Russian borders. He travelled under Russian-endorsed documents bearing the name Ludwig Michalsky—the identity that would carry him to his eventual destiny in the Dutch East Indies.[4]

Michalsky crossed the border and joined the insurgent forces of Colonel Franz Kopernicki, operating in the Piotrków and Kalisz governorates. His military acumen quickly earned him a lieutenant's commission, where he trained and led a 46-man unit to a bloodless engagement, capturing significant enemy supplies through tactical brilliance. Michalsky also led a successful ambush against a superior Russian force at Grzybowa Gora, causing their retreat. He fought bravely throughout the guerrilla war and rose to the rank of major. These engagements formed part of the larger January Uprising (1863–1864), one of Poland's most tragic independence struggles. The conflict ultimately claimed 30,000 Polish lives, with 400 prisoners executed and over 18,000 exiled to Siberia.

Following Poland's defeat, Michalsky sought refuge in Switzerland in 1864 and enrolled at the Zürich Polytechnic (now ETH Zürich). Graduating as an engineer in 1868, Michalsky got a job with the Dutch as a road engineer in East Sumatra. In September 1868, he married Anna Breker from Thalwil, and a month later, they journeyed to Sumatra.[5] However, he didn't work as an engineer; instead, he joined his brother-in-law in cultivating tobacco. In December 1869, he secured a land lease from the Sultan of Deli. He named their enterprise Polonia in honour of his occupied homeland. The area of around 1000 bouw (700 hectares) covered land between the Deli and the Baboera rivers.[6] Michalsky's wife passed away in 1869, and a year later, he married his wife's friend, Anna Hottinger from Zürich.[7] Together, they had four children, and Michalsky even invited his brother-in-law to work at Polonia (Figs. 2.2 and 2.3).[8]

[4] *Neue Zürcher Zeitung* 07-03-1981; Florkowska-Frančić 2009.

[5] *Neue Zürcher Zeitung* 30-09-1868.

[6] Jansen1928: 36, *Begraafplaatsrapport Gemeente Medan*.

[7] *Neue Zürcher Zeitung* 09-07-1870.

[8] SP 25-04-1924.

Fig. 2.2 Michalsky's house in Polonia in 1870 (Feilberg, Nationaal Archief 815_11)

Michalsky became a close friend of the Sultan of Deli and trained a small guard corps of the Sultan using the European model. Michalsky was known for his love of horses. He kept a stable of fine horses and wore large wellington boots with turned-up brims and a dark coat.[9] He worked hard and accumulated considerable wealth from tobacco plantations.

Due to a kidney ailment, Michalsky returned to Switzerland in 1875. Arriving in Zürich penniless 11 years before, Michalsky returned as a millionaire. This financial success was made possible by the hard work of the coolies, who toiled on his plantations. This aspect of his fortune is rarely acknowledged in celebratory accounts. He maintained the ownership of the plantation under Michalsky & Co. and eventually sold to the Deli Maatschappij in 1889.

In 1879, Michalsky bought Hilfikon Castle in the canton of Aargau for 70,000 francs. He refurbished it, and the castle became a meeting place

[9] DC 10-05-1938.

Fig. 2.3 Mrs. and Mr. Michalsky of Polonia (Nationaal Archief, 2.20.46_802_05)

for Polish emigrants. He also helped establish the Polish League in Switzerland in 1887.[10]

Michalsky dedicated his life to supporting his Polish compatriots across Europe. He became the president of Polish associations in Switzerland and generously utilised his resources and efforts to support his fellow Poles, including the establishment of the Polish Museum in Rapperswil and the proposal of a National Fund. Anna Michalsky supported her husband's patriotic and philanthropic activities, making Hilfikon Castle a refuge for Polish exiles. Due to his long lung illness, Michalsky passed away on June 27, 1888, and was buried in the Wohlen cemetery, his tombstone marked with the Polish eagle.[11] In his will, he left 20,000 francs to his

[10] DC 20-04-1938.

[11] *Neue Zürcher Zeitung* 07-03-1981.

hometown of Krakow and 10,000 francs each to the school funds of the communities of Hilfikon and Stallikon, but none to the place where he reaped his fortune.[12]

2.1.1 Swiss Association

In 1871, there were about 40 Europeans on the east coast of Sumatra, 17 were Dutch, 6 were German, 4 were British, and 9 were Swiss. There were 9 women and 31 men.[13] Nienhuys and Janssen, founders of the Deli Company, continued to promote the Deli region to young merchants and clerks working in Singapore. Funds were drawn from Holland, Batavia, Singapore, and Penang. The Sultan of Deli offered inexpensive land leases to cultivate high-quality tobacco on fertile land. Ambitious European clerks working in Singaporean trading houses were lured by this offer and seized the opportunity to relocate to Deli. They were able to secure funding from the trading houses or the Deli Company, which provided an advance on their future harvest. But most of them lacked knowledge about cultivating tobacco or any crops; some managed to succeed, others faced failures, and a few even encountered life-altering experiences (Fig. 2.4).

By 1884, the East Coast of Sumatra had 688 Europeans, comprising 540 males and 148 females, with the following nationalities: 380 Dutch, 88 English, 123 German, 40 Swiss, 12 French, and 11 Austrian.[14] As the number of Swiss planters reached 50 in 1886, they formed a Swiss Association called "Schweizer Verein Helvetia Deli," headed by F. Hirzel, the head administrator in Soengei Sikambing of the Guigné brothers.[15] A meeting took place at the "Nieuwe Deli Hotel" on Serdangweg, where about 30 Swiss individuals gathered, including Hans Bluntschli. The objectives were to support needy Swiss citizens and promote friendship among Swiss nationals living far from their homeland.[16] Anna Michalsky-Hottinger became the first female honorary member, and she was the first European woman to live in Deli with courage and determination in exploring the rugged territory.

[12] *Zuger Volksblatt* 28-07-1888.
[13] Cremer 1924: 53.
[14] *Deli Gids* 1938: 18.
[15] *Neue Zürcher Zeitung* 20-12-1886.
[16] SP 29-07-1936.

Fig. 2.4 Planters in the 1870s. Cremer, Straatmann, De Munnick from Deli Maatschappij, van Lee of Soengei Sipoet, Römer of Padang Boelan, Michalsky of Polonia, Ritgen of Rotterdam, Gomberg of Danemark, Peyer of Persévérance, Breker of Helvetia, Grob of Senembah (Feilberg, Nationaal Archief 815_19)

The association was later named "Schweizer Verein," where the community held an annual celebration on August 1, Swiss national day, commemorating the foundation of the country in 1291. The Swiss in the region gathered for activities such as shooting and bowling, speeches, and fireworks.[17] They frequently donated money to Switzerland, including to the country's treasury, the shooting club, etc.[18] The membership fluctuated over the years. In 1886, the group began with 42 members, which grew to 83 by 1891, with a slight dip in membership in 1889. However, it faced challenges during financial crises, first in the tobacco industry and subsequently in the coffee industry. By 1904, only 45 members remained. However, after 1910, the Swiss community experienced great prosperity. By 1916, approximately 130 Swiss nationals were residing on the East Coast of Sumatra, and thus they petitioned the Swiss government to install

[17] DC 05-08-1891.

[18] *Neue Zürcher Zeitung* 08-12-1886; *Der Bund* 17-07-1885.

a consul in Medan.[19] And a year later, a Swiss consul for the East Coast of Sumatra was appointed.[20] In 1920, the Schweizer Verein reached its peak with 152 members. But it only lasted one year as the rubber market slumped, resulting in only 85 members in 1936.[21]

2.2 Saëntis and Maryland

In the summer of 1870, Hermann Küng came to Deli to try his luck as a tobacco planter. Hermann Küng (1842–1871) was the son of a well-known medical doctor in Heiden, Switzerland. He went to Singapore in 1864, secured a position at the Swiss company Remé & Co. in Singapore, and worked there for six years. He married Mary Ganno, who had an American father and a Moluccan mother. His marriage to an Indo-European did not make him fit in the European community; thus, he had to leave and tried his luck in the new land of Deli. However, Hermann had no idea how to grow tobacco and had to rely on information from other planters. It was a sharp learning curve.[22]

Hermann received a 1400-hectare piece of land from the Sultan of Deli for a 75-year leasehold in the Pertjoet district. To remind him of his home country, he named his plantation Saëntis, a famous mountain in Switzerland, despite the land being a plain. There were no roads, minimal medical care and policing. The workers were troublesome, and planters often had to assert their authority by behaving roughly and brutally. They also had to look out for their own safety, including attacks from the Batak people and even from their workers.

In August 1871, Hermann Küng, along with his assistant Theodore Meyer, a Chinese cook, and 25 coolies from Penang, set out to establish his plantation in Deli. His wife and son remained in Singapore. Initially, Küng resided with a manager from the Deli Company whom he had met in Singapore. After constructing the first house on his plantation, he moved in with his coolies, which turned out to be a fatal decision. Other plantation owners advised him to keep his distance from the coolies and employ a *tandil*, or Chinese foreman, who would act as a mediator between the workers and the manager while also keeping them in check. However, Hermann disregarded this advice.[23]

[19] *Pinang Gazette and Straits Chronicle* 19-02-1916.
[20] DC 11-07-1917.
[21] SP 29-07-1936.
[22] Zangger et al. 2020: 46–52.
[23] Idem.

On October 14, 1871, planters in Deli became concerned when Hermann and Theo had not been seen for several days, prompting them to launch an investigation. The search ultimately uncovered their bodies buried near the house. It was discovered that on October 8, they were brutally attacked and killed by the coolies. The day before the incident, Theo Meyer had received $200 from Singapore, and the Chinese coolies who lived downstairs from the house heard him counting the money. The following morning, the coolies surrounded Theo Meyer and attacked him from behind with an axe, severing his head from his shoulders. Hermann Küng, who heard the disturbance, tried to intervene but was also brutally attacked, causing his skull to split in two.[24] Both had arrived in Deli only two months earlier with little experience.

After murdering Hermann Küng and Theodore Meyer, the coolies returned to work as if nothing had happened. However, the Dutch police managed to apprehend 25 coolies, who were found with the stolen dollars braided into their hair. They were chained up and sent to Laboean prison to await judgement. Hermann and Theo's bodies were transported to Laboean Deli in coffins and were buried in the presence of the Europeans, the Sultan, and a large entourage.[25]

At the request of the planters, the Sultan was asked to try the coolies involved in the murder. However, the Sultan hesitated to decide and sought permission from the resident of the East Coast of Sumatra, Schiff.[26] After consulting with the government in Batavia, the resident authorised the Sultan to hold the coolies accountable for their crime according to local customs, provided that no torture or mutilation was involved.[27] The Sultan carried out severe punishment, sentencing 7 of the coolies to death by hanging and sending 15 others to hard labour.[28]

Meanwhile, in Switzerland, Johannes Küng-Mösli, unaware of the incident, received a letter from his brother, Hermann, outlining a promising career as a tobacco planter in Sumatra. Johannes decided to join his brother. However, upon his arrival in Deli in late 1871, he learned of his brother's tragic death. Nevertheless, Johannes was determined to carry on his brother's legacy and took over the plantation.

[24] *Straits Times Overland Journal* 25-10-1871.

[25] *Straits Times Overland Journal* 25-10-1871.

[26] Cremer 1924: 48

[27] John Anderson, who travelled to Deli in 1823, wrote about the execution conducted by the then Sultan of Deli as "truly barbarous and horrible" (Anderson 1826: 277).

[28] SP 27-03-1924.

Cremer recounted that in 1872, 75 Europeans settled in Deli with 13 companies, along with 4000 Chinese and several hundred Javanese, Klingalese, and other workers, with almost no administrative support. Nevertheless, they sold about 6400 packs of tobacco worth a million guilder.[29]

Deli continued to attract Swiss migrants. Karl Krüsi, a cousin of Hermann Küng from Appenzell, Switzerland, arrived in Deli in 1873 and joined the Saëntis estate. He even married Mary Ganno, the widow of Hermann Küng. After seven years of work, he seized an opportunity when the Sultan of Deli offered land for lease. In partnership with Kaufmann, he established the Maryland estate in 1881, in honour of his wife. Krüsi worked hard and achieved a remarkable harvest, 16 quintals[30] of tobacco per coolie, which earned him $25,000 in cash. Using the profits, he rapidly expanded his operations, employing 200 coolies the following year and developing a second plantation, the Soengei Rempah estate (Fig. 2.5).[31]

Fig. 2.5 Manager's house on Maryland Estate, with a Swiss flag in front of the house. Men on balcony; left: Wiget, Röhrig; men in front, from left to right: Hirzel, Krüsi, Juchle. Karl Krüsi's wife, Mary Ganno, and her child were in a horse carriage. Photo by G.R. Lambert (KITLV PK-F-MM.1504/06)

[29] Cremer 1924: 53.

[30] 1 quintal = 100 kg.

[31] Schweizerisches Nationalmuseum LM-82526.4, https://blog.nationalmuseum.ch/2017/05/ein-appenzeller-in-der-fremde/.

Through his hard work and persistence, Johannes Küng successfully turned Saëntis into a thriving producer of high-quality tobacco. So successful was he that he eventually invited his wife to come and live with him in Deli.[32]

However, life in Deli was not easy; there was always a threat of diseases and danger from animals and robbers. Johannes Küng had acquired basic medical knowledge from his father's practice. He administered medicines and performed operations himself.

Life on the plantation was also boring, with little entertainment and work from sunrise to sunset. Some turned to hunting; others succumbed to alcohol. However, Emma Küng-Mösli was content and wrote:

> *I always enjoy being here, and despite the somewhat lonely life, I am never bored. Spend time working, reading and writing in a pleasant way and enjoy the beautiful tropical warmth, which is extremely good for me, and go for a walk every morning and evening, which is extremely beneficial to my health and protects me from any obesity. In the evenings, dear Johannes usually accompanies me on my tours and always delights me with his good sense of humour.*[33]

Saëntis grew to 500 workers, including 380 Chinese coolies. Violence was part of life on the plantations. Fugitive coolies formed gangs and occasionally raided the plantation for food supplies or money. In 1884, the Saëntis estate was the target of such an attack. Inter-ethnic or gang wars between Chinese workers occurred sporadically. The coolies could kill each other or murder European assistants. In the mid-1880s, fierce fighting raged between hostile Chinese gangs. The Chinese coolies commonly joined societies or *kongsis*, and there were rivalries among *kongsis*. The same year, the Maryland plantation suffered a blow. A group of Chinese coolies had gagged and buried alive four men belonging to another *kongsi*. This brutality shocked the planters, but it was not an isolated incident. The newspaper wrote that the loose management was partly responsible for appeasing other planters and investors.[34]

Yet the planters also perpetrated violence against their coolies; they were equipped with guns and even cannons. In 1876, a judicial commission was dispatched from Batavia to Deli in response to widespread allegations of worker abuse on tobacco plantations. The commission included a

[32] Zangger et al. 2020: 54–62.
[33] Zangger et al. 2020: 60.
[34] Zangger et al. 2020: 58.

judge from the Council of Justice, a public prosecutor, and a Chinese-language interpreter. Their task was to investigate formal complaints lodged by coolies, both Chinese and Indigenous, many of whom accused European administrators of physical mistreatment and coercion. Several of these allegations were substantiated. As a result, one European estate administrator was placed under arrest. However, while being transported by steamer to Batavia for trial, the administrator evaded prosecution by jumping overboard and was presumed drowned. Charges were also formally brought against three other European administrators or overseers.[35]

Researcher Will Davis documented an artefact in the Ethnographic Museum of Zürich: a threatening letter etched into a bamboo piece, dated between 1875 and 1880. Written in the Batak language, the letter was likely from a local man demanding the return of a woman, possibly his wife, who was being held at Grob and Näher's plantation in Kuta Jurung, a remote Karo village. The letter warned that failure to return her would result in arson and murder.[36]

Despite the violence and threat, Johannes Küng managed to make the plantation work, and in 1881, he was able to hand over the management of the plantation to his deputy. He returned to Switzerland for the first time with his wife and children, who were born in Sumatra. From then on, Emma Küng stayed in Heiden with the children. Johannes returned to Sumatra and managed the plantation, which he was forced to sell in 1886 due to a lack of capital. He remained a partner in the business until 1896. He finally retired to Heiden and died in 1908.[37] Karl Krüsi also amassed a fortune, and he sold his estate holdings and returned to Switzerland a wealthy man, where he built the Villa Sumatra in Zürich. Today, the only legacy remaining in Medan is the names: Helvetia, Saëntis, and Maryland (Marelan) (Figs. 2.6 and 2.7).

2.3 Patoembah

Karl Fürchtegott Grob (1830–1892), born in Zürich to a baker and city councillor, had a troubled youth marked by restlessness, leading to his early removal from school. He began a clerkship in Basel at 21. In 1858, he relocated to Messina in Sicily, where he met Hermann Näher

[35] Schaadee 1918: 32–33.
[36] Davis 2024. *ABE Journal: Architecture beyond Europe* (24).
[37] Zangger et al. 2020: 62.

Fig. 2.6 Manager's house of Maryland. Photo by G.R. Lambert (KITLV PK-F-MM.1504/06)

(1838–1908) of Lindau (Bavaria). They were introduced to the possibilities in the Dutch Indies, particularly in Deli, by the Swiss man Albert Breker. Initially, the duo experimented with coffee and nutmeg cultivation but soon recognised that tobacco held the most promise for profit in the region. In 1871, they obtained a land concession of 7588 bouw (5300 hectares) on the banks of the Blumei River near Tandjong Morawa on the border of Deli and Serdang. The area was under the Sultanate of Deli. It was an *oerung* (small kingdom) of Senembah, with the capital of Patumbak or Patoembah. The company then successively expanded and founded Patoembah, Tandjong Morawa, Tandjong Morawa Kiri, Dolok Naga and Sungei Behasa plantations, adding another 2500 hectares by 1889. They were the first to open tobacco culture in the district of Padang and Bedagei.[38]

The plantation lands stretched along the navigable Bloemei River (now known as Sei Belumai), with a trading post of Rantau Pandjang, forming

[38] Janssen 1914:1–7; https://de.wikipedia.org/wiki/Karl_F%C3%BCrchtegott_Grob.

Fig. 2.7 Grob and Näher (Nationaal Archief 2.20.46_802_02)

a self-sufficient German-Swiss enclave. This strategic location allowed them to transport tobacco in small sampan boats directly to the harbour for export. They also secured river-mouth land for nipa palm to make *atap* roofing (Fig. 2.8).

Grob and Näher employed experienced agriculturists to manage their farms. They employed compatriots of Prussian, Northern German, Southern German and Bavaria, Swiss German, Austrian, the Grisons Kanton of Switzerland, and Slovak. They also had two physicians. Although the soil was not ideal, the plantations produced dark, heavy tobacco leaves, favoured in Europe and benefiting from lower US tariffs (55¢/lb vs 75¢ for lighter leaves). However, by 1887, market preferences shifted towards lighter tobacco, and US policymakers pushed to abolish the duty

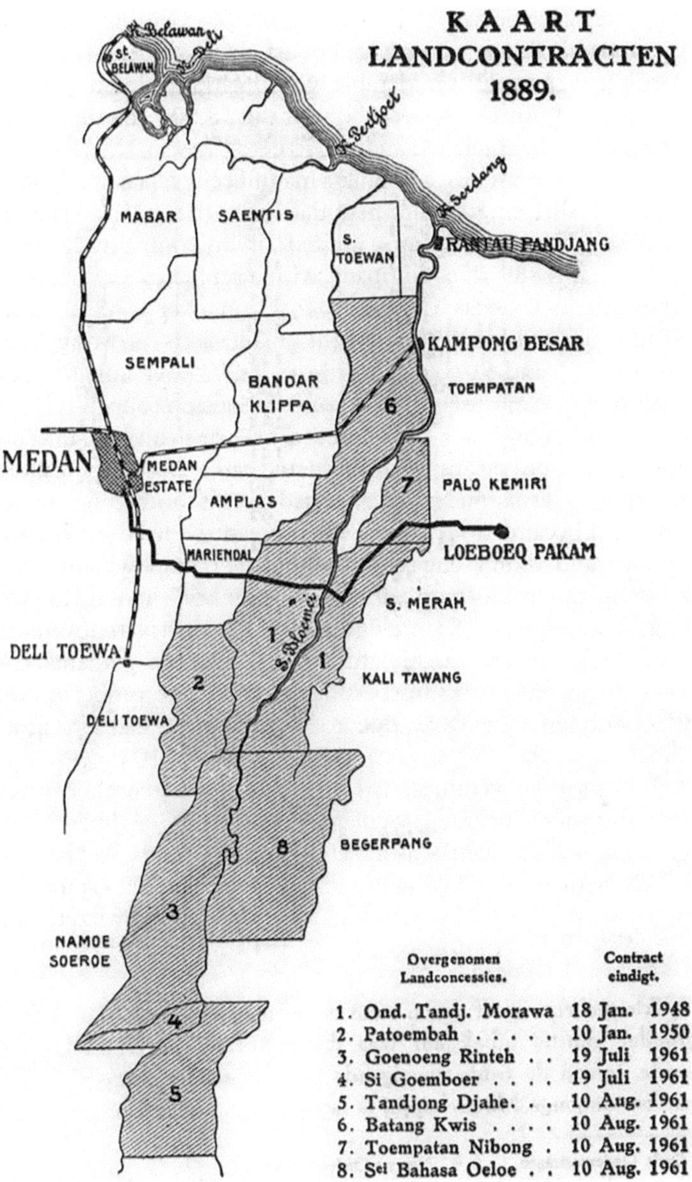

Fig. 2.8 The area of Patumbah plantation in 1889 along the Bloemei River (Janssen and Bool 1939: 49)

advantage for heavy leaves. A drought in 1887 worsened their position, yielding an overly fatty crop that sold poorly in 1888.[39]

As Grob had amassed considerable wealth within a decade, he returned to Zürich in 1879. In 1883, Grob bought the 13,000-square-metre property in Switzerland, which had an unobstructed view of the city of Zürich, the lake, and the mountains, and built a magnificent villa named Patumbah.

Grob and Näher entered into negotiations with the Deli Maatschappij, transforming their enterprise into a limited liability company, the Senembah Maatschappij, in 1889. This company, with a capital of *f*1,500,000, managed the extensive assets of Näher & Grob over 17,800 hectares.[40] Senembah expanded by absorbing other plantations, growing to 36,188 hectares in 1914 and 90,875 hectares in 1939.[41] Senembah, under the directorship of C.W. Janssen, the son of P.W. Janssen (one of the founders of Deli Maatschappij), was considered a progressive plantation with its own hospital and physicians who conducted research on tropical diseases.

Meanwhile, Hermann Näher returned to his hometown in Lindau, Germany, and became a *privatier*, which meant he lived off his accumulated wealth and didn't engage in business or employment. In 1906, Näher purchased the former Gasthaus "Rosenhof" in Lindau-Aeschach and a substantial piece of land. He had the property renovated in the *Jugendstil* (*Art Nouveau*) architectural style under the guidance of architect Josef Bichlmeier. After his passing in 1908, the property remained empty.[42] Grob died in 1892 due to a disease he had brought from Patoembah.

Other Swiss who ventured to Deli in the nineteenth century and amassed fortunes included Schlatter (Poengei), Hüber (Amplas), Sturzenegger (Rotterdam), Roemer (Bekalla), and Weber (Boenda Hara).[43] Once they earned enough money, they sold their estates to larger companies, such as Deli Maatschappij, and returned to Switzerland.

[39] Janssen and Bool 1939: 3–15.

[40] *De locomotief* 13-11-1929.

[41] Janssen and Bool 1939: 49.

[42] Schweizer, Karl. 2019. Als Sumatra-Kulis nicht nur den Liindauer Hermann Näher reich mactten.

[43] SP 01-08-1936; https://www.swiss-spectator.ch/nederlands-de-sumatra-zwitsers/

2.4 Soengei Bamban

Hans Caspar Bluntschli was born in Zürich in 1865 to a father who served as president of the Zürich city council. In 1885, he arrived in Sumatra to work for Krüse & Kaufmann before becoming a shareholder and administrator at Soengei Bamban plantation from 1889 to 1895. Soengei Bamban was part of the German-Swiss plantation company, Deutsch-Schweizerische Plantagen-Gesellschaft, based in Bremen.[44] By 1890, Bluntschli became the administrator of three tobacco plantation lands in Bedagai, including Soengei Bamban and Paja Mabar.[45]

On December 11, 1893, while assistant Ernst Ziehm of Soengei Bamban was in the field organising the distribution of labourers, he was ambushed by five Chinese coolies from the nearby forest. He was brutally murdered with axe blows and knife stabs.

The five Teochew Chinese coolies confessed to killing the young assistant, Ernst Ziehm. They had formed a sworn brotherhood and had pledged to admit to the crime together and face death together. They were all jailed in Medan, brought to trial at the Landraad (native court), and sentenced to death. On the morning of July 31, 1894, they were hanged together at Petisah. Despite their fate, they remained defiant and insulted the Europeans at the execution ground. The local Chinese community regarded their integrity as a bold and courageous act. They buried the five men in the Teochew cemetery and erected a tomb in their honour. They were revered as the "five ancestors," and people began to worship them and built a temple housing the tomb. See also the "Chinese Temples for Solidarity" chapter.

Two years after the incident, perhaps profoundly affected by it, Bluntschli decided to give up the Soengei Bamban plantation.[46] The following year, he started a new company called Liberia Sumatra AG, which traded coffee in Zürich. He also ventured into the Straits Settlements & Sumatra Ramie Syndicate two years later. Unfortunately, both companies were not successful. Later, Bluntschli acquired a concession in Siak, where he traded in wood products and cultivated ramie and other crops. He hoped to explore coal deposits in his concession area but faced difficulties, as he lived partly in the jungle and had no contacts in Batavia to develop the necessary infrastructure. Eventually, he passed away from Malaria in a hospital in Pekan Baroe in 1942 (Fig. 2.9).[47]

[44] DC 12-06-1889.
[45] Zangger 2011:267–268.
[46] DC 08-09-1894.
[47] Zangger 2011:267–268.

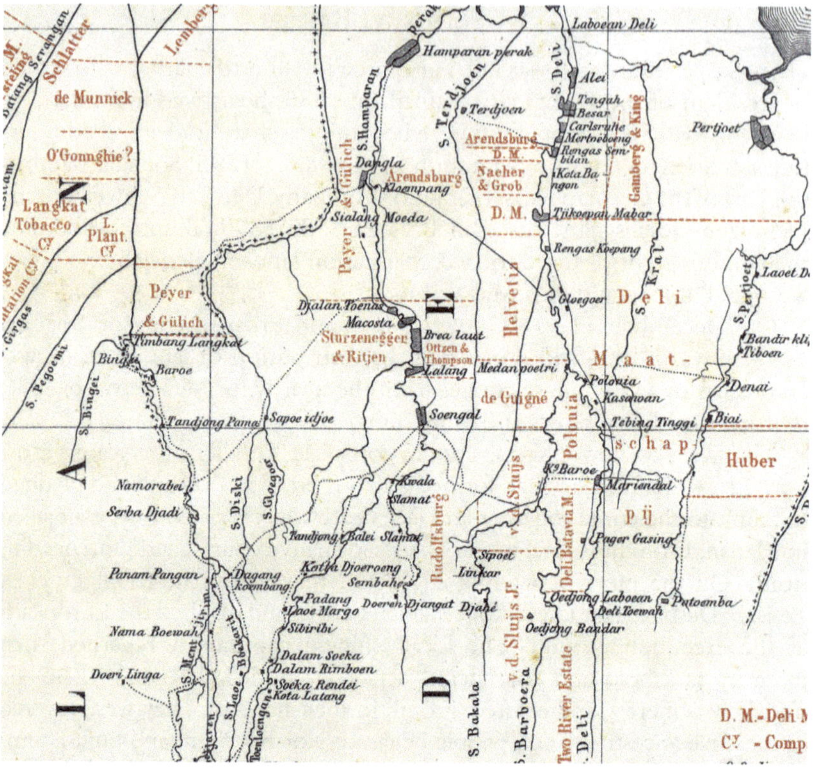

Fig. 2.9 A map of Deli by D.D. Veth (1875) shows how the landscape was carved up by European plantations. The villages were along the Deli River, and Medan Poetri was on the convergence of Deli and Baboera rivers (KITLV D C 53,6)

2.5 Surbeck and Badak

Decades later, another notable Swiss, Heinrich Surbeck, successfully established industries in the region. Heinrich was born in 1876 in the small town of Hallau, Switzerland, in the Schaffhausen Canton. He was a chemical engineer who attended the Technical College in Zürich. After graduating in 1900 and recovering from a severe lung infection, he accepted a position at the Gambir Plantation Gading Estate in Indragiri, which was owned by Swiss investors. Arriving in Sumatra around 1904, Heinrich faced numerous challenges, as the plantation's infrastructure was rudimentary. Having studied dyes and bleaches, he invented and built new equipment and machinery to produce high-quality, pure gambir dye for the silk industry. He successfully transformed the plantation's operations, resulting in substantial profits for the company.[48]

After fulfilling his contract, Heinrich took an entrepreneurial path. Around 1906, he co-founded the Goenoeng Malajoe Plantagen-Gesellschaft, another Swiss-owned enterprise. The company had a 600-hectare concession and cleared a portion of the Asahan jungle for firewood, as well as established gambir plantations and produced products for the European leather industry.[49]

Heinrich's success in the gambir industry allowed him to diversify his interests. He moved to Pematang Siantar and established the Siantar Ijsfabriek ice factory in 1916.[50] He further expanded with a lemonade factory and, in 1924, established a carbonated drink factory with the lemonade brand "*Kepala Badak.*"[51] His company was incorporated with a capital of *f*100,000 in 1920 and increased to *f*600,000 in 1940. Surbeck also had a repair workshop for automobiles, small machines, typewriters, and services for all types of firearms.[52] Surbeck built an electric hydropower station to supply electricity in Siantar, followed by another in Padang Sidempoean.[53]

In 1917, Surbeck purchased the Siantar Hotel, which had started in 1914 as a small establishment. He continued his expansion, with the management of the hotel being carried out by his two daughters, Lydia and Hedwig Sürbeck.

Despite his bustling business activities, Heinrich still pursued his passion for botany. He often explored the lush surroundings of Pematang Siantar, Toba Lake, and the Soeroengan summit, collecting ferns, lycophytes, and flowering plants.[54]

During the Japanese occupation, Switzerland's neutrality allowed Heinrich Surbeck and his two daughters to remain free and continue

[48] Meyer 1945: 259–263; Zangger 2011: 228–231.
[49] Zangger 2011: 228–231.
[50] DC 15-09-1916.
[51] SP 01-03-1924.
[52] SP 22-03-1922.
[53] SP 04-07-1934.
[54] DC 01-12-1938.

running their business. Although the Japanese suspected him of aiding the Allies, they were unable to take significant action against him.[55]

After the war ended, Indonesia proclaimed its independence, and soon the relationship between Indonesians and Europeans grew hostile. In October 1945, young Indonesian revolutionaries surrounded the Siantar Hotel and set it on fire. The Ambonese, Dutch, and Swiss residents were murdered. Surbeck and another Swiss national, Schuepp, were abducted and killed.[56]

The company Ijsfabriek Siantar continued to operate under the director Eugen Ralph Otto, the husband of Lydia Rosa Surbeck. It ran until 1957, when Soekarno announced the nationalisation of foreign companies. N.V. Ijsfabriek Siantar was then sold to Bujung Djafar.[57] The company was later acquired by a local entrepreneur, Hutabarat, and became famous for its *Cap Badak* carbonated soft drink.

2.5.1 Rubber Boom

Rubber cultivation in Sumatra began in 1905 and quickly became the most significant plantation crop. Latex became essential in the second industrialisation phase with the rise of electrical engineering, chemical, and automobile industries. Initially, latex was used for raincoats, shoes, and erasers, giving rise to "rubber." The development of vulcanisation in 1839 allowed for varying and stabilising the stiffness of latex, making it important for cable insulation, especially for oceanic telegraph cables.

As demand for rubber exceeded supply, prices soared, triggering the first rubber boom in the Amazon region. The early twentieth century saw another surge in rubber demand due to the automobile industry. Coffee and other smaller plantations were converted into rubber plantations. Native trees like ramboeng, gutta percha, and jelutong, which were traditionally grown by Malays, became a source of latex.

In 1906, Arthur Lampard of Harrisons & Crosfield visited Deli and saw the potential for applying the tobacco industry's large-scale organisational methods to rubber cultivation. Harrisons & Crosfield had already opened

[55] Surbeck was reported to help the European prisoners and apparently had a secret radio transmitter hidden in the basement of Siantar Hotel (Fusayama 2020:163).

[56] *Algemeen Handelsblad* 21-11-1945; *Het dagblad: uitgave van de Nederlandsche Dagbladpers te Batavia* 09-11-1945; *Nieuwe courant* 24-09-1946; Fusayama 1933: 29–32; https://theindoproject.org/a-festive-massacre/

[57] *Het Nieuwsblad voor Sumatra* 26-04-1957.

large estates in Ceylon (Sri Lanka) and British Malaya.[58] Victor Ris was a Swiss who worked for Tjinta Radja plantation. Ris was approached by Arthur Lampard, who was seeking to enter the Sumatran plantation economy. Ris began collaborating with Lampard around 1906, helping to facilitate Harrisons & Crosfield's early acquisitions in Sumatra. He managed an estate that was eventually bought out by the firm and converted to rubber production. In 1907, this estate was sold to the United Serdang (Sumatra) Rubber Plantations Ltd., one of the first rubber companies floated by Harrisons & Crosfield on the London market. As the British firm rapidly acquired land and founded new companies, Ris' fluency in Dutch and his connections with local authorities facilitated British investments while minimising Dutch suspicions. Ris later became the first president of the AVROS or Algemeene Vereeniging van Rubber Ondernemers ter Oostkust van Sumatra (General Association for Rubber Cultivation on the East Coast of Sumatra), overseeing industry advancements.[59] AVROS established its research station, Algemeen Proefstation der AVROS (APA) in 1916 at Kampoeng Baroe, Medan. Many of its researchers were graduates from ETH in Switzerland who were escaping financial difficulties in Europe and found well-paid jobs in Medan, including Albert Frey-Wyssling (1900–1988), a famous botanist.[60]

2.5.2 Swiss Neutrality

During the early years of the tobacco plantations in Deli, Chinese and Javanese coolies were often subjected to harsh treatment, including beatings, torture, imprisonment, and even death. As a result, the region gained a reputation as the worst place in the Dutch Indies. When van den Brand released *De Millioenen van Deli* (The Millions from Deli) in 1902, news quickly reached Switzerland, prompting *Der Bund* newspaper to publish excerpts from his booklet.[61] The paper featured additional articles highlighting the mistreatment of coolies in Sumatra. This was followed by the *Journal du Jura*, which reported Dutch atrocities in Deli. But neither publication mentioned the involvement of Swiss planters.[62]

[58] Stoler 1985: 18; Thee 1977: 15.
[59] Zangger 2011: 231–245.
[60] Zangger 2011: 387–389.
[61] *De Bund* 10-02-1903; 11-02-1903.
[62] *De Bund* 24-04-1904; *Journal du Jura* 18-10-1904.

Swiss historian Andreas Zangger raised questions about the neutral stance of Swiss sojourners, as the coolies paid the price for the wealth accumulated by plantation owners. As with other extractive colonial practices, millions of francs flowed to Switzerland from the profits of the Deli tobacco industry. Villas such as Patumbah, Sumatra, and Hilfikon were financed by wealth extracted from the labour of the coolies of Deli and in Zürich there is even a street called Sumatrastrasse. Zangger characterised the system as a form of temporary slavery and expressed surprise at how easily Swiss neutrality could coexist with colonial practices and business.[63]

[63] *WOZ.* Kultur/Wissen 45 5. November 2020: 25.

CHAPTER 3

German and French Planter Capitalism on Sumatra's East Coast

Since the 1870s, Germans and French had established themselves on the East Coast of Sumatra, each contributing differently to the region's plantation economy. German merchants such as Hüttenbach and Kehding developed Medan into a commercial hub through import–export businesses, plantation supply chains, and shipping networks. Their firms supported tobacco, rubber, and tea enterprises and maintained influence through a consulate and the German Association.

French settlers, led by the de Guigné family, built plantations at Soengai Sikambing, recruiting Tamil labour via Pondicherry and integrating Catholic missions into estate life. Others, like Brau de Saint-Pol Lias, combined exploration and business, documenting Deli's early plantation society.

While both communities helped transform Medan into a plantation centre, their fortunes changed with global events. German planters faced scrutiny over labour conditions, then severe disruption during World War I and political backlash in the 1930s, ending with internments in 1940. The smaller French presence declined through consolidation and economic downturns.

This chapter traces how German enterprise and French family ventures shaped East Sumatra's early plantation system and how war, politics, and economic change brought their influence to an end (Fig. 3.1).

B. Minasny, D. A. Buiskool, *Stories from Medan, Volume 1*,
https://doi.org/10.1007/978-981-95-7707-1_3

Fig. 3.1 Office of Handel Maatschappij Güntzel & Schumacher in Medan in 1900 (KITLV 1403431)

3.1 Pioneering German Planters and Post-war Challenges

By the late nineteenth century, a sizable German community had taken root along the East Coast of Sumatra, particularly in Deli and Medan. Germans made up roughly 15% of the European population in the region during the 1880s–1890s, forming one of the most active foreign groups in trade and plantation development. Among the first was Hermann Näher, a merchant from Aeschach in Bavaria, who became an early plantation owner in the 1870s and inspired others to follow.

The early presence soon developed into a wider commercial network. Motivated by economic opportunity and adventure, young German entrepreneurs such as Hüttenbach and Kehding established some of the earliest commercial enterprises in Laboean Deli, laying the foundation for a growing trading network. In 1880, Gustav Güntzel and F.A. Schumacher founded the import–export firm Handel Maatschappij Güntzel & Schumacher in Medan. By 1884, the German presence had expanded enough for the German government to appoint Franz Kehding as its first consul in Laboean Deli.[1]

The entrepreneurial momentum continued. In 1892, Carl Hick and August Jaenichen, who had been working on plantations in Deli, acquired the Güntzel & Schumacher business from its original partners. Carl Hick was later appointed German consul in Medan in 1898.[2] Meanwhile, in Langkat, Paul Sandel from München settled in Tandjoeng Poera around 1885 and set up an import–export business. Sandel operated 20 ships navigating the Wampoe and Batang Serangan rivers and owned many plantations in Langkat.[3] Germans were also widely employed as administrators on plantations throughout the East Coast of Sumatra.

Siegmund Ehrlich (1867–1928), from Fürth near Nuremberg, went to Deli in the 1890s and first worked at the Hüttenbach shop, He later became a procurement officer and manager and after working for more than ten years, he started his own business. Over time, Ehrlich successfully expanded his business, Firma S. Ehrlich at Kesawan, as a supplier to plantations, including cylinder oil, roofing tiles, nails, barbed wire, axes, coolie buckets, coal, De Wars Whisky, Italian Vermouth, dinner sherry liqueur, and Nordstern life insurance.[4]

German migration to Deli was not limited to merchants. Young Germans also sought jobs as plantation assistants, as recorded by Dutch author Louis Couperus:

> *Twenty years ago, I travelled with the German mail to the Indies; many young German men were on board, and their destination was at some company at Deli to try as an assistant. There were considerable German names among them. It had not happened in Germany: the family sent the young scapegoats away to the Far East. There were those who were drunk every night. It was a sad sight. I remember a nice, most lovable, handsome-looking boy with a great German name: he was drunk almost every evening ... He sometimes remained invisible for a day, and then came out refreshed and most sympathetic. After two years he died in Deli, barely twenty-two years old.*[5]

[1] DC 20-03-1886. See the chapters on Hüttenbach and Kehding in the Colonial Business and Trade section.

[2] Wright 1909: 199; *Bataviaasch nieuwsblad* 15-04-1898.

[3] Boom 2005: 243–269.

[4] DC 29-04-1914; SP 22-02-1928.

[5] Couperus 1923:43.

Following Hermann Näher's success with Senembah, several of his compatriots from Lindau, Bavaria, were drawn to Deli's lucrative tobacco industry. Among them was Richard Seutter von Loetzen, a relative of Näher, who served as director of one of Näher & Grob's plantations between 1878 and 1890. His brother, Emil Martin von Seutter, later joined the firm, eventually becoming the chief administrator for the Senembah Maatschappij. Both men accumulated substantial fortunes and returned to Lindau, where they invested in grand villas and enjoyed privileged lives. Others from Lindau, such as Anton Maria Poll and Fritz Zeiß, found employment as plantation engineers or administrators, overseeing hundreds of coolies and managing plantation infrastructure.[6]

German capital also entered the plantation sector. In 1887, German investors established the Deutsche Plantage-Maatschappij en de Sumatra-Tabak, consolidating their entry into Sumatra's plantation industry.[7] Yet it was not without controversy. Decades later, German media attention turned to labour abuses when the *Frankfurter Zeitung* (April–May 1904) published scathing critiques based on van den Brand's *De Millioenen uit Deli*, which exposed the mistreatment of indentured labourers.

German planters, led by Th.L.A. Runge (Deli Moeda estate) and backed by figures like J. Hallermann (*De Sumatra Post*), issued a rebuttal. They defended Deli's labour system, asserting that Chinese and Javanese workers migrated voluntarily under fixed-term contracts, with legal protections in place. They denied systemic abuse, insisting that employer misconduct was prosecuted.[8]

The growing German community developed its own social institution. In 1899, Carl Hick, as the German consul, convened an inaugural meeting at the Medan Hotel and founded the German Association, *Deutscher Verein*. One of its annual celebrations was the German emperor's birthday in January, followed by social events. The association even welcomed German warships visiting Deli. Notable visitors included the Duke and Duchess Johann Albrecht of Mecklenburg in February 1910. The association's leadership evolved over time, with various individuals serving as chairmen, including E. Hick, E. Tweer, Dr G. Maurer, A. Tameling, and Prof. Dr W. Schüffner.[9]

[6] Schweizer, Karl. 2019.
[7] DC 29-01-1887.
[8] DC 15-05-1905.
[9] SP 02-10-1929.

German companies were also important suppliers to the plantation economy. Notably Carl Schlieper, was known for supplying hardware and iron and steel products. Another important firm was Kerkhoff & Co., established by B.H. Kerkhoff in 1897 as a general merchant and iron and machinery importer.

The East Coast of Sumatra also attracted larger-scale German investors. Georg Hirsch, an entrepreneur from Bavaria, had a successful dyeing business in Germany. Hirsch invested in coal mines in Germany and other places, including in the US state of Illinois. He also had textile manufacturing facilities in New Jersey, as well as cotton and rubber plantations near Morogoro in German East Africa. In 1909, he acquired large plantations near Pematang Siantar, known as the Marihat Sumatra Plantations Company, a limited liability company that produced tea, rubber, palm oil, and coffee. His comrade, G. W. Th. von Guèrard, was in charge of the Marihat plantations, about 10,000 hectares consisting of four estates: Marihat Baris, Marihat Oeloe, Mahanda, and Kasinder.[10]

German presence in East Sumatra was diverse. Besides merchants, Germans also came to Deli as physicians, photographers, planters, or assistants in the tobacco plantations. Another important group was the Rheinische Mission, led by the well-known missionary Ludwig Ingwer Nommensen, who actively promoted the Christian Protestant faith, particularly in the Toba area. The Hennemann & Co. stores in Pematang Siantar and Sibolga were closely related to the missionaries.[11]

3.1.1 World War I

In August 1914, Germany declared war on Russia, France, and Belgium. Subsequently, Great Britain declared war on Germany, and in 1917, the United States declared war on Germany. The Netherlands and the Dutch Indies remained neutral. However, the outbreak of the war caused considerable confusion, and the German Society suggested that Germans in Sumatra should stay and continue working, awaiting further developments. The German trade and mail service to and from the Dutch Indies came to a standstill as German steamers in Asian waters were seized by the British.[12]

As the maritime war escalated, commercial shipping to and from Rotterdam and Amsterdam came to a halt. Due to the dangerous sea conditions, there was hardly any connection between Europe and the Dutch Indies. This disruption in trade and imports resulted in price hikes. In

[10] Marihat plantation still exists today as part of the national plantation company.
[11] *Het nieuws van den dag voor Nederlandsch-Indië* 08-05-1934.
[12] Van Dijk 2007: 137.

addition, the Allies enacted trade sanctions against Germany as part of an effort to weaken the German economy and isolate its commercial interests. German beer was replaced with Japanese Asahi beer.[13] As a result, direct trade with Japan and the United States via Penang and Singapore started. By 1918, imports from Singapore and Penang accounted for 67.4% of the total imports. This level dropped to 38% in 1932.

As the British colonial government in India commandeered rice shipments from Burma, Siam, and Indochina for military needs, Sumatra's East Coast, which imported 100,000 tonnes annually, faced catastrophic shortages. By 1918, prices had skyrocketed 700% to *f*70 per 100 kg bag. The plantation companies had to subsidise worker rations at the pre-war price of *f*10 to prevent mass desertions or uprisings.

In response to the food shortage on the East Coast of Sumatra, a meeting was convened by the Dutch Resident, involving plantation owners and shipping agencies. Fearing a worsening situation, they decided to purchase 120,000 bags of rice from Rangoon and Siam, even if it meant paying any price demanded. Plantation managers also attempted to cultivate alternative staple crops, such as sweet potatoes, maize, and soybeans. However, some planters opposed the shift, fearing disease risks to the precious tobacco.[14]

Desperate adaptations reshaped colonial agriculture. Dutch authorities mandated emergency food crops, 7100 m^2 of sweet potatoes (*ubi jalar*) and cornfields for every 100 labourers. At Senembah's estates, housing 8492 coolies, monthly rice rations were slashed from 16 kg to 10 kg, with 6 kg replaced by starchy substitutes. While workers initially accepted these measures, productivity plummeted as malnutrition spread throughout the workforce. The crisis revealed the absurd dependency of European planters: their cash-crop empire, generating millions in tobacco profits, relied entirely on imported staple foods.[15]

Initially, Europeans in Deli did not exhibit overt hostility towards the Germans, in contrast to Java. The local press refrained from inciting discord, and certain British and German businessmen still maintained their connections. The governor skilfully engaged with both British and German leaders. Still, the British company Harrisons & Crosfield dismissed 6 managers and 20 German or Austrian assistants from their rubber

[13] Van Dijk 2007: 152.
[14] Dehne 2019: 153.
[15] Janssen and Bool 1939: 40–43.

plantations.[16] Although there might be anti-German sentiments in certain cases, in general, the Dutch did not choose sides during World War I.

However, as the war continued, anti-German sentiment grew among the Dutch and their European allies. The submarine warfare in the North Sea heightened tensions, causing Germans in Deli to retreat from public life. Mass torpedoing incidents strained relations further, leading some Dutch to distance themselves from the Germans. Dr Schüffner, the chairman of the German association, reminded his compatriots to uphold their dignity and not tarnish the German name.[17]

Britain and the United States enacted the Trading with the Enemy Act, which defined the offence of engaging in business transactions with individuals of "enemy character." The Allies, including Britain, France, and later the United States, sought to regulate international trade and control access through an "Inter-Allied Blockade." It identified and seized German goods at sea, withholding credit in international financial records and utilising control over global shipping assets and supply chains to disrupt Germany's overseas commercial ties.[18]

The British compiled and published a blacklist of names in the *London Gazette*, listing companies and persons with whom British subjects should not trade. The United States published *Trading with the Enemy: Enemy Trading List*, prohibiting trade with the enemy or anyone associated with the enemy.[19] The list included German companies in Medan, such as Goldenberg and Co., F. Kehding, J. Hallermann, Güntzel and Schumacher, S. Ehrlich, S. Katz and Co., and Chinese merchants who were cooperating with them.[20] Businesses in the Dutch Indies refrained from engaging in trade with German merchants listed on the blacklist due to concerns that such transactions might lead to their own blacklisting, resulting in a loss of access to shipping and international banking services.

The situation continued until the end of 1919. Due to the animosity towards Germans, many, including Hallermann and Kleingrothe, decided to return to Germany after the war. The German companies were acquired and sold to the Dutch, including Hallermann, which became Varekamp & Co. Güntzel and Schumacher were taken over by a Dutch-owned capital,

[16] *Pinang Gazette and Straits Chronicle*, 17-07-1915.
[17] *De Locomotief* 19-03-1917.
[18] Idem.
[19] War Trade Board of the USA, 1917.
[20] *Algemeen Handelsblad* 25-03-1916.

and Kehding was incorporated into Internatio Rotterdam. S. Ehrlich happened to be in Europe when the war started and couldn't return to Medan. Immediately after the war, he returned to Medan and successfully revived his business. Ehrlich died in 1928, and not long after, his company was liquidated.[21]

As time progressed, the situation returned to normal, and German beer, such as Beck's or Tjap Koentji, became available again. New German companies were established under Dutch company laws, sometimes partnering with Dutch merchants.[22] German companies active in Medan include Carl Schlieper and Schnitzler & Co. specialised in iron and steel products.[23] There were Köhler printing firm, Herbert Delius office equipment supplier, Eduard Graaf watches and jewellery, and café Epperlein.[24]

3.1.2 German National Socialist Party and Its Dutch Supporters

With the rise of the Nazi Party in Germany in 1932, the German community in East Sumatra also began to embrace the *Nationalsozialistische Deutsche Arbeiterpartei* (National Socialist German Workers' Party). In 1933, the German community celebrated the Nazi government's *Der Tag der Nationalen Arbeit* or Labour Day on May 1 (Fig. 3.2).[25] A subsequent celebration in 1935 at the Medan Hotel, attended by German consul E. Dollmann, indicates that the Nazi Party maintained an active presence in the region. At another event at the Medan Hotel, the German Association held a German book exhibition showcasing Hitler's book *Mein Kampf*. The hall was decorated with German and Dutch flags, and the portraits of Queen Wilhelmina and Adolf Hitler were displayed side by side.[26] Every year, Hitler's birthday was celebrated with the Nazi flag. In 1938, a special film of the Führer was shown at the Rex theatre.[27]

At the same time, in 1931, the Dutch *Nationaal Socialistische Bond* (NSB), or National Socialist Movement, was founded by Ir. Anton Adriaan Mussert in Utrecht as a convergence of nationalism, fascism, and Nazi

[21] SP 23-02-1928; DC 11-07-1931.
[22] Fowler 1923: 234–235.
[23] Fowler 1923: 239–240.
[24] SP 15-07-1940.
[25] SP 02-05-1933.
[26] DC 21-11-1936.
[27] SP 20-04-1938.

Fig. 3.2 The German community celebrating the *Der Tag der Nationalen Arbeit* or labour day on May 1, 1933 at Medan Hotel (DC 02-05-1933)

sympathisers. As an equivalent of the National Socialist German Workers' Party, it initially had only a thousand members. In the second year, it rose to 18,000, and in the third year, it reached 35,000 members. One of its earliest members was Simon Plekker, who had worked in Deli for 23 years before returning to the Netherlands. Plekker was an administrator for many large plantations, including Senembah.[28] The NSB attracted a considerable number of mixed Dutch-Indonesian (Indo) followers, constituting approximately 70% of its membership. This affiliation was motivated by the party's staunch ultranationalist Dutch identity, and for the Indos, it offered a platform to publicly express their aspiration to align with Dutch culture and address their concerns regarding the growing Indonesian nationalism.[29]

NSB in the colony had a distinct character and societal role compared to its counterpart in the Netherlands. It grew rapidly in the Dutch Indies, especially in the planters' community of Deli, which embraced fascism. The Medan branch was inaugurated in 1934, forming groups in Medan,

[28] *Het nationale dagblad: voor het Nederlandsche volk* 07-03-1941.

[29] *De Groene Amsterdammer*. 2009. What motivates Geert Wilders? https://www.groene.nl/artikel/what-motivates-geert-wilders.

Kisaran, Poelau Radja, and Pematang Siantar.[30] At its fifth anniversary, its membership reached 55,000, and the Medan branch donated 2400 guilders.[31]

Initially, the NSB was not antisemitic. However, its leader, Anton Mussert, acknowledged that after Adolf Hitler and the Nazi Party came to power in Germany, the NSB began to see the Jews as a problem. Mussert aligned himself with Mussolini's view, asserting that "the majority of Jews should be deported." Following the invasion of the Netherlands in May 1940, members who continued to support the German fascists became actively involved in the persecution of Jews.[32]

Anton Mussert made his journey to the Dutch Indies in July 1935, first arriving in Medan from Rangoon. He was greeted at the airport by around 80 NSB members and gave the fascist salute, raising his right arm, shouting "*Hou zee.*"[33] After a detour to Singapore and Java, he was warmly welcomed back to Medan a couple of weeks later, giving lectures in Pematang Siantar and Kisaran at the Boenoet rubber factory.[34] His speech in Medan at the Orion theatre was attended by 800 people. Mussert emphasised the importance of the NSB's "efforts to awaken the Dutch people to their national identity and fight against both left-wing and right-wing governments that had harmed the nation's interests." He further applauded the rise of fascism in Italy and Germany, which, according to him, should be followed in the Netherlands. He further emphasised his support for Hitler.[35] His visit was widely covered in the newspapers, and Governor-General De Jonge even received him twice.

Mussert, in an interview, said the Dutch Indies were big and grand:

> *We can be proud of what has been achieved here in three centuries.*

Mussert, being an engineer, was particularly impressed with the good roads in Medan, which had a surface that had less dust and was easy to walk on due to the good Dutch engineering.[36] He further added that the Dutch nationalistic feeling was stronger in the Dutch Indies than in the

[30] SP 28-05-1934.
[31] SP 14-12-1936.
[32] SP 20-04-1940.
[33] SP 24-07-1935.
[34] SP 22-08-1935.
[35] SP 28-08-1935.
[36] SP 15-08-1935.

Fig. 3.3 Mussert arrived in Medan in 1935 with a fascist salute (left) (SP 24-07-1935)

Netherlands, as he saw many Dutch flags flown on buildings and even on ox carts (Fig. 3.3).[37]

A year later, Gerrit van Duyl, a propagandist for the NSB, visited the Dutch Indies and was warmly welcomed in Medan. In Soerabaja, van Duyl stated that the Chinese had no rightful place in the colony and that Dutch interests must take precedence. Later, in Medan, he reiterated the anti-immigrant rhetoric that the Chinese population outnumbered Europeans in the Dutch Indies and expressed concern about the economic displacement of Europeans by cheaper Asian labour. Despite the Dutch being immigrants themselves, he emphasised the need to protect European labour and economic opportunities. He maintained that he and the NSB did not incite anti-Chinese campaigns. In his speech in Medan, van Duyl stressed the importance of preserving Dutch racial and political dominance in the Dutch Indies. He proposed an imperial structure in which ultimate authority would remain with the Dutch, with limited participation by Indigenous elites permitted.[38]

[37] DC 26-08-1935.
[38] DC 03-09-1936, 05-09-1936.

Fig. 3.4 Café Epperlein celebrated Princess Juliana and Prince Bernhard's wedding in 1937 with the Netherlands and Nazi flags flown together (Bouwes Bavink 1937)

The ties between Germany and the Netherlands were further bonded in January 1937, when Princess Juliana, the sole heir to the Dutch empire, wed Prince Bernhard, a German aristocrat. The city of Medan had a three-day celebration; the city was ornamented with extravagant decorations, and lights lit up the town at night, displaying Dutch people's unwavering patriotism. There were bonfires, church services, a historical open-air play with parades, a gala evening at the Witte Sociëteit, Dutch nationalistic music performance, school parties, two big parades, a general procession, popular plays and films exhibition, and fireworks.[39] At Epperlein restaurant in Kesawan, the Dutch and Nazi flags were flown together, and the same scene could also be seen in Pasar Baroe in Batavia (Fig. 3.4).[40] Hotel

[39] SP 02-10-1936.

[40] See the picture: *Pasar Baroe te Batavia, gezien vanaf de Sawah Besar, verlicht ter gelegenheid van het huwelijk van prinses Juliana en prins Bernhard*, KITLV 54507 http://hdl.handle.net/1887.1/item:936526.

de Boer in Medan became a hub of celebration, where Dutch and German residents joined together for parties.[41] Australian entertainer Billy Heaton, who was performing in Medan at the time, wrote:

> *Here at the hotel, the Dutchmen and their lady friends and wives have been singing their lungs to a standstill; they have been going for hours, singing patriotic songs. Every so often, the band strikes up the Dutch equivalent to our 'God Save the King.' Everybody rises, some holding their hands out stretched in the Fascist salute.*[42]

Interestingly, in 1936, the editor of the *Pewarta Deli* newspaper received a pamphlet distributed by the NSB's Sumatra division, which discussed the implications of revolutionary actions in Japan. This pamphlet hinted at Japan's proximity to the Dutch Indies and argued for the need to expand local defences. However, this pamphlet was dismissed by the Dutch as the military revolution in Japan was related solely to issues in mainland Asia and not relevant to the Dutch Indies.[43]

In 1938, Count Felix von Luckner, a German naval officer who had served as the commander of the German sailing cruiser "Seeadler" during World War I, arrived in Belawan. Von Luckner, known for his support of the Nazi regime and often referred to as a Nazi apostle, gave a lecture in Medan on December 13, 1938, a month after the *Reichskristallnacht* pogrom against Jews.[44] On November 18, 1938, *De Sumatra Post* wrote an entire page about the persecution of the Jews in Germany.[45] Thus, residents of Medan were aware of the events in Germany. However, *Deli Courant* and *De Sumatra Post* published articles on Hitler's movements in Europe on a daily basis, including Hitler's birthday celebration and seven years of Nazi rule speech.[46]

[41] Idem.

[42] Idem.

[43] Overzicht van de Inlandsche en Maleisisch-Chineesche pers, 1936, no. 13, 28-03-1936.

[44] SP 13-12-1938; *The Straits Times* 17-01-1939.

[45] *De Sumatra Post* reported in detail about the pogrom against the Jews, Kristallnacht, on November 9–10, 1938, in Germany, when thousands of Jews were deported to concentration camps and many were killed (SP 18-11-1938).

[46] DC 12-02-1940; SP 20-04-1940.

3.1.3 Eduard Du Perron and Anti-fascism

In the late 1930s, not all Dutch intellectuals in the East Indies supported the growing sympathies towards fascism. One of the most prominent critics was Eduard Du Perron, a Dutch-Indies-born writer and intellectual.[47] In 1938, Du Perron published a series of articles in the progressive journal *Kritiek en Opbouw*, where he made his political stance unmistakably clear. He expressed his unwavering opposition to all forms of dictatorship, whether Stalinist, Nazi, or fascist, and affirmed his commitment to democracy. He proudly noted his membership in *Waakzaamheid* (Vigilance), a Dutch anti-fascist group founded by intellectuals like Menno ter Braak and Hendrik Marsman.[48] He emphasised that if the NSB ever seized power in the Netherlands, he and his colleagues would likely be imprisoned or forced into exile.

Du Perron criticised the complacency of many Europeans living safely in the Dutch Indies while his friends in Europe faced threats of bombings and violence.

> *I have exactly as little desire to be cowed by the tyranny of Stalin as I do by that of Hitler or Mussolini. I am also pro-democracy and anti-dictatorship; I was also a member of "Waakbaarheid" (Vigilance) from the start, and as the N.S.B. ever wins in Holland, I am, with Ter Braak and Greshoff, very much on the list of people for emigration or the concentration camp. No one doubts that. ... And to simply let it come down to the facts; I cannot afford to be in relative safety here in Netherlands India, while the day after tomorrow my friends in Europe could be bombed and gassed.*[49]

Du Perron referred to World War I, during which gas attacks were used in the trenches. In 1939, he could not have known about the gas chambers that would later be built in German concentration camps, as these were

[47] Eduard Du Perron (1899–1940) was born in Java and later lived in France and Belgium. He was a leading Dutch intellectual in the 1930s. His most famous book was *Het land van herkomst* (The Land of Origin) about his youth in Java in reflection on European culture. He died in May 1940 from a heart attack. His articles in *Kritiek en Opbouw* from 1938 and 1939 were posthumously published in *Indies Memorandum* in 1946.

[48] Menno ter Braak (1902–1940) was a Dutch author and friend of Eduard Du Perron. He was one of the most vocal anti-fascist Dutch writers in the 1930s. Ter Braak committed suicide on 10-5-1940 when the Germans invaded the Netherlands. Jan Greshof (1888–1971) was a Dutch author and poet.

[49] *Indies Memorandum*. Eduard Du Perron 1946:146, 147.

only constructed from 1941 onwards. Nor could he have foreseen that Japan would occupy the Netherlands Indies and that all Dutch civilians there would be interned in concentration camps. In hindsight, the Dutch in the Netherlands, so long as they were not Jewish or involved in the resistance, were in a far more comfortable position than those who remained in the Indies, where internment by the Japanese led to widespread malnutrition, disease, and death.

Du Perron voiced his solidarity with Indonesians, stressing that in the colonial context, his role was only to behave politely and respectfully towards the local population, rather than assert Dutch supremacy.[50] He confronted pro-Nazi sympathisers in the colony, including journalist W. Zentgraaff, the editor of the conservative *Java-Bode* newspaper, accusing him of intellectual dishonesty, slander, and the propagation of fascist ideology:

> *This old abruti - who cannot count, cannot think logically, cannot read, cannot write, cannot copy, who can only falsify text and interpret it like an innkeeper, who cannot do without the help of a psychiatrist and a bailiff for his rumination, he is here presented as a "great polemicist!"*

He compared the press in the Netherlands Indies with the press in Europe in favour of the latter, as there were more different independent newspapers:

> *The organisation of the lie is no weaker in Europe: only there one finds a counterbalance in newspapers of a different direction, an opportunity to at least approach the truth, while here an opportunistic press, occasionally with a very timid groan of half-smothered conscience, reigns everywhere.*[51]

He also denounced the broader cultural decay he saw emerging: pastors advocating for Nazi-style book burnings, literature being censored, and a growing acceptance of racial theories and authoritarian nationalism. Despite a worsening political climate in Europe, Du Perron remained outspoken. For Du Perron, the real danger lay not only in European fascism but also in the Dutch nationalists in the Indies who, under the guise of patriotism, were preparing the colony for an eventual "Anschluss" (union

[50] Du Perron 1946:149. Du Perron supported Indonesian independence and nationalistic movements.

[51] Du Perron 1946:21.

or annexation) with Nazi Germany. Through his writing, Du Perron stood as a rare and courageous voice of resistance in a colonial society increasingly permeated by authoritarian ideas.

3.1.4 *German Aggression*

By 1939, Germany's aggression in Europe had raised concerns among Dutch businesses. Güntzel and Schumacher, which had become a Dutch company by then, was not widely acknowledged as such. The last German director had stepped down in 1936. In some cases, shipping companies initially declined cargo, mistakenly believing that Güntzel and Schumacher was still German. To dispel any notion of being linked to Germany, 17 German employees were dismissed due to fears that the company might be blacklisted, as in World War I.145F174[52]

On May 10, 1940, Germany launched an invasion of the Netherlands. This aggressive move swiftly led to the Netherlands' capitulation within just five days, following the devastating bombing of Rotterdam and a subsequent threat from Germany to bomb Utrecht. In response to these events, the Dutch Indies government on the East Coast of Sumatra acted promptly. The very next day after Germany's invasion, they took decisive measures, rounding up 209 German nationals and 16 NSB members. 146F The German missionaries and doctors working in Tapanoeli were interned, and the government declared that the Rhenish Mission officially ceased its activities in the Dutch East Indies. The Dutch took over all the churches, mission schools, and hospitals.[53]

These individuals were then interned in camps located near Pematang Siantar.[54] The chief police commissioner of Medan announced that any German citizen should report to the police station.[55] At the same time, German companies were taken over by Dutch companies.

[52] *De Locomotief* 02-11-1939.

[53] Seventy-five missionaries and doctors were interned in Silindoeng (SP 11-05-1940); SP 25-05-1940; 24-07-1940; 16-08-1940. In July 1940, German internees from all of the Dutch Indies were shipped to Belawan for Koeta Tjane in Atjeh. They were then moved to Sibolga in December 1941 to be transported to India in three ships. The last ship left in January 1942 and was bombed by a Japanese warplane. Many died and some of the survivors managed to reach and settle in Nias.

[54] SP 11-05-1940.

[55] SP 11-05-1940.

The municipality of Medan released its latest census of the population of Europeans in Medan: 4183 Dutch, 262 Japanese, 208 equals, 91 British, 34 stateless, 30 American, 20 Portuguese, 19 German, 16 Swiss, 11 Danish, 11 Belgian, 5 Czechoslovakian, 4 Italian, 3 French, 3 Polish, 2 Hungarian, and 1 Yugoslav. The 19 Germans were German women and children designated by the Government Decree as non-hostile subjects.[56]

A German article claimed that German scientists in the Dutch East Indies led colonial scientific progress. *De Sumatra Post* quickly denounced German contributions to agricultural development in the Dutch East Indies, clarifying that Jacobus Nienhuys, not German capitalists, pioneered the tobacco industry in Deli. Nienhuys secured financing from the German-born P.W. Janssen, leading to the founding of the Deli Maatschappij in 1869. However, this was a Dutch company. Janssen was naturalised as a Dutch citizen. The Senembah Company was originally German, but became a Dutch-owned enterprise.[57]

Similarly, claims were made about German innovations in other agricultural areas, such as cinchona (Junghuhn) and oil palm (Belgian Galet) efforts. It argued that science is a universal endeavour and highlighted how many prominent German-born researchers, such as Rumphius, Junghuhn, and Reinwardt, either remained in the Indies or worked in Dutch institutions rather than in Germany. The article dismissed claims about German contributions to the Buitenzorg Botanical Garden and colonial medicine, emphasising that key achievements were often made by Dutch or international collaborative efforts.[58]

In 1941, the Japanese arrived in Medan. As allies, the Germans were freed and cooperated with the Japanese. Even in Padang, there was a Hitler youth organisation.[59] After the war, the German population in Medan dwindled.[60]

[56] SP 06-02-1941.
[57] SP 01-08-1941.
[58] SP 31-07-1941.
[59] United States. Office of Strategic Services 1945: 43.
[60] In the 1950s, the Indonesian government invited German doctors to work in the remote areas of the newly independent countries; about 300 German doctors went to work all over Indonesia (Geerken, Horst H. *A Gecko for Luck. 18 Years in Indonesia*. 2015: 303–304).

3.1.5 Si Hitler Hamonangan

In 1937, a Batak father took his son to be baptised, and the tradition was that the boy would adopt a Christian (Western) name. They usually adopted biblical names, but some also adopted contemporary names. During the ceremony, the missionary asked what the boy's name was. The father replied, "Si Hitler Hamonangan" (Hitler, who leads to victory). The missionary responded with *Liulang boi* (that's not allowed). "Choose another name. I cannot baptise the child with the name Hitler." The father insisted that his child would be named "Hitler Hamonangan" and left the crowded church. A few days later, the father hosted a traditional Batak adat ceremony *hordja mangoepa*. The child was given the name "Hitler Hamonangan" in accordance with Batak customs and rituals.[61]

Batak people tend to give exotic names to their children, such as Bismarck, Mussolini, and Jan Jacobson van den Berg, or Tieleman & Dros (after famous Dutch companies). And in 1941, a boy in the Karo region was named Nippon Sembiring.[62] A Batak reader wrote in *De Sumatra Post* that he rejected the portrayal of Batak as backward or barbaric, citing examples of Western misunderstanding and prejudice, such as the alleged cannibalism among Bataks being misinterpreted without understanding its cultural context. The writer pointed out the contrast between how Westerners and Bataks name their children, with Batak names reflecting significant hopes for the child's future. If a boy was given the name Hitler or Mussolini, the father hoped that his son would later become a leader among his people. If a boy was given the name Tieleman and Dros, the father hoped that the boy would become a successful trader.[63]

3.2 French Entrepreneurs and Adventurers in Deli

Alongside the Dutch and Germans, a small but influential group of French settlers also helped shape the early plantation landscape of East Sumatra. Among the first was the de Guigné family, who established the Soengai Sikambing plantation in the early 1870s. At the same time, the adventurer and ethnographer Xavier Brau de Saint-Pol Lias arrived in Deli with a

[61] SP 18-11-1937.
[62] *Soerabaijasch Handelsblad* 11-03-1937; SP 10-11-1937.
[63] SP 10-11-1937.

Fig. 3.5 Plantation at Soengai Sikambing. The European headman, Laurent, in front of his residence (on the right). His Chinese boy near him; a group of coolies behind; on the left, the tandil (Chinese foreman); the bandol d'état, a former boy (1876–1877), in front of the group; in the background, Chinese coolies on the path to the bangsals, large thatched sheds where all the harvested tobacco leaves are hung to dry, while waiting to be taken to the large fermentation bangsal of the factory. Deli, Sumatra 1880–1881 (Brau Saint-Pol Lias, Bibliothèque nationale de France, département Société de Géographie, SG WG-6)

team of explorers and entrepreneurs. Combining colonial enterprise with scientific curiosity, he documented the early years of Deli's plantation frontier and the lives of the Batak people (Fig. 3.5).

3.2.1 De Guignés: Building a Legacy Through Tobacco and Faith

The de Guigné family was one of the earliest French families living on Réunion Island, east of Madagascar. When they faced difficulties in sugarcane plantations on the island, in 1871, Albert de Guigné explored the land in North Sumatra and obtained a concession from the Sultan of Deli. Later, his brothers Paul and Georges joined him in establishing the plantation Soengai Sikambing in 1873.[64] They travelled to Deli via the South of India, where the father of the family held a high administrative post.

Paul de Guigné, the eldest in the family, a magistrate in the French administration in Pondicherry on India's east coast, became the director of the Soengai Sikambing plantation. Georges de Guigné, the younger of the two brothers, received a university education in France and was responsible for managing the plantation. Their sister Gabrielle married Joseph Jules David de Floris, a former officer in the French army from Pondicherry. De Floris moved to Deli in 1874 and managed the Soengai Poetih plantation.[65]

Since the family had a connection with the French administration, they were able to transport Tamil workers from southern India (Pondicherry and Tiruchirappalli) to Deli.

The de Guigné established a large family in Deli with extensive descendants, relying on connections between Réunion, India, Sumatra, and Singapore. They managed prosperous tobacco plantations with the help of Indians and Chinese coolies. They also provided hospitality to passing French people in a setting inspired by their Catholic beliefs.

In 1873, the Dutch Catholic Pastor de Vries from the Catholic church made the first official trip to Deli and wrote:

Heaven does not seem to be much wanted by the planters.[66]

In 1876, Father de Vries visited the de Guigné family, who were devout Catholics and promised to construct a small church once they received regular visits from a clergyman. Five years later, in November 1878, Dutch Pastor Carolus Wenneker arrived in Deli to establish a mission as the first pastor. The de Guigné family warmly welcomed him and generously provided him with hospitality until the new presbytery and church in Medan were completed in January 1881.159F That first Catholic church was located on the site of today's Catholic cathedral at Jl. Pemuda, Medan.

Paul and Julie de Guigné had two daughters and a son, while Joseph de Floris and Gabrielle had five of their nine children born in Sumatra

[64] Labrousse 2009: 83–116.
[65] Brau Saint-Pol Lias 1884: 307–309.
[66] Missie Kapucijnen 1917: 91–92.

between 1872 and 1884. Albert de Guigné settled later and married Marie Brasier de Thuy in 1875 in Singapore.

Initially funded through advances from the Deli Company, they later secured French investment. Paul built a chapel for his Catholic Tamil workers, where they could pray and educate their children in religion. However, they soon sold their companies.

In 1898, the Franco-Deli Tabak Maatschappij was incorporated in Amsterdam with a capital of 3 million guilders and a plantation area of 5200 bouw (about 3645 hectares).[67] De Guigné and De Floris brought into the company their plantations Soengei-Sikambing, Gambier, Loening, Oedjong-Deleng, Namoe-Rambai, and Soengei-Poetih. They received cash and shares worth 2.5 million guilders.[68]

The de Guigné family made enough money and decided to return to France. Before they left Deli, they offered the Catholic Tamils whom they had brought over a free passage back to India. Some took advantage of the offer, but many returned to Deli seeking employment. After De Guigné's departure, the Tamil Catholic community dispersed across various plantations for work. The new owners demolished the chapel, but the remaining Catholics built a bamboo hut as a temporary place of worship. Later, the plantation provided four coolie houses to the workers, which they converted into a chapel.[69]

In 1886, Paul and Julie de Guigné decided to return to France and settled in the Bordeaux region. Their son Jacques de Guigné became a second lieutenant of the French army. In World War I, Jacques died leading an attack against the Germans in 1915. His daughter, Anne de Guigné, although she only had a short life, is considered a saint in the Roman Catholic Church. She was declared Venerable by Pope John Paul II on March 3, 1990.[70]

The French were still making a living on the East Coast of Sumatra, and in 1910, Dutchman M. Chits, an agent for the shipping line KPM, was appointed as the French Consul Agent in Medan (Figs. 3.6 and 3.7).[71]

[67] 1 bouw = 0.7 hectares.

[68] *Bataviaasch nieuwsblad* 22-06-1895. Harm Kamerlingh Onnes met Mr and Mrs Chits in 1923 in Medan and even made a sketch of him.

[69] *Nieuwsblad van het Zuiden* 21-07-1923.

[70] https://www.annedeguigne.fr/fr/evenements/2015-centenaire-de-la-mort-du-capitaine-de-guigne/171-notice-biographique-jacques-de-guigne-1883-1915.html.

[71] *Bataviaasch Nieuwsblad* 27-04-1910.

Fig. 3.6 Mr and Mrs Chits, by Harm Kamerlingh Onnes, February 1923 (Buiskool, D.A. *De reis van Harm Kamerlingh Onnes* 1999: 163)

In 1920, the famous French aviator Poulet flew to Medan to give a flight demonstration.[72] However, by then, the economic crisis had struck Deli, and many plantations had been abandoned. Dutch author Annie Salomons, who lived in Deli in 1924–1925, wrote:

> *Saint Cyr… it invoked the memory of Napoleon, heroism, panache, and yes, a former French officer had given that name to the enterprise to preserve a beautiful memory of his youth. Later, when it had become a highly profitable kebon, the administrator's house was built. It wasn't like any other Indies house, but rather resembled a stately, imposing European country house with an upper floor, a monumental staircase, and oak panelling along the walls. A wide driveway had led there, and in the evening, when one drove to the hospitable home, the light of the lanterns on the high gate could be seen shining through the trees from a distance. Splendid celebrations had taken place there; the spacious dining room had echoed with exuberant joy. …*
> *All of this came to mind as we entered the wide driveway; the ground was covered in grass, and the tree trunks were overgrown with vines. The lanterns had been removed from the tall fence posts, replaced by small trees of varying heights and types…*
> *Then we stood in front of what used to be the house; a local wandered about, and no one knew what he wanted there. It was desolate; the shutters had been taken away, with only a few remaining at the top, not worth the effort to remove. …*
> *… Here, it had been barely two years ago that young, cheerful people, in the prime of their lives, had celebrated life with joy and exuberance… Did a house*

[72] SP 25-02-1921.

Fig. 3.7 Bridge in Medan over the Soengai Deli to the tobacco plantation Soengei Sikambing (Bibliothèque nationale de France, département Société de Géographie, SG WG-6). "*M. de Guigné had built there according to the architecture used in Hindustan, as primitive as it is ingenious. Long pieces of wood planted in the river support the planked deck and the thatched roof, inclined two by two and meeting at the end, well above the roof.*" (Brau Saint-Pol Lias 1884:302)

deteriorate faster here than a human being? Or was all existence and flourishing equally unreliable?[73]

[73] Salomons 1933: 43–46.

3.3 The Adventures of Brau Saint-Paul Lias

A notable Frenchman who ventured to Deli was Xavier Brau de Saint-Pol Lias, a larger-than-life adventurer, ethnologist, and geographer. He studied at the college of Pamiers and worked at the Banque de France before joining the Geographical Society, the Colonial Studies Society, and the Commercial Geography Society (Fig. 3.8).[74]

In 1875, Brau de Saint-Pol established the "Société des Colons-Explorateurs" or Society of the Colonial Exploration in Paris. It aimed to combine ethnographic research with the establishment of agricultural enterprises in overseas colonial territories. The association allowed engineers, industrialists, farmers, doctors, and merchants with some capital to conduct scientific research and establish agricultural, industrial, and

Fig. 3.8 Xavier Brau de St.-Pol Lias by Alexandre Quinet (Bibliothèque nationale de France, département Société de Géographie, SG PORTRAIT-1342)

[74] https://fr.wikipedia.org/wiki/Xavier_Brau_de_Saint_Pol_Lias

commercial enterprises. A team of agriculturists, an engineer, a physician, a merchant, a scientist, and an administrator was formed.[75]

Brau de Saint-Pol initially focused on the Dutch East Indies. He arrived in Batavia in July 1876. He obtained approval from the governor-general to establish the society in the Dutch Indies. His team was made up of Walloon, Laurent, Tabel, Guillaume, Chapel, and Doctor O'Roorke. The Dutch government pointed to Deli, an area just being developed for tobacco cultivation. Brau sent his colleagues ahead to Deli to take a survey.

In October 1876, Brau de Saint-Pol arrived at Laboean Deli and visited the de Guigné family in Soengei Sikambing. He obtained a land lease from the Sultan of Deli. However, they faced many difficulties and illnesses. They had rented a large house from the Datoe Bandar, but sudden rain put them more than a foot underwater, causing some of them to catch a fever, while the engineer suffered from an eye infection.[76]

Brau de Saint-Pol realised they could not stay in the Laboean area and had to look for a piece of higher ground. He was given a concession area of 3000 bouw [77] in Bedagei, where his companions had already surveyed the land. The group was able to raise capital of 87,000 francs.[78] However, the land was at the southern frontier of the tobacco plantation area at the time. Brau's concession on the Bedagei River was not easy to access; one had to take a boat from Belawan to the mouth of the Bedagei, then travel up the river and sometimes switch to another type of boat. The area became known as "Jungle Brau" in honour of the leader, but it was locally known as a gathering place for elephants.

The jungle was inhabited by tigers, crocodiles, monkeys, and rhinoceroses. This surreal experience fuelled the enthusiasm of Brau. And he never failed to write to the newspapers, such as *L'Explorateur, L'Exploration, Journal des Voyages*, etc. about the celebrated exploits of the colony.[79]

They started a tobacco company with Chinese and Batak workers. The first crop was good, but the second was disappointing. But they managed to plant over sixty thousand tobacco plants and constructed 2 drying sheds, huts for the coolies, a mansion for the administrator, 2 fine houses on a hill for 2 families, and 4 tents for the other partners. There was also a

[75] Labrousse 2009: 83–116.
[76] Idem.
[77] 1 bahu or baoe = 0.7 hectares.
[78] Broersma 1919: 99–100.
[79] Labrousse 2009: 83–116.

garden, a park with goats, pigs, geese, ducks, chickens, and pigeons.[80] The management of the workforce was challenged by differences in enthusiasm levels. The team was disillusioned by spotting a large vein of gold in the area, and they started to fall out with each other.[81]

Nevertheless, Brau did not forget the ethnographic goal of his association. He wrote for journals, outlining his observations on animals, plants and the study of the Batak people. He returned to Paris in the summer of 1877 and gave a lecture at a geographical society meeting. He tried to search for new capital but was unsuccessful. Back in Bedagei, the plantation was abandoned by its team in 1878. Tabel and Laurent left and were hired as assistant administrators by de Guigné.[82] Later, the engineer and the doctor of the company received a subsidy of 12,000 francs each from the French government for their scientific research.

Despite this, Brau de Saint-Pol continued to pursue his dream of exploring the colony in Sumatra and eventually secured a mission from the Ministry of Public Instruction. He returned to Singapore in 1880 with a new team. He departed in the company of John Errington de la Croix, a mining engineer, to Meulaboh, Labuan Haji, Singkel, Lhoong, then Malaysia, and returned via Java. He made a third expedition (1884–1885), again with Errington de la Croix, to India, Burma, Malaysia, Indochina, and Siam, and also returned via Java.

Brau de Saint-Pol gave lectures in Europe and published several books about his adventure, notably *De France à Sumatra par Java, Singapour et Pinang. Les anthropophages* (1884), detailing his adventure in Deli. In the book, he provided a detailed account of how a Deli tobacco plantation was physically built, financed, and operated. First, he obtained a concession sealed by the Sultan and approved by Dutch authorities. The work was then driven by a multiethnic labour hierarchy and a capital-intensive colonial system. The Europeans served as administrators, assistants, surveyors, and overseers. Chinese workers, recruited through brokers in Penang, Singapore, and Swatow, formed the backbone of field labour. Organised into *kongsi* work gangs under foremen (*tandil* or *baba tandil*), they cleared forest, tilled soil, and handled the delicate curing of tobacco leaves. Some also became carpenters, blacksmiths, or small traders in the estate towns. Malays worked as boatmen, herdsmen, or auxiliary guards, forming the

[80] Broersma 1919: 99–100.
[81] SP 15-12-1913.
[82] Labrousse 2009: 83–116.

local mediating class between Europeans and upland Bataks. Indian labourers were skilled ditch-diggers, drain builders, and cattle-keepers. Boyan or Baweanese craftsmen were prized for their expertise in rattan and thatch construction, essential for the *bangsal* sheds and coolie barracks. Batak highlanders, drawn down from the mountains by cash wages, appeared sporadically as clan-based contract workers. From the planter's verandah, the estate appeared as a small industrial colony: coolies working the fields, Klings driving ox carts, Boyans roofing sheds, Chinese traders running shops, and Europeans on horseback overseeing it all.[83]

His photographs of the early residents of the region are now in the French National Library. Here, we reproduce his interesting observation (Fig. 3.9).

3.4 The Study of the Batak People

The Batak people are an Indigenous group of North Sumatra who inhabit the rugged highlands. They are known for their distinct languages, a clan system, and culture and traditions. The Batak people developed a rich culture long before European contact. Their first appearance in European records dates to the late thirteenth century, when Marco Polo, sailing along Sumatra's coast in 1292, described the story of a tribe of "man-eaters" in the interior. Though shaped by myth and fear, this account attracted Europeans to study what they believed to be the primitive people (Fig. 3.10).

However, this is a colonial narrative; Batak communities were not isolated societies but were deeply embedded in long-standing networks linking the plateau, the foothill *doesoen* (village), and the Malay-dominated coast. Highland Batak populations supplied labour, forest products, and migrants to Indigenous cultivation zones and coastal trade circuits. There were also genealogical ties connected to the inland and lowland elites. This interdependence was gradually transformed as coastal Malay sultanates, through Islamisation and "Malayisation," positioned themselves as intermediaries to the outside world and increasingly framed non-Muslim inland peoples as Batak, socially inferior outsiders.[84]

According to historian Ichwan Azhari and philologist Ulrich Kozok, the term Batak is an exonym, originally a name used by coastal Malay communities to refer to the peoples of the interior highlands, which was

[83] Brau Saint-Pol Lias 1884:302–336.
[84] Perret 2009: 143–168.

Fig. 3.9 The drying of tobacco leaves. Deli's tobacco harvest ran on a tight, staged workflow. Cut plants were hung head-down in bangsals-verts on anak-kayou racks (10 stalks per stick), where assistants graded quality (worth 1–8 dollars per thousand stalks) and dried the leaf for ~3 weeks. Workers then stripped leaves into small ikat (bundles) (paid 1 douit each), hauled them by ox-cart to a central fermentation shed, piled them into monitored heaps (≈50 °C), repeatedly re-stacked for even colour, and finely sorted into four principal hues (brown dark/light, green, yellow) with many nuances and texture classes. After a final long fermentation, leaves were press-baled (often in January) and shipped via Labouan/Pinang to Amsterdam, Rotterdam, and London, valued in Europe as premium cigar-wrapper leaf (Brau Saint-Pol Lias 1884: 338–339)

later adopted by European observers. As Western tobacco plantation expansion intensified, the Dutch colonial administration then solidified these changes by codifying *adat*, drawing administrative borders, and institutionalising the Batak–Malay divide as an ethnic and legal category. By the end of the century, Batak identity had been reshaped as a category embedded in plantation capitalism and colonial governance.[85]

[85] Personal communication with Ichwan Azhari and Uli Kozok.

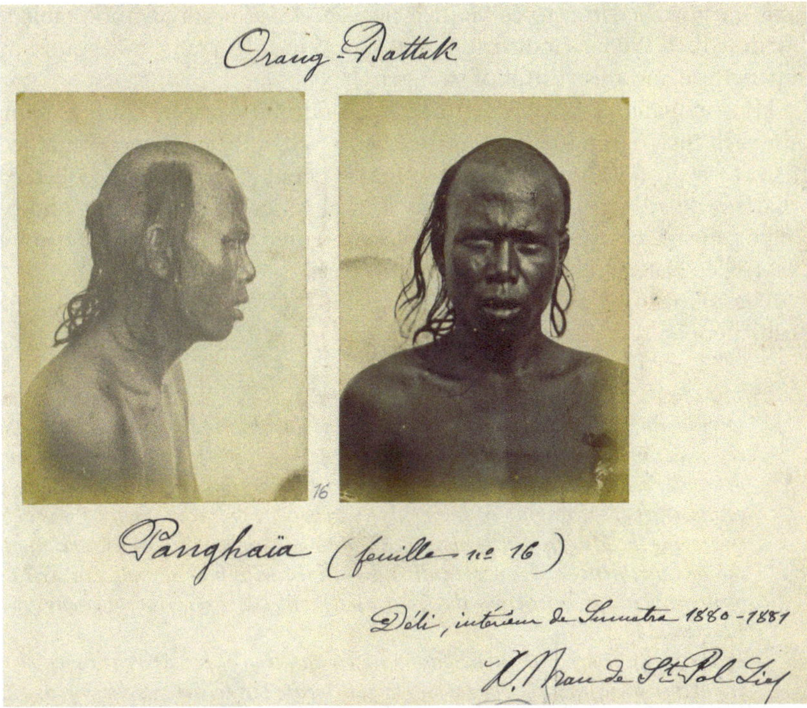

Fig. 3.10 Profile of a Batak penghulu (Brau Saint-Pol Lias, Bibliothèque nationale de France, département Société de Géographie, SG WG-6)

Curious Western explorers and officials began to venture into what they called "Batakland."

Brau Saint-Pol Lias travelled for several days into the highlands and a Batak village. He described the Bataks as the principal inland race of Sumatra, occupying the fertile volcanic mountains stretching from Atjeh to Palembang. They lived in well-cultivated plateaus and valleys planted with rice, betel, and bananas, and raised buffaloes, cattle, small but vigorous horses, goats, and pigs, showing none of the Islamic restrictions of the coastal Malays. Physically, they were taller and stronger than the Malays, with darker complexions, more prominent features, and an expression of savage pride and independence. Their clothing was woven by themselves from thick blue, white, and black cloth, and they adorned themselves with silver ornaments. Every man carried a *parang* and a *pisso* (machete and knife), using the latter to carve their peculiar script upon bamboo tablets. He described them as industrious and skilled in their crafts, but bound by superstition and mistrustful of strangers.[86]

He conducted anthropometric studies and photography among them, admired their strength, intelligence, and self-sufficiency, yet regarded them as a proud and primitive mountain people. He proudly collected what he called a complete anthropological series of the Bataks: photographs, measurements, and hair samples presented to the Musée d'Histoire Naturelle (Natural History Museum) in Paris.

The following is an extract of Brau Saint-Pol Lias' encounter with the Batak people.

> *The editorial staff of the dictionary published by the Société d'Anthropologie in Paris declares that it does not possess scientific documents about the Bataks and is content to give some ethnographic information drawn from good sources and generally correct. During my last trip, I tried to fill this gap; equipped with a complete set of measuring instruments and photographic equipment, I was able to provide the Museum with what is called an anthropological series, that is, all the measurements of twenty adult individuals, with hair samples, as well as photographic portraits from the front and profile. My series covers twenty-two Bataks. …*
>
> *By the way, the general public has no understanding of the effort it takes for a researcher to acquire the objects they seek, to locate the documents they need. The Bataks are not easy people. They are extremely difficult, and to convince them to allow themselves to be measured and photographed, I had to pay each individual and bring along the village leaders. Even then, I faced many difficulties during the execution. For example, when I asked for a lock of hair, it seemed like a never-ending political issue; endless negotiations, and sometimes I had to exhaust my Malay eloquence and other persuasive means. Panghaia, one of them, never agreed to give me a lock of hair.*
>
> *"As soon as toewan (sir) returns to his country," he repeated stubbornly, "and he has a lock of hair from me, he can make me sick or let me die…"*
>
> *Perhaps one does not have to look far in our country for similar superstitions.*
>
> *Once I returned from Kampoeng Sounggal, disappointed with the gap that this stubbornness caused in my collection, when I met a Batak whose beautiful hair immediately aroused my desire. I stopped him, showed him a Spanish mat of the kind that the Malays call "ringgit mariam" (cannon ringgit), the only currency they will accept, and asked, "Do you know this money?" Ringgit allous, he replied.*

[86] Brau Saint-Pol Lias 1884:345–356.

"Do you want it?" "Yes."
However, I had not directly asked for his hair yet and had taken a detour. "You have long hair. Doesn't it bother you?" "No."
"They must be very warm." "No, not really."
"Of course, you don't wear your hair in a way that makes you feel uncomfortable." He looked as if to say, "Where is this going?"
"Do you want to trade it for a coin?" He understood me now and declined.
"Two coins?" "No!" "Three." He remained silent and seemed to waver. With ringgits and patience, I might still get what I wanted.
The native who accompanied me came to my aid. "Well," he said, "toewan (sir) wants to relieve you of your useless hair and even gives you mats, and you refuse?" "Yes, he has too much hair; his head is too hot. I don't want that man to get sick and give him four ringgits." He neither said yes nor no.
Finally, when he agreed, I took him away immediately. One must not give him time to think, otherwise, he will change his mind. But how to cut his hair? I only had a "bowie-knife." Luckily, I saw a seamstress nearby with a copper scissors. She kindly made it available to me.
And then, passers-by saw me bent over my Batak for more than fifteen minutes on the roadside, while he sat on the ground, and as I sweated, learning an operation that Parisian hairdressers do with such ease and that I had not thought would be so difficult. The hair was quite tangled, but I cannot reveal why so much merit was hidden in my work. But must we not endure much for science? [87]

[87] Brau Saint-Pol Lias 1884:357–364.

CHAPTER 4

The Influence and Dynamics of Japanese in Medan

During colonial times, the Dutch government established a social hierarchy that categorised different ethnic groups living in the region. The population was categorised into three distinct groups for administrative purposes: Europeans, Natives, and Foreign Orientals. In the early twentieth century, the European category was expanded to include Europeans and their equals, which also encompassed Japanese residents. Meanwhile, the Foreign Orientals comprised individuals mainly from Asia and the Middle East, including Arabs, Indians, and Chinese. This division primarily served administrative, taxation, and educational purposes (Fig. 4.1).

The Japanese had settled in Medan and the east coast of Sumatra since the late nineteenth century; however, the number remained relatively small. The Japanese worked in various professions, including traders, servants, manual labourers, and skilled roles such as photographers.

When Britain and France defeated China in the Opium Wars and the US Navy demanded similar concessions from Japan in 1854, Japanese leaders initially considered armed resistance. They soon realised that Japan was technologically and militarily inferior to the western powers, making resistance futile. Consequently, they adopted a strategy of modernisation. Starting in 1868, Japan eliminated feudal domains, restructured power,

B. Minasny, D. A. Buiskool, *Stories from Medan, Volume 1*,
https://doi.org/10.1007/978-981-95-7707-1_4

Fig. 4.1 Hüttenbachstraat was known for its *toko* Japan, or Japanese shops, and the well-known Asahi photographer on the right (Asahi postcard, KITLV 1403436)

and gradually introduced modern systems in education, the military, finance, law, and government.[1]

In 1894, the British-Japanese treaty, based on reciprocity, prompted other Western countries, including the Netherlands, to establish similar relations with Japan. These agreements provided both sides with privileged access to each other's markets and established legal equality between the Japanese and Europeans, particularly in matters of justice administration. The Dutch, in particular, were concerned about Japan's potential interest in colonising New Guinea, a weakly controlled part of the Dutch colony. Recognising Japan's increased influence, the Dutch granted the

[1] Key milestones included compulsory elementary education in 1872, the creation of the Army General Staff in 1878, the establishment of the Bank of Japan and a new criminal code in 1882, the formation of a cabinet in 1885, and the introduction of a constitution by 1890. Paine 2010: 66–67.

Japanese European legal status in 1899, setting them apart from other Asians living in the Dutch East Indies.[2]

Upon hearing the news, the Japanese residents in Medan rejoiced. But they were also aware of their unique circumstances. A discussion was held to discontinue the customs of the Japanese people living on the island, but it was not agreed upon.[3] Classifying the Japanese in the same category as Europeans did not necessarily mean that Japanese individuals were treated exactly the same as Dutch or other European colonists. However, it granted them certain privileges and a relatively higher social status than the Indigenous groups and the Chinese.

4.1 The Japanese in Medan

The Dutch Indies in the late nineteenth and early twentieth centuries saw the arrival of many Japanese women working as prostitutes. The women mainly came from impoverished areas in Kyushu, dominated by poor farmers during the Meiji period (1868–1912). Around 1889–1892, these women crossed the Malacca Strait, arrived at Belawan, and came to Medan by ox cart. These women were unofficially welcomed as there were a disproportionate number of males to females in the region. (This topic will be discussed in Volume II.)

According to Dutch colonial government statistics from 1896, there were 463 Japanese residents in the Dutch East Indies, with 376 women. In Medan, there were 209 Japanese residents, with 79 women working in 15 brothels and 92 working as female maids. Naokichi Nakamura, a self-proclaimed world explorer, visited Medan in 1902 and found numerous Japanese women engaged in what he termed "ugly businesses". He reported that there were around 80–90 Japanese residents in Medan, with three Japanese stores.[4]

Japanese men worked as labourers, merchants, and photographers. One of the earliest merchants was I. Mazaraki; initially a tailor, he later established his own outfit-making shop, offering the white uniform known as *jas toetoep*, a white cotton suit with a high collar, specially designed for a tropical climate.[5] At the same time, it is unknown whether they were

[2] Houben 2013: 227–237.
[3] Aoki 2013.
[4] Aoki 2013.
[5] DC 15-06-1898.

related, M. Mazaraki established his photography shop in Medan in August 1899, and Ms R. Mazaraki had a dress shop at Polonia.[6]

As the Japanese population grew, in 1897, the Japanese of Medan founded the Foundation Association, with three men and three women elected as committee members, and registered 55 members. It was the first Japanese association in Southeast Asia. The women of the association primarily handled fundraising, while the men worked on acquiring land for a cemetery. They purchased land at Petisah, next to the Hokkien cemetery, and established the Japanese cemetery. A Japanese woman drowned in a flood and became the first occupant of the cemetery. In 1900, the association changed its name to Sumatra Nihonjin kai or Sumatra Japanese Association. The association expanded, and in 1913, the Japanese erected six *Jizo* (protector deity) statues in the cemetery and invited a Japanese Buddhist monk from Penang for the opening ceremony.[7]

In 1904, when the Russo-Japanese War broke out, the Japanese women of Medan eagerly donated, contributing $400 to the Japanese military. After the fall of Port Arthur in 1905, the Japanese of Medan, led by Shibuya, Matsuzaki, and Konishi, organised a procession through the city. Japan emerged triumphant, forcing Russia to relinquish its colonising ambitions in East Asia. A party was held at the Konishi shop with music and dance, *De Sumatra Post* reported:

> *Some Europeans, including us, who had been invited by our hairdresser to come and take a look, were received with great enthusiasm by Japan upon their arrival in the most beautifully decorated hall and when one of the guests, a cheerful planter, expressed his feelings and shouted "Banzai" in a loud voice. The excitement of the partygoers knew no bounds anymore.*[8]

The Dutch did not realise that 33 years later, they would be conquered. This victory established Japan as a major modern Asian power that defeated a European power and impressed Dutch colonial officials.[9] The Dutch Indies and Japan saw an improvement in their economic and political relations.

In 1907, the Dutch appointed a military attaché in Tokyo, and two years later, Japan opened a consulate in Batavia. The two countries became

[6] DC 16-07-1898; SP 03-12-1902, 14-03-1905.

[7] Aoki 2013.

[8] *Het nieuws van den dag voor Nederlandsch-Indië* 26-01-1905.

[9] Houben 2013: 220.

good friends, and in 1912, a Dutch-Japanese treaty on trade and shipping granted Japan "most favoured nation" status. A year later, a new Japanese government led by Admiral Yamamoto Gonbei, who advocated expansion southward, came to power. Japan acknowledged Dutch neutrality during World War I. During the interwar period, Japanese economic activities in the Dutch Indies grew significantly, driven by the region's abundant natural resources, labour reserves, and strategic importance. The Osaka shipping company's vessel, the Tenchi Maru, visited Medan's Belawan harbour, the first ship that sailed directly from Japan. [10]

4.1.1 *Toko Japan and Japanese Entrepreneurs in Medan*

The first Japanese shop, *toko* Japan, was opened on Djalan Hüttenbach in 1894 by Matsujiro Hayashi from Yokohama. This pioneering venture paved the way for others to follow suit, including Tomizo Konishi (Konishi shop), Toranosuke Matsuzaki (Matsuzaki store), Tora Mitsuo Higuchi (Mikiya shokai), K. Sugimoto, Y. Ikeda, Sowaki, and Yamato, each contributing to the vibrant tapestry of Medan's Japanese presence.

These *toko* Japan offered a diverse array of Japanese products—ceramics, glassware, as well as everyday essentials like sandals and ornaments. One young man, Tsunegoro Shibuya from Misaka Village (present-day Chiba Prefecture), arrived in Medan in the late 1890s with little money. He heard that when Dutch people returned to their homeland, they would purchase Japanese art, and thus, he became an art dealer. At that time, Medan already had established businesses like Hayashi and Konishi. Shibuya, however, was not discouraged by his limited capital. Shibuya worked hard to conquer commerce in Medan. His relentless efforts bore fruit, gradually earning the respect of the local administration. In an unexpected twist of fate, Konishi was forced to return to Japan, while Hayashi passed away, leaving Shibuya as the victor in this battle of enterprise in Medan.

As the years passed, Shibuya amassed a vast fortune, becoming one of the founding members of the Japanese Association. He also served as the sixth president of the Sumatra Japanese Association. By 1915, his store diversified its offerings, selling art supplies, cement, porcelain tea sets, and more, including agricultural tools. Shibuya acted as the Sumatra agent for Tokyo Daihei Insurance Company and was the exclusive dealer for Asahi

[10] The ship arrived in Belawan in 1916, Aoki 2013.

Beer on the Sumatra east coast. Shibuya's shop also catered to Japanese women, offering an array of daily necessities such as make-up, kimonos, and other goods.

Around 1914, a visitor from Japan was taken aback by a startling discovery when he visited Shibuya's store. He found that Japanese women were being openly sold there. Shibuya not only dealt with daily necessities but also engaged in the business of procuring women. Every Sunday, Shibuya would arrange five or ten Japanese women in front of his store and auction them off. His clientele consisted mainly of patrons of brothels, but even passersby couldn't resist joining in the bidding.[11]

Shibuya's empire continued to expand. Following World War I, Japanese products began dominating the market as European shipments were disrupted. By 1918, with 14 Japanese employees, Shibuya boasted remarkable sales of *f*2.5 million. The year also saw many Japanese firms in Medan thriving. Matsuzaki and Nisso trading company were among the top contenders, each raking *f*80,000 in trading volume. Daiwa, Satsuma, and Tanaka followed closely with *f*40,000–50,000, and Kakimoto at *f*30,000, while Harashima, Misono, Hayashi, and Mikawa at *f*20,000 guilders and Taisho pharmacy at *f*10,000.

Despite his remarkable achievements, Shibuya faced an insurmountable debt. The Dutch Indies government imposed a high war profit tax to capture the profits earned by businesses due to the wartime economy. In 1921, after over 30 years of business, Shibuya went bankrupt, and all his goods were auctioned.[12]

The influence of these Japanese merchants extended beyond Hüttenbachstraat, spilling into the neighbouring Oudemarktstraat and Moskeestraat. Another notable establishment was T. Harashima's *toko* Japan, established by Sadakichi Harashima, nestled at the corner of Moskeestraat and Oudemarktstraat (Fig. 4.2). Harashima's store supplied more than daily necessities; it also provided tools for plantations, spades, shovels, grasscutters, and *tjangkol* for the hardworking women.[13] Adjacent to this bustling shop, Harashima opened Japan Hotel, which welcomed travellers and locals alike. Similar to Shibuya, Harashima offered both general goods and brothel services.

[11] Aoki 2013.

[12] *Bataviaasch nieuwsblad* 16-08-1921; DC 12-08-1921.

[13] DC 01-02-1917.

Fig. 4.2 Sadakichi Harashima and Japan Hotel and T. Harashima on the corner of Oudemarktstraat and Moskeestraat (from *Picture Book of the South Sea Islands*, Itoh, 1914, photo courtesy of Sumio Aoki)

A hundred metres away, one of the renowned Japanese hotels was the Hindia Hotel, sometimes spelled India Hotel, located at Oudemarktstraat No. 52-54 (present jl. Perdana). The India Hotel opened in 1907 and was operated by Keiji Shiki, who also ran other Japanese hotels in Medan. These hotels, run by Japanese women, were often clandestine brothels, serving European planters seeking respite on their days off. The Japanese hotels sprouted when the Dutch government banned prostitution in 1911. In 1925, there were 3 European hotels, 5 guest houses, 42 Japanese hotels, 2 Chinese and 6 Malay hotels, 114 coffee houses, 47 eateries, and 6 billiard houses in Medan.[14]

[14] Gemeente Medan 1925.

Other notable Japanese businesses include Bosin & Co., a drugstore owned by Keitaro Takeuchi which specialised in medicines, chemicals, and medicinal goods. Meanwhile, Yamato & Co. was directed by Akira Yagi, a young and dynamic businessman. This store was renowned for its collection of Japanese art objects and an assortment of general goods. Over at Mikiya & Co., the proprietor Tomio Higuchi curated a delightful selection of Japanese art objects, ceramics, and a variety of general merchandise (Fig. 4.3). T. Matsuzaki & Co., owned by Toranosuke Matsuzaki, also provided Japanese art objects and an assortment of general goods.

Adding to the cultural mosaic, T.Y. Yamaguchi, a Japanese barber, set up a thriving barber shop in Oudemarktstraat in 1912. His establishment continued to flourish well into the 1940s, serving as a testament to the enduring presence of the Japanese in Medan. Beyond commercial and

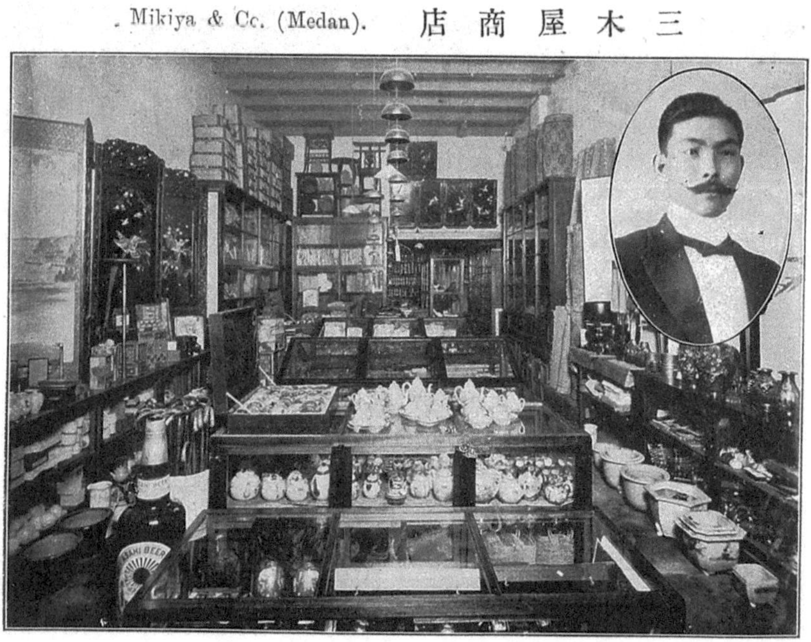

Fig. 4.3 Mikiya & Co. owned by Torao Higuchi, who sold fine arts, general goods, and foodstuffs (from *Picture Book of the South Sea Islands*, Itoh, 1914, photo courtesy of Sumio Aoki)

hospitality ventures, the Japanese also invested in rubber and oil palm plantations in East Sumatra. For example, Nanyo Para Rubber Cultuur Mij (Nanyo Gomu Saibai Kaisha) was incorporated in Medan at a capital of *f*500,000 for a rubber plantation in Tanah Hitam Hilir.[15]

4.1.2 Japanese Photographers

Japanese men were also known as photographers in Sumatra. One of the earliest photographers was M. Mazaraki, who opened a Photographisch Atelier in 1899 and captured pictures of Medan until 1904.[16]

Masuo Makida (or Makita) originated from Okawara Village in Kyoto Prefecture and went to Singapore to try his luck in 1895. However, he was not successful and thus headed to Medan in September 1896. Arriving in Medan, Makida led a wandering life, including working as a manager for the Konishi shop. Later, he partnered with Keitaro Takeuchi, who was successful in Medan, and in 1905, they opened a general store called M. Makita. Takeuchi himself established a successful drugstore called Botchin in Medan in the same year. Makida also managed a clothing and tailoring shop Jamato, alongside his general store and prospered enough to employ over ten staff members. However, due to corruption by a chief employee whom he trusted, he had to close the store.

In 1907, Makida took over a photography studio operated by a Japanese named Watanabe, K.Y. Asahi Photo Studio Art Nouveau, also known as Asahi Fotograaf (Fig. 4.4). The business was a success. Asahi was celebrated for its photography with European clientele. However, Makida, a graduate of the commerce school, aspired to succeed in business, not just running a photography studio.

Makida served as president of the Japanese Association in the East Coast States from 1911 to 1918. Under his leadership, the association had 480 members. He was well-respected and called upon to assist in various police matters involving the Japanese community. His fluency in Malay made him an invaluable translator in the courtroom, bridging the gap between cultures and laws.[17] In 1915, the Chinese ran a boycott campaign

[15] SP 20-08-1929.
[16] SP 28-10-1899.
[17] SP 06-04-1918.

Fig. 4.4 Masuo Makida and the Asahi photoshop (from *Picture Book of the South Sea Islands*, Itoh, 1914, photo courtesy of Sumio Aoki)

against the Japanese in Medan, including an article in a Chinese newspaper. Makida was called into court as a witness and expressed his concern that the Japanese trade suffered due to leaflets that encouraged a boycott of Japanese goods.[18]

However, in 1919, a twist of fate once again altered the course of Makida's life. Due to financial problems, the Asahi Photo Studio had to be sold and was acquired by a Japanese company and renamed Asahi & Co.

[18] SP 15-06-1915.

Under the new management, Asahi & Co. expanded, producing postcards depicting Medan views and the scenery of East Sumatra. It also had a branch in Brastagi, operated by Y. Asada. Subsequently, Makida spent his life in Medan as a "living encyclopedia" of the Japanese community. In 1940, Makida was serving as the accountant for a Japanese company.[19]

Another notable Japanese photographer was Ichitaro Fujisaki from Nagasaki. In 1901, he opened photography studios in Singapore and Medan. He subsequently closed his shop in Singapore and settled in Medan. Fujisaki took many scenes of Medan and its surroundings and, like Asahi, also created and sold postcards featuring the people and landscapes of Sumatra under the name I. Fujisaki & Co. Similar to Makida, Ichitaro Fujisaki went bankrupt around 1919. Ichitaro Fujisaki's Fujisaki Photo Studio operated in Medan from 1901 until around 1919. Other Japanese photographers in Medan include Taisho, who was also a druggist in the 1910s, and T. Kaneo in the 1920s.

4.2 Japan's Trade and Community

In 1909, the Japanese community of Medan celebrated the birth of Dutch Princess Juliana with a parade of Japanese tradition. In the same year, a consulate was established in Batavia, and Japanese residents, who had previously been under the jurisdiction of the Singapore Consulate, began to contact the Batavia Consulate even for minor matters. The consulate reported about 600 Japanese living in Sumatra; two-thirds were women (Fig. 4.5).[20]

The outbreak of World War I disrupted the import of European products, which in turn vitalised Japanese businesses in Sumatra. Japanese shops made huge profits as Japanese products flooded the market. In 1918, companies like Sumatra Kogyo from Japan expanded into the Medan area, acquiring rubber plantations and extending their reach to the Atjeh region.

Since 1919, there had been a discussion on opening a Japanese consulate in Medan.[21] In 1924, there was a plan to establish a Japanese-Dutch

[19] Aoki 2013.

[20] Idem.

[21] *Algemeen Handelsblad* 17-02-1919.

Fig. 4.5 The Japanese community of Medan celebrated the birth of Dutch Princess Juliana in 1909 in front of Toko Shibuya with Tsunegoro Shibuya standing in the middle (Tropenmuseum 60036739)

iron company in Sumatra.[22] However, it was not realised. It was not until 1928 that the first Japanese Consul of Medan, Tsutomu Suwa Jorocui, was appointed.[23] By then, the number of *karayuki san* had declined, the existing mistresses had retired or gone back to Japan and there were no newcomers.

In the 1920 census, the number of Japanese men and women in Java was 1266 men and 468 women. For other regions, there were 1359 men and 1055 women. In the 1930 census, there were 373 Japanese men versus 416 Japanese women on Sumatra's East Coast. There was still a relatively larger number of women than men. However, the number of newborn Japanese in Medan was quite low; over 1919–1928, there were only 49 births registered, or an average of 5 births per year.[24]

[22] SP 15-04-1924.
[23] SP 07-04-1928.
[24] Gemeente Medan 1929.

In 1932, the Japanese Sumatra Association recorded 433 Japanese residents. The association maintained a Japanese school and a cemetery, while the Japansche Handelsvereeniging was also established as the trade association.

The primary school Medan Nippon Shogakko was established in 1920 and registered only 35 students in 1925.[25] A Japanese temple called Hongwanji was established in 1924 at Kroesenstraat.[26] The construction of a Japanese school near the temple was proposed, and donations were collected from the Japanese residents, resulting in a total of *f*8235. Aided by Japanese government funds, in January 1930, a new school building was completed.[27]

4.3 Japan's Aggression

Japan's modernisation transformed it into a formidable power, enabling it to defeat major empires and form a significant alliance with Britain. After its victory over Russia in 1905, Japan saw itself as a world power, fuelling its imperialist ambitions to dominate parts of China alongside European imperialist countries. Japanese leaders believed that becoming an imperial power was the best defence against Western imperialism and thought their model of modernisation could benefit neighbouring countries.[28]

After the outbreak of World War I in 1914, Japan saw an opportunity to further advance its ambitions. It joined the Allied forces and sent a secret ultimatum to China demanding regional authority in Manchuria and Shandong as well as in the German spheres of influence in China. Together with the ultimatum, Japan threatened war in April 1915 with the "Twenty-one demands." Sun Yat-sen declared that these demands were a secret deal between President Yuan Shi Kai and Japan, with the purpose of allowing Yuan Shi Kai to be accepted as an emperor. China realised that it was powerless against Japan and reluctantly agreed. At the same time, China leaked the "Twenty-one demands" in the hope that the Western powers would stop Japan's aggression, as it could also affect Western interests. But the Japanese had entered into secret deals with other Allied powers. During the Versailles Peace Conference that concluded World

[25] Medan municipality yearbook, Gemeente Verslag, 1925.
[26] Jansen 1934: 79.
[27] Aoki 2013.
[28] Paine 2010: 67–69.

War I in 1919, the Allies transferred control of the eastern Chinese province of Shandong, which had been previously held by imperial Germany, to Japan. When the 21 demands became known among the Chinese, there were strong nationalistic and anti-Japanese reactions, resulting in the "May Fourth Movement" in China and abroad.

The 21 demands also included the insistence that China seek Japanese loans and military and financial advisors. All this stirred nationalist sentiment among the Chinese community in the Dutch Indies, with calls for a boycott of Japanese products sold by Chinese shops.[29] The Dutch Indies government urged the Chinese residents, "as guests in the colony," not to strain their host's relationship with Japan. In Medan, a Chinese newspaper faced a libel lawsuit for its derogatory remarks about the Japanese, resulting in three individuals receiving two months' imprisonment.[30] In 1915, the Chinese boycott ended after an agreement between China and Japan.[31]

Japan's aggressive actions escalated again in 1925 and reached a climax in 1937 when Japanese forces initiated an assault on Shanghai, signifying the outset of the Second Sino-Japanese War. In 1937, the Nanking massacre took place.[32] In response, Sumatra's Chinese community again launched an extensive boycott of Japanese products. The large Chinese community vigorously championed an anti-Japanese campaign, which the Dutch Indies government prohibited as a measure of its neutral stance. The boycotts against Japanese goods were most prominent in Medan.[33] Shops that were known to sell Japanese goods were smeared with tar, dirt, or rotten eggs.[34]

Japanese imports in the Dutch Indies were just over 1% before 1930, mainly earthenware, porcelain, and glassware. In the years following the Great Depression, Japan emerged from its own depression through aggressive trade in glassware, textiles, and other light industrial goods in the East Asian and US markets, severely undercutting British and European manufacturers. Japan used high tariffs to limit imports of American and European industrial products, but dumped cheap goods into Asia.

Consequently, Japan's imports to the Dutch Indies grew rapidly, reaching 32% in 1933. In contrast, the Dutch share of imports declined from

[29] Anti-Japanese sentiments in the press (Buiskool 2025: 274–276).
[30] Van Kees 2007: 242.
[31] SP 18-11-1912, 10-1-1913, 12-4-1915, 21-5-1915, 22-12-1915.
[32] During the Nanking massacre, at least 300,000 Chinese civilians were killed.
[33] SP 13-08-1930.
[34] DC 10-11-1937.

32% before 1913 to 18% between 1925 and 1929 and then dropped to a low of 9.5% in 1933.[35]

The Japanese products, through the dumping economy, were cheaper than European and Chinese products and of higher quality. The cheaper Japanese products during the economic depression made them very attractive, and the depreciating yen made Japanese imports cheaper. For example, Japanese bicycles were three to four times cheaper than European products. Japanese manufacturers could copy the same printed textiles that originated from Manchester and were sold for less than half the price. The import of cotton cloths from the Netherlands fell by 50% in 1933.[36] Japanese beers were sold at half their price in Japan.[37] The Japanese also made copies of fine products such as Lux soaps and Parker pens.[38] Even batik clothing was produced in Japan. Another popular product was matches, which were cheaper than those conventionally produced in Sweden. By 1934, cheaper Japanese goods swept throughout Singapore, and even European companies that complained about the cheapness of Japanese goods abandoned British goods for Japanese goods.[39]

The Japanese captured a significant portion of the Dutch Indies market and expanded into shipping and distribution. To counter this commercial invasion, the Dutch Indies government imposed quotas and import licences, which helped Western countries, including the Netherlands, regain a significant share of the Dutch Indies market. By 1937, Japanese imports had been reduced to 25%, while Dutch imports had increased to 19%, higher than before the Great Depression. The Japanese were not happy with these quota restrictions and protested, leading to a conference in Batavia, but it produced no resolution. Japanese imports to the East Coast of Sumatra were still significant in 1936, amounting to 43%, 36.6% in 1937, and 31.4% in 1938.[40]

By 1930, the Dutch increasingly feared Japanese expansion in the Netherlands Indies, viewing it as both a political and an economic threat. Dutch newspapers warned that Japan was influencing Indonesians by portraying the Dutch as exploitative rulers. At the same time, concerns grew

[35] Vandenbosch 1940: 257.

[36] *The Brisbane Courier* 14-07-1933.

[37] *The Straits Times* 04-02-1933.

[38] Jin, Denis Koh Soo, and Kyoko Tanaka. "Japanese Competition in the Trade of Malaya in the 1930s." *Japanese Journal of Southeast Asian Studies* 21.4 (1984): 374–399.

[39] *The Straits Times* 14-02-1934.

[40] *Het nieuws van den dag voor Nederlandsch-Indië* 26-05-1939.

that Indonesian nationalist leaders were drawing closer to Japan. Reductions in educational funding by the colonial government further intensified these anxieties. As opportunities diminished locally, a growing number of young Indonesians pursued studies in Japan, supported by a Japanese organisation established to facilitate this movement. Indonesian journalists also travelled to Japan, strengthening intellectual and political connections between the two countries.[41]

Japan was positioning itself as a leader of Asia, with the "Asia for Asians" propaganda, and courted Indonesian leaders. The Dai Nippon Kaikyō Kyōkai (Great Japan Islamic Association) was established to promote friendship with Islamic nations, increase trade, and broaden knowledge of Islam within Japan. Initiatives included building an Islamic centre in Tokyo, hosting exhibitions and conferences, offering scholarships, and encouraging academic and cultural exchanges. A major Islamic exhibition in Tokyo and Osaka drew 1.5 million visitors and hosted 40 Muslim delegates from across Asia, including prominent Indonesians like H. Abdul Kahar Moedzakkir.[42]

C. Lekkerkerker, an archivist of the Nederlandsch Java Instituut, warned about Japanese immigration in the Indies with a fear of political or military aims.[43] However, the Japanese population in the Indies was relatively small, and the Dutch didn't see them as a threat. Lekkerkerker wrote:

> *Incidentally, who would not applaud that these industrious people participate in the production process in Ned. Indies?*

A conference was convened in Tokyo between the Dutch and Japan, during which the Japanese Prime Minister explicitly stated that Japan had no territorial ambitions in the Dutch East Indies.[44] However, as the Netherlands succumbed to German occupation, the Dutch Indies found themselves vulnerable to Japanese threats and actively pursued favourable terms to avert a potential conflict.

In September 1940, Japan's Minister for Commerce led a Japanese Economic Mission to Batavia. Minister Kobayashi emphasised the primary objective of fostering stronger economic bonds between Japan and the

[41] Vandenbosch 1935: 424–428.
[42] SP 07-02-1940
[43] *Algemeen handelsblad voor Nederlandsch-Indië* 19-06-1930.
[44] *News* (Adelaide) 01-03-1937.

Dutch East Indies, underpinned by a foundation of friendship. Of particular interest to Japan were the minerals and the securing of a reliable oil supply.[45] Just a month later, news broke that English-Dutch and American companies had agreed to provide Japan with substantial oil from the Dutch East Indies. This development stirred controversy, as it was perceived that such an oil supply would bolster Japan's military efforts in China.[46]

The Dutch insisted on their resolve to prevent essential war materials from reaching Germany through Japan. In response, Japan urged the Dutch Indies to collaborate, citing the "Greater East Asia Co-Prosperity Sphere" as a compelling reason for cooperation.[47] However, tensions escalated when, in May 1940, a Dutch Indies seaplane fired upon a Japanese vessel. In light of this incident, the Dutch Minister issued a formal apology to the Japanese government, expressing deep regret for the irresponsible actions of the crew and acknowledging their failure to uphold their promise of refraining from provocative acts against Japan in the Dutch Indies.[48]

Newspapers alleged that Japanese spies were operating covertly within the *toko* Japan. More Japanese started photography businesses and were seen travelling between cities and ports taking pictures.[49] In July 1940, US President Franklin Roosevelt took a significant step by halting shipments of scrap iron, steel, and aviation fuel to Japan while permitting American oil exports to continue. In response, Japan made several strategic moves: it entered resource-rich French Indochina with the consent of Nazi-occupied France and solidified its alliance with Germany and Italy as part of the Axis powers. In July 1941, Japan extended its presence into southern Indochina, signalling preparations for an attack on British Malaya, a crucial source of rice, rubber, and tin, as well as the oil-rich Dutch Indies. This prompted President Roosevelt to freeze all Japanese assets in the United States on July 26, 1941, followed by the British.[50]

In response, Japan dispatched ships to Dutch Indies ports to repatriate its citizens.[51] A significant number of evacuees were closely tied to companies affected by Dutch measures, including the freezing of credits and the

[45] *Newcastle Morning Herald and Miners' Advocate* 14-09-1940.

[46] *Border Morning Mail* 21-10-1940.

[47] *Kalgoorlie Miner* 23-05-1941.

[48] *The Age* 24-02-1940.

[49] *The Courier Mail* 04-03-1939.

[50] https://en.wikipedia.org/wiki/July_1941.

[51] *Syonan Shimbun* 05-07-1942.

suspension of oil exports to Japan. Customs officials in the Dutch East Indies made alarming discoveries. They stumbled upon concealed maps and sketches with military significance hidden in the luggage of Japanese evacuees. In one instance, a Japanese individual was found in possession of sketches and 35,000 yen secreted within a portable gramophone. In Semarang, customs officers uncovered secret writings sewn into the seams of a kimono.[52]

A month later, Japan launched an attack on Pearl Harbour on Sunday morning, December 7, 1941. The next day, the Dutch declared war against Japan. Japanese nationals were classified as Dutch enemies, resulting in the arrest of around 2000 Japanese citizens in the Dutch Indies and the seizure of all assets owned by Japanese citizens.[53] The prisoners were sent to intern camps in Australia. In March 1942, the Japanese launched an invasion of Sumatra, swiftly conquering the Dutch East Indies. Following the capitulation, the Japanese military assumed control of the territory, with the 25th Army taking charge of Sumatra.

4.3.1 Endnote

Before the outbreak of World War II, the Japanese community had a good presence in Medan. From small shops on Hüttenbachstraat to thriving businesses, photography studios, and plantations, the Japanese played an active role in the city's economic and cultural life. Their status as "Europeans and equals" granted them privileges that helped establish strong commercial networks and social organisations, including schools and temples. However, Japan's increasing militarism and aggressive policies in East Asia strained these relations, culminating in growing suspicion and boycotts led by the Chinese community. By the late 1930s, despite their earlier success and integration, the Japanese in Medan found themselves caught between thriving commerce and mounting political tensions that foreshadowed the coming conflict.

[52] *The Daily Telegraph* (Sydney) 12-11-1941.
[53] *Soerabaijasch Handelsblad* 11-12-1941.

CHAPTER 5

The Indian Communities' Journey in Deli

The Indian immigrant population in the Dutch East Indies was relatively small, numbering about 30,000 in the 1930s within a total population of roughly 60 million. The majority, approximately 17,000, lived on Sumatra's East Coast, particularly in the Deli region, working as coolies, while others were concentrated in major cities on Java. In Medan, the 1892 census recorded 776 Indians out of 12,924 residents. This number grew to around 2000 by 1920 and increased to 3000 by 1930, representing about 5–6% of the city's population (Fig. 5.1).[1]

Archaeological findings in Kota China, a village near Medan, suggest that traders from South India had settled in the region as early as the eleventh century. Over subsequent centuries, Gujarati Muslim traders also played an important role in spreading Islam in the archipelago. Notably, Nuruddin ibn Ali ar-Raniri, an Islamic mystic from Surat, lived for several years in the Sumatran court of the Sultan of Atjeh in the seventeenth century.[2]

According to *Hikayat Deli* or the Legend of Deli, the sultans of Deli and Serdang were descendants of Sri Paduka Gocah Pahlawan Laksamana Kud Bintan, who was a son of an Indian king. He was stranded in Atjeh and helped the local leader to subdue enemies. Later, he went to Soenggal and married Puteri Nang Baloean, the sister of the leader of Kedjoeroean Hitam. The son of Gocah Pahlawan was Tuanku Panglima Perunggit,

[1] *Het nieuws van den dag voor Nederlandsch-Indië* 14-12-1934.
[2] https://en.wikipedia.org/wiki/Nuruddin_ar-Raniri.

B. Minasny, D. A. Buiskool, *Stories from Medan, Volume 1*,
https://doi.org/10.1007/978-981-95-7707-1_5

Fig. 5.1 A group of Indian workers at a bridge of the plant road on a tobacco plantation (photo from: *Album van Deli* (Stafhel and Kleingrothe, 1894)

who conquered Kesawan and established Kedjoeroean Padang (1634–1700), thereby establishing Deli as an independent kingdom.[3]

Several location names around Medan have Hindu origins, including Medan (from Maidan), Kesawan (from Keshava, or Lord Vishnu), Serbanyaman (possibly from Subramaniya). The more recent migration of Indians to the Deli region occurred with the development of the tobacco industries starting in the 1860s. Indian migration to the Deli region was driven by the demand for labour on tobacco plantations and, subsequently, merchants and traders who followed the city's development.

Colonial administrators commonly categorised Indians into three groups: Kling, Bengalese, and Bombayer. These names, also used in the Straits Settlements, were derived from the English trading ports in India during the colonial period. The three key presidencies in British India—Madras, Bengal, and Bombay—were major provinces initially governed by the East India Company and, after 1857, by the British government.

[3] Tengku Luckman Sinar 1996: 23–24.

Centred on the cities of Madras (present Chennai), Calcutta (Kolkata), and Bombay (Mumbai), these presidencies served as vital hubs for British trade and commerce in India. Indians arriving in the Straits Settlements were identified by their ports of origin: South Indians departed from Madras were called "Kling," North Indians departed from Bengal were called "Bengalese," and West Indians who departed from Bombay were called "Bombayer." However, as we will discuss, these labels reflected ports of embarkation rather than ethnicity, language, or religion.

5.1 Tamil Coolies

The expanding tobacco industry in Deli, Langkat, and Serdang fuelled the need for a steady labour force. Planters regarded Tamil workers, imported from the Straits Settlement, as efficient and reliable, making them a key solution to labour shortages. However, the British-Indian government prohibited the direct recruitment of Tamil workers to the Dutch Indies without formal agreements. The British-Indian government insisted on appointing a British-Indian Protector in Deli who could speak Tamil to oversee the welfare of Tamil workers.[4]

The Dutch Minister of Colonies appeared hesitant to provide such an officer. Deli Tobacco administrator J.Th. Cremer criticised British policies as unfairly obstructing their access to labour and stressed the need to reduce dependency on British-controlled territories for labour supply. He wished to establish direct steamship routes between Madras and Deli to encourage voluntary migration without formal recruitment processes. In particular, the southeast coast, such as Madras (current Chennai)—a major port for emigration, Tanjore—a district in southern India, Negapatam (Nagapattinam)—another coastal port in Tamil Nadu, and Karikal (Karaikal)—a French colonial enclave in Tamil Nadu.[5]

Negotiations between the British-Indian and Dutch Indies governments in 1876 and 1888 failed, primarily due to the Dutch refusal to allow British agents in East Sumatra to oversee the welfare of Tamil workers. Consequently, planters turned to intermediaries or *kanganies* in the Straits Settlements. The *kanganies*, experienced plantation workers, acted as intermediaries to recruit labourers from South India, advancing their travel and recruitment expenses. The system tied workers to plantations

[4] DC 03-04-1886.

[5] Cremer 1885: 205–213.

through debt-bondage, hierarchical control, and low wages, enabling planters to maintain a cheap and stable labour supply.[6] However, the Protector of Indian Immigration in Penang boarded every steamer departing the port to ensure that no Indians were en route to Deli. The Straits government was obligated to prohibit the emigration of Indian coolies to any country that did not have a formal labour convention with the British Indian government.[7]

Despite restrictions on emigration from these settlements, the relatively lax enforcement allowed the flow of labour to continue.[8] South Indian workers primarily came from the regions within the Madras Presidency of the British colonial rule. The areas included districts along the Coromandel Coast, such as Tanjore (Thanjavur), Madura (Madurai), Trichinopaly (Tiruchirappalli), and Tinnevelly (Tirunelveli).[9]

The South Indians (primarily Tamils) were employed in physically demanding tasks such as constructing roads, digging trenches, building dykes, and driving bullock carts. Their economic conditions were harsh, with monthly earnings often less than six dollars after deductions for fees and down payments. The number of South Indian workers in the East Coast of Sumatra was around 250 in 1870, 459 in 1874, increased to 1500 in 1884, 1930 in 1894, and 4140 in 1901. However, the number declined to 2010 by 1920, and 1200 in 1927 as planters shifted to employing cheaper Javanese labour.[10]

The planters preferred Tamil workers for their diligence, agricultural skills, and perceived docility. In the 1880s, the Deli Planters Association pushed for direct recruitment from South India to streamline labour supply, alongside cultural accommodations like Hindu temples and Tamil translators to ease settlement. Economic incentives—tax breaks, housing, and farmland—were proposed to retain workers long term. However, due

[6] Behal 2013: 23–25.

[7] *Pinang Gazette and Straits Chronicle* 01-08-1890.

[8] Wiselius 1884: 356–370.

[9] Idem.

[10] In 1894 the 72 companies affiliated to the Deli Planters Association, employed 10 616 Javanese, 33 469 Chinese, 1930 Klingalese, 1939 Boyans and Bandjarese. Chinese workers remained the dominant labour force, with their numbers reaching 54,489 in 1901 and 209,459 by 1920. In 1927, 74,000 workers were employed in tobacco companies under the coolie ordinance and 21,500 as free labour. Of the 74,000, 28,000 were Chinese, 37,000 Javanese men, 8000 Javanese women, and 1000 Klingen. Of the 21,500, 12,000 were Javanese women, 2500 Javanese men, 3100 Bantammere and Bandjarese, 3400 Javanese, so-called colonists, and 200 Klingen. (Broersma 1919:131; Volker 1928:15, 67).

to high costs and a lack of sustained government support, Tamil migration declined by the 1920s.[11]

5.1.1 South Indians

In Southeast Asia, the South Indians or Tamils were referred to as Kling, or Keling or Klingaleezen or Klingen in Dutch.[12] The term Kling is often linked to the ancient Kalinga region, covering the present-day part of Odisha and northern Andhra Pradesh. In fact, an early Hindu kingdom in central Java in the sixth century was called Kalingga. However, the Indians objected to the term Kling due to its derogatory and sometimes insulting connotation.[13]

The South Indians represented the largest group of Indians in the Dutch Indies. Among them were Muslim and Hindu communities. The Dutch referred to the Muslim Indians as Mooren or Kodjah. The term Mooren is a misnomer, as Moor is a term used by Europeans for Muslims from North Africa, partly living in Spain. While Kodjah (Khoja) are a minority of followers of Shia Islam from western India, particularly in Gujarat, Sindh, and Maharashtra.[14]

The Hindu Tamils were the majority and worked as plantation labourers and cart drivers. Due to economic challenges, most could not afford to return to India and formed a community in Deli. Their society was influenced by caste divisions. A large portion of the Tamil workers were considered outcasts, separated by occupation and place of residence, and they were forbidden to enter Hindu temples. Thus, many converted to Buddhism and Catholicism. [15] Another Southern Indian group, the Telugus, was integrated into the Tamil community.

[11] Idem.

[12] Langereis 1919: 709–712.

[13] It was even suggested to have an offensive connotation of "killing." SP 18-09-1915; Jansen 1934: 11.

[14] In Java, the Indian Muslims have integrated with the native Muslim population, forming neighbourhoods like Pekodjan (after Kodjah) in Semarang. Indian Muslims in Medan consisted of Tamil and Urdu speakers. There were also Muslim Indians from Bengals who often worked as tailors and bakers (Jansen 1934: 40–42).

[15] In traditional Hinduism, the society was divided into 4 castes: Brahmins who were scholars, priests or teachers; Kshatriyas, the rulers, administrators or warriors; Vaishyas as farmers or merchants; and Shudras as artisans, labourers, or servants. Below the castes were the Dalits or untouchables, or called Adi Dravidar or Pariah in Tamil Nadu. (Pallavi Aiyar. *Medan: A chequered history of Hinduism, Islam, colonialism and tobacco.* Sep 08, 2022).

In Medan, the Indian quarter was called Kampong Kling near Polonia. However, the Indians also settled near Kesawan at Djalan Hindoo (Hindu), which was confusingly also called Kampong Kling. Colonial newspapers often described Indian quarters in racialised, moralising terms; *De Sumatra Post* in 1903 reported:

> *In the kampong Kling behind the shop Hüttenbach, for example, in the evenings it is again swarming with those greasy, shiny brown young ladies, many a young man has already experienced this to his detriment.*[16]

Similar to the Chinese Captain, the Dutch also elected leaders of the Indian community, commonly referred to as Kapitein Kling. In 1887, Bawadji, who owned a slaughterhouse, was appointed as the Kling leader.[17] These leaders, titled captains and lieutenants of the Klingalezen, were appointed by the Dutch Indies government as advisors to administrative officials on matters concerning their compatriots in major cities with large Indian populations, including Padang, Sibolga, Palembang, Medan, and Boeleleng (Singaradja, Bali).

In 1908, we read a *Deli Courant* advertisement:

> *To all esteemed gentlemen, princes, and merchants,*
> *On the 19th, 20th, and 21st of January 1908, the major religious festival of the Hindu temple in Kampong Kling Hindu Polonia, named Taipoosam, will be celebrated for all Hindus in the plantations and in Medan.*
> *To the Hindu community, on the 18th, 19th, and 20th of January 1908, we, the Chitty people, humbly request the assistance of your esteemed authorities in granting leave for all Hindu Kling labourers in the plantations so they may attend their religious duties.*
> *To all esteemed plantation authorities, this is a significant religious event in the Hindu faith. There are two such major festivals annually. One was Tibawali, which occurred on November 4th, 1907. The second is Taipoosam, a grand celebration for the Hindu community from January 19th to January 22nd, 1908. During this time, it is obligatory for all Hindus to perform great prayers at the temple of Swami Subramaniam.*
> *Therefore, we humbly request the assistance of the plantation authorities to allow all Hindu Kling labourers four days of leave. On January 20th, there will also be a ceremonial fire ritual held in the open field near the office of the Controleur.*

[16] SP 07-07-1903.
[17] DC 23-11-1887.

With respect,
The Captain of the Hindu Kling Community, K. MOETOE, Bindjey.[18]

The Indian immigrants in Sumatra brought with them their cultural and religious practices. There were two important holidays for the Indians: Diwali and Taipoosam. Taipoosam or Thaipusam is a Tamil Hindu festival celebrated with the procession of the statue of Swami Subramanian across the streets of Medan. It featured ornately decorated wagons and objects adorned with gold and diamonds. Some participants performed acts of penance, including piercing large gold pins through their tongues, walking on wooden blocks embedded with nails, and beating their heads against temple steps until they bled, among other acts of self-inflicted pain. Diwali, also known as Deepavali, is a religious festival in Hinduism, Jainism, and Sikhism, symbolising the victory of light over darkness.

Hindu temples were built in Medan, and community life centred around these temples, which provided not only spiritual support but also cultural continuity.[19] There were two main temples, the Subramaniam temple on Parkstraat (Jl. Kejaksaan, Kebun Bunga) managed by the Chettys, and the Mariamman Temple, a Shaivite Hindu temple.[20] The latter, now called Sri Mariamman temple, is dedicated to Parvati, Shiva's consort, revered as Mariamman, the protector against infectious diseases. Located at the corner of Kroesenstraat and Calcuttastraat, Mariamman temple was originally established in Laboean Deli around 1880 during a cholera epidemic and moved to its current location in 1909.[21]

In addition to the Sri Mariamman Temple, Tamils in Medan supported the Kaliamman Temple (also known as Kali Kuil) and the Thandayuthapani Temple located on Parkstraat. The Kaliamman Temple, located near the Baboera River and about 100 metres from the Sri Mariamman Temple, originated in the early twentieth century. Appasamy Chettiar, was rewarded a piece of land by the Dutch and dedicated a place of worship to Murugan's weapon, the vel. Later, when the Chettiar returned to Tamil Nadu, he sold the land to a Chinese Captain (Tjong A Fie). As a replacement, the Captain

[18] DC 16-01-1908.

[19] Jansen 1942: 70–81.

[20] Shaivite refers to a follower of Shaivism, one of the major traditions within Hinduism that reveres Shiva as the supreme deity.

[21] Jansen 1934: 40–42; https://en.wikipedia.org/wiki/Sri_Mariamman_Temple,_Medan.

donated land by the river and funded a new temple, leading to the establishment of the Kaliamman Temple.[22]

In Medan, Mohamad Ali, an Indian Muslim, was appointed head of the Kling (*hoofd van de Klingalleezen*) since 1899.[23] In 1911, Mohamad Ali held the official title of Lieutenant of foreign orientals (other than Chinese). However, the Hindus were unhappy with his appointment and sent a petition to the then-governor, requesting a separate leader further noting that there was also no Hindu *wijkmeester* or local leader. The controleur, or district officer, responded that there would be no separate Hindu head as long as Mohamad Ali remained in office.[24] Finally, in 1924, the Dutch government established Lieutenants of the Bengalese and Bombayer, Ranjit Singh and Lieutenant of the Klingaleezen and Chettys Gulam Mahamad Japi Sahib bin Bahadur.[25]

Prominent Indian leaders also visited Medan. In 1927, Indian writer and poet Rabindranath Tagore visited Java and Bali. He arrived at Belawan as a stopover and stayed at Hotel de Boer.[26] Two years later, another prominent Indian, Sir Annamalai Chettiar, a statesman, educator, financier and philanthropist, visited Medan.[27]

By the 1920, the Indian community started to establish themselves as the Federated Indian Community, with A.L.R.K. Somasundaram Chettyar serving as its secretary.[28] The Federation petitioned the Dutch East Indies government to replace the term "Kling" with "Voor-Indiër." The Governor-General approved the request, and a 1928 government decree prohibited using "Kling" in official documents, officially designating Indians as "Voor-Indiërs." "Kampong Kling" was renamed Kampong Madras and the title "Chetty" was changed to "Chettyar" supported by the Governor of the East Coast.[29]

[22] Mani 2006.

[23] *Regerings-almanak voor Nederlandsch-Indië* 1899.

[24] SP 07-04-1921.

[25] *Regerings-almanak voor Nederlandsch-Indië* 1927.

[26] The visit was organised by Harnam Singh the wijkmeester (local head), Lilaram Hotchand Mahtani, representing the Bombayers, A.R.S. Murugappa Chettiar on behalf of the Tamils, F. Odimal Libeh Maricar for the Muslims and S.K.S. Sinnamuthu Pillai and Somasundaram on behalf of the Chettys. SP 17-08-1927; *The Straits Echo* 24-08-1927; *Rotterdamsch nieuwsblad* 14-12-1928.

[27] Sir Annamalai Chettiar was a member of the Council of State of Delhi, founder of the Rajah Annamalai University, and one of the founders of the Indian Bank. In Medan, he stayed at the house of the Mayor of Chinese (Khoe Tjin Tek). SP 04-12-1929.

[28] SP 16-11-1927.

[29] SP 16-11-1927; *Het nieuws van den dag voor Nederlandsch-Indië* 10-09-1927; the "ar" in Chettyar refers to an honorific name (Singaram 2019).

the Indians in Sumatra had a drinking habit, *De Sumatra Post* reported in 1905:

A Klingalese who had apparently consumed too much "gin" last night or night and had lain down in a parrit (gutter) along the Padang Boelanweg to sleep off his intoxication, was rudely disturbed in his rest this morning by a fellow countryman passing by. The not yet completely sober drunkard became so angry that he jumped up, threw his arms around the neck of his unknown countryman and bit off a piece of his ear. At the sight of blood, the perpetrator suddenly became calmer, fell to his knees and begged for forgiveness - which was granted to him, on condition that he would give up the remainder of the gin he had left over from the previous evening, for the benefit of the wounded man. Peace was then made. [30]

The Indians were considered British-Indian or British subjects. In 1919, they formed the British-Indian Association, and in 1931, the British Indian Merchants Association of North Sumatra.[31] In response to Mahatma Gandhi's arrest on May 5, 1930, by the British, the Indian community of the East Coast of Sumatra closed their shops and halted business activities as a form of protest. A prayer session was held at the Hindu temple in Medan. The British Indian Association sent telegrams to the Viceroy of British India and the national congress expressing regret over Gandhi's arrest, proclaimed a *hartal* (strike) for the day, and prayed for his swift release.[32]

Nevertheless, in 1935, we read an ad in the *Deli Courant*[33]:

SILVER JUBILEE OF HIS MAJESTY THE KING EMPEROR GEORGE V.
His Britannic Majesty's Consul and The Vice Consul,
Following up on the order issued for the delivery of a short address about the above Silver Jubilee, we, the Trustees of The 'Mariyamman' Temple of Medan, hereby most humbly beg to submit and express that we are filled with unbounded joy and enthusiasm to observe that His Majesty the King Emperor George V, through the Grace of His Almighty Providence, has been gifted with the Bliss of governing us for a period of 25 years, which has led to the commemoration of the present occasion with grandeur and glamour. Further, we doubtless feel that God will be compassionate enough to pour on His Majesty His Choicest Blessings

[30] SP 3-5-1905.
[31] *De locomotief* 11-01-1919; *Bataviaasch nieuwsblad* 25-09-1931.
[32] SP 06-05-1930.
[33] DC 07-05-1935.

> *for long life and prosperity, to enable the forthcoming Golden Jubilee being extolled with increased magnificence on the completion of a further 25 years.*
> *Your Most Obedient Servants,*
> *TRUSTEES OF THE 'MARIYAMMAN' 'VEREENIGING'.*

A prominent leader among the Tamil community in Medan was D. Kumaraswamy, born in 1906 to Tamil migrants from Pondicherry. He revitalised the dormant Deli Hindu Sabah in 1931 and chaired it until 1941, using it as a platform for social reform. He established divisions for women, theology, sports, drama, and music, and authored songs and plays to inspire change. Kumaraswamy also founded the Indian Boy Scout Movement in 1936, a hockey team, the Djalan Darat Tamil School in 1935, and co-founded the Indian Welfare Association in 1937 to assist impoverished Tamils in East Sumatra.[34]

5.2 Chettys: Financiers and Moneylenders

Chettis, Chettiars, or Chettys, a prominent caste from Chettinad, Tamil Nadu, are traditionally known for their roles as both large-scale bankers and small-scale moneylenders. The Chetty community established a sophisticated commercial organisation based on a network of interconnected family business firms, many of which evolved into partnership firms. The firms were headquartered in South India, while agents, typically unrelated to the owners, managed operations in Southeast Asia. Aspiring Chetty agents underwent rigorous apprenticeships in other firms, progressing through roles such as accountant and cashier before becoming subagents and ultimately agents, typically between the ages of 22 and 25 (Fig. 5.2).

The Chetty agents were sent to Sumatra and Malaya under three-year contracts written on palm leaves, during which they received capital, salary and allowances for travel, housing, food, and clothing. Upon completing their term, they returned to India to report their accounts to their principals and typically received a 10% share of the profits. Chettys did not return abroad immediately but alternated with other agents who replaced them for the subsequent three-year terms. While living overseas, Chettys adhered to strict cultural practices. Their customs prohibited women from

[34] Deli Sabah Hindu English Section was presided by J.W. Bicknell (DC 08-09-1914). Mani 2006: 64-67.

Fig. 5.2 A Chetty and his helper (Westenenk 1922)

leaving their homeland, so they remained unmarried abroad or engaged in relationships with local women. [35]

The first Chettiar in Deli was Moenawian Chetti, who arrived in Laboean Deli in 1879. Many others followed from Ramanadhapuram district, Tamil Nadu and some of the 96 villages of their district.[36] The

[35] *Encyclopaedie van Nederlandsch-Indië*, Vijfde deel, 1917–1939.

[36] Westenenk 1922: 1-17. In Penang and Medan, Chettys usually referred to Tamils involved in the moneylender business, while in other countries, Chetty is a profession. The

Chettys established a temple for the worship of Lord Subramanian, a representative of Shiva, also known as Murugan. Their original shrine was in Laboean Deli, and it was moved when merchants and traders relocated to Medan, where it was replaced by the Thandayuthapani Temple at Parkstraat. During the Taipoesam Festival in January/February, the statue of Swami Subramanian was carried out of the temple and processed through Moskeestraat and Hindoestraat. Chettyars had their homes and offices decorated with greenery, and garlands were stretched across the street.[37]

In the 1920s, Medan served as a hub for Chetty's business in Southeast Asia, centred on Moskeestraat, which hosted 70 agencies with a combined capital estimated at *f*10–12 million.[38]

Chetty introduced instalment credit, with loans typically ranging from under *f*100 to *f*3000, occasionally reaching *f*50,000. Large loans required collateral, such as gold, jewels, or land mortgages. The borrower had to sign an acknowledgement of debt for an amount much larger than the amount borrowed. They charged high interest rates, often disguised as advanced repayments, and operated within strict conditions that made default costly for borrowers. Their lending model was based on adding a year's worth of interest (typically 18%) to the principal upfront, requiring repayment in ten monthly instalments. Many borrowers failed to realise that they were paying interest on the entire original loan amount throughout the repayment period. Late payments triggered penalties of 2% per month on outstanding amounts, along with legal and administrative costs. Defaulting on a single instalment rendered the entire debt immediately collectible. In some cases, borrowers were offered additional loans on harsher terms, trapping them further in a cycle of debt.[39]

Chettys received 10% of the net profit from their activities, which often amounted to substantial sums, from *f*2000 to 5000 and occasionally up to

building where the moneylending business is located is called *kittanggi*, the shop has a manager (agent or aesandu), bench boys or helper, and a cook (Singaram 1985).

[37] SP 04-02-1928; DC 24-01-1933.

[38] Westenenk 1922: 1–17. Their initial capital was around *f*25,000. At Moskeestraat No. 2 was R.M.R.M. Ramanathan, No. 4 was S.K. Sinnamuthu, No. 10 was P.L.R.M. Palaniappa & Ramasamy Chettyar, P.L.S. Lethumanan; No. 26 was Murugappa with a trading name Annamalay. No. 36 was Somasundaram with a trading name Anna Lana Kana Roena. The first two or three initials of the name refer to the name of the person's great-gradfather, grandfather, and father (Singaram 2019).

[39] *Algemeen Handelsblad* 17-04-1926.

*f*20,000. Some firms reportedly reaped gold worth *f*200,000 in three years from Medan alone.[40]

Their interest rates varied between 6% and 36%, depending on collateral, yet still compared favourably with those charged by village banks (35–130% p.a.) and government pawnshops (up to 72% p.a.). In the absence of local banks and cooperative institutions, moneylenders, who also included Chinese, Arabs, and Sikhs, exploited borrowers through exorbitant interest rates and unethical practices. Victims ranged from locals to government employees, who often became ensnared in unmanageable debts. Some cases include individuals surrendering property or even family members to settle debts.

In 1907, after the opening of the Java Bank (Javasche Bank, the central bank of the Netherlands Indies) in Medan,[41] the Java Bank directly supported the newly founded Deli Bank of the Tjong brothers. The reason was that the Java Bank saw the Deli Bank as a development bank for East Sumatra and a tool to keep small traders out of the hands of the Chetty usurers.[42] Many years later, in 1931, the Anti-Usury Association (Anti Woeker Vereeniging, AWV) was established in Medan in 1931 to combat this exploitation. The association sought to negotiate fairer terms for victims and advocate for legal reforms. For example, a European woman borrowed 350 guilders from a Chetty in 1933, but had to sign that she had received 490 guilders. Despite paying 675 guilders in total, she still owed 455 guilders. The AWV negotiated the debt to 245 guilders, payable in instalments of 15 guilders per month.[43]

De Sumatra Post mentioned the Chettys in relation to the caste system:

> *The caste system reveals itself in the temples, the pariahs are not allowed in the temples. They want to be treated more on an equal footing but the Chetties who belong to the highest caste do not seem to want to give in and some time ago even a pariah is said to have been seriously abused in one of the temples. The case was then hushed up so that the police would not find out. Eventually it leaked out*

[40] Westenenk 1922 1:17.

[41] Godley 1981: 129; Claver 2006: 286.

[42] The loan concerned a road construction project from the Chinese N.V. Deli Bank and Chunghwa Shangyeh Maatschappij (Company), for a minimum of *f*100,000 and a maximum of *f*500,000 (*Gemeenteblad* 12-4-1920; SP 5-5-1916; SP 2-8-1918; SP 11-9-1918) (Buiskool 2025: 124).

[43] DC 04-05-1935; *Lustrum-uitgave der Anti-woeker vereeniging te Medan* 1936.

anyway. In Kampong Kling signs were placed in front of several kedehs with the inscription "Paria's and Pella's dilarang masoek (not allowed to enter).[44]

5.3 Bengalese Guards and Milkmen to Entrepreneurs

In Medan, the Sikhs were referred to as Bengalese, which was incorrect, as they were not from Bengal but from Punjab, the Five Rivers Land in North-West India. Some came from Amritsar and Jalandhar in the eighteenth century. Some early Sikh traders circulated through Atjeh earlier, but settlement expanded markedly in the late nineteenth and early twentieth centuries.

The North Indians usually travelled to Malaya on ships from the port in Bengal, and thus they were referred to as Bengalis. They stood out for their distinctive physical appearance, marked by turbans and beards. They were hired mainly as security guards, porters, and watchmen. Some Sikhs reared cows and sold milk; others were bread makers or *toekang roti*, and others were moneylenders.[45]

Their religion, Sikhism, was influenced by Hinduism and Islam. Their last name Singh, means lion. The first Sikh temple, or Gurdwara Sahib, in Medan was established in 1911, located next to the Tamil temple.[46]

Some Sikhs became merchants in cosmetics, textiles, and sporting goods. In 1920, the Sikh community established the Deli Tatta Khalsa Sabha in Medan to promote the moral and spiritual development of its members by establishing reading rooms. While Sikhs rejected the caste system, the members of the reading room were limited to Sikhs of the first four castes. It was opened to Europeans and Christians, provided they did not belong to the lowest caste.[47] In 1931, the Sikh community established the Khalsa English School on Kroesenstraat under the management of the Gurdwara Parbandhak Committee.[48] The school was open to all communities, offering daytime and nighttime classes.

[44] SP 14-6-1926.

[45] Jansen 1934: 40–42.

[46] Jansen 1928: 20–25.

[47] SP 15-12-1920.

[48] Ranjit Singh, the leader of the Sikhs, contributed *f*5000 out of the total *f*30,000 capital for the school. Luckman Sinar 1996: 84.

Prominent Sikh figures included the brothers Hakam and Gurdit Singh, wealthy entrepreneurs renowned for their real estate ventures. Hakam began his career modestly as a milkman, owning a few cows and personally delivering milk to customers before gradually expanding into property and other businesses. The brothers Singh started around 1900 with property projects in the Chinese quarter with the help of the Sultan of Deli. Later, they cooperated with Tjong A Fie in house-building projects.[49] The brothers initiated projects in the Indian quarter, constructing rows of houses that they rented out. Additionally, they developed real estate in Tebing Tinggi.[50]

5.4 The Commercial Role of Bombayers

The *Orang Bombay* were primarily involved in commerce, running *toko Bombay* shops specialising in silks, fabrics and accessories for women's clothing. They were not from Bombay, but originally from Sindh and Karachi.

Their stores were often branches of larger companies operating across East Asia. The workers, predominantly Hindu men on contracts, lived on-site and rarely had families, leading to a detached lifestyle. They sold wares including ivory and ebony figurines, workboxes, walking sticks, colourful scarves, silk wall hangings, gold and silver jewellery, and precious stones such as diamonds and rubies (Fig. 5.3).

Their names typically include a reference to a deity from the vast Hindu pantheon, followed by a suffix such as "mall," "das," or "chand." These suffixes signify devotion to the mentioned deity or to a particular aspect of that deity represented by the name, such as Hoondamall, Govindamall, Bagawandas, and Bulchand.[51] There were also Hindi-speaking Uttar Pradesh Muslims.

[49] Hakam and Gurdit Singh were also active in promoting Medan for their fellow Indian countrymen. They invited Indian families from Punjab to Deli to settle in Medan, gave them land and some cows and hereby stimulated the settlement of an Indian community in Medan. Later on, Dalim Singh, the son of Hakam Singh, went into the cinema business. He owned the Oranje Bioscoop and Medan Bioscoop. (Information from Mrs. Miki Singh, Medan. October 2003; Information from Tan Boen Djin and Margaret Wee, Medan 18-10-1995 in: Buiskool 2025:79)

[50] Medan in 2020 had around 850 Sikh families.

[51] Jansen 1934: 40–42.

Fig. 5.3 The first toko Bombay in Medan on the corner of Kesawan (Nationaal Archief 803_06)

Jhamatmal Gurbamal Melwani journeyed from Penang to Medan in 1882 with nothing but a case of leather slippers. Determined, he began his venture, cycling through the streets of Medan to sell his wares. Within just two years, at the age of 27, he had saved enough to establish his own shop, Jhamatmall Gurbamall & Co. in Kesawan, specialising in silk, embroideries and fine clothing materials. By 1890, the business had expanded significantly, with offices based in Singapore, Yokohama, Calcutta, and Padang. In 1897, he returned to India to oversee his firm in his hometown of Hyderabad, Sindh.[52]

Another prominent business was Hoondamall, established by Bhai Khemchand Hundamal Mahtani from Hyderabad, founded in Medan in 1900.[53] The business continued under the name F.K. Hoondamall (Fatelechand & Khemchand), and Hoondamall and Sons had branches in Singapore and Kobe. There were also Kundamall Brothers (which declared bankruptcy in 1933) and Mohanlal Hansraj. Indian Shops in Kesawan in the 1920s–1930s included Hari Bros and Rose & Co. (head office in

[52] DC 05-10-1935; https://shakunkimatrai.com/chapter-12/.

[53] SP 12-08-1935.

Sialkot with branches in Singapore, Soerabaja, Batavia, and Medan) for sports equipment, and Iserdas & Bulchand, Galani for fashion items.[54]

In 1923, due to the economic crisis, a group of workers at a *toko Bombay* in Medan went on strike, citing poor wages, heavy workloads, and unmet contractual promises of food and housing. The shop workers, engaged on three-year contracts in their homeland, faced harsh conditions upon arriving in Medan. Complaints include excessively long working hours, from 6 a.m. to 9 p.m. daily, without any days off, and inadequate pay that has not been adjusted despite the rising cost of living. These workers, left unsupported by fellow countrymen due to fear of reprisals, seek mediation to either enforce their contracts or facilitate their return to India. Mohamed Ali, the designated Kapitein Kling was the representative for non-Chinese foreigners. Despite his role, there were calls for appointing a specific intermediary for the Bombay workers to better address their grievances.[55]

A counterstatement, signed by other Indian employees, appeared a few days later, declaring they had no complaints. The letter, signed by 23 employees of a major Bombay store, stated that Captain Kling, Mohamed Ali, took excellent care of them, treated them well, and was highly regarded by British Indians. They also confirmed they received adequate food, were satisfied with their accommodations, found their salaries sufficient, and felt content in their employment.[56]

5.4.1 Religious Conversion and Missionary Influence

The Catholic presence among the Tamils in Deli dated back to 1873, when Father Johannes de Vries first visited the region. He discovered a small Catholic community comprising Tamil labourers from Pondicherry and Tichinopoly, brought to Deli by French tobacco plantation owners. The French manager of the Soengei Sikambing plantation, de Guigné, established a chapel and facilitated religious education for the Tamil workers and their families. However, following de Guigné's departure to France, the community lost its cohesion. The chapel fell into disrepair and was eventually dismantled. The remaining Catholics built a makeshift bamboo hut to serve as a place of worship.

[54] *De Indische courant* 31-01-1938.
[55] SP 14-08-1923; 21-12-1923.
[56] SP 28-12-1923.

The Catholic mission gained new momentum when the Jesuits, who had struggled to provide sufficient support due to a lack of personnel, handed over their work to the Capuchin Fathers. In 1914, the Capuchins sent two Dutch priests, Father Camillus Kerkhof from Borneo and Father Ferdinandus from the Netherlands to Medan. Father Ferdinandus, who had studied Tamil, was assigned to minister to the Tamil Catholics. The community welcomed the Capuchins with great enthusiasm. For the first time, they had a dedicated pastor who spoke their language and could provide consistent spiritual guidance. A school was completed in 1914, followed by a church in 1915, and a rectory shortly thereafter.[57] *De Sumatra Post*:

> *Kampong was built through the mediation of the Roman Catholic church here, with the construction costs covered by voluntary contributions. The kampong consists of 9 houses, a school and a church. This kampong is a continuation of the one in Soengei Sikambing. In Medan, there are many Catholic Klingalese, in British India also many Catholic Klingalese.*

The School was also intended for non-Catholics, and education was provided by two Indian teachers. Interestingly, all subjects were taught in English. The Indians said that the Dutch language was of no use to them because they could never get a good job with it. Education was given almost for free. A total of 60 pupils were registered, but usually 40 to 50 children attended lessons.[58]

The Hindu community established the Deli Hindu Sabha in 1913 to counter Tamil conversions to Catholicism and promote Hindu unity. D. Kumarasamy Pillay (1931–1941) reformed it by lifting bans on widow remarriage, encouraging inter-caste marriages, and simplifying ceremonies, while opening schools to combat illiteracy. The Tamil Muslim community formed the Indian Muslim Association in 1941, led by trader Abdoel Gafoer Barkata. In 1926, Buddhist Tamils founded the Hadie Dravidan Sabah (Adi-Dravida Sabai) to provide household training and combat caste-based exclusion from the Tamil Hindu society.[59]

[57] *Nieuwsblad van het Zuiden* 07-07-1923; 14-07-1923; 21-07-1923.
[58] SP 01-12-1915.
[59] Rivai et al. 2021.

5.5 Japanese Occupation and the Indonesian Independence Struggle Period

During the Japanese occupation, many Indians joined the Provisional Government of Free India (Azad Hind), led by Subhas Chandra Bose, an anti-British colonial government. In early 1945, Chandra Bose went to Medan, where the Indian community reportedly raised 1 million guilders to support Bose. The Indians regularly donated to support the Japanese war and formed Lembaga India Merdeka Sumatra.[60] The Japanese organised a unit of the Indian National Army (INA), which included volunteers from Medan trained in Penang and other places, and deployed it to fight against the British in Burma.

After Japan's surrender in 1945, the British Army, including 800 Indian soldiers, arrived in North Sumatra, particularly Medan, to disarm Japanese forces and maintain order. However, Indonesian revolutionaries saw this as an act of imperialism, opposing their fight for independence, leading to tensions as the local population viewed the Indian troops as helping the imperialists. Clashes between the Indonesian fighters and British Indian soldiers resulted in many casualties. Amid worsening conditions, many rural Tamils moved to towns like Medan, where they found refuge with the British Indian forces. While there were a few British Indian soldiers who deserted and joined the Indonesian army, during the Dutch-Indonesian conflict, many Indians lost their livelihoods, prompting the Indian government in 1946 to repatriate approximately 3000–4000 Indians who faced persecution and destitution.[61]

When India gained independence in 1947, it was one of the few countries that played a crucial role in supporting Indonesia's fight for independence from Dutch colonial rule. Indian leaders, including Jawaharlal Nehru, advocated for Indonesia's cause on the international stage, bringing global attention to their struggle, particularly during the 1947 Asian Relations Conference in New Delhi and later at the UN. India also provided diplomatic and logistical and material support, including arms and resources, to the Indonesian Republican forces. This solidarity reflected a shared anti-colonial vision and strengthened ties between the two nations during their fights for freedom.[62]

[60] The leader was L.H. Mahtani and vice leader Pritam Singh. *Syonan Shimbun* 09-01-1945, *Kita Sumatora Sinbun* 22-11-1943, 08-01-1944, 28-01-1944, 23-06-1944.

[61] Mani 2006: 59–60; *The Straits Times* 13-03-1946.

[62] Jagtiani 2022.

5.5.1 *Endnote*

The history of Indian immigrants in the Dutch East Indies is one of resilience, adaptation, and enduring cultural identity. From Tamil labourers on Sumatra's plantations to Sikh guards, Chetty financiers, and Sindhi entrepreneurs, Indian communities played a crucial role in Deli's development. They were plantation labourers, waiters, barbers, dhobis (washermen), traders in silk and jewellery, night watchmen, policemen, money-lenders, and breadmakers. They were skilled performers, with magicians, snake charmers, and pedicures. Fakirs demonstrated impressive feats, while fortune-tellers offered services that intrigued many, though some were advised to avoid them. Despite occasional issues like excessive drinking among some, they were seen as hardworking people, known for their flavourful curry dishes and sweets.[63] Many descendants of plantation labourers are now integrated into North Sumatran society. Their legacy is a testament to their ability to navigate migration challenges, preserve their cultural heritage, and contribute to the Medan society.

[63] Langereis 1919: 709–712.

CHAPTER 6

How the Suez Canal Facilitated the Colonial Extractive Economy

A new and fertilising stream of trade set in with the utilisation of the shortened ocean route, giving prosperity to trade and strengthening the finances of the possessions.[1]

In March 2021, the Suez Canal in Egypt garnered global attention when a massive cargo ship became stuck in the canal, disrupting shipping operations worldwide for six days. This canal, which links the Mediterranean Sea to the Red Sea, provides the shortest route between Europe and Asia, and approximately 12% of the world's sea cargo passes through it. The opening of the Suez Canal in 1869 facilitated the colonial extraction of resources from Asia. This waterway was especially advantageous for the Dutch colonial power, as it accelerated the extraction and shipment of resources from the Dutch East Indies to Europe (Fig. 6.1).

6.1 Impetus for Colonial Commerce

The late nineteenth century saw the rapid development of trade and the extraction of resources from the Dutch Indies to Europe. This rapid economic development was due to a confluence of several factors. First, the Dutch colonial government abolished the *cultuurstelsel* (or enforced culture system) in 1870 and implemented a liberal economic system in the

[1] Wright 1909: 104.

B. Minasny, D. A. Buiskool, *Stories from Medan, Volume 1*,
https://doi.org/10.1007/978-981-95-7707-1_6

Fig. 6.1 Port Said and the entrance to the Suez Canal in 1869 (Édouard Riou, Wikimedia)

Dutch Indies.[2] This liberal system allowed private companies to conduct business directly in the Indies. Next was the availability of new lands, which provided new agricultural products. The tobacco in Deli had its first export in 1864, and by 1870, it had gained a reputation as a high-quality product, attracting buyers from Europe and the United States. After years of conflict, Dutch military campaigns expanded control in 1880, although resistance in Atjeh continued well into the twentieth century.

The opening of the Suez Canal in 1869 significantly shortened the travel time between the Netherlands and the East Indies. In typical schedules, the canal reduced voyage distance substantially (often described as roughly a third), and could cut travel time from about six weeks to around a month. Without the canal, ships had to go around Africa's Cape of Good Hope. A journey that took 40 days became 28 days, saving significant amounts of fuel and costs. The introduction of large steamships further made transport cheaper and more efficient.

The canal provided a tremendous impetus to the colonial mercantile economy. The news of the canal's opening excited the Dutch merchants and government. Agricultural and mining products could be shipped more efficiently to Europe, resulting in greater profits.

[2] The Cultuurstelsel (Cultivation System) was a colonial agricultural policy implemented by the Dutch in Java from 1830 to around 1870. Indonesian peasants were forced to grow cash crops—such as sugar, coffee, indigo, tea, and tobacco—on part of their land (usually 20%). These crops were then delivered to the Dutch colonial government at fixed prices, often below market value.

Some of the valuable products include cinchona bark, the main ingredient of quinine. The Dutch started experimenting with growing cinchona, which originated from South America, in West Java in 1854. Soon, it became an industrial-scale production system in West Java. Java was also known for its tea, sugar, coffee, rubber, tobacco, cocoa, kapok, and other agricultural products.[3]

In addition to transportation, communications technology also advanced colonial extraction. Telegraph was established in Java in 1856, and in 1859, Batavia was connected to the Netherlands via a telegraph line to Singapore. In 1863, a railway system was established in Java to move agricultural products.[4]

6.1.1 *Trains, Ships, and Automobiles*

Deli tobacco brought four times the price of tobacco from Java. Initially, tobaccos grown from various places on the east coast of Sumatra were shipped using small boats via canals and rivers to Laboean Deli. From there, all collected commodities were shipped to Belawan via the Deli River (Fig. 6.2).

To make transportation more efficient, under the initiative of J.T. Cremer, the Deli Tobacco Company established a subsidiary, the Deli Railway Company (Deli Spoorweg Maatschappij, or DSM). DSM, a private railway company, was established in 1883 to move agricultural products from all over the East Coast to the sea. The rail works were challenging due to the region's swampy terrain. Malaria was widespread, and in 1884 and 1885, cholera epidemics further compounded the dangers. Tragically, a considerable number of Chinese labourers lost their lives during the construction of the railway.[5] The first line connecting Medan and Laboean Deli opened in 1886.[6]

Building a railway line through the demanding landscape of Sumatra proved to be a formidable undertaking. Before the railway's construction began, a system of roads had to be established, as it was unfeasible to lay railway tracks directly across such challenging terrain. Hence, the initial step involved creating a network of roads, and once this groundwork was

[3] Wright 1909: 104.
[4] Idem.
[5] *NRC Handelsblad* 17-06-1988.
[6] Wright 1909: 199.

Fig. 6.2 The Shipping of Deli tobacco in 1879 (KITLV 1402029)

completed, railway construction could commence. The construction of the railway presented numerous challenges, including dense jungles, swamps, rivers, and mountainous landscapes.

Belawan was strategically situated near the Strait of Malacca at the mouth of the Deli River. Belawan was originally owned by DSM to transport tobacco from plantations to the port. In February 1888, a short railway track connecting Laboean and Belawan was established, but it faced significant challenges. Contractors, labourers, and materials had to be sourced from distant locations. Malaria was a constant threat to the workers.[7] A notable feature includes the Belawan Bridge, the bridge over the Oelar River with a span of 60 metres, numerous bridges with spans of 36 and 32 metres, and the reinforced concrete crossing near Medan. The assembly of iron bridges was often hindered by the sudden rise of river levels (flash floods), which carried fallen trees downstream. These trees would become lodged against the assembly structures, potentially blocking the river and endangering the partially assembled bridges. Workers had to work intensely, even at night, to remove these blockages, tasks that were often perilous. Furthermore, the local population was mistrustful of

[7] Buiskool 2025: 60–62.

railways, often associating accidents with malevolent spirits. This belief gave rise to ceremonies intended to appease these spirits. One particularly tragic incident involved a fireman who was found burned to death in his locomotive. Rumours circulated that bridge-building required "human sacrifices," and the traumatic fatalities associated with construction. As a result, both local inhabitants and Chinese workers avoided lonely roads near major bridge construction sites, fearing they might be captured and killed for such sacrificial purposes.[8] The railway, finally completed in 1909, covered 22 kilometres (km) from Medan to Laboean Deli and Belawan, and saw five daily trips, each taking an hour and ten minutes (Fig. 6.3). Over time, Belawan evolved into the principal seaport, while Laboean Deli gradually returned to a fishing village.

Railway lines continued to be built connecting most tobacco plantation areas, east to west and north to south of the Deli region, spanning over 100 km. The railway expanded to include new areas of cultivation, such as coffee and oil wells, and by 1900 it had been extended to 260 km.[9]

Fig. 6.3 Belawan train station (Kleingrothe, KITLV 26883)

[8] Langereis 1918: 21–23.
[9] United States Bureau of Foreign Commerce 1899: 596.

Another notable achievement was the construction of large bridges, including the railway bridge over Soengei Asahan. The 75-metre-long bridge, designed by Dr. P. Joosting of Dutch Railways, was the largest span ever built by the DSM.[10] These bridges were essential for spanning rivers and gorges in the demanding terrain.[11]

In 1888, during the first eight months of operation, DSM transported 378,861 passengers and 42,199 tons of goods. The following year, in 1889, the company saw significant growth in its services, with 743,619 passengers and approximately 79,866 tons of goods transported. As rubber and palm oil became important, the railway network was extended to the southern part of the region: Soengei Bamban to Tebing Tinggi in 1904, Dolok Merangir to Pematang Siantar in 1916, and Tandjong Balei in 1927.

DSM also established a telephone network along the railway initially for its own use, but later expanded to serve the public due to demand from European officials and companies. DSM applied for a concession to operate the telephone network in Deli, Langkat, and Serdang, which was granted in 1885. By 1888, the network had 32 connections, increasing to 213 by 1900.

Telegraph connections were also developed, with lines from Medan to various locations, connecting Deli to the outside world. In 1887, a post office was opened in Medan, and by 1891, a direct connection between Medan and Penang was established. The cable to Penang was laid and operated by the Eastern Extension Australasia and China Telegraph Company. Another telegraph line connected Belawan to Koetaradja in 1892, followed by an overland line to Sumatra's West Coast. The line extended from Medan through Serdang, Asahan, and Padang Lawas to Padang Sidimpuan and from there to Padang, cutting through Sumatra and traversing dense jungles inhabited by large herds of elephants. These elephants frequently knocked over the line's supports, once even over a stretch of more than 5 km. Additionally, large trees would often fall on the line, disrupting the connection, and workers would sometimes have to trek for days to reach these locations and restore the line. The integration of telegraph and telephone services was crucial for railway operations. It facilitated communication between different stations, helped manage train schedules, and ensured the safety and efficiency of railway services. Cable

[10] https://doi.org/10.5169/seals-2704
[11] *NRC Handelsblad* 17-06-1988.

maintenance faced significant challenges due to frequent damage from fishermen's hooks, requiring constant retrieval and repair. Initially, the Dutch Indies government lacked its own cable-laying ship and had to hire a vessel from an English company at a high cost. Subsequently, the Dutch Indies government acquired its cable-laying ship.[12]

In 1927, DSM reached its peak in terms of passenger and freight transport. During this year, 6,988,089 passengers and 1,000,874 tons of goods were transported. Another line from Kisaran to Rantau Prapat was completed in 1937. By 1940, the total length of the east Sumatra railway network was about 540 km.[13] DSM played a crucial role in the economic development of Sumatra. This infrastructure facilitated the transport of goods, particularly from the lucrative plantation economy, boosting local and colonial economies. However, this progress came at the expense of the local workforce, who often endured harsh working conditions such as malaria, cholera epidemics, and extreme physical challenges. This exploitative nature of labour practices is rarely discussed.

6.1.2 Roads

Roads were built mainly for the transportation of agricultural products. Initially, planters had to construct their own roads for their plantations. Eventually, the roads were opened to public traffic, though ox cart transport could be temporarily suspended during rainy weather. This restriction was soon lifted, and planters were obliged to keep the roads open for public use without limitations after two years of general use. However, they were also tasked with maintaining the roads, including bridges and other infrastructure. To compensate for this, they were granted the right to collect tolls, with the rates set by the government. Gradually, all these roads were brought under government management, and tolls were abolished.

Colonial accounts categorised roads in ways that mirrored racial hierarchies. The highest-grade roads, or "European roads," were for horse-drawn vehicles, mostly in Medan, becoming less common farther from the city. These European-style roads were primarily supported by the tobacco industry rather than general transportation. The second tier of roads, known as "coolie paths," was narrower, suitable for horses or people, and

[12] Langereis 1918: 22–23.

[13] *Deli Data 1863–1938.*

zigzagged through hilly terrains, sometimes crossing streams with simple bridges. The most basic type, referred to as "Batak paths," was wide enough only for a person on foot, traversed steep inclines, and passed directly through streams and rivers.[14]

The Laboean-Medan road, crucial for transportation, was constructed through collaboration between the planters and the Sultan. It was followed by the construction of roads from Medan to Bindjai and Deli-Toewa. The Dutch Indies government did not provide support for maintaining and developing essential infrastructure. It was not until 1892 that the government finally refurbished the 17.5 km road, and roads connecting the region were constructed. Roads were built north to south, parallel to the coastline of Sumatra. Significant routes included the roads from Bindjei to Tandjoeng-Poera and from Medan through Perbaoengan to Tebing-Tinggi, with the government fully funding the road from Tebing-Tinggi to Tandjoeng-Balai. Due to the lack of maintenance by planters, many roads became nearly impassable during the rainy season, leading to significant transportation challenges and exorbitant travel costs. For instance, a trip from Medan to Laboean could skyrocket from 2–3 guilders to 12–15 guilders during the rainy season, often resulting in travellers having to continue their journey on foot due to vehicle breakdowns or muddy conditions. Most goods were transported by railways. However, a significant amount of goods was moved by two-wheeled carts drawn by oxen. Long caravans of these carts, driven by Indian or Malay drivers, who often slept stretched out on their carts during long routes, were a common sight on the roads.[15]

In the late 1920s, roads were built to the highland in Simaloengoen, over the Toba plains and north of Lake Toba. Tea plantations like Balimbingan, owned by the Handels Vereeniging Amsterdam (HVA) or Amsterdam Trading Company, near Pematang Siantar were established at the same time.[16]

6.1.3 Shipping Lines

The development of shipping lines was vital for ensuring steady connections between the Dutch East Indies, Europe, and regional trade hubs. In

[14] Kipp 1990: 65.
[15] Langereis 1918: 5–6.
[16] Buiskool 2025: 26.

August 1869, the Dutch held a public meeting in Amsterdam to discuss the opening of the Suez Canal. The participants were enthusiastic about the possibility of establishing a shipping line from the Netherlands to Batavia via Port Said. As a result, a commission was formed to establish a regular steamship line, and in February 1870, the commission signed a contract with the Dutch government. This led to the establishment of the Stoomvaart Maatschappij Nederland (SMN) (The Netherlands Steamship Company), which transported all Dutch government goods, including its monopoly of coffee and sugar from Java. With a capital of 3,000,000 guilders, the company ordered its first steamers from John Elder & Co. of Glasgow.[17]

On May 17, 1871, the maiden voyage of Willem III was launched, but two days later, it caught fire and beached off Portsmouth. Another ship also crashed on a rock in the Red Sea. Reliable sailings were eventually established in 1874, starting with a monthly schedule. By 1877, the shipping line was operating on a three-week schedule, and by 1879, it offered a fortnightly service. The shipping line further improved, with departures scheduled every ten days by 1882. In 1892, the Nederland line entered into a partnership with Koninklijke Rotterdamsche Lloyd (KRL), also known as Rotterdam Lloyd. The two companies agreed that their ships would sail to the Indies every alternate week. The Dutch government signed an agreement with both companies to ensure the maintenance of its mail service.[18]

By the late nineteenth century (1890s), at least five companies offered fortnightly travel from Java to Europe.

- The Stoomvaart Maatschappij Nederland or SMN (Netherlands Steamship Company) sailed from Batavia to Amsterdam via Genoa, calling at Padang, Aden, Suez, and Port Said at a distance of 9100 miles in 28 days, with a first-class ticket at US$301.50
- The Koninklijke Rotterdamsche Lloyd or KRL (Royal Dutch Rotterdam Lloyd) ran between Batavia and Rotterdam via Marseilles with a distance of 9000 miles, calling at Colombo, Pirim, Suez, and Port Said, which took 28 days.
- The British Queensland Royal Mail Line steamers ran between Batavia and London via Colombo, Aden, Suez, Port Said, and Naples, first class at $201, and took 33 days.

[17] Wright 1909:104.
[18] Wright 1909:176–180.

- The British Peninsular and Oriental Royal Mail Line travelled between Batavia and London, via Brindisi, calling at Singapore, Colombo, Aden, Suez, and Port Said.
- The French Messageries Maritimes boats ran between Batavia and Marseilles, calling at Singapore, Point de Galle, Aden, Suez, and Port Said.

For the Europe–Indies route, SMN and Rotterdamsche Lloyd coordinated sailings and mail contracts. Separately, the Koninklijke Paketvaart Maatschappij (KPM) developed packet services within the archipelago, linking major hubs (Batavia, Singapore) with regional ports, including Sumatra (Fig. 6.4).[19]

The trade between Deli, Penang and Singapore had always been intense. The number of commercial ships arriving at Laboean Deli and Belawan ports grew significantly over the years. In 1880, Laboean Deli saw 513 ships with a net tonnage of 53,951 m^3. By 1890, Belawan substantially increased with 932 ships and a net tonnage of

Fig. 6.4 The ship Ophir of the Royal Paketvaart Maatschappij (KPM) enters the port of Belawan (Tropenmuseum 10010654)

[19] Wright 1909:183–187.

546,294 m^3. A regular shipping service between Belawan, Penang and Singapore commenced. Shipping company Stoomvaart-Maatschappij Deli, with steamships Medan and J. Nienhuijs, approximately 500 tons, sailed between Belawan and Penang, under the management of Jacob van Nie.[20] A Chinese company in Penang, Chong Moh Steamship Cy, had the steamship Ho Kwei of 200 tons sailed between Penang and Belawan and steamships Langkat (60 tons) and Rosa (75 tons), sailing between Penang and the smaller ports on the East Coast.[21] This was followed by Hebe and Calypso, which travelled from Singapore to Penang and Belawan. Later, the steamship Medan plied the route between Singapore and Belawan.[22] In 1889, an average of 8000 tons of goods were shipped to and from Singapore and 7000 tons from Penang to Laboean Deli.[23] The first direct shipping route from Belawan to Batavia was established in 1892. Ships had to anchor outside the harbour, in the roadstead near the Deli River's mouth, and cargo was transferred using small sampans or *praoes*. Passengers had to transfer to smaller boats to reach the shore.[24]

Prior to 1890, all tobacco shipments were routed through Penang and Singapore via the British Ocean Steamship Company from Liverpool and the German Nord-Deutscher Lloyd Line from Bremen. From 1891, the Koninklijke Paketvaart Maatschappij (Royal Package Navigation Company) began shipping tobacco to Tanjung Priok and Sabang, where it was subsequently loaded onto Dutch steamers.[25]

For connecting Deli with Chinese ports such as Amoy, Swatow, and Hong Kong, primarily for the transport of Chinese workers, several large ships were commissioned by the Deli Planters Association. These ships, capable of accommodating over 500 passengers, were used to ship Chinese workers from Swatow to Belawan on a 7-day trip.[26]

[20] Schadee 1919: 241–242.

[21] Ho Kwei was later sold to Hüttenbach and Liebert.

[22] Hebe and Calypso owned by W. Mansfield & Co. (Singapore) with F. Kehding as the agent in Medan. Sumatra and Medan was owned by Behn, Meyer & Co. (Singapore) with Güntzel & Schumacher as an agent. Ho Kwei was owned by Hüttenbach and Liebert (Penang) with van Nie as an agent (*Reclame 1903–1904*, N.V. Algemeen Reclame Bureau Excelsior, Bandoeng).

[23] *The Straits Independent and Penang Chronicle* 23-08-1889

[24] Buiskool 2025: 59–62.

[25] Idem.

[26] Langereis 1917: 23.

In 1900, significant developments began at Belawan's harbour, including dredging and the construction of docks for small vessels. The harbour underwent further expansion in 1912, enabling it to accommodate large steamships and reducing dependence on Singapore as a transit port. Due to its distinctive red paint, the harbour became widely known as goedang merah or the red warehouse.[27]

In 1920, the creation of a deepwater port named Oedjoeng Baroe, equipped with a railway transportation system, marked another milestone. It wasn't until 1923 that large ocean-going steamers were able to reach Belawan. That year, a direct weekly mailboat was established between the Netherlands and Java. In the 1930s, about 70% of the exports from East Sumatra were through Belawan. The year 1936 saw a remarkable expansion, with 2763 ships arriving at these ports, and a massive net tonnage of 14,798,319 m^3.[28] Belawan was one of the principal ports in Sumatra for Muslim pilgrims embarking on the hajj to Mecca, serving hundreds of travellers annually from East Sumatra.[29]

6.2 Extractive Economy

The Suez Canal accelerated the mining of resources out of the Dutch Indies. In 1910, the customs houses of the East Coast of Sumatra brought in 3.27 million guilders and in 1915, 3.92 million guilders.[30]

Feldwick gave an account of export from the East Coast of Sumatra in 1915:

Kerosene, 140,280,021 litres; benzene and gasolene, 84,600,762 litres; liquid fuel, 629,620 litres; forest products, 6,006,621 kilogram (kg); rubber: *Hevea*, 9,085,943 kg; *Ficus* plantation, 441,222 kg; *Ficus* jungle, 32,213 kg; other sorts, 1693 kg; Copra, 5,105,240 kg; gambier, 2, 124,979; gutta-percha, 583,421 kg; charcoal, 916,704 kg; Coffee: Liberia, 2,174,106 kg; Robusta, 1,188,552 kg; Java, 11,047 kg; other sorts, 97,264 kg; black pepper, 1,487,555 kg; Penang nuts, 4,006,294 kg; rattan, 4,517,462 kg: sago flour, 176,586 kg; Deli tobacco leaf, 20,821,722

[27] Song 2015:118.

[28] *Deli Data 1863–1938.*

[29] DC 05-10-1936; 20-08-1938.

[30] *Pinang Gazette and Straits Chronicle* 23-05-1916.

kg; tea leaves, 638,118 kg; trassi, 8,717,755 kg; salt or dried fish, 26,092,005 kg; fresh fruit, 47,092 kg.[31]

In 1915, there were 372 plantation companies with a cultivated area of close to 1 million hectares. The total investment in agriculture was 200,019,632 guilders, with Dutch capital: 93,419,000, Dutch Indies: 11,682,000; British 65,284,123; French: 4,750,000; German: 2,500,000; Belgium: 18,787,500; Swiss 3,585,000; Shanghai (British) 390,000; Straits Settlements 183,000; Hong Kong 489,000.[32]

The main agricultural products exported from the East Coast of Sumatra were[33]:

Tobacco: In the year 1864, approximately 50 tons of tobacco were harvested, yielding 4000 Dutch guilders. Fast forward to around 1912, and the tobacco industry flourished, with exports reaching an impressive 282,920 tons, translating to a staggering 60,000,000 guilders. British companies produced nearly 10% of the tobacco crop on Sumatra's East Coast, and over 30% of the crop was shipped via British vessels. However, by 1936, the figures had declined, with 141,766 tons of tobacco valued at 30,600,000 guilders being exported.

Rubber: Before the rubber boom of 1909, several British rubber companies were already operating in Sumatra. Notable companies included the Anglo-Sumatra Rubber Company (£90,000 capital, 1907), Sumatra-Deli Rubber Estates (£240,000, 1907), and the United Langkat Plantations Company, which originally cultivated tobacco (£450,000, 1889). Other key ventures were the Asahan Rubber Estates (£250,000, 1910), Insulinde (Sumatra) Rubber and Tobacco Estates (£100,000, 1910), and Mendaris (Sumatra) Rubber and Produce Estates (£300,000, 1911). By the eve of World War I, British firms controlled around 36,000 acres of Hevea rubber, about half of the total in Sumatra, with an invested capital reaching approximately £6 million by 1913.[34] The Americans were in as well with the Hollandsch Amerikaansche Plantage Maatschappij (Dutch American Plantation Company), which later became the United States Rubber Plantation Inc. in Kisaran. The Belgians had Société Financière des Caoutchoucs (Socfin) (Rubber Finance Company) with oil palm plantations in Asahan. Rubber production substantially increased

[31] Feldwick 1917:1178–1179.

[32] Idem.

[33] *Deli Data 1893–1933.*

[34] Great Britain Foreign Office 1920: 62–63.

between 1910 and 1937. In 1910, 390 tons of rubber were exported. By 1937, this figure had skyrocketed to 112,923 tons of estate and 27,866 tons of peasant rubber. In 1924, the total export of rubber from the Dutch East Indies was 179,747 tons or 42.7% of world's production. Of the total planted area, about 480,000 acres were in Sumatra, and 420,000 acres were in Java, and the remainder was in other regions.[35] That meant rubber from the East coast of Sumatra was about 20% of the world's production.

Tea: By the end of 1913, around 2428 hectares of tea had been planted on Sumatra's East Coast, with all but approximately 202 hectares established using British capital. In 1914, 203,355 kg of tea were exported. This peaked in 1934, with 11,844,725 kg of tea leaves and 1,448,403 kg of tea dust. By 1937, the figures remained high, with 9,756,276 kg of tea leaves and 975,201 kg of tea dust being exported.

Palm Oil: Exports started with 180,685 kg in 1919, but they saw a significant boost by 1937, with 190,626,675 kg of palm oil and 39,630,425 kg of palm kernels being exported.

Fibre: In 1920, 717,802 kg of fibre were exported. Although it reached its peak in 1933, with 64,148,776 kg, the industry remained robust, exporting 53,059,900 kg in 1937.

Gambir: In 1908, 460,234 kg of gambir were exported. The peak came in 1922, with 5,322,401 kg. By 1936, the figures had reduced but were still significant, with 3,061,673 kg being exported.

Copra: In 1915, 130,000 kg of estate and 4,978,210 kg of peasant copra were produced. The peak occurred in 1926, with 4,309,248 kg of estate and 10,925,549 kg of population copra. By 1936, the numbers remained substantial, with 3,577,384 kg of estate and 21,738,222 kg of population copra.

Coffee: The coffee industry saw modest production around 1893, with approximately 1700 kg. However, it reached its peak in 1914, with exports totalling 3,677,747 kg. By 1936, the figures had reduced but were still notable, with 1,852,000 kg being exported.

Derrio (Akar Toeba): The export of Derrio was relatively low in 1930, with 3 tons. However, this number significantly increased by 1937, with 39 tons being exported, indicating growth in this particular industry.

[35] *The Singapore Free Press and Mercantile Advertiser* 28-12-1925.

Petroleum: In 1892, approximately 5,000,000 litres were exported, and peaked in 1904 with 154,882,616 litres, and rose to 654,392,000 litres in 1936.

And there was virtually no manufacturing industry developed in the early twentieth century. Thanks to Suez, the exports from Indonesia reached 500 million guilders in 1910 and peaked in the 1920s with a value of more than 2000 million guilders per year. From the East coast, annual export was 200–300 million guilders per year, with a trade deficit of 100 million guilders per year. A large share of profits was repatriated to metropolitan investors and financial centres in Europe.

In 1923, the Dutch Chamber of Commerce of Medan compiled statistics on the nationality of plantation owners in Deli (excluding tobacco).[36]

	Planted area (ha)	*In bearing (ha)*	*Yield (kg)*
Rubber			
Dutch	51,373	31,665	11,866,896
British	47,300	37,283	12,284,260
American	26,623	18,117	6,422,755
Franco/Belgian	14,491	10,759	3,897,641
Neth. Indian	11,554	6671	2,275,243
German	1760	1660	852,504
Japanese	4709	1080	381,858
Swiss	1862	985	380,632
Scandinavian	2943		
Shanghai	1012	447	38,200
Tea			
Dutch	4095	2960	2,145,089
British	5609	5259	3,806,457
German	671	622	596,759
Neth. Indian	643	454	115,108
Palm Oil			
Franco/Belgian	5407		1,955,032
Dutch	4583	1849	1,690,306
British	61	1407	
German	2159		
Shanghai	151		
Swiss	18		
Coffee			
Dutch	5684	4293	658,650

(*continued*)

[36] *The Straits Echo* 24-04-1923.

(continued)

	Planted area (ha)	*In bearing (ha)*	*Yield (kg)*
British	1284	1011	293,820
Neth. Indian	460	43	23,580
Shanghai	405	405	92,100
German	1291	837	141,840
Copra			
Neth. Indian	3470	1424	964,277
Dutch	3311	791	363,130
British	2439	1805	1,557,850

CHAPTER 7

De Witte Sociëteit and the White Society of Medan

The first thing I learned in Sumatra was that there are two kinds of people in the world: white and coloured. The white man is the master; master and ruler in the strictest sense of the word. It is reflected in his manner of speech. He does not ask, he commands.[1]

The Sociëteit, a private club exclusive to Europeans, was established in every major city in the Dutch Indies. There were also clubs exclusively for the Chinese and the Malay nobility, but the most prominent was the Dutch Sociëteit. Known colloquially as "Soos" among the Dutch, these clubs were central social hubs for Europeans. The oldest of these, Harmonie, was founded in Batavia in 1814. These clubs were popular spots for Europeans to gather, socialise, and enjoy drinks (Fig. 7.1).

7.1 The Soos

In Medan, De Witte Sociëteit was founded on September 19, 1879 by Major General Demmenie, the military commander on Sumatra's east coast.[2] Originally, the club was exclusive to officers and civil servants, but in the 1880s, it opened its doors to civilians. In 1882, a temporary building was constructed at the Esplanade near the Medan Hotel, where the club hosted theatre performances, readings, and musical events.

[1] Székely 1979: 45.
[2] There is also a Witte Sociëteit in Den Haag, the Netherlands.

B. Minasny, D. A. Buiskool, *Stories from Medan, Volume 1*, https://doi.org/10.1007/978-981-95-7707-1_7

Fig. 7.1 Medan Witte Sociëteit around 1900 (Kleingrothe, KITLV 1403412)

In his book about the Deli Railway Company, Ir. H. Meijer, an engineer at the company, recalled that in the early days, officers stationed at the nearby military compound (currently known as Lapangan Benteng) would return late at night from the Witte Sociëteit on the Esplanade to their barracks. For safety, they carried a lantern and a goat: the lantern to avoid potholes and other hazards in the track, and the goat as a bait in case of tiger attacks.[3]

In January 1886, the Soos leased a piece of land on the other side of the Esplanade from Deli Maatschappij. It was next to the post office, with a rent of one guilder per year. The building was inaugurated on October 18, 1886, with about 100 members.[4] The club provided a place for European members to unwind and enjoy themselves in Medan. The remote location of the plantations often resulted in lonely evenings for the planters, but the club offered a chance to socialise twice a month. In 1890, the club was expanded to include a billiard room and a front porch. Next to the club was a music tent where bands played. Club members could participate in a variety of activities, including drinking at the bar, playing billiards, listening

[3] Meijer 1987: 17; *NRC Handelsblad* 09-07-1987.
[4] *Het nieuwsblad voor Sumatra* 17-09-1954.

to music, dancing, and attending concerts. Dance music would be played on Sunday evenings from 6 to 9 o'clock. Unsurprisingly, it remained a European male society. The *Deli Courant* of March 3, 1897, wrote:

> *Although we cannot boast of a large female audience that likes to dance, there were still about ten dance couples, which has been enormous for Deli recently. The young ladies usually enjoy the greatest pleasure in dancing, but the region here can count them by hand.*[5]

Beyond social gatherings, the Soos also hosted serious musical concerts. The *Deli Courant* on March 31, 1897, wrote:

> *This evening was very important for the history of the association, because of the new decorations, recently done by the well-known decorative painter Joh. C. Mondaag of Amsterdam. ...*
>
> *Both the solos for violin "Vorspiel und Sicillana aus der Cavalleria Rusticana" and "Gavotte Parisienne" as well as the trio for alto, violin and piano "Der Fischer", in association with Mrs. G.O. and Mr. v.K elicited thunderous applause from the attentive audience.*[6]

Dutch author Justus van Maurik wrote:

> *"Erst das Geschäft - aber dann das Vergnügen" (Business first - then pleasure) is the slogan of the Soos. Anything entertaining from Singapore or elsewhere is brought to the Soos in Medan as soon as possible to cheer up the evening hours of the members.*[7]
>
> *I attended, among other things, a few performances by the Willard Troop, an English operetta company, which gave some performances at the expense of the Society, which was very favourably enjoyed and was paid better than they deserved, ..., and the artists, who are lucky enough to be received there, always return satisfied and with a well-filled pouch, unanimously declaring: "Medan people are the nicest people in the world."*[8]

St. Nicholas' Day (December 5), an important family feast in the Netherlands, was also celebrated in the Sociëteit de Witte.[9] *De Sumatra Post* wrote:

[5] DC 31-03-1897.
[6] DC 31-03-1897.
[7] Maurik 1897: 437.
[8] Idem.
[9] SP 06-12-1899.

St. Nicholas's Day celebration at De Witte.

A successful St. Nicholas's Day celebration at Sociëteit de Witte. The good Saint arrived from the station in an open carriage drawn by four horses, kindly provided by Captain of the Chinese Tjong A Fie and Mr. D. Rens, and escorted by a large procession, including members of the board of "Gezelligheid in Deli". The avenue of De Witte was illuminated with Chinese balloons in many colours. The hall was electric. The children sang a few songs loudly and brightly, and then the Spanish Saint departed.[10]

In November 1897, Medan experienced the first motion picture at the Witte Sociëteit, played by Louis Talbot with his cinematograph. Not long after, the club decided to build a more permanent structure and took out a loan of *f*60,000 with a 6% annual interest rate. As a final parting event, members were given the opportunity to demolish the old wooden building.

In August 1904, the new white stone building was completed, and roller skating on the marble floor of the front gallery became a popular attraction. A bowling alley was added in 1906. Musical bands were brought from Europe and Australia for Saturday night dances.[11] There were *bal masqué* or masquerade balls where Europeans dressed up in Chinese golden dresses, pierrots of different colours, harems, and even as Chinese coolies.[12]

A.J. Lievegoed, the chief editor of *De Sumatra Post* found that the town lacked cultural and intellectual pursuits. Thus, the Deli Cultural Circle (Delische Kunstkring) was founded in 1912 to promote intellectual and cultural interests among the people of Deli. Lievegoed worked closely with the Witte club to organise evening events.[13]

Artist Harm Kamerlingh Onnes visited the Sociëteit and wrote in 1923:

Afterwards, we go to the "Soos" where dancing is taking place. It's 8 o'clock, and we do some dancing. The club is actually what our auditorium (in the city of Leiden, the Netherlands) is. Something like the foyer, very spacious, quite funny, such a whole crowd in white. It definitely brightens things up. – The ladies wear regular dresses in colours. – Dancing is quite warm here, especially with a cardigan, which is only worn in the presence of ladies.*[14]

[10] SP 06-12-1900.

[11] *Het nieuwsblad voor Sumatra* 17-09-1954.

[12] *Pinang Gazette and Straits Chronicle* 09-10-1916.

[13] SP 09-09-1912; 30-09-1912.

[14] Buiskool 1999:89.

When Harm was in Medan, the Dutch singer Geertruida van Vladeracken performed in the Witte Sociëteit. *De Sumatra Post* wrote in March 1923:

> *Geertruida van Vladeracken sings folk songs. She sings them with freshness, she acts well in her various costumes... After the interval, first came French songs, among them the well-known "Le roy a fait battre tambour." Geertruida van Vladeracken put more into it than in many of her other songs, but she didn't get the most out of it, so it didn't become a small drama, as precisely these chansons, with their striking portrayal, can be. The Kunstkringbestuur presented the singer with beautiful flowers.*[15]

7.2 All One Needed Was a White Skin[16]

> *In one respect the Witte Sociëteit differs from other cities in the Indies; people of coloured blood are not encouraged within its doors. In Java, which was colonised much earlier than Sumatra, and where important Government positions are held by men whose blood is not 100 per cent European, there is no discrimination against a touch of colour. But Sumatra has not long been civilised and it still has a prejudice against mixed breeds, as in the United States, South Africa and other countries where miscegenation has been common in the past.*[17]

Locally, the club was called *roemah bola* (ball house, or a place where one plays ball games), but the Witte Sociëteit was established as a club exclusively for the white population of Deli. These white workers referred to themselves as Deliaan (Fig. 7.2). Regardless of their background, any European could come to Deli and find work, as long as they were white. The European lifestyle in Deli has been the subject of numerous novels, including works by Ladislao Székely and his wife, Madelon. Madelon Lulofs wrote that white Europeans did not come to Deli to settle and raise families; instead, they aimed to accumulate wealth quickly and return to Europe to live comfortably.[18] Székely wrote:

> *There are two worlds: the white and the coloured. There are separate compartments in the trains for the whites. Not that "Only for white gentlemen!" - is written on the outside; there is no written law for it, but everyone knows and*

[15] DC 17-3-1923.
[16] Based on the title of a chapter in Anthony Reid's Witnesses to Sumatra.
[17] *Newcastle Morning Herald and Miners' Advocate* 05-11-1938.
[18] Székely Lulofs 1933:39.

Fig. 7.2 The white members of De Witte Sociëteit (Wright 1909)

observes it. It goes without saying that the hotels, clubs and restaurants of the white man are not open to the coloured.[19]

You're in Deli here. Whites travel first, get that straight! You're a tuan here. Forget what you were in Holland; that makes no difference here. Here you're a White. That's what counts. And don't forget it when you deal with Orientals. …

If a white walks into a store, let us say into the store of a Hindu millionaire, the millionaire will bow low before the tuan, who may be a runaway sailor, a card-sharper or an adventurer. But he is a white tuan.

If you want to get into a cab and a coloured woman happens to be sitting in it, waiting for her husband who is shopping in a store, she will immediately get out and offer you the carriage.[20]

The Whites laid down rules on how the "Natives" should behave. Madelon Lulofs in *De Andere Wereld* wrote:

A white man never greets a native, at most - if you want to be really friendly - you say: tabeh… Of course you can't know that, but don't forget it. And now I'll teach you a few other things, the ABC of our relationship with the natives.

[19] Székely 1979: 46.
[20] Idem.

> *Each native is obliged to get off his vehicle or bicycle and walk beside it for twenty yards, ten ahead and ten beyond a white person, and even when passing a company building like an office, a shed or a house. …*
>
> *If they're riding a bike, they also have to get off it, and if they pass by with a topi (hat), they also have to take that headgear off their head ten meters before and ten meters after ….*
>
> *You may think this silly or exaggerated, but don't forget that we whites were alone, facing a mass. We can hold our own only if there are strict, conventional regulations. These rules should impose discipline.*[21]

And for the Chinese who had a queue:

> *The Chinese labourer, dressed in his Sunday best, wears dark blue silk trousers, a wide jacket without shape made of the same material, a brown or grey felt hat, and the peculiar small Chinese slippers. The queue, which is braided, is usually coiled up and tied into a bundle at the back of the head. If he wishes to speak to a European, he must remove his hat from a distance and also uncoil the bundle and let his braid hang down.*[22]

Despite having an international population, the white population, who made up less than 10% of the total population, were in charge. Prior to the 1910s, all planters were men, and marriage was prohibited as it was believed that it would distract young white men from their work. In 1884, out of the 688 Europeans on the East Coast, 540 were men and only 148 were women. By 1900, not much had changed, with 1578 men out of 2079 Europeans residing in Deli.

As with any colony, racism was prevalent in Deli. The Deliaan world was divided into social classes: assistant, manager, and chief manager. The *sinkeh*, or novice assistant, held the lowest rank, while the experienced ones were known as *laukeh*. The new assistant had to supervise the coolies and ensure that the work was completed, placing them at the bottom of the social ladder. To be accepted as a Deliaan, one had to work tirelessly in the fields under the scorching sun. This challenging task required individuals to prove themselves and work their way up the social ranks.[23]

[21] Székely Lulofs 1946:100–101.

[22] *Zutphensche courant* 25-08-1891.

[23] Sinkeh originated from the Hokkien word meaning newcomer (fresh from the boat). It was commonly used to refer to newly arrived coolies, but the term was also applied to planters.

Within Medan's White society, the elite separated themselves from the others. Europeans in Medan used to enjoy the music of the Manilla Band in the Esplanade in a shared space in front of the bandstand. The Electric Company generously provided free lighting, making these gatherings a pleasant communal experience. However, the elite members of Medan's society, particularly those from the Soos, began to distance themselves from the loud planters who often enjoyed drinking their beers. The community called it the Medan Chic.[24]

An anecdote was shared about a fourteen-year-old girl who caught the eye of an eager young suitor. The boy, full of youthful passion, fell in love with the girl, the daughter of a prominent official. The girl's father held an esteemed position, while the boy's father owned a shop that sold fancy goods, a profession viewed with disdain by the upper echelons of society. Despite societal barriers, the young man wrote a love letter, albeit riddled with spelling errors, expressing his desire to meet her. Unfortunately, the girl's father intercepted the letter. The father decided to intervene by dressing up as a woman, complete with a bonnet, dress, and high heels, to impersonate his daughter at a planned rendezvous. When the unsuspecting boy approached, thinking he was meeting his love interest, the father revealed himself and gave the boy a firm scolding, putting an abrupt end to the youthful romance. The daughter was sent to Europe.[25]

7.2.1 Hari Besar

After working 12 hours a day in the scorching tropical sun for two weeks, the planters would receive their pay and a well-deserved holiday, known as *hari besar* (the big day). Some of them would rent a car or take the train to Medan to enjoy themselves. Those who were not able to travel could still party at the plantation clubhouse. In Medan, they would greet each other in English (Fig. 7.3),

> *Hello guys, where are you going tonight?*
>
> *Two weeks of slave service, but one day of a gentleman's life, with champagne and an extra nice dinner. A dog job in the jungle for two weeks, but spent one day in a tuxedo and pumps. We are Delians.*[26]
>
> *A hari besar at Deli was always something special, Medan turning into a seething cauldron, the walls of Medan Hotel were bulging and at the De Boer hotel personnel brought out their coarsest crockery, in anticipation of breakage*

[24] *Het nieuws van den dag voor Nederlandsch-Indië* 09-08-1902.
[25] Idem.
[26] Bormann 1926: 45.

Fig. 7.3 Medan during hari besar in 1925 (Rijtuigen op een weg te Medan, KITLV 182253)

> *once people took to spinning plates on the marble floor....Have you ever experienced what is going on inside of you when you hear the ringing sound of soup plates spinning on marble at forty places at once?* [27]

And best of all, in the era before credit cards, the planters had an unlimited credit system:

> *Of course, the checks come at the end of every month. This frequent use of checks - the so-called ticket system - is something that occurs all over the East Indies. No European pays with cash here in a hotel and often also in one or another business. A very easy attitude and also a discreet way to get into debt in a hotel, but with a very dangerous side to it!* [28]

[27] Veersema 1936:205.
[28] Bormann 1926:46.

7.2.2 Members Only

The Witte Sociëteit is an exclusive club, with membership decided by ballot, existing members voted on the admission of new members. Dutch journalist Willem Brandt noted:

> *There is no question that an Indonesian could ever become a member.*[29]

But of course, there were a few exceptions, such as the Sultans and their families.

In 1913, Van Kaathoven obtained permission from the club's board to rent the hall for cinema screenings, exclusively for Europeans and those deemed their equals. Soon after, the "Wife of a Soos member" published a letter in *De Sumatra Post*, expressing shock and concern over the decision. The author questioned who the "equals" were, and suggested that it mainly referred to the Japanese population in Medan, many of whom were public women (prostitutes). The author urged the board to respect the women members by keeping those women out of the White Society.[30] Against this racist remark, one reader reacted that these Japanese women did not bother anyone and wrote:

> *If everybody would behave themselves as decently as these Japanese women, the police would never need to interfere. What happens now is that Japanese women will not give irritation, but that some gentlemen who sit in their vicinity do.*[31]

Another reader, "Planter woman" in the name of sisterhood, wrote:

> *Justice is a beautiful virtue, but to practice it is very difficult; because: where is the line if we start banning public women? If we exclude the Japanese, we must also exclude the Europeans. And how do we know that Europeans are so highly superior to their Japanese sisters? We cannot judge by appearance alone. And then… all the young and sore men who have an intimate relationship with those women? Should we keep them out too?*[32]

The chairman of the Town Council, S. van der Plas, responded that such a restriction would upset many citizens (Fig. 7.4). Van der Plas said:

[29] *Het nieuwsblad voor Sumatra* 17-09-1954.
[30] SP 10-04-1913.
[31] SP 11-04-1913.
[32] SP 15-04-1913.

Fig. 7.4 Governor S. Van der Plas (KITLV 4402)

> *Europeans of the lowest quality could demand entry, while Indigenous and Chinese of high esteem, yes, even to members of this council, entry could be denied! […] something like this is exactly what we do not want.*[33]

Van der Plas asserted that the club could charge a high admission fee to prevent that and keep the lower classes out.

As a response, the elite Indigenous community established their clubs. Bangsawan Club at Djalan Radja was also called de club der Tengkoe's or the club for the Tengku's (nobility). In 1930, the Indigenous community proposed the society Sociëteit Taman Persahabatan Indonesia (Garden of

[33] SP 16-04-1913.

the Friends of Indonesia). However, some leaders found it political and decided to omit the word "Indonesia" from the name. Thus, Taman Persahabatan was established at Wilhelminastraat No. 36 (Jl. Sutomo) also called the De Inlandsche sociëteit. Chinese Major Tjong Yong Hian established the Yan Kin Hian Club at Hongkongstraat (jl. Cirebon) No. 11. Also known as the Chinese Club (Chineesche-sociëteit) or Sociëteit Yan Kin Hian, it served as a social venue for Chinese merchants and elites, featuring a restaurant and a gambling room.[34]

7.2.3 We're Not Going Home Yet

Membership of the Soos was a coveted social position, but it was not attainable for everyone, particularly the *sinkeh*. Only Europeans who had worked in Deli for more than six years, earned a good income and had a respectable reputation were eligible to become members. Moreover, the Soos had a tradition of excluding middle-class traders or shop owners, as it was considered a sanctuary free from creditors. In the Deli society, most planters did not have to pay in cash.

Non-members of the White Club were only allowed to enter the club during the Kunstkring performances held in the large theatre hall. However, they were restricted to attending the performance only and were not permitted to visit the bar. Afterwards, they had to find somewhere else to enjoy their drinks.

The white community enjoyed lavish parties, with gallons of booze flowing through the night, and music played until the early morning hours. The motto was

> *We're not going home yet, not yet!* [35]
>
> *At the Witte Sociëteit (White Club) in Medan the food and drinks would satisfy the most exacting gourmet: and on Saturday and Sunday nights women are allowed to dance with their menfolk on the large marble flagstones in the garden. Marble is the most usual dance floor in the East Indies. It is an ideal surface.*[36]

In the 1930s, it was also a tradition that when the party was over and leaving the soos, planters headed straight to café Epperlein, a German

[34] DC 05-05-1930; SP 07-12-1935.

[35] *Het Nieuwsblad voor Sumatra* 17-09-1954.

[36] *Newcastle Morning Herald and Miners' Advocate* 5-11-1938.

bakery in Kesawan, where the Epperlein brothers always opened at five o'clock in the morning. They could have hot coffee, fresh ham rolls, and after that, they immediately dove into the pool.[37]

In 1930, the Soos had 716 members, but this number decreased to 394 by the end of 1934 due to the economic crisis. In 1940, at its 60th anniversary celebrations, it increased back to 625 members.[38]

All activities stopped on the eve of Medan's capture by Japan. The Australian newspaper *The Sun* wrote:

> *When night falls in Medan, the streets are brightly lit up in peacetime. The natives enjoy their time at Amusement Parks, while the Europeans head to the "White Club," which boasts a luxurious swimming pool, the best European band, and stage performances that provide ample entertainment for homesick Dutch. The "White Club" is a symbol of the wealth and prosperity of the white community in Medan, consisting mostly of middle-class settlers whose lives are closely tied to the fate of Sumatra. Although its members do not come from the aristocracy, the club reflects the Dutch colonists' attempt to transplant Holland into this faraway and exotic part of the world. Medan is also one of the cultural centres of the Indies. In peacetime, the Medan Art Circle organised annual exhibitions and musical performances, inviting world-famous artists and arranging lectures and film exhibitions while paying large sums.*[39]

7.3 After the War

After the war, the British military occupied the Witte Sociëteit building. In March 1948, the Allied forces offered the Hirohara shrine, a Shinto temple built in 1944 by forced labour behind the Deli Proefstation (Deli Research Station for Tobacco), as the new venue. This is now known as the Medan Club at Jl. Kartini. The original sociëteit building was demolished and converted into office buildings in the 1950s.

The management of the Soos was entrusted to Mr. and Mrs. Mettier, with Louis Mettier, a Swiss and a long-standing member of the Soos, at the helm. Mettier arrived in Deli in 1913 and worked for Senembah company. With his wife, they settled in Medan in 1930 and established the Medan Garden and a night security service, while also having a nursery in Kabanjahe. Under their leadership, the membership grew from 200 to 800 by 1954, with many old Deliaans leaving and new members joining.

[37] Idem.

[38] Idem.

[39] *The Sun* 09-01-1942 (There was no swimming pool at the White Club).

In May 1954, on its 75th anniversary, the Witte Sociëteit was officially renamed the Medan Club, marking the end of decades of white dominance and exclusivity. The Medan Club, which operated at Jalan Kartini until 2022, offered a range of activities beyond drinking and dancing, including a movie night, tennis, bowling, and other Western-oriented pursuits.[40]

On October 28, 2021, the Medan Club site was designated a cultural heritage site by the Medan City Government. However, on July 9, 2022, the North Sumatra Provincial Government, led by Governor Edy Rahmayadi, barred the sale of the land to any third party and announced plans to purchase the 1.4-hectare site to expand government offices. The purchase price was over Rp.457 billion (~$28.5 million USD). This move sparked criticism over the urgency and high cost. Edy Rahmayadi defended the decision, warning that if the land was not bought, it could be redeveloped privately into high-rise buildings. The heirs of the Sultanate of Deli claimed ownership, arguing the land had only been conceded to Deli Maatschappij and never properly compensated. Lawsuits were filed, but

Fig. 7.5 A garden party in Medan (Wright 1909)

[40] *Het nieuwsblad voor Sumatra* 17-09-1954. The building at Jalan Kartini was a Japanese shinto temple constructed by forced labour by European and others. Chinese lawyer Tan Tjeng Bie was forced to work on the building in 1943 and 1944.

Fig. 7.6 Scene at the Esplanade and De Boer (*Pertja Timoer* 04-02-1928, *Sumatra* 14-05-1927)

the North Sumatra High Prosecutor's Office later ruled the purchase legal.[41] With that decision, the remain of the Witte Sociëteit in Medan came to an end (Figs. 7.5 and 7.6).

[41] https://en.wikipedia.org/wiki/Hirohara_Shrine

CHAPTER 8

The Evolving Kesawan

Kesawan, the heart of Medan, has long been the city's most iconic urban corridor, where colonial ambition, commercial energy, and multicultural life converged. Emerging in the late nineteenth century as the commercial road of the Deli tobacco empire, Kesawan grew into a bustling district lined with grand European offices, Chinese shophouses, and Indian and Malay trading establishments. Its central artery, Jalan Kesawan (now Jalan Ahmad Yani), became both a showcase of architectural splendour and a stage for everyday encounters: rickshaws rattling past art deco façades, coolies unloading goods at godowns, and well-dressed families strolling between cafés and department stores. Kesawan symbolised Medan's transformation from a remote plantation hub into a cosmopolitan colonial city. Today, despite modern pressures, its surviving buildings and street rhythms continue to reflect the stories of the people who shaped it (Fig. 8.1).

8.1 From a Village to an Urban Centre

Medan was first developed in 1870 with the establishment of the Deli Maatschappij (Deli Company) headquarters on the east bank of the Deli River, at the confluence with Sungei Baboera, making it navigable for loading small boats. Medan Poetri was a small *kampong* fortified by an earthen wall among *ladangs*,[1] nutmeg gardens and forests with around 50

[1] Ladang = field.

B. Minasny, D. A. Buiskool, *Stories from Medan, Volume 1*,
https://doi.org/10.1007/978-981-95-7707-1_8

Fig. 8.1 Kesawan around 1905 by Kleingrothe. On the right was Toko Soey Tek Bie, followed by the intersection with Marktstraat (Kleingrothe, KITLV 26913)

households. Neighbouring *kampongs* were Kesawan, Binoewang, Merbau and Tebing Tinggi.[2] The Deli company's headquarters started with a rudimentary building. At the same time, the Medan estate was established, followed by the Kesawan estate in 1873.

Several decades previously, Kedjoeroean Padang,[3] the forefather of the Sultanate of Deli, had conquered the region of Kesawan, a lowland plain on the banks of the Deli river. The Malays inhabited Kampong Kesawan under the *oeroeng* (district) Soekapiring or *soekoe* Kampong Baroe led by Datoek Kesawan. In 1875, Kesawan consisted of only 37 households. With the development of Medan and Kesawan, the Datoek moved to Kampung Baroe.[4]

According to Veersema in the Guide Book, *Gids voor de Oostkust van Sumatra,* the name Kesawan was suggested to come from the Malay word

[2] Broersma 1919:148; *De Locomotief* 13-03-1925.

[3] "Kedjoeroean" (or "Kejuruan") in Malay refers to a specific area, district, or region under the administrative control of a ruling power. Anderson wrote Kassawan as one of the tribes lead by Santun, Orang Kaya Kassawan (Anderson 1826: 306).

[4] Halewijn 1876: 154; Jansen 1925:9. In pre-colonial time, the Deli region was separated by customary territories of *soekoe* (in Malay) or oeroeng (in Karo), they were the same system under the rule of the Sultan of Deli.

"Kesawahan," meaning "to sawah," referring to its rural past.[5] A more likely origin is from the Indian name *Keshavan* (also spelled *Kesawan* or *Kesavan*), a common name in southern India. Keshava is one of the names of the Hindu God Vishnu, and the name *Keshavan* was commonly used during the Hindu kingdoms in ancient Indonesia.[6] Similarly, the name Medan was derived from the Indian word Maidan.[7] The Deli region had a long history of Hindu influences, dating back to well before the tenth century.[8]

As early as 1874, the Deli Company designated an area for the *kedehs* (shops) along the road of Kampong Kesawan. On *hari besar*, a Chinese worker would say he was going to shop "pigi sawah."[9] Chinese merchants from the British Straits Settlements (mainly from Penang) soon established a foothold in Kesawan by establishing shops to serve European needs. It was not until 1880 that roads were built and the Esplanade was established. This coincided with the development of photography in the late nineteenth century. Thus, historical pictures captured the development of Kesawan from rows of wooden shops to a modern shopping street. These photos allow us to partly reconstruct the history and evolution of Kesawan.

8.1.1 In the Beginning

From its earliest days, Kesawan served as Medan's commercial district, predominantly led by Chinese merchants. Initially, it was dominated by makeshift wooden *kedeh*s or shops, lining the muddy street. Shops were built to cater to the needs of the European population and plantation owners in the surrounding areas. The area around Kesawan was also the first Chinese settlement, with an area designated as *Chineesche kamp* (Chinese camp).[10]

[5] Veersema 1940: 28.

[6] For example, king Balitung (898–910) of Mataram kingdom in Java had a title Śrī Īsvara keśavo tsavatuṅga (meaning glorious, Īśvara and Keśava [a.k.a. Śiva and Viṣṇu]) (information from Dr. Jarrah Sastrawan).

[7] https://en.wikipedia.org/wiki/Maidan; Feldwick 1917: 1180; Buiskool 2025: 46.

[8] A Vishnu statue with Buddha statues were discovered in Kota China (McKinnon 1984:79–82).

[9] *De Locomotief* 13-03-1925. The Chinese term for Kesawan is Shawan, and the area was called Deli Shawan.

[10] DC 11-12-1886, 16-11-1887; 14-05-1890.

The earliest picture of Kesawan from 1885 shows a row of wooden two-storey *kedehs*. At that time, Medan had about sixty shops, mostly Chinese. These shophouses had a commercial area on the ground floor and a living area upstairs. A notable shop in the picture is Su Yeu Nam, a gold and silversmith, as well as a watchmaker (Fig. 8.2).

Khoe Tay Liam arrived in Deli as a coolie. Over time, he became a *kelontong* [11] or peddler in the Batak region, where he established strong connections with the local population by learning their language and customs. He became wealthy, with an estimated wealth of 30,000 guilders. He owned shops in Laboean Deli and five houses in Kesawan Nos. 1, 2, 3, 4, and 6, which were rented to Seng Hap, Hong Tjong Tjan, Lie Tek Kie, Soei Nam, and Kong Lam Sing. Khoe Tay Liam's influence extended to

Fig. 8.2 Kesawan with wooden stores around 1885 (Tropenmuseum 60001774)

[11] *Kelontong* originally means a peddler or hawker. The word came from the sound made by a little drum carried by a Chinese peddler while the person was walking and selling his stuff. It evolved to *toko kelontong* which means a shop that sells any basic needs.

the colonial administration, as he was closely associated with the Resident of Deli. This connection allowed him to wield considerable power. But his bold actions and increasing influence alarmed colonial officials, who feared potential regional destabilisation. Allegedly, he organised local resistance against colonial authorities, leading to his arrest. He hosted seven Batak tribal leaders, who returned to their tribes with plans, reportedly, to mobilise a mass protest, possibly involving 2000 followers, to protest to the Sultan on his detention by the Assistant Resident. His supporters, marked by the red flag, raised 20,000 guilders to cover his expenses. Khoe Tay Liam died in 1895 and the government sold his assets.[12]

The next photo from Stafhell & Kleingrothe, taken around 1895, depicts an ox cart watering the Kesawan road. It shows the same location as the 1885 picture (Fig. 8.3). The road was slightly busier, the wooden

Fig. 8.3 Kesawan 1895 with an ox cart watering the road. By Stafhell and Kleingrothe (KITLV 80217)

[12] *Bataviaasch handelsblad* 26-11-1880; DC 15-06-1895, 06-04-1898.

shops persisted, but now the shop on the corner of Kesawan was made of bricks. Su Yeu Nam was the third house from the corner.

Merchants and traders from China, India, Java, and Malacca found their way to Medan, where money was earned easily and spent freely. The picture "*Hoek Kesawan en Esplanade te Medan*" (Corner Kesawan and Esplanade in Medan)[13] taken by Jan Willem Schut around a similar time, provides a clearer picture (Fig. 8.4). The corner shop was a two-storey shop called *Toko Bombay* operated by Jaramul Tilokchand, selling Chinese and Japanese goods. Next to it was Seng Hap & Co.

Tan Tang Ho, a *peranakan* from Batavia, founded the *kelontong* shop Seng Hap, recognising an opportunity to cater to the European market by importing goods from Penang, such as beer, gin, cognac, food items, and cigars. He had many Europeans *langganan* (customers). Similarly, Oei Soei Boe from Penang established the Soey Tek Bie store in Kesawan in

Fig. 8.4 Hoek Kesawan en Esplanade te Medan 1897 (photo by Willem Schut, J., Nationaal Archief 803_06)

[13]Toko Bombay usually means shops run by Indian merchants selling clothing materials.

1887, offering a range of imported products, including wine, spirits, cigars, biscuits, ham, sausage, cheese, chocolate, butter, and soaps. Tjong Yong Hian set up his shop Chong Lee, with imported food items, whiskey from Scotland, port from Portugal, sherry from Spain, milk and butter from Australia.

In 1887, E.B. Salomon established Kesawan Hotel, a Café and Restaurant with a billiard table.[14] While Kesawan was already a shopping street, it was still dominated by small timber shophouses. The Chinese camp around it was notorious for the makeshift houses. This caused the area to be prone to fire. On February 24, 1890, *Deli Courant* reported a fire at 4 o'clock in the morning:

> *Finally it happened, a fire broke out on the Kesawan and the result fully met expectations: much, very much was burned and, as predicted, little could be done about it.*[15]

The fire wiped out a block of 62 houses and shops on Kesawan and its back street at Djalan Padjak (current Jl. Kumango). The damage was estimated to be 150,000–300,000 guilders. But most houses were insured. Tjong A Fie and Tjong Yong Hian owned 40 *kedehs* insured for $37,000.[16] Two days later, Tjong A Fie and Tjong Yong Hian advertised that they planned to build a series of commercial houses with office spaces above the site where the fire broke out.[17]

Within the next few years, the Tjong brothers led the rebuilding of Kesawan, and wooden shops were replaced with buildings made of brick (Fig. 8.5). They erected two-level Chinese-style shophouses that spanned the entire block, creating a cohesive and unified look. The rebuilding is part of a broader trend in the community, with numerous new structures being added, each contributing to the town's growth and modernisation.[18]

European shops were also established. *Deli Courant* wrote:

> *While our electricity company will soon begin stringing the lines that will light up our streets and roads, as well as our large buildings and houses, trade and*

[14] DC 08-10-1887.
[15] DC 24-02-1900; SP 26-02-1900.
[16] *Haagsche courant* 05-04-1900; DC 24-02-1900.
[17] SP 28-02-1900.
[18] DC 24-03-1900.

Fig. 8.5 The rebuilding of Kesawan (WereldMuseum RV-A440-q-169)

industry are working to increasingly develop into metropolitan enterprises. The building of the firm S. Katz & Co. has given a significant push in the direction of elegant shop spaces, filled with fancy goods, and this example was followed by a similar establishment next door, where now Soei Tek Bie & Co. also offer an exceptionally rich collection of delicacies to the public. This was followed by the neat and tidy premise of the Delische Bazar, stocked with various fine and neat items for household use or luxury. After that, the large establishment of Cornfield made its mark, which, besides offering a substantial tailoring service, also provided the public with the opportunity to purchase fine gifts in various fields.

Finally, on Monday the 11th, the grand opening took place in the magnificent building of Messrs. Goldenberg & Zeitlin. Under a large turnout of Medanese ladies and gentlemen, and under the rarely seen phenomenon here of a curious Native crowd onlookers, the aforementioned gentlemen presented their new premise to the public on Monday evening. We have already mentioned that the modern appearance of the building would make a very good impression on the main streets of our capital cities, but now that we have seen the interior, we do not hesitate to declare that the richness and luxury of the display truly surpass everything we have seen so far in the Indies. The gentlemen G. & Z., who have been in the business here in Medan for so many years and are thus well acquainted with the nature of Delische needs, especially regarding luxury items, have arranged a selection of luxury objects in Europe that simply astonishes us.[19]

Katz & Co. opened in 1887 and offered clothing materials and fashion items for both men and women. Another notable store was Goldenberg & Zeitlin, which opened in 1898 at the corner of Kesawan and Djalan Datoek. The magnificent building was built by Langereis & Co., which did not earn much profit, but established itself as a grand architect in the new town.[20] This store specialised in a fine range of products, including jewellery, hunting rifles, lamps, glassware, sheets, cigars, wines, and more. Next to Goldenberg & Zeitlin was W. Cornfield, which carried a complete range of clothes and luxury items imported from London and Paris. These European shops were an important part of the commercial landscape of the area, catering to the needs and desires of the growing European community in the region.

8.1.2 Kesawan in 1900

Medan differed from cities in Java as it was built from scratch and planned with a European urban design. Its proximity to the Straits Settlements influenced its urban characteristics, reflecting some English city traits. Unlike in Java, where the famous Rijsttafel was a customary dining experience, it was not a popular dish in Medan, where the Dutch preferred dishes and foods from the Netherlands.[21] The Malay used in Medan was more closely related to the Malay used in Penang. In Java, it was referred to as "barracks Malay," but in Medan, it was called "Chinese-Malay." The boy servant known as *djongos*[22] didn't address his mistress "Nyonya" instead "Mem," derived from "Madam." The stable boy was called "syce." People don't say "lihat" (to see) but "tengok," "cakap" instead of "bicara" or "omong" (to speak).[23]

By 1900, Kesawan had evolved into a new shopping street (Fig. 8.6). Dutch writer Justus van Maurik, who visited Medan, wrote:

[19] DC 23-11-1898.
[20] *Bataviaasch nieuwsblad* 14-12-1898.
[21] *Nieuwe Haarlemsche Courant* 18-12-1928.
[22] *Djongos* was from Dutch jongen means boy.
[23] *Soerabaijasch handelsblad* 11-06-1906.

Fig. 8.6 Kesawan in the early 1900s, the first two houses on the left remain until today (Kleingrothe, KITLV 78466)

> *Medan, the capital of Deli, immediately makes a very pleasant impression. One can see that one is in a young city, in a prosperous place, full of vigorous and lively activity. Medan could rightly be called "the tobacco city," because in fact it owes its origin and ever-increasing growth to tobacco. You can see from the neat, well-built and lavishly furnished houses that you don't have to be on the penny in Medan, that people there understand that money is round and must roll, and that comfort and luxury can very well be combined with tireless and hard work.*[24]

In March 1900, Tan Tang Ho opened his new Seng Hap store, featuring a Roman temple-style facade distinguished by two large columns.[25] The corner building next to Seng Hap, at the intersection of Kesawan and Esplanade, was initially occupied by the S. Katz & Co. fashion store and later by the Dutch shipping company, Nederlandsche Lloyd. The evolution of Kesawan is depicted in the picture by Kleingrothe. The first two buildings from the corner of Kesawan on the left remain until today. The

[24] Maurik 1897: 435–436.
[25] SP 26-3-1900; Buiskool 1999: 95.

Chinese-style shophouses featured semicircular window frames, wooden shutters, and a walking arcade.

In December 1900, Tjong A Fie moved to his new mansion, *Deli Courant* reported:

The house itself is a masterpiece, exuding simplicity, symmetry, and practicality. The front yard is lined with the main road, Kesawan, and features a "grand gate" of wood and stone, crowned impressively. Through this gate, visitors enter a quiet forecourt and approach the main building, square and primarily tinted in a light coffee-cream colour, topped with a traditional Chinese roof with large, calm lines and tasteful cement decorations that aren't overbearing. The sidewalls are elegant in plain white, with rectangular lattice windows made of green tiles, adding a unique decorative touch to the otherwise large, quiet surface.

Upon entering, one passes through a wide central gallery, reaching a triptych-style portico, spacious and open, decorated with red and gold wood carvings partially imported from China. This leads into an inner courtyard, where a fountain will later be installed to bring freshness. The entrance area is roomy and bright, with small, pot-grown bonsai trees in the courtyard, showcasing the art of tree trimming. High above, glistening plaques display proverbs in faded letters that exude wisdom and, at night, glow with electric light, casting a soft glow over the entire building.

Through another courtyard decorated with red silk drapery, we enter the tepekong, the house temple, a spacious hall adorned with inscriptions, silk drapes, and wall hangings. Ebony chairs line the walls, and on the back wall sits a black and red wooden altar, where the household gods will be placed. The altar's niches are framed with gilded carvings harmonising with the solemn surfaces. The ebony furniture, including stools, tables, and stands, is inlaid with mother-of-pearl.[26]

Fireworks were set off, drums were beaten and flutes were blown. *De Sumatra Post* wrote:

Saturday at half past three a deafening noise started; it was more like the whole house collapsing or just a simple fireworks display. Then there were tam-tams, flutes, and strange click-clack machines, the sound of which resembled eating

[26] DC 27-12-1900.

> *chestnuts, and all kinds of beautifully coloured papers written with incantations were burned.*[27]

Two years later, on an auspicious day, January 2, 1903, Tjong Yong Hian moved to his new house in Kesawan, next to Tjong A Fie's mansion. Chinese opera and fireworks marked the occasion.[28] At the same time, Hallermann established *De Sumatra Post* in a small house next to Tjong A Fie's mansion.

In February 1900, a major fire erupted in Kesawan, devastating an entire block adjacent to Padjak Street. The fire destroyed 62 houses, including the Delische Bazaar and Robinsons Piano Company. Despite minimal wind, the blaze spread to a nearby block, exacerbated by inadequate firefighting equipment. One insurer assessed the loss at 150,000 guilders, while the Chinese captain estimated it at 300,000 guilders. The fire consumed 40 kedehs owned by Tjong A Fie and Tjong Yong Hian, which were insured for a total of $37,000.[29]

The photo by Japanese photographer Mazaraki in 1905 showed a combination of timber and brick houses in Kesawan. The photo was taken from South to North, with a view of the protestant church at the Esplanade in the far distance. To the right, there was the fence of the Tjong Yong Hian mansion. On the left, there was Kong Soen Ho, who specialised in *meubels* or furniture (Fig. 8.7). Sindhi merchant Bhai Khemchand Hundamal Mahtani established Khemchand & Sons, known as Hoondamall & Sons, which had the best imported silks and textiles.

Kesawan became the lively centre of Chinese commercial, social, and cultural life in Medan (Fig. 8.8). During Chinese New Year, fireworks exploded joyously across Kesawan, making loud cracking noise all day, annoying the Dutch residents, who wrote in *De Sumatra Post*:

> *Medan, however, is a Dutch-Indies city and not a Chinese one, and therefore the loud festivities do not belong on the commonly used thoroughfare.*[30]

The construction of metropolitan Medan began around the Esplanade. The Protestant church at the Esplanade was completed in 1900, built with

[27] SP 17-12-1900.
[28] SP 03-01-1903.
[29] SP 26-02-1900; *Haagsche courant* 05-04-1900.
[30] SP 04-02-1913

Fig. 8.7 Kesawan around 1905 (Mazaraki, M. KITLV 35766)

a German-inspired design in the Romanesque style. Later, in 1928, it was demolished to make way for the Dutch trading company, Nederlandsche Handel-Maatschappij (NHM) office.

The Javasche Bank established a branch in Medan and entrusted the design and construction of a new building to architect Ch. Boon of the Deli Maatschappij.[31] However, upon its completion, the bank's central management found the building unsuitable for their needs. Subsequently, the Deli Maatschappij acquired the building and repurposed it into the Town Hall for the newly formed municipality of Medan. To complete the building's transformation, Tjong A Fie generously donated a large clock in 1912.[32] In 1909, a new Javasche Bank was designed by architect Ed Cuypers and constructed next to the town hall.[33]

[31] *Indische Mercuur* 08-10-1907. Charles Marinus Boon was born in Den Ham on 29-4-1871, and died in Wassenaar on 13-11-1947, son of preacher Albert Goswin Boon.

[32] Buiskool 2025: 142,322.

[33] Eduard Gerard Hendrik Hubert Cuypers (1859–1927) was the nephew of the famous architect Pierre Cuypers (1827–1921), of the Rijksmuseum and Central Station in Amsterdam.

Hotel de Boer at the Esplanade was completed in 1902.[34] Offices of the Güntzel & Schumacher company and the Chartered Bank were built on Nienhuysweg (Jl. Pinang) with dark grey stone classical architecture. The new headquarters of the Deli Maatschappij was completed in 1910 (Jl. Tembakau Deli). The building of a new post office began to be discussed in 1910 with architect Ch. Boon. However, as the progress was slow, a new design by Simon Snuyf of Burgerlijke Openbare Werken (BOW) or the Department of Civil Public Works was selected. The post office was inaugurated on the night of February 12, 1913.[35]

Fig. 8.8 The centre of Kesawan faced the Esplanade, with Goldenberg, Zeitlin, Cornfield on the left, Atelier Kleingrothe on the right, and Firma Hoondamal on the right (Wereldmuseum RV-A440-q-168)

[34] SP 17-07-1902, After Dutch modernist architect H.P. Berlage (1856–1934).
[35] DC 13-02-1913. Ir. Simon Snuijf, born Amsterdam 11-6-1880, d. Batavia 15-9-1944.

8.1.3 Kesawan in the 1910s

The next stage of Kesawan's development was the construction of the building at the entrance corner. The building, built by Harrisons & Crosfield featured a colonial and classical British style, designed by Englishman Herbert Walker. It was constructed using Aberdeen granite shipped from Scotland. The building was named Julianahuis or Juliana House, in honour of Dutch Princess Juliana's birth in 1909. The Victorian-style building was officially occupied in November 1914 (Fig. 8.9). Harrisons & Crosfield operated in the rubber industry and also as a general importer and agent for British shipping companies and insurance banks. Among its notable features, Juliana House boasted the first elevator in Sumatra, which was designed by R. Waygood & Co.[36] A copy of the Harrisons & Crosfield building was constructed in Great Tower Street in London, England and was occupied in 1912.[37] Another British trading company from the Straits, Guthrie & Co., also set foot in Kesawan in 1913. They supplied British goods ranging from beer, stout, and brandy to motor oil.

Fig. 8.9 Julianahuis at the corner of Kesawan (WereldMuseum 7082-nf-353-26-2)

[36] Pugh 1990: 59; Loderichs 1997:19; SP 04-11-1914.
[37] Pugh 1990:56; See https://maps.app.goo.gl/HK3i6vgiy9MAmLkx5

In 1911, residents of Kesawan paid their final respects to Tjong Yong Hian (1850–1911), who served as the Chinese Major of Medan. His sudden passing was mourned by all residents of Medan, including Europeans and the Sultan. Tjong Yong Hian had lived through the entire period of Deli's rise and was highly regarded as an excellent advisor, known for his sharp mind and vast business knowledge. As a Mandarin of the second class, he played a significant role in the region's development. His funeral procession was a solemn occasion as the people of Kesawan bid farewell to a beloved figure who had left an indelible mark on the community.[38]

As the year 1910 rolled in, new stores were built, including Kleingrothe Atelier's studio and Hallermann's bookstore. Smaller Chinese and Indigenous wooden shops on Kesawan were gradually replaced with brick buildings.[39] Kesawan had firmly established itself as Medan's premier *winkelstraat* (shopping street), renowned for its luxury offerings. It catered to the needs of the European population and the planters during their *hari besar* celebrations. The street was adorned with electric lights and road lamps and boasted sealed road surfaces, pavements, and galleries, protecting pedestrians from the sun and the rain. The shopping experience on Kesawan was supreme, featuring a diverse array of shops, department stores, and trading companies offering items ranging from furniture, tailoring, and shoemaking to photography, clocks, and jewellery, and everything in between. Indian shops sold beautiful fabrics, Chinese shops offered exquisite gold and silver craftsmanship and intricate ivory carvings, and Javanese shops proudly displayed an array of colourful wayang figures.

In 1912, P.W. Duson and his wife A. Duson-Galis opened Maison Duson at Kesawan 31, specialising in ladies' fashion and dressmaking and bringing Paris fashion to Medan.[40] Maison E. Mesters was the renowned barber in the vicinity, and Deli Slachterij (slaughterhouse) operated by J.C. Mann was the trusted butcher. Rathkamp & Co. was the esteemed *apotheker* or chemist on Soekamoelia Street (now Kimia Farma), and another notable chemist, J. Sijpesteyn & Co., established itself in Kesawan. This bustling area had undeniably transformed into a vibrant epicentre of commerce and luxury, symbolic of the growth and prosperity during Medan's colonial era.

[38] Stade ten Brink *Koloniaal Weekblad* 29-11-1906.; 12-9-1911; SP 19-9-1911; DC 11-9-1911.

[39] SP 07-02-1913.

[40] DC 05-10-1912.

Automobile Company Van Marle was among the first companies that introduced car sales in Medan. D. Rens, who previously specialised in making horse carriages, transformed their business into a car dealer and garage to service cars. Without clear traffic rules, cars zigzagged across the road, drivers honked their horns every five yards, and vehicles were parked wherever they pleased, leading to frequent traffic jams in Kesawan. To address this, a traffic rule was established by painting a white line down the middle of Kesawan Road, prohibiting cars from crossing it. Violators were fined (Fig. 8.10).[41]

In 1918, another significant transformation took place at the corner of Kesawan and Paleisweg with the construction of the AVROS building. AVROS stands for Algemeene Vereeniging van Rubberplanters ter Oostkust van Sumatra, or the General Association of Rubber Planters of Sumatra's East Coast. Architect G. H. Mulder designed the building, featuring a green globe crown equipped with a bell that told the time of the

Fig. 8.10 J.W. Meijsters with his photoshop around 1920s on Kesawan (KITLV 181211)

[41] *The Straits Times* 22-12-1927.

day. Adjacent to the AVROS office was the office of Tjong A Fie. *De Sumatra Post* wrote:

> *The AVROS office will form an architectural unity with another office building next to it, which is owned by Major Tjong A Fie. The tower of the AVROS office is the main architectural moment of the entire building. Furthermore, it has been fortunately obtained that the two parts, AVROS and the office building of Tjong A Fie, each speak separately and for themselves and nevertheless form an architectural whole.*[42]

Three years later, the insurance company, Nederlandsch-Indische Levensverzekering en Lijfrente Maatschappij (NILLMIJ) or the Netherlands Indies Life Insurance and Annuity Company, now known as Asuransi Jiwasraya, was built adjacent to the AVROS building. Designed by architect S. Snuyf, the two buildings are abruptly separated. Originally, the NILLMIJ building was intended to be a two-story structure connected to the AVROS building. When Mulder designed the AVROS building, he considered extending it along Soekamoelia and Paleisweg to connect with Tjong A Fie's building. However, this plan was never realised, and thus the AVROS and NILLMIJ buildings remained distinct structures.[43]

In 1921, Kesawan said goodbye to another important leader, Tjong A Fie (1860–1921), the Major of the Chinese. His funeral in March of that year was a grand affair, attended by people from all walks of life. The procession to his final resting place at Poelo Brayan was more than 1 km long, a testament to the respect and admiration that he had earned during his lifetime. The funeral was the talk of the town.[44]

8.1.4 Kesawan in the 1930s

By the 1930s, Kesawan was regarded as the "Kalverstraat" of the capital of Sumatra.[45] It boasted a number of European shops, including fashion stores Tokra Sascha and Modehuis Roelofs, which imported fashion items from Gerzon, the fashion house in Amsterdam. In 1935, Gerzon opened

[42] SP 31-01-1918.

[43] SP 31-01-1918.

[44] SP 28-03-1921; DC 29-03-1921.

[45] Kalverstraat is a busy shopping street of Amsterdam (Brandt 1948:175); Buiskool 2025: 149-153.

its Medan branch at Kesawan.[46] For men's fashion, J. Th. Maal had white suits, shoes, and hats.[47] There was the Goud en Zilversmid Co. or Gold and Silversmith Company which doesn't need an explanation. Geo Wehry was an import-export firm for liquors and food items. Firma S.D. Kaper had the latest motorsports bike and was an agent of "His Master's Voice" gramophone. Chinese shops include Ban Sin, selling imported foods from Australia and Europe; Tjo Kie & Co., a fine tailor; Hwa Nam furniture; Sin Huat Hin Lie Kie bicycle shops; Poo Tai Foo dispensary, selling herbs and medicines; and Anggoer Obat Tjap Boelan, medical wine. There were also branches of Aw Boon Haw's Tiger Balm and Singapore's Tan Kah Kee branch that offered rubber shoes under the brand Bell or Tjap Lontjeng. [48] For sports equipment, Liang You had badminton and tennis racquets. You could also find the national anthem "Indonesia Raja" on a gramophone record. Yick's and Japanese Y. Ebata had the latest photography equipment.

Banks were also available, with the Chartered Bank of India, China and Australia being the oldest bank in town. Meanwhile, the Tjong brothers established the Deli Bank. Khoe Tjin Tek and colleagues established Chunghwa Shangyeh Maatschappij, known as the Hokkien bank, with a capital of *f*1,000,000 in 1913, occupying Kesawan No. 25 in 1925.

At the end of the corner of Kesawan, next to the bookshop and printing company Varekamp, stood the Nederlandsch-Indische Escompto Maatschappij, a Dutch bank founded in 1857 in Batavia. In 1928, the bank established a new office in Medan, opposite the AVROS building (now known as Bank Mandiri, previously Bank Dagang Negara). The building was designed by architect Ed Cuypers and the architectural firm Fermont and Cuypers. There is a tile with an inscription in the hall of the bank (Fig. 8.11).

The financial crisis of 1931 had a significant impact on Kesawan, resulting in the closure of several shops. Maison Duson closed its doors after 22 years in operation. Yet, in 1933, the architecture and construction company Langereis rebuilt the old Cornfield building into Cornfield Magazijn, adopting a modern style building. Unfortunately, despite its renovation, the Cornfield business struggled and was liquidated in 1939

[46] SP 31-12-1935.
[47] SP 20-04-1933.
[48] Buiskool 2025: 187.

Fig. 8.11 The first stone of this building of the Ned. Ind. (Netherlands Indies) Escompto Company Medan designed and build by the Architects and Engineers Office Fermont and Cuypers Weltevr (Weltevreden) (today's Lapangan Banteng, the large square directly across from Hotel Borobudur) and Amsterdam was laid on 27th of August 1927 by Alex van Cuyk, four-year-old son of W.A. van Cuyk, Director of the Company in Batavia (photo by Dirk Buiskool)

after more than 50 years in Kesawan. The building was subsequently taken over by Bata shoes store and became more famously known as the Bata building.[49]

In 1933, the Lunchroom Café Epperlein opened its doors in Kesawan, serving German baked goods, food, and the best ice cream in town. Five years later, in June 1938, Tip Top opened its Lunch Room. In October 1939, the fashion house De Zon, which was owned by a Chinese group and had branches in Batavia, Bandoeng, and Singapore, opened its department store in Kesawan with air conditioning. It offered a wide range of fashion items for both men and women.[50]

Kesawan was a bustling street, but it became congested with traffic. Critics claim it was too narrow and chaotic, but an editor of *De Sumatra Post* satirically argued the lively, sociable character (*gezelligheid*) of Kesawan was essential to the city's identity. Rather than forcing order through

[49] DC 20-05-1933.
[50] SP 17-10-1939.

one-way traffic or parking rules, the street should remain a free-flowing commercial and social hub. Minor delays were insignificant compared to the social and economic value Kesawan provides. The author satirically suggested bromide vending machines for impatient drivers instead of bureaucratic interference that would stifle their spirit.[51]

However, the thriving heartbeat of Kesawan fell silent when the Japanese invaded Medan in 1942. Kesawan was called Tiyodadori Kita 1-Tjome, but only a few shops were operating.

8.1.5 Kesawan after 1945

Following the Second World War, Medan's colonial grandeur faded as homes, gardens, and landmarks were neglected; iconic buildings like Hotel de Boer and the Esplanade were run-down or repurposed. However, Kesawan remains the commercial hub of Medan. After 1945, trade continued, and most Chinese businesses were operating again. Epperlein no longer existed, but two Chinese-run establishments, Medan Restaurant and Broadway, had taken its place.[52]

Over time, Kesawan retained its status as Medan's premier destination for luxury shopping, showcasing a wide range of fashion shops, fine fabrics, sports equipment, radio and electronics stores. The Chinese newspaper Democracy Daily had its office next to the Bata building. Business was booming for the newly independent country. However, prices had tripled by the end of the 1950s due to rampant inflation, devastatingly impacting the economy. In August 1959, the Rupiah was devalued by a staggering 90%. Inflation continued, with rates soaring from 27% in 1961 to a staggering 174% in 1962, and eventually reaching an inconceivable 600% by 1965.

The severe economic conditions, coupled with the political turmoil, prompted the government to introduce the new Rupiah. Then, one afternoon on December 13, 1965, the Soekarno government dropped a bombshell by announcing that the new Rupiah was worth 1000 of the old unit; 10,000 Rupiah became a mere 10 Rupiah.[53] The sudden news caught many people off guard, and some shops were unaware of the change. On that day, Toko De Zon was packed with shoppers grabbing goods.

[51] SP 06-07-1938.

[52] *Amigoe di Curacao* 19-06-1947.

[53] https://en.wikipedia.org/wiki/History_of_the_Indonesian_rupiah

Despite the currency turmoil, Kesawan managed to maintain its status as a high-end shopping street in the 1970s. European shops and companies were taken over and nationalised, and Varekamp and Deli bookshops became Toko Buku Deli. Indian shops sold sporting equipment and textiles, while Chinese shops offered clothing materials and antiques. However, as time passed, the buildings in Kesawan fell into disrepair, with many dilapidated houses lining the streets. While Seng Hap's Roman pillar still remained, many buildings were left empty, some even became more profitable as swallow nests.

During the 2000s, Kesawan square provided an area for nighttime dining, but unfortunately, it was short-lived. Similar to other historic areas in Indonesia, such as Jalan Braga in Bandung and Kota Lama in Semarang, Kesawan holds significant historical value. However, many of its historic buildings are now in decay, and the addition of unsightly new constructions threatens to compromise the street's unique character. In 2023, a change in local government policy saw many buildings in Kesawan being painted and refurbished. The Cornfield Magazijn building was finally restored. Whether this restoration effort will continue remains to be seen.

8.2 The Water Tower and Railway Viaduct of Medan

Medan's most iconic landmark is the water tower, standing about 43 metres high, and the railway viaduct or *titi gantung* has provided pedestrians crossing over the railway for more than 110 years (Fig. 8.12).

8.2.1 The Water Tower

When Medan became the capital of the residency of the East Coast of Sumatra in 1886, the local government sought to improve its infrastructure. The city underwent significant upgrades, including the implementation of drainage systems, road sealing, and the installation of electric lighting. However, the absence of clean drinking water remained a major issue. Various plans were proposed to provide Medan with a reliable water supply, but the high estimated cost made it difficult to secure funding. As usual, the Dutch Indies government did not want to invest.

Eventually, Deli Maatschappij took on the project with the contributions of P. Kolff and J. van Vollenhoven. In June 1903, Boshuyer was sent to study the issue, and plans were developed to bring water from springs

Fig. 8.12 The water tower of Medan (Tropenmuseum 60012538)

at Roemah Soemboel, on the border of Siboelangit plateau, about 500 metres above and 37 km from Medan. Water quality tests confirmed its excellence. A concession was sought to establish a high-pressure channel for supplying water to Medan and Two Rivers, Deli-Toewa, Mariendal, and Polonia tobacco estates.[54]

In March 1905, a concession was granted to the Ayer Bersih Waterleiding Maatschappij (Clean Water Company), founded in Amsterdam, to establish and operate a high-pressure water channel for Medan and nearby tobacco estates. They were required to maintain hydrants, fountains, and public baths and provide water for firefighting free of charge.

The water channel that stretches from Roemah Soemboel springs to the high reservoir in Medan spans approximately 37.5 km. It comprises cast-iron pipes with diameters ranging from 125 to 250 millimetres, designed to maintain controlled water pressure. At 1-km intervals along the channel, there are components like shut-off-cocks, draw-off cocks, safety valves, and pressure gauges to regulate water flow and facilitate pipe maintenance.

Boshuyer drafted the initial plan for the water pipeline, but he passed away, and thus, the project was continued by W.H.M. Schadee and further completed and executed by Polis. Construction began in January 1906, and by August 1907, Medan received its first water supply.

A water tower was constructed to hold and supply water to Medan. The construction of the tower began in May 1908, employing local Chinese and Javanese labourers. The concrete foundation was 4 metres deep in the ground and weighed 1700 tons to withstand earthquakes. This solid foundation proved to be lasting until today. The tower and tank, when full, were 1275 tons. The tank was made from iron with a wooden casing and Monier roofing. It was built according to the Intze system, where the support surface is smaller than the width of the tank, which has a technical advantage over a completely cylindrical basin. The tank has a diameter of 14 metres and a height of 9 metres, with the upper edge of the basin standing 39 metres above ground level. It can hold about 1200 cubic metres or 1.2 million litres of water. The total length of piping in Medan was about 21 km.

The total cost of the project was *f*733,317, with the high reservoir accounting for *f*149,494. By January 1909, the tower delivered water to 732 houses, and in 1908, 233,000 cubic metres of water were provided to the city.[55]

[54] SP 06-01-1909.

[55] Wright 1909: 568–569.

A water tower was also built in the Two Rivers estate to supply water to the plantation; it stands along the route from Sibolangit to Medan. This tower and a large channel in Namo Rambe still exist. The water tower is now called Tugu Trepes. Its walls, riddled with bullet holes, are crowned by a statue of an Indonesian fighter. After the Japanese surrender in 1945, the Two Rivers plantation, known locally as Trepes, served as the headquarters for Indonesian fighters under the leadership of Nip Xarim. By the end of 1945, the English army clashed with these Indonesian fighters, eventually seizing control of the Medan region by July 1947. This tower was a key battleground, witnessing fierce conflicts between Indonesian revolutionaries led by Nip Xarim, and the Dutch and English forces. [56]

8.2.2 The Viaduct or Titi Gantung

The Deli Spoorweg Maatschappij (DSM) or Deli Railway Company was founded in 1883 with a capital of 2 million guilders to build railway networks across the East Coast of Sumatra. A concession was obtained, and construction of the railway began in October 1883. The first railway line from Laboean Deli to Medan opened to the public on July 25, 1886, and then extended to Belawan, a total of 56 km, which was completed in February 1888. The next railway line was a 37-km line from Medan to Serdang, Loeboek Pakam and Perbaoengan, which opened in February 1890.[57]

The railways facilitated the transport of people and goods across the region. However, the railway was built through the middle of Medan, cutting the town into two parts: the western part from the Esplanade and the eastern part of the Chinese quarter. There were only a few crossings, and long trains frequently blocked the railway crossing during peak hours, causing delays for vehicles and pedestrians. Some expressed frustration with the Deli Railway Company, which was perceived as having exercised a form of tyranny over the locals due to frequent traffic disruptions. This situation was tolerated by the local government because of their business prominence.[58]

After a long period of complaint, in 1903, the Deli Railway Company planned to construct a footbridge at Djalan Tepehkong. However, the

[56] Reid 2014: 179.
[57] Meijer 1987: 23.
[58] *Het nieuws van den dag voor Nederlandsch-Indië* 02-07-1902.

discussion of this railway crossing continued for several years, with proposals for either a viaduct or an underground tunnel. After a long debate, it was finally decided to build a viaduct. It took another seven years to complete, and the viaduct was officially opened on April 1, 1910.

However, the bridge, known locally as titi gantung, soon faced issues. Users found it to be unsafe for vehicles, including carriages and bicycles, due to steep inclines and inadequate safety measures. A Chinese cyclist suffered injuries due to ineffective brakes, and difficulties were also faced by horse-drawn carriages and pedestrians. The local police, noting these safety concerns, prohibited the use of the viaduct for bicycles just days after its opening. Meanwhile, the railway crossing gates remained closed throughout the day, causing significant inconvenience and traffic problems, as this crossing was a major traffic route.[59]

After the initial hiccup, the viaduct became well used by pedestrians, cyclists, and rickshaws. But some were also unimpressed as it is rather narrow.[60] With the first Oranje cinema building and a poffertjes[61] stall, Medan had become a metropolitan city. The viaduct allowed pedestrians to walk across from the Esplanade to the cinema at Djalan Bali. As the viaduct stands on poles and, between those poles, there are many spaces, a reader of *De Sumatra Post* suggested it could become the Catacombs of Medan-Metropolis![62] The space under the viaduct can be used for *poffertjes* stalls and café.[63]

The Medan railway station, originally constructed as a modest building in 1884, remained operational until 1938. That year, a new design was proposed, leading to a renovation that lasted nearly a year and culminating in the inauguration of the new station in June 1939. The modern design features a prominent 20-metre-high tower equipped with a clock, a structure that notably towered over other buildings in the city at that time.[64] Despite various extensions and modifications over the years, the building still stands and continues to serve its original purpose to this day (Figs. 8.13 and 8.14).

[59] *De locomotief* 16-04-1910.
[60] SP 08-11-1923.
[61] Small Dutch pancakes.
[62] Catacomb is an underground passageway for religious practice or burial place.
[63] SP 06-08-1910.
[64] SP 17-06-1939.

Fig. 8.13 The Medan station viaduct (Tropenmuseum 10015041)

DE SUMATRA POST VAN ZATERDAG 4 JUNI 1938 – EERSTE BLAD

Station Medan krijgt een modern aanzien

Strakke lijnen en een twintig meter hooge toren.

Begin van het volgend jaar gereed.

Fig. 8.14 The modern railway station of Medan, starting to be built in 1938 (SP 04-04-1938)

CHAPTER 9

Hobbit House to Kota China: The Archaeological Rediscovery of North Sumatra's Deep Past

The sun was setting over the dense forests when Dr. Pieter Vincent van Stein Callenfels, a distinguished Dutch archaeologist, arrived at the "*Roemah Koemang*" or house of the gnomes near Sibolangit in 1920 (Fig. 9.1). Local legends believe the massive tuff block carved with a small chamber was the home of *homin*, mythical dwarf-like beings.[1] These spirits could steal children or adults. For generations, villagers had whispered of its hidden secrets, hinting at underground chambers and relics of an ancient civilisation long forgotten. But van Stein Callenfels, the Director of the Archaeological Department of the Netherlands Indies, wasn't interested in folklore; he sought facts. Standing 1.9 metres tall and weighing well over 125 kilograms, Callenfels was formidable, instantly recognisable by his bushy beard and booming voice. Known for his irreverent humour and a remarkable tolerance for whisky, his academic prowess matched his unconventional personality.

9.1 Van Stein Callenfels and the Prehistoric Deli

The tale begins with a wealthy Dutch planter, grieving the recent loss of his wife, who turned to a *doekoen* or clairvoyant medium for a connection with the deceased. Over time, he began to doubt the medium, prompting

[1] The little people were called *homing* in Toba Batak, *homin* in Simelungun (Timor) Batak, *umang* or *kemang* in Karo and *omang* in Mandailing (McKinnon 2011).

B. Minasny, D. A. Buiskool, *Stories from Medan, Volume 1*,
https://doi.org/10.1007/978-981-95-7707-1_9

Fig. 9.1 The Batoe Kemang "hobbit house," near Sibolangit (KITLV 30907)

him to test the legitimacy of the medium's supposed abilities. The planter heard stories from an elderly local about the house of gnomes, which was said to have ancient underground chambers or tombs. The planter then funded an excavation at a location where the medium claimed to see through clairvoyant visions.[2]

To the planter's disappointment, the dig found no underground tomb. But during the excavation, a labourer found a notably heavy stone among the surrounding volcanic tuffs and handed it to the excavation leader. Closer inspection revealed blue lines on its flat grey surface, resembling an inscription in an old Indian script. Years later, it was handed to Dr. A. Kruyft, who was researching megalithic culture in the archipelago. Kruyft identified the stone as a Palaeolithic hand axe, similar to those found in Europe but previously unseen in the Dutch Indies. Thus, he brought it to the Archaeological

[2] SP 06-04-1932.

Bureau in Batavia. Returning from the Netherlands, van Stein Callenfels saw the rock and recognised it as an andesite rock shaped like a hand axe of the Palaeolithic age.[3] Van Stein Callenfels immediately went to Sibolangit to investigate. Unfortunately, the excavation yielded no results, as the piece had apparently fallen from a higher mountain ridge.[4]

Earlier systematic observations of these stone structures were made by missionary J. H. Neumann, who meticulously documented the *roemah oemangs*. Together with E. J. van den Berg, they provided one of the first detailed descriptions of the "Batoe Kemang" at Doerian Tani, near the road from Medan to Bandar Baroe (now called Gua Kemang).[5] Van Stein Callenfels conducted further investigations at this site. He observed that the chamber's interior resembled a traditional Batak house, complete with a gable roof, and hypothesised that it served as a grave. This interpretation was supported by similarities with the rock-cut graves of the Toraja people in Sulawesi and in North Borneo.[6]

This discovery sparked interest in the prehistoric landscape of Sumatra's East Coast, following reports of mysterious shell mounds found in Tamiang and in plantations near Deli. Shell mounds found near plantations in the Deli region attracted the attention of researchers (Fig. 9.2). Notably, two Swiss scientists, Dr. Carl Heusser, a biologist affiliated with the AVROS, and Dr. Eric Georg Mjöberg, an entomologist from the Deli Research Station, meticulously documented the shell mounds at Boeloe Tjina and Tandem Hilir. These shell mounds, also referred to as "kitchen middens" similar to those found in Denmark,[7] contain not only shells but also the remains of mammals, birds, fish, and primitive tools such as

[3] Palaeolithic or the Old Stone Age is a period in human prehistory that is characterised by the use of stone tools extending from 3 million to around 11,000 years ago.

[4] *Soerabaijasch handelsblad* 30-03-1932.

[5] Van Den Berg, E.J., Neumann, J., 1907.

[6] SP 31-03-1932. Some *roemah oemang* chambers, such as one found near Bah Boloek, feature intriguing rock carvings. For example, the chamber at Bah Boloek had an entrance decorated with reliefs depicting a human figure in a seated, ritualistic pose and a bird, identified as a possible heron or stork, a symbol often associated with life and death in local traditions. Other carvings include geometric shapes and animal motifs, which may have held spiritual or ceremonial significance. Such symbols suggest that the roemah oemang may have served as ritual sites, tombs, or even temporary dwellings for the dead before they were transferred to final resting places.

[7] Kitchen middens are archaeological sites consisting of ancient refuse heaps created by human communities. They have been found in various locations around the world, particularly in areas where early human settlements existed near coastlines, riverbanks, or other resource-rich environments.

Fig. 9.2 The shell mound of Boeloe Tjina in 1920. (Heusser and Mjöberg. De schelpheuvel van Boeloe Tjina. *Teysmannia* 31:443–446)

Fig. 9.3 Stone tools from the shell mound in Boeloe Tjina; left, a Sumatralith (Wereldmuseum RV-3200-7, 8)

rounded stones (Fig 9.3). This composition suggests that these mounds were ancient refuse heaps, indicating early human settlements and their subsistence activities. The mound was 3.5 metres high and elliptical in shape, made up of five distinct layers of loose shells separated by thin humus layers. The Deli Company had been using the shell deposits as raw material for lime production, gradually reducing the mound's size.[8]

Building on these findings, van Stein Callenfels launched a series of excavations in 1925–1926 at the Saëntis plantation. Unlike earlier exploratory digs, his excavations were detailed and methodical, producing a wealth of material evidence. The Saëntis mound, originally situated in a swamp forest, was approximately 6–7 metres high and 30 metres wide. It primarily consisted of shells from *Meretrix meretrix*, a saltwater clam locally known as *kepah*. The way these prehistoric shells were opened was similar to the method used by local coastal fishermen.[9] The excavation revealed a range of artefacts, including unifacial stone tools typical of Sumatran Palaeolithic industries, a bifacial tool, a mortar and pestle, and pieces of haematite used for pigments or decorations.

The term "Sumatralith" emerged from this excavation, coined by van Stein Callenfels and British anthropologist Ivor Hugh Norman Evans as a tool found in Sumatra. A Sumatralith in archaeology refers to a distinctive stone tool: an oblong cobble with one side chipped and the other left in its original, water-worn state.[10]

The inland location of the shell mounds, sometimes as much as 10–15 kilometres from the current coastline and several metres above sea level, raised further questions about the environment in which they were formed. Van Stein Callenfels argued that these sites must have been near the coast at the time of their formation. Either the sea level was higher, or the land has since risen, pushing the coastline farther eastward. This would mean that the ancient coastline once extended much further inland, encompassing sites like Boeloe Tjina and Saëntis.

The presence of advanced stone tools, including mortars and pestles, suggests that the communities were not only hunter-gatherers but also engaged in more complex subsistence activities, possibly including plant processing and crafting. The bones of tigers, rhinoceroses, monkeys, and dolphins suggest a diverse diet that included both terrestrial and marine resources. Some bones bore marks of marrow extraction, indicating that the inhabitants had developed sophisticated butchering techniques.

[8] Heusser and Mjöberg 1920, *Teysmannia* 31:443–446. There was also a club exclusively for the Chinese, of which Europeans could not become a member, but the most prominent was the Dutch *Sociëteit*.

[9] JC van der Meer Mohr. 1940.

[10] Louys, Julien, 2024. *Quaternary palaeontological and archaeological research in Sumatra*.

The discoveries didn't stop there. Similar stone tools began to appear in other locations, including Borneo and across the sea in Indochina. In the limestone caves of the Bac Son Massif, north of Hanoi, archaeologists unearthed axes almost identical to the Sumatraliths. Van Stein Callenfels proposed a joint expedition with Evans, the British government ethnographer in Malaya. Together, they scoured the Malay Peninsula, piecing together the puzzle of a culture that had traversed hundreds of miles, carrying their distinct tools and traditions. Their expedition was a success. The stone axes they discovered matched the Sumatraliths, suggesting that this prehistoric culture was not confined to Sumatra but extended across Southeast Asia, connecting distant regions through a shared Palaeolithic heritage (Fig. 9.4).

Fig. 9.4 Top: P. V. van Stein Callenfels and the shell mound of Saëntis (KITLV 67181, 122987). Bottom: Shells and stone tools found from the shell mounds in Deli by P.V. van Stein Callenfels in 1926 excavation (KITLV 123051, 123005)

9.1.1 Professor Challenger

Dutch author Rudy Kousbroek, who was born in East Sumatra, remembered many stories about Van Stein Callenfels.

> *On the east coast of Sumatra, where I grew up, countless legends circulated about him – about his height, his appetites and other desires, his knowledge of Javanese and Old Javanese texts, his limited respect for authority (and often related practical jokes). How Stein, dressed in pajamas and mounted on an elephant, made his appearance at the Resident's, how he, with his dog Labbie (named after the well-known Buitenzorg vegetarian Labberton from Hinloopen), convinced a pawnshop inspector that dogs were naturally vegetarian, and especially the story of the discovery of a Neolithic skull with a French flag inside. This was Stein's response to a suggestion from higher authorities during the visit to the Dutch East Indies of a French dignitary —Clemenceau, according to some accounts — who had expressed a desire to be present at the making of an important prehistoric discovery.*
>
> *Van Stein Callenfels rarely missed opportunities to poke fun at officials, especially as they became more self-important. To a resident who had inquired by official letter whether anything had been done about the monkey nuisance in Semarang, he telegraphed: "Since your departure, Resident, we haven't seen a monkey here." The impression all this made in "the posh colony" is easy to imagine.*
>
> *Other anecdotes concern his fabulous knowledge of Javanese; measures that other government officials couldn't explain to the population in long explanations, he managed to explain in a short speech. This was due to Stein's ability to borrow examples from traditional literature, and not least, to his ability to make people laugh. He could captivate Javanese for hours with improvised stories and knew how to get them to do anything. Just as is sometimes said of Du Perron, Stein Callenfels managed to instill a sense of self-respect in the Indonesians: he was courteous and knew their culture, both elements that other Dutchmen in the Indies usually lacked.*[11]

Van Stein Callenfels' larger-than-life persona inspired Sir Arthur Conan Doyle's character, Professor Challenger, in *The Lost World*. Doyle had reportedly met the towering archaeologist in Kuala Lumpur in 1913 and immortalised him as the brilliant but eccentric scientist. Dutch writer Rudy Kousbroek wrote in his memoir:

[11] Kousbroek, R. *Het Oostindisch Kampsyndroom* 1992:57, 58.

"His face and beard reminded me of an Assyrian bull: the former highly colored, and the latter so black as to have a bluish sheen about it, and hanging down long to his breast." This is a quote from Arthur Conan Doyle, whom Stein met and used as a character in his novels ("Professor Challenger" in The Lost World); Stein is also described in Jan de Hartog's "God's Geuzen," in the guise of Dr. Breszinsky-Jansen.

In all these descriptions, much attention is paid to Stein's thunderous voice and gargantuan appetite. Fantastic stories circulated about the number of meals he could devour in a row, feats he was said to equal in eroticism; but as far as I know, no details about this have been recorded anywhere, and that's how it should remain.

Stein Callenfels also appears in various memoirs of the Indies, such as "Jeugherinneringen uit de Rimboe" (Youth Memories from the Rimboe) by Wijnands van Resandt, and he is one of the very few Dutchmen about whom another Dutchman has ever dedicated a biography ("Ivan the Terrible, Life and Works of Dr. P.V. Stein Callenfels", by B.D. Swanenburg, from which I have quoted here and there). However, I have some stories about him firsthand, because my father met him a few times.

My father's first encounter with Stein Callenfels probably occurred during his visit to Medan in March 1920, but it is certain that my father attended a lecture by Stein Callenfels on the prehistoric excavations in Deli at the Medan Hotel in 1925. He told me about it more than once, and what I particularly remember is that the planters treated him to a fantastic party afterward, which lasted until the next day. On that occasion, Stein also seems to have received his famous "piring" (plate) from the Deli planters, a large flat dish which he then took with him everywhere and on which he always had himself served: "then he didn't have to keep asking for new portions".

Stein's visits to Deli were related to the Kitchen-Middens discovered there: the latter part of his career focused more on prehistory than archaeology, but he did pioneering work in both fields. Incidentally, he started out as a planter and amateur archaeologist; in 1921 he returned to Leiden to complete his studies; by 1924 he was back in the Indies.[12]

People called him "Ivan the Terrible" due to his fierce demeanour. Van Stein Callenfels often required a sedan chair carried by local labourers to traverse field sites. He passed away unexpectedly in Colombo in 1936.

Yet, time took its toll on the archaeological treasures he had uncovered. Van Stein Callenfels suggested the preservation of these sites and asked the plantation companies not to mine the shell for lime. The archaeological

[12] Kousbroek, R. *Het Oostindisch Kampsyndroom* 1992:59, 60.

interest in these sites continued until 1940. Unfortunately, most of these shell mounds slowly disappeared.

9.2 Ed McKinnon and the Discovery of the Lost Kota China

Half a century after van Stein Callenfels's death, Scottish archaeologist Ed McKinnon (1936–2023) continued this legacy by uncovering the maritime and urban dimensions of North Sumatra's past (Fig. 9.5).

Edmund Edwards McKinnon, a Scotsman, was born on February 12, 1936, in Strawberry Hill of Twickenham, nestled within the County of Middlesex, United Kingdom. His educational journey began at Owen's School for Boys in London from 1947 to 1952. Then, he pursued his passion for agricultural engineering at the Kesteven (Lincolnshire) Farm Institute in Caythorpe between 1953 and 1954. He further studied at the Edinburgh and East of Scotland College of Agriculture from 1954 to 1956, culminating in the Scottish and National Diplomas in Agriculture.

Fig. 9.5 Tony Milner, Ed McKinnon and Lim Ken Chian on the site of Putri Hijau, December 2004 (Photo by Dirk A. Buiskool)

A new chapter opened in his life as he joined the 1st Battalion Seaforth Highlanders, serving from 1956 to 1958 in Gibraltar and Münster, Germany. Upon his release from National Service, he entered the potato marketing industry.

However, destiny had other plans for Ed McKinnon. In November 1960, he took on a position as an Assistant Manager for the British-owned London Sumatra plantation (formerly Harrisons & Crosfield). He was assigned to the Turangi Plantation in the Bahorok Subdistrict of Langkat Regency. He was curious about the history of the area within the plantation and asked his manager, who replied that the plantation was previously uninhabited before being occupied by the Dutch. Ed McKinnon discovered several artefacts, including stone tools, in Langkat. He thought that it was quite evident that the region had a deep history. McKinnon's true awakening to the art and archaeology of Sumatra occurred during a trip in 1962 to the Padang Lawas area of South Tapanoeli, where he explored the Panei complex of brick-built temples previously investigated by Schnitger in the 1930s. This journey kindled a fervent interest in Sumatran art and archaeology. Unfortunately, his time was cut short in 1964 by the Indonesian government's takeover of the plantations during the confrontation with Malaysia.

Venturing further, he took on the role of assistant manager at the Westworth tea estate in the Nilgiri Wynaad region of Madras, South India, in 1965. This experience exposed him to linguistic and cultural ties between Tamil Nadu and North Sumatra, revealing the interconnectedness of these distant lands.

Returning to Scotland, Ed spent three years working with agricultural business consultants in Berwickshire. However, the allure of Sumatra proved irresistible, and in 1969, he was called back to assist in managing a British-owned plantation company in North Sumatra.[13]

Around 1973, a trader of antique items named Abdurrahman Lubis offered him a stone statue. Ed declined to purchase it but expressed an interest in seeing it. Abdurrahman then took him to Paya Pasir, part of the subdistrict Marelan,[14] which was still a remote area on the coast of Medan. McKinnon was astonished as he walked along a narrow path in Paya Pasir and noticed archaeological remains on the ground, including Chinese

[13] McKinnon 1984: ii–iii.

[14] Formerly Maryland plantation.

coins, beads, glass fragments, and ceramic shards. He then observed the statue in a local resident's house.[15]

A few months later, McKinnon returned to Paya Pasir and encountered a second sculpture that was discovered by a local resident while digging a well. McKinnon then reached out to several local researchers, including Tengku Luckman Sinar, as well as other researchers from both within and outside the country. Subsequently, McKinnon embarked on initial explorations of the area and identified it as the lost Kota China site, last mentioned in 1823.

After that, he dedicated his spare time to investigating archaeological sites in the area, unearthing artefacts in Kota China and identifying previously unrecorded sites such as Kota Bangun, Kota Rentang, and Pulau Kompei. His relentless passion was bolstered by the support of Indonesian friends, including Tengku Luckman Sinar S.H., Dr. E.K. Siahaan, Dr. Terbit Sembiring, and Dr. Ichwan Azhari.

Driven by his fascination for art and archaeology, McKinnon decided to depart from his role in the plantation company. He pursued further studies, obtaining master's and doctoral degrees in the Art History program at Cornell University in the United States. He not only found professional fulfilment but also had a fateful meeting with his future wife, Sinta Dermawan.

His PhD dissertation at Cornell in 1984 brought Kota China into the international spotlight with the title, *Kota China: Its Context and Meaning In The Trade of Southeast Asia In The Twelfth to Fourteenth Centuries.* Following McKinnon's research, at least 12 foreign researchers from the UK and France embarked on explorations at the Kota China site, which has gained significant international recognition.

McKinnon had great experience in archaeological survey and ceramic analysis, which earned him the Oriental Ceramic Society's George de Menasce Bursary Award in 1976 and election as a Fellow of the Royal Asiatic Society.

McKinnon followed up on van Stein Callenfels' clues on the prehistoric human settlement in the region. In 1974, Ed found three shell mounds in Langkat, which had been used as a quarry. McKinnon recovered skeletons of 12 individuals from the heap. McKinnon considered these to be part of the Hoabinhian tradition of stone tool making, which can be found throughout mainland Southeast Asia, China, and Taiwan.

[15] *Kompas* 25-03-2023.

McKinnon also found the description of the gnome houses in a publication by German G.L. Tichelman's "Felsengänge an Sumatras Ostküste," published in a German journal, *Paiduma*, in 1939.[16] Tichelman described these rock structures at various locations in Deli and Langkat, including at Kwala Mencirim plantation, Namo Trassi, Durian Tani near Sibolangit, Limau Mungkur Estate near Tandjong Morawa, and others. The age of these rock-cut chambers is unknown, but McKinnon estimated it to be in the range from the end of the first millennium to as late as the sixteenth century. Tichelman suggested that these chambers were likely constructed by the present-day Karo and Timor Batak ancestors, who may have been influenced by Tamil culture. Similar caves in southern India reflect a mix of Buddhist and Hindu influences. The chambers likely served as ossuaries for storing bones, and some were sealed with cut stones, a trace of medieval Tamil Buddhist and Hindu influences in the region.

By the 1980s, the shell mounds had become quarries, where ancient refuse heaps were ground into lime powder. Only a few mounds, including the one in Tamiang, now known as Bukit Kerang, remained intact. Similarly, once scattered across the landscape, the hobbit houses of the Karo and Toba regions have all but vanished, with only a few surviving as silent witnesses to a lost world that van Stein Callenfels once uncovered.

McKinnon further discovered archaeological sites such as the Putri Hijau fortress in the village of Deli Tua at Namo Rambe, Deli Serdang Regency. The discovery of this site shed light on the existence of the Aru Kingdom, which flourished in Sumatra from the foutrteenth to the sixteenth century but remained shrouded in mystery. Despite being one of the largest kingdoms in Sumatra and being mentioned in various written sources, its whereabouts were unknown. By combining written history with folklore, McKinnon began exploring the Putri Hijau (Green Princess) Fortress site in 1972. Various excavations revealed artefacts such as ceramic fragments, pottery, earthenware, stone tools, lead bullets, iron slag, and Acehnese dirham metal coins. The Princess Hijau Fortress was finally discovered and designated as a provincial-level cultural heritage site in 2019.[17]

Ed McKinnon retired with his wife in Bogor but was still active and came regularly to Medan. He last visited Medan in March 2023 and passed away three months later.

[16] McKinnon 2011.
[17] Idem.

9.2.1 The Discovery of Kota China

"Kota China" was first mentioned in the report by John Anderson, an official of the East India Company stationed in Penang, who published his 1823 mission to the East Coast of Sumatra. Anderson wrote about the antiquities in Deli:

> *At Delli Tuah, or Old Delli, there are the remains of an old fort, with large square stones, the walls thirty feet in height, and two hundred fathoms in circumference. Rajah putri Iju, the celebrated princess, is stated to have built it. It is now, however, in a very imperfect state; and possibly my information as to the size may be incorrect. At Kota Jawa there are the remains of a Javanese fortification, which I had an opportunity of examining. The intrenchment of earth is about a mile, or a mile and a quarter in circumference. Here there was formerly a colony of 5000 Javanese. At Meidan, higher up, there is a well attached to a mesjid or mosque, formerly built of large square hewn granite stones, two feet in length, by one foot wide. At Kota China is a stone of a very large size, with an inscription upon it, in characters not understood by any of the natives.*[18]

In 1882, shortly after the Dutch had established their presence in the Deli region, the Controleur of Laboean Deli, responding to a request to locate the inscription at Kota China, personally visited the site but found no evidence. However, another stone, known locally as the *lumpang batu* or stone mortar, seemingly a "yoni" or the base of a statue, was moved to the Controleur's compound in Laboean. Concurrently, the Controleur documented an oral tradition at Kota China, indicating that the Chinese occupied the site many years prior. Afterwards, the site appears to have faded into obscurity until 1972.[19]

Initially, Ed McKinnon pursued leads from late 1969 until October 1972, concerning the unearthing of caches and individual ceramic artefacts, primarily consisting of Chinese pieces from the Song Dynasty (960–1279 AD) and the Yuan Dynasty (1280–1368 AD) in the Medan vicinity. Subsequently, the site was thoroughly surveyed, and an excavation effort was initiated to procure stratified materials from the locations. McKinnon found statues of Buddha, Vishnu, and Shiva, and an inscription. He also discovered gold and silver workings, copper-bronze statues,

[18] Anderson 1826: 203–204.
[19] McKinnon 1984: 6.

beads, lamps, rings, etc., ceramics and coins. Chinese coins appeared as surface finds, pointing to their use in daily transactions.

The archaeological remains found at Kota China provide substantial evidence of foreign settlements and direct commercial interactions between South India and South China. Religious artefacts from South India at Kota China reflect the Indian influence in Southeast Asia, as traders established permanent bases and brought along stone images of their deities. This site also reveals early bronze images that could have originated from Indian and Sinhalese sources.

Local oral tradition holds that Kota China was originally an Indian coastal settlement; the village thrived on commerce until Chinese newcomers arrived, sparking conflict and displacing the Indians. A precious silver statue with diamond eyes, once present in the village, was lost. The Chinese prevailed but faced divine wrath. A shellfish plague from the sea led to their defeat, infiltrating their lives and forcing them to flee.[20]

Historically, the roots of Kota China can be traced back to the Srivijaya Empire, a grand unifier of the fragmented Malay kingdoms from the seventh to thirteenth century. Acknowledged as a vassal state by the Middle Kingdom or China, Srivijaya functioned as a trade nexus in Southeast Asia. In this historical context, the absence of Kota China from earlier records is probably because it was under the Srivijayan umbrella.[21]

The decline of Srivijaya in the twelfth century set the stage for the Kingdom of Aru or Haru, established by the Karo people. Smaller ports like Kota China appeared as maritime trade centres. As Srivijaya faded, Kota China rose, filling the void and serving as a new hub for traders.

The initial wave of Chinese immigrants establishing roots in Kota China was estimated to have been during the mid-to-late twelfth century. This period coincided with a notable surge in the presence of Chinese ships navigating the northeast coast of Sumatra en route to Sri Lanka and South India. Over time, the population of Chinese settlers likely grew, eventually leading to the area being recognised as Kota China.

Contemporary evidence suggests that Chinese Buddhists would have seamlessly integrated into an existing Indian Buddhist sanctuary. The extensive presence of cash coins and other artefacts, some of which fall beyond the scope of typical trade items, strongly indicates a Chinese influence at the site. Remains of ceramic figurines, potentially linked to Taoist

[20] McKinnon 1984: 7.
[21] Milner et al. 1978: 1–42.

religious practices, and a partially preserved talisman bearing Chinese characters further support this notion. Kota China emerged as a cosmopolitan settlement.

As this new phase unfolded, the region experienced another shift. The Kingdom of Aru was mentioned in Chinese records when it submitted to the Mongol ruler Kublai Khan in 1282. During the Southern Song Dynasty, China's maritime commerce surged, reaching the most far-flung corners of the Srivijayan Empire. This surge bolstered restless vassals like Aru and Tamiang, who were noted not just in Chinese but also in Javanese and Arab chronicles.[22]

Over time, Kota China's fortunes dwindled. While the exact reasons remain unknown, tensions between foreign settlers and indigenous peoples might have played a part. Historical texts from fifteenth-century Malacca suggested ethnic conflicts at Kota China, and it's possible that external threats from rival polities added to the strain.[23] The Putri Hijau legend suggests that the Aru Kingdom was constantly attacked by the Atjeh kingdom, and was finally conquered in the late sixteenth century.

Despite a lack of monumental structures and signs of calamity, such as evidence of burning, Kota China stands as a silent witness to a past era of vibrant commerce, cultural amalgamation, and shifting powers. Nowadays, there is a site museum established by Dr. Ichwan Azhari of Universitas Negeri Medan, open to the public by arrangement.[24]

From van Stein Callenfels to Ed McKinnon, they turned myth to evidence, from the gnome houses of Sibolangit to the cosmopolitan harbour of Kota China. North Sumatra emerges not as a colonial frontier, but as a crossroads of humanity, where ancient hunters, sailors, traders, and storytellers left their mark on the ground.

9.2.2 The Legend of Poetri Hidjau

Poetri Hidjau (the Green Princess) is a famous folktale from Deli that blends themes of beauty, power, loyalty, and the fall of a kingdom. It is deeply tied to the history of the Aru/Haru Kingdom and the origins of Deli.

[22] Idem.
[23] Idem.
[24] http://disbudpar.sumutprov.go.id/objek_wisata/museum-situs-kota-cina/

Long ago, in the ancient kingdom of Deli Toewa, a mighty Datoek (chieftain) and his wife were blessed with three extraordinary triplets. The first was Meriam Puntung, a mighty cannon; the second, Ular Simangombus, a serpent of great power; and the third, a radiant girl named Poetri Hidjau.

As the years passed, the cannon remained in her father's arsenal, a silent guardian of Deli Toewa. The snake, restless and wise, slithered away to the northern highlands near Lake Toba, where it grew into a fearsome dragon. Poetri Hidjau, meanwhile, blossomed into a woman of such ethereal beauty that princes and warriors from distant lands sought her hand.

Among them was the proud and ruthless Toekoe of Atjeh, a prince who would not be refused. When Poetri Hidjau rejected his proposal, his pride turned to fury. He raised an army and marched upon Deli Toewa, determined to take her by force.

The people of Deli fought bravely, their defences bolstered by the mighty Meriam Puntung, whose thunderous roars shook the earth. Yet the Atjehnese were cunning. Toekoe ordered his men to rain gold coins upon the defenders, and greed overcame duty. The Deli warriors abandoned their posts to gather the treasure, and in that moment of weakness, the Atjehnese struck.

With her people slaughtered and her home in ruins, Poetri Hidjau agreed to Toekoe's demand—but on one condition: the war must end, and she would be taken to Atjeh in a glass coffin. Toekoe, triumphant, accepted.

As the princess prepared to leave, her brother, the cannon, roared one last time—a final, desperate shot. The blast split Meriam Puntung in two: one half flew to Laboean, the other to the northern highlands, where the great dragon, Ular Simangombus, felt his sister's sorrow.

Enraged, the dragon surged towards Deli, his massive body carving rivers through the land. But he was too late.

Poetri Hidjau, her heart heavy with grief, cast a curse upon her homeland: "Never again shall perfect beauty be born in Deli." Then she allowed herself to be sealed in the glass coffin, carried away to Atjeh.

When she arrived, she gave a strange command: "Let all who greet me bring an egg and place it upon the shore." The people obeyed, and when the coffin opened, Poetri Hidjau stepped forth—so dazzling that the king and his court fainted at the sight.

Yet the princess had one last request. "Before I marry you," she told Toekoe, "I must seek my brother's counsel."

The winds howled. The waves of Djamboe Ajer rose like mountains. And from the depths, the dragon emerged, his golden eyes burning, his jaws wide. He devoured every egg upon the shore, and the people trembled in terror.

Poetri Hidjau called to him, "Brother, may I become queen of Atjeh?"

The dragon shook his mighty head. No.

With a sorrowful smile, the princess climbed onto his head. The waters churned, and together, they vanished beneath the waves.

According to legend, Poetri Hidjau resides in the whirlpool of Djamboe Ajer, within a golden palace beneath the sea. Sailors shipwrecked and lost are said to be welcomed by her, offered food and shelter, before being gently returned to the world above.[25]

Centuries later, in the 1990s, McKinnon and colleagues uncovered the ruins of Poetri Hidjau's fortress in Deli Tua, which was mentioned in John Anderson's book. Scholars believe she was a real historical figure, a Batak Karo princess of the Sembiring Meliala clan from Siberaya. Her tale is entwined with the fall of the Aru Kingdom, destroyed by the relentless attacks of the Atjeh Sultanate in the sixteenth century.

The last king of Aru was betrayed and slain. Fleeing on an elephant, his queen escaped to Johor, where she married its Sultan. With his aid, she reclaimed her throne in 1540, but Atjeh struck again in 1564, sacking Johor Lama.[26]

9.2.3 *The Rise of the Sultanate of Deli*

In 1612, Atjeh launched a campaign along Sumatra's east coast, conquering Aru. The conquest was led by Muhammad Dalik, better known as Sri Paduka Tuanku Gocah Pahlawan, an Atjehnese commander of noble descent from Pasai and India. As a reward, Iskandar Muda appointed him to govern the former Aru territories in 1632, tasking him to suppress resistance, spread Islam, and integrate the region into Atjeh.[27]

To consolidate his rule, Gocah Pahlawan allied with local Karo Batak leaders and married Princess Nang Baluan Beru Surbakti, daughter of King Undo Sunggal, establishing both political and familial legitimacy. He was recognised by four Karo urung (clans) as Datuk Tunggal, laying the

[25] DC 24-03-1886; Soerabaijasch handelsblad 22-10-1881.

[26] https://en.wikipedia.org/wiki/Aru_kingdom.

[27] Sinar Luckman1996: 23–28.

foundation for what would become the Sultanate of Deli. After his death in 1641, his son Tuanku Panglima Perunggit succeeded him. Taking advantage of Atjeh's weakening after Sultan Iskandar Thani's death, Perunggit proclaimed Deli's independence in 1669 and opened diplomatic ties with the Dutch in Malacca.

Laboean Deli became a growing river port and political centre. By the late seventeenth century, the Dutch East India Company (VOC) archives already recorded Deli as a trading post. Over the next century, Deli's rulers maintained fragile autonomy amid regional rivalries involving Siak, Johor, and Atjeh, all of whom sought control of Sumatra's east coast and its resources.

Internal conflicts over succession weakened Deli in the early eighteenth century. After the death of Tuanku Panglima Paderap (r. 1700–1720), his sons fought for power. The civil war split the realm: the victor Tuanku Panglima Pasutan ruled Deli, while his half-brother Tuanku Umar Johan Alamsyah, supported by Karo allies, founded the Sultanate of Serdang in 1723.

Through the eighteenth and nineteenth centuries, Deli's fortunes fluctuated under the influence of Siak, Johor, and Atjeh. It remained rich in natural resources, camphor, sandalwood, pepper, and rice. The Dutch, eager to secure commercial interests, cultivated alliances with both sultanates. In 1862, Sultan Mahmud Al Rashid Perkasa Alam Shah formalised Deli's political contract with the Dutch East Indies government, ensuring protection in exchange for recognition of Dutch supremacy.[28]

[28] Idem.

PART II

In the Chinese Quarter

We drive into Medan. Chinese inscriptions, Chinese streets. Rikshas roll over the asphalt.[1]

The temple served as the gateway to the Chinese quarter. Everywhere in Medan you encountered Chinese but here they ruled the roost completely. The houses were two-storied stucco affairs, the living quarters located upstairs, the ground floor opening like a windowless store-front directly onto the street. It was within those yawning caverns, closed in by wooden blinds at night, that the Chinese merchants and artisans conducted their operations within full view of all passers-by. The coppersmith's journeymen, stripped to the waist, were belaboring their metal and setting up a din which I heard from afar. A barber was wielding his machine clippers, a dentist was digging and drilling right under my nose, so to speak, as I passed. Shoemakers, bicycle repair men, merchants—all were performing their routine tasks like actors on an open stage.[2]

[1] Schuh, Gotthard. *Eilanden der Goden: Java, Sumatra, Bali*, 1943: 86.
[2] H. Tscherning Petersen. *Tropical Adventure*, 1948: 24–25.

CHAPTER 10

Chinese Officers of Medan

Architect and builder G.D. Langereis wrote:

> *As soon as one arrives in Deli, one is struck by the overwhelming presence of Chinese. It feels more like being in China than on one of the islands of the Indian Archipelago.*
>
> *Barely has the ship docked before swarms of Chinese rush on board, offering their services to carry your luggage and so forth. Walking through the streets of the harbour town Belawan, one sees a few Malay shops here and there, but by far, most are Chinese-owned shops (toko's), displaying and selling a wide variety of goods.*
>
> *Passing construction sites, it is again almost exclusively Chinese labourers—carpenters, masons, and so on—working there. On the railway platforms, it is the Chinese who load and unload the wagons. In short, one gets the complete impression that the Chinese are the natives, and other races seen among them do not truly belong here.*
>
> *This impression lingers in the first days of one's stay, during a cursory but superficial acquaintance with the land.*
>
> *In the main town, Medan, where every newcomer typically begins their stay, one finds Chinese servants in hotels, Chinese cashiers and clerks in banks and trading offices, and shops mostly owned by the Chinese. The crowds on the streets consist largely of Chinese people.*
>
> *Visiting European households, one often finds Chinese as house servants, though this is less common on Sumatra's East Coast than in the British possessions across the Straits of Malacca. However, the water boy, the servant*

B. Minasny, D. A. Buiskool, *Stories from Medan, Volume 1*,
https://doi.org/10.1007/978-981-95-7707-1_10

> *responsible for filling bathtubs and performing heavy household tasks, is almost invariably Chinese.*
>
> *On the plantations, especially the tobacco estates, it is again predominantly the Chinese who work as labourers. They are the true planters, while other groups, such as Javanese and Tamils, handle auxiliary tasks like carting, clearing forests, building barns, and constructing roads and drainage systems.*
>
> *The Chinese are not only prominent among the labourers but also in higher circles and even in semi-official positions. This includes the leaders of the Chinese community, who are appointed by the Dutch East Indies government with titles such as Major, Captain, and Lieutenant. These leaders act as advisors to Dutch officials on Chinese matters and often wield considerable influence and power. Additionally, there are ward chiefs and lessees of government monopolies, such as the former opium and alcohol trades and the operation of gambling houses.*
>
> *In private enterprise, one finds flourishing Chinese businesses, including Chinese-owned banks and insurance companies. However, as landowners and managers of plantations, the Chinese have not been officially granted a place on Sumatra's East Coast, and it is even forbidden for them to establish themselves in such capacities. Whether this prohibition is circumvented, I cannot say.*[1]

Medan and its surroundings were well known for their large Chinese population. The development of Medan has been profoundly shaped by the overseas Chinese community, with notable figures such as Tjong Yong Hian, Tjong A Fie and Khoe Tjin Tek. They served as community leaders and played important roles in the city's early growth. Their significant contributions laid the foundation upon which the Chinese presence in Medan continues to thrive to this day (Fig. 10.1).

The Dutch Indies government regarded the Chinese as a "necessary evil." The Chinese had a network of traders and served as intermediaries for importing and exporting various goods. The Dutch wanted revenue, and the Chinese had the skills to facilitate trade across the country and region. The early Dutch governor J.P. Coen of the Dutch East Indies wrote in 1623:

> *daer is geen volck in de werelt die ons beter dienen dan de Chineesen.*

There is no people in the world who can serve us better than the Chinese.[2]

[1] Langereis 1918: 581–582.
[2] Quoted by Vandenbosch, 1930: 1001.

Fig. 10.1 Tjong Yong Hian and Chinese officers with Dutch personnel at a gathering in Medan around 1905 (photo courtesy of Rebecca Chandra)

Madame Wellington Koo, the daughter of tycoon Oei Tiong Ham of Semarang, wrote:

> *They complained that they did not mingle, did not intermarry, educated their own, refused to be assimilated.*[3]

She was, in fact, referring to the Dutch, who resented the Chinese for their shrewdness and ability to work around the rules.[4]

The Dutch installed local Chinese leaders to control their community, or "let the Chinese take care of their own affairs."[5] As early as the establishment of Batavia in 1619 by the Dutch East India Company (VOC), Chinese headmen were appointed to assume leadership roles. Among them, Souw Beng Kong became the first Chinese captain in Batavia.[6] The Dutch left the Indigenous and Chinese alone and never attempted to improve their lives. When a crime victim was Chinese, the Chinese leader was tasked with handling the matter. However, if the victim were a European, the Dutch would pursue the matter seriously.[7]

[3] Koo and Taves 1975: 18.

[4] Interestingly Oei Hui-lan (Madame Wellington Koo) was first married to British consular agent Beauchamp Caulfield-Stoker, then to Chinese statesman Wellington Koo.

[5] Godley 1981: 20. Lohanda 1996: 76–86.

[6] Godley 1981:16; Lohanda 1996: 86

[7] Eastwick 1893.

In Dutch, Chinese leaders were referred to as *Hoofden der Chinezen*, which translates to "Heads of the Chinese." Locally, they were known as *Kapitan Cina*. These Chinese officials were chosen from among individuals of high social stature, typically wealthy Chinese merchants with strong connections to European administrations and Indigenous leaders. The officers were granted certain administrative and judicial authority within their communities. Part of their duties included tax collection from the Chinese populace, including taxes on income, property, household utensils, carriage, as well as life events like weddings and funerals. They also received a substantial salary. In 1887, the Chinese Captain of Medan received a yearly salary of *f*3000, while a Lieutenant received *f*1800.[8]

An effective means of formalising the business partnership between the Dutch government and Chinese officers was through revenue farming. In this system, wealthy individuals, merchants, or Chinese heads were granted exclusive privileges to monopolise particular commodities or services within a defined area for a set period. Public auctions were conducted where affluent merchants competed to obtain these licenses by submitting the highest bids. Among the various revenue-generating enterprises, some proved highly profitable, including licenses for opium, alcohol, pawnshops, and gambling. Moreover, certain goods that were not controlled by European traders, such as pork, salt, and sago, were also subject to this arrangement. Revenue farms also encompassed a range of services, including ferry operations, toll collection, and *wajang* performances, among others. The auction was announced in local newspapers and the Straits Settlement. The Dutch government found this approach to be a practical means of generating income, and Chinese officials overseeing one or multiple revenue farms could accumulate significant wealth through this arrangement.[9]

The January 1, 1876 contract granted the Dutch Indies government the right to collect taxes and operate monopolies, compensating Sultan Deli with an annual indemnity of *f*123,100.[10] Under the Sultan's rule, gambling was prohibited on plantations, and it was only permitted at the main station in Laboean. The first lease was sold in February 1876, for opium, spirit, gambling, and toddy farms for a monthly fee of $12,410 in

[8] *Staatsblad van Nederlandsch Indië* 1884–1888: 526.
[9] Buiskool 2025: 82–83.
[10] *Deli Gids* 1938: 19.

Perak, under British auspices.[11] Once colonial government consolidated control, the gambling and opium farms were pushed to maximise revenue. On the main road between Laboean and Medan, a distance of less than 12 miles, there were seven gambling houses. The first gambling lease alone yielded *f*119,400.[12] The opium lease generated even greater revenue. By 1884, the region's revenue had risen to *f*2,382,188.[13]

The Chinese officers were given ranks based on military titles, such as *Majoor* (Major), *Kapitein* (Captain), and *Luitenant* (Lieutenant), depending on the size of the local Chinese population. A Major oversaw the community in larger cities, whereas a Captain or a Lieutenant assumed leadership in smaller locations. Beneath these officers, there were Chinese *Wijkmeesters*, also known as district wardens, who held authority over specific local areas. These district wardens played an important role in managing and maintaining order within their assigned regions.[14]

These Chinese officers functioned as middlemen between the government and the Chinese population, including collecting taxes for the colonial government, and settling various civic affairs, such as marriage, birth, divorce, those who wanted to return to China, problems between the coolies and the Dutch planters, etc.[15] The Lieutenant had the most contact with the Chinese community. All matters, from complaints to rewards, were handled by the Lieutenants. The Lieutenant signed residence permits for all Chinese in his controlled regions. The Captain primarily undertook external duties, including attending regular meetings at the Resident's office to discuss matters of local government, representing the Chinese community on government committees, and sitting in court to resolve conflicts between the Chinese and the indigenous or Europeans. The Chinese Major was the most prestigious and had the highest responsibility for the community. The Major also served *ex officio* as a member of the *Landraad*[16] (district court). Chinese businesses frequently sought the Major's assistance for matters relating to the government.[17]

[11] Toddy is alcoholic beverage from palm tree. *The Straits Times* 12-02-1876.

[12] *Het Vaderland* 02-10-1876.

[13] *Deli Gids* 1938: 19. The lease of opium for Deli in 1888 was *f*295,000 per month and dropped to *f*140,000 in 1896 (*Pinang Gazette and Straits Chronicle* 02-11-1888; *The Straits Budget* 21-11-1896). The spirit farm was *f*11,000 per month.

[14] Lohanda 1996:77–79.

[15] Jansen 1940: 86.

[16] Landraad is a lower district court for indigenous and Chinese people.

[17] Buiskool 2025: 113–114.

Until the early twentieth century, colonial regulations and police practice often required Chinese residents to retain traditional dress and the queue, especially in public and in formal contexts.[18] On official occasions, the Chinese officers wore Qing imperial officer or Mandarin uniforms despite holding no official rank in the Chinese court. During its early days, Medan was segregated into distinct living quarters, organised to facilitate local administration along ethnic lines. As a result, the Chinese community could only live in their designated quarter. Any Chinese individual wishing to travel beyond their designated area was required to obtain a travel pass issued by a Chinese officer.[19]

10.1 Early Chinese Leaders

When Laboean Deli became the capital of the region in 1873, it already had a sizeable Chinese population operating shops and small ships (*tongkang*). The Chinese settlers were mainly from Penang, who had already traded with the people from Deli decades earlier. Chinese shops offered all kinds of merchandise, alongside carpenters and goldsmiths. The houses along the Deli river resembled a riverside town in China, with the backs of the houses facing the river.

The first Chinese officer of Laboean Deli was Tjioe Tjoe Jen, appointed as Captain in 1874. He was probably from the Hokkien Chew clan of Penang. In 1881, he was appointed as a Captain, overseeing both Medan and Laboean Deli. Another Hokkien leader, Oen Ghan The, was appointed as the Lieutenant of Medan. Meanwhile, Lim Tek Swee and Khoe Teng Ko served as Lieutenants in Laboean Deli. They were influential Hokkien merchants who held lucrative revenue farms in opium and gambling.

The Chinese first settled in Medan in the area near Kesawan, known as the Chinese camp. Jacob Cremer described the condition:

> *Here the coolie of the enterprise finds on holidays and rest days everything his heart desires, shops with all kinds of delicacies, medicines and clothing from the Heavenly Kingdom. Furthermore, the healing juice of the poppy (opium), which is forbidden to him back home, pork, strong drinks, opportunities to squander or pawn his money and possessions, girls to comfort him. All these pleasures—except for the women, oddly enough—are supplied under the*

[18] Godley 1996:76–86.

[19] The quarter system was abolished in 1918.

watchful eye of the colonial administration. So far, no clever financier has yet turned the women into a government monopoly lease.[20]

Many of the Chinese heads died at relatively young ages. Tjioe Tjoe Jen, who also ran a shipping business and held an opium license, died in 1885. Khoe Teng Ko, the father of Khoe Tjin Tek, died in 1893 at the age of 44, and Lim Tek Swee died in 1901. After their untimely deaths, Medan lacked strong leadership until Tjong Yong Hian emerged to assume the role.

10.2 Tjong Yong Hian and Tjong A Fie

Few figures shaped Medan's early colonial economy more visibly than the brothers Tjong Yong Hian and Tjong A Fie. Born into a Hakka family in Songkou village, Meixian, Guangdong, the brothers carried with them the values of diligence and ambition as they ventured into the Nanyang (South Seas) in search of fortune.[21]

The elder brother, Tjong Yong Hian (Zhang Rongxuan, 1850–1911), was the first to seek opportunities abroad. After completing his primary education, he sailed for Batavia around 1872, where he worked under Thio Tiauw Siat (Zhang Bishi), a self-made tycoon who had risen from humble origins to become one of the wealthiest businessmen in the Dutch East Indies (Fig. 10.2).

Thio Tiauw Siat had journeyed to Batavia at a young age and started working as a store assistant. Through hard work, he married the daughter of the shop's owner and with her father-in-law's initial support, he eventually established his own shop and rose to great heights. Thio's business ventures in Batavia were diverse, earning him the trust of the Dutch government. As a result, he flourished by supplying goods to the Dutch army and navy, and also gained considerable wealth through managing several revenue farms.[22]

Thio Tiauw Siat took Tjong Yong Hian under his guidance as they had the same surname and were fellow Hakka. Under Thio's guidance, Tjong Yong Hian thrived, earning a pawnbroker's license and gaining the trust of the Dutch colonial government. By 1877, at just 27 years old, he was

[20] *Eigen haard; geïllustreerd volkstijdschrift*, 1889, no. 5, 01-01-1889.
[21] Buiskool 2025: 117.
[22] Buiskool 2025: 122–124; Godley 1981: 10–12.

Fig. 10.2 Tjong Yong Hian (TM-FV-0451-13)

appointed Chinese Lieutenant of Onrust Island.[23] When the Dutch expanded their activities in Sumatra in 1875, Thio Tiauw Siat extended his business to Deli and Atjeh. Around the year 1880, Tjong Yong Hian relocated to Laboean Deli.

His younger brother, Tjong A Fie (Zhang Yaoxuan, 1860–1921), followed in his footsteps. At 18, he left China for Laboean Deli, where he initially worked for a Chinese merchant before establishing his own shop. His natural talent for negotiation and dispute resolution quickly won him respect among the Chinese community.[24]

The brothers soon formed a formidable business alliance with Thio Tiauw Siat under the firm Ban Yoen Tjong, supplying provisions to labourers and managing lucrative revenue farms—monopolies on opium, gambling, spirits, and pawnshops. Their ventures expanded rapidly, and by the 1880s, they were key players in Medan's economic boom, fuelled by the tobacco industries.[25]

Tjong Yong Hian's commercial activities spanned shipping, trade, finance, and infrastructure across Southeast Asia and South China. He owned and invested in vessels, transporting rice, sugar, textiles, tea, and daily goods between Singapore, Penang, Medan, and Chaozhou–Shantou. He had businesses in tobacco, liquor, and mining. His networks managed remittances and pooled capital. Beyond trade, he invested in the Chaozhou-Shantou Railway, bridges, and schools, blending business with philanthropy. Tjong Yong Hian was not a labour recruiter, but he mediated in Chinese labour contracts and disputes, acting as a broker between overseas Chinese, local rulers (in Deli and Malaya), and Qing officials. Thus, Tjong Yong Hian acted as an entrepreneur, community leader, and political intermediary).[26]

10.2.1 Ranks and Businesses

In 1879, the Assistant Resident of Deli decided to relocate the capital from Laboean Deli to Medan. During this time, Tjong Yong Hian demonstrated his capabilities and earned the trust of the government, leading

[23] Known as Pulau Kapal, part of Kepulauan Seribu. In the colonial times was a docking place for commercial ships.

[24] Buiskool 2025: 122–126.

[25] Buiskool 2025: 122–126.

[26] Xiao Wenping & Rao Ganzhong 2021: 183–383.

to his appointment as the titular Chinese Lieutenant of Medan in 1884. The incumbent Chinese Lieutenant Oen Gan The did not have much influence, and when he passed away in 1887, the *Deli Courant* wrote:

> *There is neither much good nor any evil to be said about the deceased, and in a Chinese society like Deli's, this is already commendable in itself. Among the Chinese, he never held much influence, nor did he attempt to acquire it in any way.*[27]

Tjong Yong Hian's promotion to Lieutenant of the Chinese was a testament to his exceptional capabilities—not only as an astute businessman but also as a respected leader, trusted advisor, and skilled mediator. His sharp intellect, diplomatic acumen, and deep understanding of local affairs earned him the confidence of the Dutch colonial government, the Sultans, and the Chinese community alike.

With his unparalleled knowledge of Medan's economic and social landscape, he became an indispensable consultant for Dutch officials and plantation owners, who frequently sought his counsel. His influence extended beyond formal duties; during New Year celebrations, he cultivated goodwill by presenting Dutch officials with lavish gifts—some worth hundreds of guilders—even to those he had never met. Such strategic generosity strengthened his political and commercial networks, ensuring smoother dealings in both business and governance.[28]

Tjong Yong Hian was promoted to the Captain position in 1893.[29] Similarly, Tjong A Fie was appointed Lieutenant-titular of the Chinese of Laboean Deli in 1885, and a year later, he became the Head of the Hakka. In August 1898, Queen Wilhelmina of the Netherlands was crowned and in honour of this occasion, both Tjong Yong Hian and Tjong A Fie received promotions. Tjong Yong Hian ascended to the rank of Major and Tjong A Fie became Captain of the Chinese (Fig. 10.3). The Chinese community celebrated this significant milestone with a grand public reception, commemorating the achievements and contributions of these two esteemed individuals to their community.[30] In 1904, Tjong Yong Hian received a gold medal from the Dutch government for his service.[31]

[27] DC 17-09-1887.
[28] Van Den Brand 1902: 25–26.
[29] DC 01-04-1893.
[30] DC 24-8-1898; DC 3-9-1898; DC 24-9-1898; DC 28-9-1898.
[31] Wright 1909: 580, 581; SP 12-9-1911.

Fig. 10.3 Tjong A Fie (Tropenmuseum TM-FV-0451-32)

As a Lieutenant of the Chinese, Tjong A Fie served as an informal judge within the Chinese community. At that time, Deli's police force was limited, overseen by a superintendent-magistrate. Tjong A Fie was tasked with conducting preliminary investigations for the police whenever a Chinese individual was involved. He attended the *politie-rol* four times a week to handle preliminary investigations of minor offences. Tjong A Fie acted as a mediator and problem solver among the Chinese, particularly in instances of frequent disputes. Fluent across many Chinese dialects used in Deli, Tjong A Fie was the go-to person during coolie riots, playing a crucial role in managing these conflicts.[32]

The thriving tobacco industry spurred the rapid growth of Medan's town construction and commercial development. Tjong Yong Hian and Tjong A Fie owned much of Medan's land, and also owned a brick factory.[33] Amid the housing shortage between 1900 and 1915, they capitalised on their advanced knowledge as Chinese officers and city council members, strategically purchasing land near planned infrastructure. They built popular Chinese-style shophouses with businesses on the ground floor and living quarters upstairs. Tjong A Fie bought land at low prices, such as in Kampong Dalam, and developed housing to address local housing shortages, keeping rents affordable. Contemporary accounts (and local traditions) claimed that Tjong A Fie controlled an extraordinary share of Medan's property market, as high as three-quarters, though the exact proportion is difficult to verify. They also controlled the city's markets, leasing land from the Deli Company to build covered markets for meat, fish, and vegetables.[34]

In 1907, the Tjong brothers, with Thio Tiauw Siat, established the Deli Bank, the first Chinese bank in Medan, with a capital of 3 million guilders.[35] The bank offered comprehensive banking services: loans, cash accounts, consignment contracts, and the sale of products to a third party (Fig. 10.4).[36]

10.2.2 Philanthropy

In Medan, the Tjong brothers were known for their philanthropy. They followed Confucius's teaching that stressed benevolence and righteousness; thus, giving is part of being a good person with high morale. Tjong Yong Hian and Tjong A Fie rebuilt the oldest mosque in Medan, Mesjid Gang Bengkok. In 1897, they handed the newly built mosque to the

[32] Buiskool 2025: 139–141.
[33] DC 31-08-1887.
[34] Buiskool 2025: 122–123.
[35] SP 09-09-1907.
[36] Buiskool 2025: 123–125.

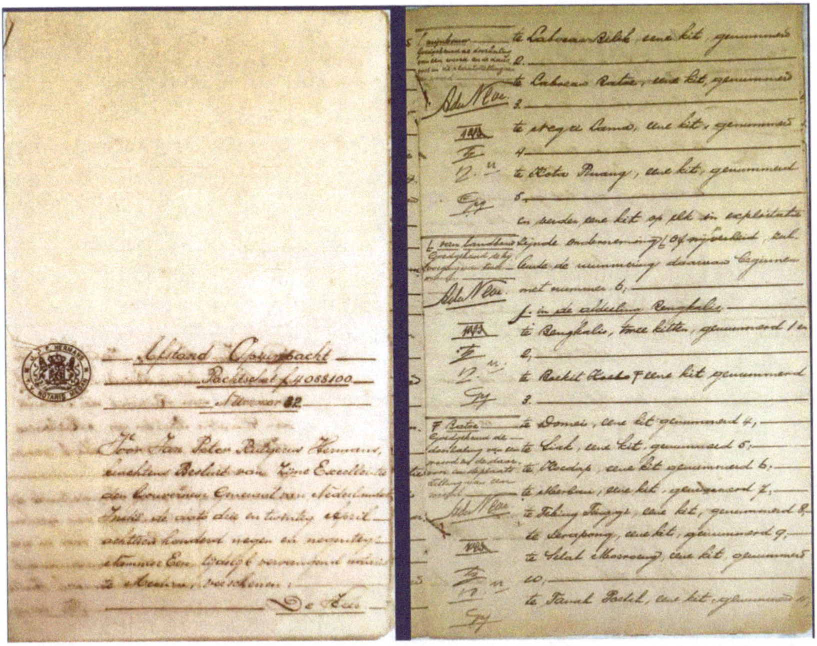
Afstand Opiumpacht
Pachtschat f4058100
Nummer 82

Fig. 10.4 A contract for the Opiumpacht or opium farm for the East Coast of Sumatra and Bengkalis in 1899 awarded to Tjong A Fie, with Tjong Jong Hian and Khoe Tjiauw Tiong as guarantors. The lease was from January 1, 1900 until March 1902, with a monthly payment of *f*150,300, amounting to a total of *f*4,058,100 over the duration of the contract

Sultan of Deli.[37] Tjong Yong Hian and Tjong A Fie donated to Chinese temples in Medan and Penang, a hospital in Medan, Hindu temples, Muslim mosques, Catholic and Christian churches, and schools in Medan and China.

In 1890, the Tjong brothers established the Tjie On Jie Jan Hospital and Asylum—a charitable institution dedicated to serving Medan's most vulnerable. Built on land donated by the Deli Maatschappij, the complex stood along Hospitaalweg (now Jl. Sambu). The hospital provided free medical care to impoverished and disabled members of the Chinese community, while the adjacent asylum offered free shelter, food, and support

[37] Buiskool 2025: 129–130, 141–144, 318–323; DC 30-01-1897.

for the elderly and destitute. Funding came from the brothers' market operations in Medan.[38]

In 1896, Tjong Yong Hian received 92,300 m^2 of land from the Deli Maatschappij on Kampung Doerian for a Chinese public cemetery. In 1903, the Tjong brothers established the first Chinese school in Medan, the Dunben or Tun Pun School. Five years later, The Deli Company donated a land of 4635 m^2 to the brothers for use as the school. In China, they donated funds to build roads, bridges, hospitals, schools and provided relief to natural disaster survivors. Consequently, the Qing government awarded the brothers honorary official titles.

On September 10, 1911, Tjong Yong Hian suddenly passed away.[39] Because Tjong A Fie and some of his family members were in China, his body was preserved until all family members were present to bid farewell. He was dressed in 12 garments, some of which were almost entirely made of gold.[40] His funeral was held two months later. It was a grand funeral; houses and shops hoisted the Dutch flag at half mast, showing his importance as a Dutch officer.[41]

Tjong Yong Hian was buried in his garden house, Keboen Boenga, next to the Baboera river. A street in the Chinese quarter was named after him, and a bridge was built by his family in his honour. In the 1960s, all Chinese road names were changed to Indonesian. In 2013, his great-grandson successfully appealed to Medan's government to restore the original name, Jalan Tjong Yong Hian, in recognition of his contributions to the city.

10.2.3 Majoor Tjong A Fie

Exactly one month after Tjong Yong Hian's passing, the Chinese revolution known as the Wuchang Uprising erupted on October 10, 1911. This revolution marked the end of the Qing Empire and the traditional Chinese monarchy. Five months later, on February 5, 1912, Tjong A Fie was appointed as *Majoor der Chinezen* (Major of the Chinese community), entering a new era with the establishment of the Republic of China.[42]

[38] Buiskool 2025: 130,223,224.
[39] SP 12-9-1911; SP 19-9-1911; DC 11-9-1911.
[40] *Indische Mercuur* 10-10-1911.
[41] SP 02-11-1911.
[42] SP 13-1-1912, 5-2-1912, 7-2-1912, 3-3-1912.

From then on, he was known as Majoor Tjong A Fie and he embraced European-style attire.

Tjong A Fie's business interests expanded from real estate to include the Medan hotel, and rubber plantations. He was the first Chinese person in the region to employ a Dutch person, Dolf Kamerlingh Onnes, to manage his business portfolio.[43] His fortune was estimated between 30 and 40 million guilders through wise investments in real estate and various enterprises.

Tjong A Fie was renowned for his generosity and philanthropic spirit. He cared for his fellow Chinese compatriots and actively supported all ethnic groups within the community. Whenever public, religious, or social organisations needed funding, they would turn to Tjong A Fie, and without hesitation, he would make significant contributions. In times of disaster striking a *kampong*, Tjong A Fie promptly provided aid in the form of money and rice to those affected. The less fortunate and needy could walk up to the front of Tjong A Fie's house and receive alms.[44] He donated rice and money directly to elderly, sick individuals, mothers with large families, and their children, significantly aiding over 350 families, approximately a thousand people in total.[45]

Tjong A Fie initiated many social projects, including donations and financing the building of mosques and schools. Tjong A Fie donated one-third of the cost of Mesjid Raya and paid for the building of mosques in Petisah, Sibolga, and Sipirok. He donated a piece of land for a cemetery for the Arabs. As the fasting period culminated in Hari Raya, lines of people would form outside his house, receiving his heartfelt alms. This act of kindness and respect for their traditions endeared him to the Muslim people.[46] For the Catholics, he donated half the cost of building the Cathedral at Jalan Pemuda in 1904.[47] In 1912, Missionary Nommensen and Ed

[43] See the chapter on Kamerlingh Onnes.

[44] SP 04-02-1921; *Bataviaasch Nieuwsblad* 14-02-1921.

[45] Het nieuws van den dag voor Nederlandsch-Indië 22-01-1920.

[46] *De Locomotief* 19-08-1918: Tjong A Fie donated *f*4000 for the mosque in the main town of Sibolga, with a pledge to increase this gift by another *f*4500. *Pewarta Deli* 27-7-1917. Journalist Mohammad Said remembered that on Hari Raya. Hundreds, thousands of Malay, Javanese and other Indigenous queed up in a long row in front of the Tjong A Fie's mansion to receive an alm (Mohammad Said, interview with D.A. Buiskool 19-11-1994). Tjong A Fie started this distribution from around 1916. (*Andalas* 15-6-1920).

[47] Tjong A Fie donated 7000 guilders for the Church of the Immaculate conception at Jl. Pemuda.

Muller talked to Tjong A Fie to request a location to build a church for the Batak in Medan, and he duly provided them with land.[48]

Tjong A Fie also helped improve the city's infrastructure. Prior to 1911, Medan lacked an organised waste removal service, relying on informal, unsanitary disposal by Chinese labourers. Thus, Tjong A Fie donated a pneumatic night-soil system with tank wagons and a pump, replacing unsanitary manual removal with a mechanised, closed system.[49] Tjong A Fie valued education and donated land for a kindergarten and an orphanage for the Salvation Army. He contributed to building the girls' school of *Sarikat Goeroe* (teacher's organisation) in Medan. In 1917, he initiated two vocational schools for students of all ethnicities; one was a general trade school for boys to learn construction, and another was a midwifery school for girls.[50] Tjong A Fie contributed to establishing a leper colony Sitjanang and a tuberculosis sanatorium in Kabanjahe, donated to the eye patient association in Weltevreden.[51] Additionally, Tjong A Fie actively supported the development of Medan by financing road construction and contributing to the construction of the town hall's clock tower. In honour of his late brother Tjong Yong Hian, the Tjong family funded the construction of the Baboera bridge and presented the bridge as a gift to the city of Medan. Through his thoughtful and significant contributions to various ethnic groups, Tjong A Fie set himself apart from many other capitalists, earning a reputation as a compassionate and truly remarkable philanthropist.[52]

In 1916, the Governor of Sumatra's East Coast, Simon van der Plas, wrote to the Governor-General in Buitenzorg, stating:

> *As your Excellency knows, I rate Major Tjong A Fie as one of the most remarkable amongst the prominent names that this colony enjoys. With his exceptional gifts of heart and head, and his extraordinary capacities, he would, were he a Dutchman, be able to attain any office or position.*[53]

[48] However after years the land was not being used and Tjong requested it back (SP 11-08-1937).

[49] *25 jaren decentralisatie in Nederlandsch-Indië* 1905–1930: 387–389.

[50] *De Locomotief* 10-12-1917.

[51] SP 23-10-1919; SP 16-12-1920, Tjong A Fie donated *f*10,000 to the eye patients' association.

[52] SP 03-02-1929, Tjong A Fie donated to Sanatorium for Lung Sufferers in Davos. Buiskool 2025: 141-143.

[53] *Indische Gids* I, 1919, 648.

Governor Van der Plas considered Tjong A Fie as one of the most prominent men in the colony and bestowed upon him the honorary title of advisor for Chinese Affairs of the East Coast of Sumatra.[54]

Tjong A Fie recognised the strategic importance of food self-sufficiency in Sumatra's East Coast. In 1917, rice imports to the East Coast of Sumatra were around 145,000 tons. The region had 8.5% of the Indies population but consumed 43% of the outer island imports. Only 31.5% of the consumed rice was grown locally. Thus, Tjong A Fie advocated for the local production of three essential commodities - rice, sugar, and salt - believing this would liberate the region from volatile imports. However, his vision clashed with plantation owners who prioritised lucrative export crops over food production, content to import rice from Siam and Java. [55]

The fragility of this dependence became starkly apparent during World War I. By late 1918, rice imports faltered as key sources like Rangoon, Saigon, and Siam restricted exports, causing prices to skyrocket (e.g. imported rice cost *f*75 per 100 kg, up from *f*10). This triggered a major food security crisis. By early 1919, rice reserves could barely sustain the region's 250,000 labourers for four months, triggering soaring prices and economic instability.[56] The Dutch colonial government responded by centralising rice importation and distribution, giving import licenses only to government bodies and planter associations. It fixed retail prices, using local traders, established ration card systems to prevent hoarding, and organised charity-based distributions for the poor, supported by planters and Tjong A Fie. From mid-1919 onwards, rice distribution stabilised. The government enacted several measures to reduce import dependency, including mandatory food crop cultivation (e.g. maize, cassava), and plantations were forced to diversify food supply for workers. In 1919–1920, the total rice imports dropped by 55%, despite a population increase of 160,000.

Tjong A Fie proposed a solution by establishing Chinese-operated rice fields and a local salt refinery. In 1920, he experimented with sugar cane cultivation at the Paja Mabar estate as the foundation for a grander vision—large-scale sugar plantations supported by a dedicated refinery, potentially transforming the region's agricultural landscape. But these

[54] Van der Plas. 1917. Memorie van Overgave.
[55] Koloniaal tijdschrift, jrg 11, 1922, 01-01-1922.
[56] *Het koloniaal weekblad*, jrg 19, 1919, no. 5, 30-01-1919.

were not realised. As the rice import stabilised, the government and planters did not bother to address the food self-sufficiency issues. [57]

A Catholic friend once asked Tjong A Fie:

> *Say, Major, tell me honestly, just between us—are you truly happy?"*
>
> *And the Major immediately answered him candidly: "No, my friend, not at all. I was happy, back when I was just an ordinary man going door to door selling my tobacco. Back then I had no worries. But now that I'm rich, I'm full of worries. For example, I'm worth ten million, and now I lie awake day and night thinking about how I can quickly make it fifteen million. I'm constantly afraid of competition, of financial setbacks—nothing but headaches and worry. No, no, I'm not happy at all!*[58]

The post-World War I economic downturn impacted countries like the US and UK and had significant effects elsewhere, including rubber prices. In 1921, rubber prices halved, and rising operating costs severely hampered the profitability of Tjong A Fie's rubber enterprises. During this financial strain, Tjong A Fie was compelled to pawn part of his house to Java Bank to secure liquidity. His long-standing trust and good relationship with the bank initially facilitated this process. However, after a change in bank management, his request for a half-million guilders loan was denied, indicating a loss of trust from the new directors. This refusal and perceived breach of trust greatly distressed Tjong A Fie. Additionally, there was financial turmoil at the Deli Bank, which was overdrawn by 7 million guilders due to poor administration, further complicating the economic landscape.[59] These events seriously affected Tjong's business and health.[60]

Tjong A Fie received the highest award from the Dutch government as an Officer in the Order of Oranje-Nassau on January 22, 1921. Two weeks later, Tjong A Fie died on February 4, 1921 due to a brain haemorrhage.[61] A grand funeral was held one and a half months after his passing on March 28, 1921. The procession was about one kilometre in length.[62]

[57] DC 13-08-1920.

[58] *De Java-Post; Weekblad van Nederlandsch-Indië*, jrg 23, 1925, no 37, 18-09-1925.

[59] *Indische Mercuur* 8-4-1921.

[60] Li Songyan 1984: 183–202; *Het koloniaal weekblad*, 1921, no. 37, 15-09-1921.

[61] Chang 1981: 171.

[62] DC 29-03-1921.

The funeral became the talk of the town.[63] Representatives from all walks of life came to send the Major off in honour of his deeds. Tjong A Fie is still a legend, and his mansion in Kesawan street, which was once valued at 1 million guilders, is open to the public as a museum.

10.3 The Installation of the Chinese Heads

The following is a translation of an article from the *Deli Courant* April 22, 1893, reporting a special occasion where eight Chinese heads were officially appointed in Medan. It was a special occasion, and the ceremony was described in detail. An accompanying photo was also taken by C.J. Kleingrothe (Fig. 10.5).

> *Yesterday, as we already announced, the solemn installation of the newly appointed Chinese chiefs on the East Coast of Sumatra took place. Days before, Medan's residents saw the erection of honorary arches, and were no less entertained by the deafening music.*
>
> *At about half past nine, the headmen to be installed and their friends arrived at the Landraad Hall. Beautifully attired in heavy silk robes, richly decorated with gold embroidery, and with tall caps or conical yellow hats fitted with long hanging red tassels, they made a splendid effect.*
>
> *The carriages of the chiefs were preceded by a multitude of their countrymen, each tribe separately, all with flags, music, plates and canopies including symbolic representations. The many children seated on battak ponies made a pretty sight, and we noticed two of the Chinese Captain's children, in colourful silk suits, dressed as heralds. The music made a life like judgment, especially the armed virtuosos with an instrument that was somewhere between a bassoon and a matilampu (power black out).*
>
> *When all were present, the Resident, shielded from the sun's rays by the golden pajong (umbrella), came and the proper ceremony commenced. The Resident took a seat behind the green table, with the Assistant Resident on the right and Mr M. Schaalje, interpreter for the Chinese language, on the left, the Regional Secretary, the Controleurs Sieburgh and Wagner and the First Engineer van den Waterstaat, Kerstens, all in the great gala.*
>
> *In front of the table were the Chinese heads, with Tjong Young Hian in the middle. The Secretary then read the Government Decree, whereby Tjong Young Hian was appointed captain and Tjong A Fie, Lo Loe Pioe, Khoe Teng Koh, Lim Tjeng Keh, Ang Koen Djoe, Lie Sien Seng, Joe Ik Ho and Tho Teng Poh were appointed lieutenants.*

[63] Buiskool 2025: 149–152; SP 28-03-1921.

Fig. 10.5 Installation of the Major of the Chinese by the Resident for the East Coast of Sumatra W.J.M. Michielsen, assistant-resident J.C. van Hasselt and secretary J.A. van Rijn van Alkemade (KITLV 114722). W.J.M. Michielsen is in the middle with the moustache, and on his left is Tjong A Fie. To his right is Tjong Yong Hian, followed by (possibly) assistant-resident J.C. van Hasselt, Khoo Teng Ko, Lim Tjing Keh, and possibly Ang Koen Djoe (KITLV 114722)

Tjong A Fie (Medan), Lo Loe Pioe (Laboean Deli), Khoe Teng Koh (Laboean), Lim Tjeng Keh (Bindjey), Ang Koen Djoe (Bagan Siapi Api), Lie Sien Seng (Seroewai), Joe Ik Ho (Tebing Tinggi) and Tho Teng Poh (Batoe Bahra) were appointed lieutenants.

Hearing this in profound silence, the Resident took the floor and pointed out to the newly appointed appointees in a short and impressive speech (in the Malay language) the obligations they had assumed by accepting the appointment. He especially emphasised that they were bound to set an example to their compatriots; that they should rule without regard of the persons, and further the welfare of their countrymen who had settled here.

Finally the Resident asked them if they were prepared to take the prescribed oath, according to Chinese custom, before the appointed Commission, whereupon a unanimous yes followed. With this, the session was finished.

Before the procession started moving again, Messrs. Staffhel and Kleingrothe received permission to make a photographic recording. This profession was great, because of course all Chinese wanted to be photographed in their best costume.

Afterwards the Resident and the Secretary withdrew, and the procession, now augmented by the Commission, consisting of gentlemen Hasselt and Schaalje, and the other gentlemen, proceeded to the Chinese temple. In front went two Chinese on horseback, who seemed to serve as outriders, then the Hokkien and Canton Chinese, the Sin-Leng and Sin-Weh tribes, followed by the Hui-Tsoei, Heilokhong, Gho Koan, Tsoei Tsoei, Tsei-lam and Khee Chinese, all with flags and music. Captain Tjong Young Hian followed in a carriage with two horses, Lieutenant Tjong A Fie, in the well-disposed carriage with the familiar apple-grey horse (grey with apple-round spots on the horse), then the Commission, and on it a series of carriages, rickshaws and runners. In and around the temple was crowded.

The new nominees took turns taking the oath. It is impossible to give a good description of this ceremony without proper knowledge of the meaning of the various ceremonies. To Western eyes and concepts, the solemnity was somewhat lost. It was clear, however, that the Chinese headmen took the matter "au grand seriously," which was the intention, anyway. After all were sworn in, there were some mighty strokes to the gong, and the written and signed oath forms were burned in an open urn amid the fireworks. According to Chinese concepts, the sounding of the "gong" serves as a warning to the Deity that the oaths will ascend to heaven, and the latter is by means of burning. This combination of religious ideas with the practical notions of speedy dispatch is truly genuinely Chinese and original.

After the ceremony in the temple, the procession again proceeded to the Landraad hall, where all received a written certificate of their new dignities and a congratulation from the Resident. An acknowledgment from Captain Tjong Young Hian followed, and that concluded the official part of the proceedings.

In a private conversation the Captain expressed his joy at the fact that all the tribes of the Chinese were celebrating together and that the interest was so general. We gladly add our congratulations to the rest and wish our brave Captain Tjong Young Hian and his no less sympathetic brother Tjong A Fie a long possession of their new dignity.

In the evening at 7 o'clock "le tout Paris de Medan" was gathered at the home of Captain Tjong Young Hian, where he and his brother held a reception. The Resident, H.H. de Sultan, Colonel van de Pol and many military and civil authorities were present. A Chinese wayang provided the children with great pleasure, and our cheeky Dutch boys admired the spectacle "between the wings." Early enough!

It is a pity that the writer cannot enjoy the Battalions music which cheers the troops at Seroeway, cannot be in two places at once. The Chinese music is a bit monotonous in the long run. As in the past, the two newly appointed hosts proved to be excellent and generous hosts, for which a word of thanks is due.

10.4 Khoe Tjin Tek

Following Tjong A Fie's death in 1921, Medan's Chinese leadership entered a tense interregnum. Some expected the colonial state to abolish the major's post; others insisted it remained indispensable in a town shaped by Chinese labour, commerce, and associations. In November 1922, the government appointed the Hokkien businessman Khoe Tjin Tek as Chinese Major of Medan, the first Hokkien leader in many years (Fig. 10.6).[64]

Khoe Tjin Tek (1876–1969) (Qiu Qingde) was born in 1876 in the Har Yiap village, Hai-Teng district, Zhangzhou, Fujian. His father, Khoe Teng Ko, was a successful businessman and was the Lieutenant of the

Fig. 10.6 Khoe Tjin Tek (Nationaal Archief 2.20.46)

[64] SP 29-04-1922.

Chinese in Laboean between 1887 and 1893.[65] Khoe Teng Ko was a holder of several revenue farms on the East Coast of Sumatra and invested in land in the newly developed city of Medan. He developed and constructed houses at the end of Hüttenbachstraat, which he then leased out. However, Khoe Teng Ko died at the young age of 44 in 1893 and Khoe Tjin Tek was left to continue his father's business.

The housing construction and timber business expanded with the prosperity of the Deli tobacco industry. Around 1909, Khoe Tjin Tek established a Kang Chan (Jiangzhan), a firm of timber business, sawmilling, house construction, and architectural design. Kang Chan was successful and expanded with branches in Belawan, Bindjei, and Perak, Malaya. Khoe Tjin Tek owned fruit plantations and a fish farm. He also held several revenue farms and operated as an importer and commission agent in Medan.[66]

In 1904, Khoe Tjin Tek and fellow Hokkien businessmen established the Chung Hwa Shang Yeh trading enterprise. In January 1913 it was formalised as Chung Hwa Shang Yeh Maatschappij (Chinese Trading Company Ltd.), founded by 27 businessmen, led by Khoe Tjin Tek, Oen Huat Kim, Tan Tang Ho, and others, with a registered capital of 2 million guilders. The company offered a range of financial services, including deposits, loans, money transfer, and fire insurance. People knew it as the Hokkien bank, while Deli bank was referred to as the Hakka bank.[67]

Khoe Tjin Tek was well known for his philanthropy.[68] Recognising the struggles faced by many poor Chinese in arranging funerals, Khoe and other merchants founded the Hokkien Kongsi or benevolent association in 1904. This organisation served as a charitable and welfare institution dedicated to assisting with funeral arrangements and supporting the community. As Tjong A Fie established Tun Pun school in 1904, which was regarded as a Hakka school, Khoe and the Hokkien leaders established a Hokkien School, Hua Shang (Hwa Shang) Elementary School in 1908. Khoe generously donated two of his houses on Japanese Street (current Jl. Kepribadian) as the school building.[69]

Khoe Tjin Tek actively participated in many social associations, such as the Association *Armenzorg* (poor relief) and the Chinese philanthropic

[65] Wright 1909: 580; Buiskool 2025: 157,160.

[66] Idem.

[67] Buiskool 2025: 77.

[68] Wright 1909: 580.

[69] Buiskool 2025: 161.

association or Mutual Help Provident Fund (Hwa Chiao Tzu Shan Hsieh Hui).[70] He contributed 5000 guilders for the construction of a new ward in the leper colony of Sitjanang.[71]

After Tjong A Fie's death, the major's post remained vacant. The government initially planned a small Chinese Affairs office, appointing Liong Soei Tin as a first-class officer and Yap Soen Tjai as a second-class officer. When Liong died suddenly and budgets were cut, the plan was shelved. The government then appointed Khoe Tjin Tek, without consulting the Chinese community, yet he nevertheless gained broad respect.[72]

In 1933, the Dutch Indies government expressed its appreciation for Khoe Tjin Tek's services by bestowing on him the Officer in the Order of Orange Nassau.[73] Khoe Tjin Tek remained the Major of the Chinese until the Japanese occupation. During the Japanese occupation, his position was used to facilitate community-wide fundraising and levies. Following the end of the Second World War, however, the position was dissolved. Khoe Tjin Tek lived a long life and died in 1969 in Medan.[74]

10.4.1 Chinese Festive Gate, August 1923

The *Deli Courant* of December 8, 1923 wrote:

> *Medan, celebrates the 25th anniversary of Queen Wilhelmina's government. The whole of the East Coast, even if there are still separate celebrations in the smaller towns, because here at Medan the feasts had the most official character and, moreover, very, very many people from all over the region gathered here. And we may be pleased, because the feasts got off to a smooth and good start and fulfilled their purpose. The whole population ... has had to take with them the impression of the great significance of this jubilee, which was worth celebrating for a whole week and in such a generous and loyal manner ... To those who had eyes to see, there was a pleasant festive atmosphere in the crowd, and this was remarkably evident on some evenings in particular ... almost everyone has cooperated to make this festival a success in such a way. ... The festivities, at least the official festivities, are over, now we will have to tackle doubly hard. But may the mood remain, in which we forgot for a while our worries, a mood of cheerfulness,*

[70] Idem.

[71] *The War Cry* 11-02-1926.

[72] SP 28-11-1922.

[73] Buiskool 2025: 164; SP 07-09-1933; SP 14-09-1933; SP 26-11-1934; SP 04-02-1935; SP 05-02-1935.

[74] Buiskool 2025: 164.

Fig. 10.7 A festive Chinese wooden gate was erected between the Juliana building and the Seng Hap Department Store for the 25th jubilee of Dutch Queen Wilhelmina. On the gate, it was written the year 1898 and 1923 (J.W. Meijsters, KITLV 32519)

> *in which "cheerful workers" set themselves again, to continue to work together with confidence in the future for the development of this country.*[75]

The festive gate was an initiative of the Major of the Chinese, Khoe Tjin Tek (Fig. 10.7).[76]

[75] DC 08-09-1923.
[76] DC 21-08-1923.

CHAPTER 11

Chinese Temples for Solidarity

The economic growth of Deli and the East Coast of Sumatra drew Chinese labourers and merchants to the region. Upon arrival, they constructed temples dedicated to gods and deities, seeking protection, blessings, and prosperity (Fig. 11.1).

Chinese immigrants were primarily bound by shared hometowns, dialects, and clan affiliations. Mutual assistance among those from the same region was crucial. This kinship influenced the construction of temples, the formation of guild halls, the organisation of associations, the division of *kongsi* groups, and even their choice of work and trades.

Laboean Deli served as the primary trading centre in Deli, where tobacco leaves from different parts of the region were collected and transported via the Deli River to Belawan, where they were shipped to Europe. The Chinese called Laboean Deli *Lao Wuhan,* which literally means old Wuhan. It was also known as *lao fu keng,* meaning tiger pit, due to the roaming tigers in the surrounding jungle.

When Eliza Netscher, the resident of Riau, visited Laboean Deli for the first time in 1863, he was not impressed by the dilapidated *kampong* with rundown houses, rubbish beneath stilt houses and neglected roads.[1] He estimated the Malay population at no more than 2000 alongside some 20 Chinese and a hundred "Hindus of mixed-blood."[2] Netscher noted that

[1] *Soematra Courant* 06-08-1864.

[2] Idem.

B. Minasny, D. A. Buiskool, *Stories from Medan, Volume 1*,
https://doi.org/10.1007/978-981-95-7707-1_11

Fig. 11.1 Sketch of people visiting Kwan Tee Bio in Medan. Etching of Deli and Sumatra's East Coast by Steven Andries Schouten, Amsterdam 1929 (Wereldmuseum TM-alb-0292-3)

trade in Deli was conducted almost exclusively with Penang.[3] He further noted that indigenous states were largely untouched by European influence. He emphasised the need for improvement in both local governance and the general trade situation.[4]

In 1870, a fire broke out in Laboean Deli, reportedly destroying the entire Chinese settlement of 200 houses.[5] By the time Laboean Deli became the capital of Deli in 1873, it had a sizeable Chinese population with shops, carpentry workshops, and goldsmiths. The settlement was still described as a nest of mud and mosquitoes.

[3] *Soematra Courant* 13-08-1864.
[4] *Soematra Courant* 20-08-1864.
[5] *The Straits Times* 26-03-1870.

11.1 Laboean Deli: Liesheng Gong and Shousan Gong

The earliest temple in Laboean Deli was Liesheng gong built by the Hakka community in 1879. It has a bell with an inscription dated the fifth year of Emperor Guangxu (1879). It was probably funded by Tjong Yong Hian.[6] Due to the rivalry between the Hokkien and Cantonese communities, the Hokkien community constructed a larger temple, Shoushan Gong or Siu San Keng, dedicated to the goddess of mercy, Guanyin. The building of the temple began in 1885 on the site of the old prison (Fig. 11.2).[7]

Fig. 11.2 Shousan Gong or Siu San Keng, photographed by Kleingrothe (KITLV 86745)

[6] In 1970s, the Liesheng gong was renovated and an additional temple was built in the back hall for the God of Wealth. *Harian Indonesia* 03-07-2010.

[7] DC 14-11-1885.

A stone inscription in the Shousan gong, dated 1890, stated that the Chinese had lived in the area for thirty years but did not have a proper temple for worship, prompting community leaders to gather and contribute donations to a worship place for the Guanyin Bodhisattva. Leading donors, led by Qiu Dingguo (Khoe Teng Ko), Lin Deshui (Lim Tek Soei/ Lim tek Swee, the Chinese Lieutenant of Laboean 1881–1893), and Wen Shaochang, who contributed 1160, 1000, and 1000 yuan, respectively, made up a total donation of 14,500 yuan.[8]

The temple built by the Hokkien people was inaugurated on December 10, 1890.[9] A large ceremony followed on January 10, 1891, including a statue procession (Fig. 11.3).

Early photographers of Medan, Stafhell and Kleingrothe captured images of the temple, which represented the Chinese community's strong presence in Deli. Siu San Keng is situated around 100 meters away from Masjid Al-Osmani, built in 1854 by the Sultan of Deli. Initially a wooden structure, the mosque was rebuilt into a permanent structure in 1870–1872

Fig. 11.3 An advertisement on *Deli Courant* 07-01-1891 on the procession of the statue into the Kuan Im Teng temple with a grand Chinese opera

[8] Franke 1988: 94–99.
[9] DC 07-01-1891.

by Sultan Mahmud Perkasa Alam. In 1927, the mosque was refurbished and funded by Deli Maatschappij.

Siu San Keng temple was constructed in the Fujian architectural style and features a double-layer swallowtail ridge. The swallowtail ridge refers to the edge of the roof that is slightly curved upwards, with both ends extending upwards, shaped like a swallow's tail. Adjacent to the temple stood the Hokkien Kongsi or Fujian Association. Despite several renovations and refurbishments, Shoushan Gong has retained much of its original architecture. People from Belawan to Medan come to seek blessings and prosperity from Guanyin, the benevolent goddess. The temple is particularly crowded during Goddess Guanyin's birthdays. Nowadays, the old Chinese houses lie in decay, as most Chinese have left the once-prosperous Laboean Deli.

11.1.1 Titipapan

Another important early settlement for the Chinese is Titipapan, halfway between Belawan and Medan. The Chinese called it *banlu dian*, meaning halfway shop. Titipapan is also the area where Nienhuys established the first tobacco field in Deli near Martubung.

The Temple of Zhenjun Miao is located in Titipapan and is locally known as Go Ya Kong. The main deity is Zhenjun, a deity bearing the surname Wu (or Go in Hokkien) who fought against pirates in Guangdong.[10] The temple is managed by the Lufeng people (Hailok Hong). It was built around 1895 by Chinese tobacco farm workers. It is situated near the old Helvetia tobacco estate, formerly owned by the Deli Maatschappij. A wooden tablet in the temple was donated by Zheng Cifu, from Mahua, and his fellow plantation workers, dated late 1895. The temple was rebuilt in 2019. Another Zhenjun Miao temple is located at Tanjung Mulia, also known as Haikoulu by the Chinese, between Titipapan and Laboean Deli. It was built around 1878.[11]

[10] Franke 1988: 103–105.
[11] Franke 1988: 113–114.

11.2 Temples in Medan

11.2.1 Kuan Tee Bio

As Laboean Deli's low-lying riverfront proved vulnerable to flooding, the Deli Tobacco Company shifted its administrative centre to higher ground in Medan (from the 1870s). The Chinese community soon followed, establishing themselves in Kesawan, where they set up shops catering to the needs of Europeans. When Tjong Yong Hian moved to Medan and became the Lieutenant of the Chinese community in 1884, his first act was to commission a temple. He chose to honour Guandi, the protector god who symbolises brotherhood among the Chinese (Fig. 11.4).[12]

In the early days, Chinese clans, including the Hokkien, Cantonese, Teochew, and Hakka, did not always get along. Their strong traditional beliefs added further complexity to their relationships, and even minor misunderstandings had the potential to escalate into violent

Fig. 11.4 Kwan Tee Bio (ca. 1900, Mazaraki, KITLV 35746)

[12] *Straits Times Weekly* 29-03-1892.

confrontations. Moreover, the presence of rival secret society gangs, such as Ho Seng and Ghee Hin, originating from Penang and Singapore, further intensified tensions among the clans. Despite the pressing need for harmony, no leader wielded enough power and influence to effectively quell the rivalries between the clans.

Observing the ongoing conflict between the Chinese clans, Tjong Yong Hian founded the Guandi temple to foster unity among the Chinese community and end the conflicts. The temple's establishment aimed to provide a common ground where people from different clans could come together, fostering a sense of togetherness and mutual understanding. The choice of Guandi as the temple's focal deity was significant, especially for those from Guangdong. This particular group held a profound reverence for Guandi, revered as their protector deity.[13]

Emperor Shunzhi of the Qing dynasty bestowed the following title upon Guandi or Guan Gong, summarising his role: "Guan the Holy Great Deity, God of War Manifesting Benevolence, Bravery, and Prestige, Protector of the Country and Defender of the People, Proud and Honest Supporter of Peace and Reconciliation, and Promoter of Morality, Loyalty and Righteousness."[14]

Thus, the first temple in Medan was initiated in 1884, and was locally known as Kuan Tee Bio. It is located on the Indian camp, Klingenstraat. The street was later renamed Kwanteebiostraat and is now known as Jalan Irian Barat. As Lieutenant of the Chinese of Medan, Tjong Yong Hian wrote an introduction on a stone inscription to commemorate the temple's construction. The inscription describes the Chinese people who settled in Deli Shawan (Deli Kesawan), including scholars, farmers, industrialists, and merchants. These people sought blessings from Guandi shengjun (lord Guandi), Caibe xinjun (god of fortune), and Fude zhengshen (god of virtue). One of the primary goals of establishing this temple was to promote solidarity among Guangdong's different dialect and hometown groups. The inscription was signed by Tjong Yong Hian and Tjong A Fie's family.[15]

Tjong Yong Hian and three other donors generously contributed 1000 or more silver yuan each towards the construction of the temple, resulting in a total donation of over 10,000 yuan. The temple, which cost about

[13] Franke 1988: 82–89.

[14] https://en.wikipedia.org/wiki/Guan_Yu.

[15] Buiskool 2025: 205–209; Franke 1988: 82–89.

20,000 guilders, was inaugurated with a grand festival from December 19 to 22, 1890. The rivalry between the Hokkien and Cantonese people was palpable, as just over a week prior, the Hokkien people had inaugurated Siu San Keng in Laboean Deli. In Siu San Keng, the stele inscription reads: "In the winter, in the twelfth lunar month, on an auspicious day of the Gengyin year under Heaven's mandate," referring to the year 1890. By contrast, the stele at Kwan Tee Bio reads "In the eleventh year of the Guangxu reign, in the Yiyou year, in the first month of winter (1885). The explicit reference to the Guangxu reign of the Qing dynasty reflects a political allegiance with the Qing imperial authority, whereas the Siu San Keng inscription adopts a non-political calendrical formulation.[16]

The inauguration of the Guandi temple was lavish, represented by the four tribes of Guangdong: Hakka, Hailokhong, Cantonese and Teochew, each represented in the procession by a large triangular banner. The festival featured a procession led by various Chinese clans, and it included beautifully embroidered banners, copper figurines, and wooden boards with donors' names and proverbs.[17]

The building was designed in Cantonese style, known as Lingnan architecture, featuring a wok-shaped roof with two curved walls extending from both ends. Approximately 1500 people participated in the procession, led by Tjong Yong Hian and Tjong A Fie on horseback. Visitors from Penang, Singapore, and across Deli joined the celebration, and the Deli Railway saw a surge in passenger traffic. The procession garnered the attention of thousands, including Europeans, and the evening entertainment featured a *wajang* performance.[18]

At the same time, on 19th December 1890, across the railway from Kwan Tee Bio, a new temple opposite Pachtstraat (Jalan Kumango) was also inaugurated. The temple or *Topekong* was surrounded by a small park.[19] Thus, the road was known as Djalan Tepehkong

[16] In the late Qing calendrical practice, dates were customarily recorded using a dual system. Years were first designated by the emperor's reign title, with time counted sequentially from the beginning of a particular reign, and followed by the same year identified by its position within the sexagenary cycle, a sixty-year cyclical system.

[17] DC 24-12-1890.

[18] *Wajang* is a theatrical performance, in this case, traditional Chinese opera.

[19] DC 20-12-1890. Topekong or Tepehkong is from Hokkien Tua Pek Kong or Dabogong in Pinyin, is a local god reverred by the Fujian Chinese in South East Asia, commonly referred as the God of Prosperity.

As we suspected, the eardrums of Medan's residents had a hard time yesterday and today at the inauguration of the new Chinese temple. Numerous processions marched through the streets with deafening noise - to drive away evil spirits - and were often distinguished by beautiful costumes and expensive banners: the dragon was not missing, of course.

Tomorrow is the most important day of the festival and then the Topekong will be permanently installed in the temple, nicely decorated in Chinese style, opposite the Pachtstraat, which is surrounded by a small park. This will look nice after a while and is the only place here where - apart from the Esplanade - trees have been planted for the general good.[20]

During the Chinese Ghost Festival:

The surroundings of the Chinese temple opposite Djalan Teipehkong provided a delightful scene last night. The Hokkien Chinese were making offerings to the souls of the deceased and to evil spirits. In a shed, a variety of dishes, selections of drinks, and pyramids of kwé-kwé (traditional cakes) were prepared, while three priests continuously read prayers. Hundreds of mats were laid out on the lawn, covered with all sorts of food items and lit with countless small lights. In addition, thousands of paper-made clothing items were hung on ropes as offerings — and this morning, everything was gone![21]

The temple at Djalan Topekong was long gone, but the Kwan Tee temple remained a popular place of worship. It has undergone numerous reconstructions, with the first rebuild in the late 1920s due to its deteriorating condition. Unfortunately, the restoration work caused the temple to lose its original characteristics. According to Gerard Jansen, a Dutch civil servant for ground affairs of the Medan municipality in the 1930s, the temple hosted a grand festival during the fifth lunar month, featuring bustling stalls in the temple's yard and a Chinese opera that played day and night.[22]

The temple underwent several refurbishments and extensions over the years. In 1970, it was fully renovated, but not long after, the government took a portion of its land for road expansion, leading to another significant rebuilding. The temple was refurbished once again in the 1980s and received another major extension in the 2000s. The temple houses several

[20] DC 20-12-1890.
[21] DC 22-08-1894.
[22] Jansen 1934.

historical artefacts, including a shrine built in 1890, two incense burners - one built in 1890 and the other in 1902, and two sets of couplets erected in 1906.[23]

To this day, the temple remains an important religious and cultural landmark in Medan. People seek guidance from Guan Gong for their business and personal matters, and his advice is believed to be infallible. It's common for people to make solemn vows before Guan Gong for various reasons to demonstrate their sincerity.

11.2.2 Tianhou Gong

As Medan's Fujianese community grew, they did not want to remain in the shadow of the Guangdong-dominated Guandi temple. During temple gatherings, the Guangdong people would stand in the front row while the Fujianese remained at the back. This led the Fujianese to desire a new temple of their own. To meet the needs of the community, Tjong Yong Hian initiated the establishment of a second temple dedicated to the deity Tianhou, specifically for the Fujianese community in Medan. The goddess Mazu is also known as Tianhou, meaning Queen of Heaven. She is highly revered by the coastal people of Fujian and is believed to be a powerful and benevolent heavenly queen who will protect Chinese merchants during their sea voyages (Fig. 11.5).

Tianhou gong was established at Kapiteinsweg (now Jalan Pandu) around 1906, organised by the Chinese General Chamber of Commerce of Deli. An inscription dated 1911 records that each donor, headed by Wan Lianxing, Zhang Zhenxun (Thio Tiauw Siat), and Zhang Yunan (Tjong Yong Hian), gave 2000 yuan. Zhang Hongnan (Tjong A Fie), Xie Rongguang, and Qiu Zhaozong gave 1000 yuan each. An additional 124 donors contributed, bringing the total to 20,000 yuan. Tjong Yong Hian further donated 4000 yuan to cover the shortfall.[24] Devotees believed that the Heavenly Empress brought peace and prosperity to all beings, especially to sailors who prayed for safe and prosperous voyages.

Gerard Jansen, who authored a book about the ethnic communities of Medan and their cultural characteristics in 1934, observed that the temple was built slightly askew in relation to the roads, following *feng shui*

[23] Franke 1988: 82–89.
[24] Franke 1988: 106–111.

Fig. 11.5 Tianhou gong with Medan's water tower (KITLV 377192)

principles.[25] Although dedicated to Mazu (a Fujianese sea-goddess), the temple's roofline drew on southern Chinese Lingnan style. We can still find two bronze bells in the temple, one dating back to 1906 and the other to 1907. The bells symbolise the prosperity and blessings that Mazu brings to her followers. There is also a couplet from 1907 donated by a group of Fujianese expressing hopes for prosperity and safety for the country and those seeking refuge in the temple.

As the donations indicate, it was once the largest in Medan, located opposite the water tower and occupying a large land area. Over time, the temple deteriorated due to harsh weather and was left in a dilapidated state after the war. Finally, after years of fundraising and construction, the new temple was completed in 1976. Unfortunately, it is now obscured between tailors' shops. Now called Vihara Ariya Satyani, the temple doesn't resemble the original structure, but it remains a revered spiritual site (Fig. 11.6).

[25] Jansen 1934.

Fig. 11.6 The Tianhou temple (right) in 1935, was built slightly askew towards the road for good *feng shui* (KITLV 181922)

11.2.3 Pulo Brayan

In 1886, Tjong Yong Hian erected another temple in Pulo Brayan, dedicated to the goddess Guanyin, known as Guanyin Gong. Tjong Yong Hian headed the donation with 51 yuan, followed by Liu Yuanzhen with 50 yuan. A further 86 names contributed, resulting in a total of 765 yuan.[26] Next to the temple was a burial ground for the Guangdong people. During the construction of the Deli Railway, the remains of Chinese labourers were frequently uncovered during excavation work. Tjong Yong Hian and Tjong A Fie designated a burial ground in Poeloe Brayan and founded the Guangdong Yishan Association.[27]

In the 1970s, it was rebuilt and renamed Qingyin Chansi, incorporating other deities. It is located on Jalan Jos Sudarso in Pulo Brayan and is called Vihara Avalokitesvara, managed by the Henghua (Putian/Xinghua)

[26] Franke 1988: 89–93.
[27] Chang 1921: 2.

people. Nearby, another temple called Wudi-miao, built around 1890, can be found, where Guandi is the main deity.[28]

11.3 Plantation Temples

Almost every tobacco plantation along the East Coast of Sumatra traditionally included a temple to serve as a place of worship for the Chinese labourers. Although many of these temples have since vanished, a few still stand in the vicinity of Medan, namely Bulu Cina, Klumpang, and Paya Bakong. Although the original structures have been replaced by new buildings, these temples remain a popular place of worship. These plantations were owned by the Deli Maatschappij, and the temples were constructed around the year 1900. The temple was usually constructed by the *tandil* or overseers. The setup typically included a temple and a Chinese opera stage (*wajang*) facing the temple, among the coolies' houses.The temple in Bulu Cina is known as Tua Pek Kong, with a main deity called Tham Kong Ya or Tan Gong Xian Sheng 潭公仙聖. The deity was originally from Huizhou and achieved immortality at the tender age of thirteen. According to legend, praying to him has the power to invoke sunshine or rain and bring about miraculous healing. Since he was but a child, devotees offer candies and marbles at the altar as tokens of their reverence (Fig. 11.7).

The temple in Kloempang, next to the Deli river, was built in 1900 and was beautifully captured by photographer Kleingrothe in 1903. The temple is now hidden behind a school and now known as Kwan Im temple (kelenteng), rebuilt in 1991 (Fig. 11.8).

The most complete remaining structure is at Paya Bakung. The Guandi temple, surrounded by oil palms, still attracts visitors on the first and fifteenth day of the lunar calendar. It was left abandoned in the 1990s but the temple was rebuilt in 2011. Across the road from the temple was the house of the head tandil (Chinese foreman), Lim Cai Koa, dating from 1925. Oral tradition says that the temple was built because of a disease outbreak at the plantation, which claimed many lives. The Chinese workers brought a wooden statue of Guandi from China to this temple, and miraculously, the number of deaths was reduced. This oral tradition may echo the period's recurrent cholera epidemics (notably in the mid-1880s),

[28] Franke 1988: 101–102; Known as Kuan Tee Bio, located at Jalan Pertempuran №48a, Pulo Brayan.

Fig. 11.7 Boeloe Tjina temple around 1900 (Tropenmuseum 10015614)

when long-distance labour shipping and crowded barracks amplified disease transmission. To prevent further outbreaks, the Deli Planters Association established a quarantine facility, including a station in Poeloe Berhala, in 1899, which helped reduce the outbreak.

During the tobacco plantation days, at the annual payout period, plantation workers were given three or four days off, which often turned into a time of feasting, gambling, and watching Chinese opera or *wajang*. These shows were held either in permanent venues, where admission was

Fig. 11.8 Chinese temple on the plantation Kloempang in 1903 (Kleingrothe, KITLV 12645)

charged, or in open-air theatres. The theatres were often set up opposite the Chinese temple (*Tepekong*). The event was often intertwined with the vices of gambling and opium use.[29] Local tradition says that opposite the Guandi temple was where the Chinese *wajang* was performed, and a room on the ground floor of the tandil's house was an opium den.

Until 1930, the head tandil was responsible for organising Chinese opera (*wajang*) performances on the plantations, often in conjunction with licensed gambling activities. However, in January 1931, the Governor of the East Coast of Sumatra issued a decree which banned the issuance of gambling licenses (*dobbellicenties*) on tobacco plantations during the off-harvest period. The DPV also tried to reduce the influence of the *hoofd-mandoer* (head mandor for the Javanese), the financial authority of the *hoofdtandil* (head Chinese foreman). The head *tandils* were prohibited from lending significant sums of money to workers. Estate managers were also instructed not to allow head *tandils* any opportunity to withhold money from workers' wages during pay distribution. Additionally, head *tandils* were forbidden from selling or arranging the sale of food items and

[29] Langereis 1918: 599.

goods to workers. They were also prohibited from collecting money via payroll deductions, except for small, voluntary contributions made for the purpose of organising religious festivities. The Deli Planters' Association (DPV) took over responsibility for the *wajang* performances and organised them under a single contractor. The Medan-based firm Mooi Long & Co. was commissioned to supply Teochew *wajang* troupes, such as Law Sai Poh Hong and Sam Sai Poh Hong, according to a fixed schedule. The costs of performances were borne entirely by the plantations. To discourage workers from seeking entertainment and gambling opportunities outside the estates, the DPV also requested that the Governor limit public *wajang* performances in nearby towns and centres (Figs. 11.9 and 11.10).[30]

Fig. 11.9 The Paya Bakung temple was left in a dilapidated state in the 1980s (photo collection of BM)

[30] DPV Jaarverslag 1931:6–7, 96–97.

Fig. 11.10 Head tandil house at Paya Bakung (photo by BM)

11.3.1 Pekong Lima or Temple of the Five Ancestors

The Five Ancestors Temple (Wuzhu Miao) or Vihara Pekong Lima is located on the main road from Medan to Tanjong Morawa. Unlike other Chinese temples with statues of deities, the main shrine in Wuzhu Miao is a tomb. It is a mausoleum for five Chinese coolies: Tan Pe Yak, Go Tho Seng, Li Sa Ti, Yo Kwi Lim, Ng Ge Kang. A couplet says: *A new tomb forged in kindness, binding a noble affinity; Awake in a distant land, their spirits rest in broad compassion*. Another writing says: *By courage they upheld righteousness, illuminating the ages; By steadfast loyalty of heart, their virtue endures for ten thousand years* (Fig. 11.11).[31]

The temple is now regarded as the guardian of the nearby Chinese cemetery. However, the tomb of the five coolies was originally at the Teochew cemetery at Bindjeiweg (current Jl. Gatot Subroto). The legend has it that five young men from Chaozhou (Teochew), China, signed a contract to work as coolies in tobacco fields in Deli. These five young men worked in the Soengai Bamban tobacco plantation, became close friends and sworn brothers. In charge of a tobacco field was a mean European assistant who constantly abused and mistreated the workers. Unable to

[31] 善结新坟结善缘，梦醒异域宽怀抱. 立膽為義照千古，存心從忠萬年.

Fig. 11.11 Pekong Lima in Tanjung Morawa (photo by BM)

endure continued abuse, one night, they decided to plan for an assault early the next morning. They prayed to the local god, *topekong*, and a chicken was slaughtered to seal their pact; they swore as blood brothers with an oath that they would never betray each other. Early the next morning, the assistant was out in the field. One of the brothers swung an axe on his head. The others joined in and hacked him ruthlessly with hoes until he could not move. The five did not run away but surrendered. In court, they all admitted to killing the assistant. They were all executed together.[32]

The local Chinese community was moved by the blood brothers' act and buried their bodies to honour their righteousness. They became martyrs and their tomb was known as the Five Ancestors Temple.

The legend of the five blood brothers was well known in the early twentieth century, but over time, the real story was lost. The five brothers were Chinese coolies working at Soengei Bamban and were responsible for the murder of German assistant Ernst Ziehm on December 11, 1893. The incident occurred at six o'clock in the morning while labourers were being allocated tasks on the forest side of the plantation. The five brothers launched an attack on Ziehm during this period. Following their

[32] See the Chapter on Swiss Planters in Deli.

apprehension, all of them confessed to the crime. Subsequently, they faced trial in the *Landraad* (a native court) in Medan on March 13th, 1894, and were subsequently sentenced to death.[33]

The execution day was July 31, 1894 and reported by the *Singapore Free Press and Mercantile Advertiser* (August 14, 1894):

> *At Medan on Tuesday last, at 7.30 a.m., the sentence of death by hanging was carried out on the five murderers of Mr. Ziehm of Bedagei. The hour appointed was 7 a.m. The five men preferred to walk instead of to be driven from the gaol to the place of execution.*
>
> *While on their walk to the place of execution (kampong Petissa), and during the reading of the sentence, they behaved in an insulting way towards Europeans in general and to one of the Chinese officials, calling names and spitting. All five were hanged at one time, the scaffold having been enlarged. Death was instantaneous in four cases. They were all strong, vigorous men.*

Tjong A Fie, the Lieutenant of the Chinese at that time, visited the brothers before their execution, saying that he could not help them but promised to unite them with God by building a tomb for them.[34] The brothers were buried in the Teochew grave in Bindjeiweg (Jalan Binjai, now Gatot Subroto, near Medan Fair. The Hokkien cemetery was on the north and Teochew cemetery was on the south of Bidjeiweg in Petisah). In 1898, the tomb was rebuilt with marble by Tjong A Fie. The large tomb attracted the local Chinese, who presented offerings in the hope of good luck or fortune, which led to the cult of worshipping the five ancestors.

The killing of Ziehm and the execution of the coolies were among countless incidents caused by the cruelty and violence perpetrated by Europeans in the Deli tobacco plantations. Yet, it was the courage and loyalty shown by the coolies in their resistance against the Dutch and other European planters that made the story of the five blood brothers stand out. The legend inspired a play written by Chinese political figure Wang Renshu, who described it as the brothers' heroic act against the Dutch colonial regime. In 1970, the Teochew cemetery had to make way for housing expansion, and the Five Ancestors Temple was relocated and rebuilt as a large temple at its current location.

[33] Stenberg and Minasny. *Bijdragen tot de taal-, land-en volkenkunde* 178: (2022) 159–191.

[34] Information from Mrs. Seah Peng Ee-Tjong, the granddaughter Tjong A Fie, by D.A. Buiskool, Singapore, 19-10-1993 (Buiskool 2025: 207–208, 319).

11.3.2 *Wuzu Miao or Go Co or Vihara Pekong Lima Medan*

There is another Five Ancestors temple in Medan. The Go Co temple, located at Jl. Sutomo in Medan, commemorates five young men executed by the Japanese. In March 1942, when the Japanese entered Medan, the Dutch officials had mostly fled, and there was no security in the city. People broke into the warehouses and shops and started looting. Initially, the Japanese army did not intervene. Eventually, they began shooting the looters to stop the robberies, but chaos continued elsewhere.

Near Hakkastraat (Jl. Nusantara), five innocent Chinese bystanders were watching the looted shops. The Japanese caught them and beheaded them in public. They were Huang Wen Chan, Huang A Yam, Huang Chin Phan, Liu Yin Khan, Shih Sui Ling aged between 20–30 years old.

Their heads were displayed on a pile of bricks in the middle of the road junction in front of Centrale Pasar (Pusat Pasar) for four days. From then on, no more looting occurred. The families of the beheaded victims did not dare to approach the bodies, so some local Chinese took the bodies of the five young men and buried them behind Centrale Pasar at Wilhelminastraat (Jl. Sutomo).

Their heads were on display until four days later, when the Japanese executor asked a monk to say a prayer to the five people, saying that he was executing his duty as part of the Japanese army, and the five people had sinned against Teno Heika (Japan's emperor) and obstructed peace under Japanese rule. The local Chinese took the heads and buried them together with their bodies. In 1947, the Chinese set up a fund to build a memorial temple for the five people, and now it is known as Pekong Lima at Jl. Sutomo.[35]

11.3.3 *Temples as Cultural Heritage*

As we travel from Laboean Deli to Medan, we can spot several ancient temples established during the late 1800s and early 1900s. Although some have been restored, others relocated, and a few even dismantled, Chinese temples were once present on every plantation, but most have since vanished. These temples represent the Chinese diaspora in Deli and each has its own story of aspirations and journeys. Tjong Yong Hian's goal was to establish temples that would unite the Chinese community and encourage

[35] Kho 1947: 13–14; *Nieuwe Courant* 11-01-1947.

harmony. These temples were not only places of worship. They were institutions of solidarity, anchoring migrants through dialect networks, charity, dispute mediation, festivals, and collective memory. Preserving them is therefore preserving the social history of Deli itself.

CHAPTER 12

Tjong Yong Hian Building the Chaozhou—Shantou Railway

The story of Tjong Yong Hian's railway venture bridges two worlds: the rise of Medan as a colonial entrepôt and the dawn of China's modernisation. By the turn of the twentieth century, Medan's Chinese merchants, men like Tjong Yong Hian and his brother Tjong A Fie, had built fortunes from Deli's plantations and turned commercial success into instruments of diplomacy and reform. Their wealth, earned under Dutch rule, flowed back across the South China Sea to fund schools, bridges, and famine relief in their native Guangdong.

It was within this web of trans-Asian exchange that Tjong Yong Hian undertook one of his most ambitious projects: the construction of the Chaozhou—Shantou Railway, China's first merchant-financed and managed railway (Fig. 12.1). His efforts reflected the optimism of a new Chinese diaspora, one that saw itself not as an exile, but as an agent of renewal. Medan's prosperity thus became the seedbed of China's modernisation, and its merchants the unlikely architects of a new era in Chinese industry and pride. This chapter traces how a businessman from colonial Medan, drawing on lessons learned from the Deli plantations, brought modern infrastructure to his ancestral homeland and helped reshape China's path to the twentieth century.

After the Sino-Japanese War (1894–1895), the Qing Empire found that it was lagging far behind in technology, and Empress Dowager Cixi

B. Minasny, D. A. Buiskool, *Stories from Medan, Volume 1*, https://doi.org/10.1007/978-981-95-7707-1_12

Fig. 12.1 Tjong Yong Hian at the opening ceremony of the Chao-Chow & Swatow (Chaozou-Shantou) Railway, November 25, 1906 (photo courtesy of Rebecca Chandra)

wanted to modernise China through the development of railroads.[1] However, the construction of railways in China faced challenges due to cultural beliefs in *feng shui* and superstition. Numerous ancestral tombs were located throughout the landscape, and disturbing or desecrating these sacred sites was considered taboo. Introducing iron tracks and locomotives that passed through these revered ancestral lands could trigger public unrest and resistance.[2] Additionally, the Qing Empire faced severe financial strain, dealing with many natural disasters and wars with foreign countries.

The expansion of railways also symbolised the height of European colonial influence. European powers had already started to build railroads on their concession lands in China, facilitating the transport of goods out of China. After suffering various wars and defeats at the hands of Europeans, the Qing government initiated a large-scale modernisation in 1902. It shifted from state-led enterprise to commercially funded modernisation,

[1] Chang 2013: 124–125; Buiskool 2025: 125,126
[2] Chang 2013: 124–125

particularly encouraging overseas Chinese to fund railways and industry. In 1896, a proposal was made for a railway line from Beijing to Hankou, with reformist Sheng Xuanhuai overseeing the project.[3] Sheng Xuanhuai actively sought investment from affluent overseas Chinese, among whom was Thio Tiauw Siat. Thio Tiauw Siat, a successful entrepreneur who had amassed wealth in Batavia and resided in Penang, was invited to Beijing to discuss the project. While Thio agreed to raise capital in Nanyang (Southeast Asia), he advised Sheng that a railway line in the South of China (Guangdong province), where most Chinese in Malaya and the Dutch Indies came from, would be more attractive.[4] Thio Tiauw Sat recommended Tjong Yong Hian as the ideal person to execute such a project.

12.1 Tjong Yong Hian and China

In traditional China, Chinese who lived overseas were often regarded as traitors, and merchants were the least valued profession (the first being scholars and officials). But the Qing government realised that wealthy overseas merchants could contribute to the country's ailing economy. In 1903, the Qing government established a Ministry of Commerce for the first time, electing Thio Tiauw Siat as the vice president.[5] Merchants were encouraged to establish companies and businesses in China under the motto "industry to save the country" (*zhiye jiuguo*). Those who raised sufficient shares and funds would be awarded official status.[6] A state bank was established in 1905 with the yuan as a national currency.[7]

The Qing government made use of the colonial *Kapitan* system established in Malaya and the Dutch Indies. These local Chinese leaders, in effect, could represent the Chinese people and facilitate trade with China. In addition, these merchants could donate to China's ailing economy. The Qing government set up a consul general in Singapore for the Nanyang Islands in 1877 and Penang in 1890. Thio Tiauw Sat was appointed vice-consul in Penang (1890–1894), and became the consul in Singapore in 1895. Tjong Yong Hian, a close ally of Thio Tiauw Siat, was appointed as

[3] The Beijing-Hankou (now part of Wuhan line) began construction in 1899 and completed in 1906 (Dillon 2010: 149).

[4] Yen 1984: 123.

[5] Godley 1975: 373.

[6] Chang 2013: 395.

[7] Idem.

the deputy vice-consul and the vice-consul from 1894 until 1895. The position lifted Tjong Yong Hian's position as a formal Chinese official.

The brothers Tjong Yong Hian and Tjong A Fie were famous merchants in Medan and also well-known community leaders. Tjong Yong Hian and Tjong A Fie contributed to public welfare in their hometown in Meixian by building bridges, roads, and schools. They generously donated funds to help the local government in Guangdong. They supported the compilation and publication of local literature. During floods, droughts and famines in China, they donated funds for disaster relief. The Qing court commended their charitable deeds, and they were awarded the title of Fourth Rank Jingtang in 1902.

Tjong Yong Hian and Tjong A Fie were traditional Chinese and loyal Confucian followers who would give up part of their wealth to help modernise China. Tjong Yong Hian was made a special Qing representative to the Southeast Asia Chinese and was asked to raise money for China's first merchant-run national banks.[8] The Tjong brothers donated to the Chinese Navy, built schools in their hometown of Meixian and donated to Lingnan University in Guangzhou (now part of Sun Yat-sen University). They built a dam to prevent flooding and a bridge in Songyuan in Fujian. Tjong Yong Hian received the Bottom of the First Rank from the Qing government in 1903.[9] For their philanthropic activities in Guandong, both brothers were raised to the rank of Mandarin.[10]

12.1.1 *Proposing the Railway to Empress Cixi*

Tjong Yong Hian witnessed how railways built by the Dutch in Deli modernised and facilitated economic growth. The planters in Deli initially depended on ox carts and small boats to transport tobacco leaves to the harbour for export. They recognised the need for a more efficient transportation system and desired the construction of a railway line. However, the Dutch Indies government was reluctant to make such an investment. In response, the Deli planters established the Deli Spoorweg Maatschappij, a privately owned company, to construct railways connecting the region

[8] Godley 1975: 129.

[9] Tjong Yong Hian received the Bottom of the First Rank and the brevet rank of a Third Rank in 1903 (Franke 1988:149; Godley 1981:129,181).

[10] Kühr 1921: 3–5.

and improving the export process. This initiative proved to be a great success.

Shantou (Swatow) had been an important British treaty port since 1858, with a direct shipping connection to South East Asia. It was the second most important port after the provincial capital, Guangzhou. It was a port where the British imported opium to China, and a place of coolie trade. Chaozhou was a prosperous business town, the prefectural centre and the seat of the local government.[11]

Tjong Yong Hian planned to build a railway from Shantou (Swatow) to Chaozhou and then extend the railway to his hometown in Meixian.[12] A railway line between Shantou and Chaozhou had been proposed since 1888. This was an important trade route for transporting products from Chaozhou to the port, as the local waterways were very shallow during winter. Moreover, it took a day to travel via boat from Shantou to Chaozhou. British company Jardine Matheson & Co. surveyed a route, and with the firm Bradleys, in 1888, applied to the Qing court to build the line but was strongly opposed by the people of the area.[13]

Tjong Yong Hian saw the railway construction as a critical solution to a chronic grain supply crisis in the Hakka hinterland. The Hakka town Jiaying and Chaozhou produced only three months' worth of rice annually, relying on imports from Anhui and Siam via Shantou's port. Seasonal droughts paralysed the Mei River, the region's lifeline, leading to price spikes and increased famine risks. Tjong Yong Hian, a rice importer, wanted a railway to bypass these bottlenecks, ensuring year-round transport while cutting costs and reducing middlemen's profits.

On October 24, 1903, Tjong Yong Hian was received by Empress Dowager Cixi and Emperor Guangxu in Beijing (Fig. 12.2).[14] Although Guangxu was the emperor, the empress dowager was the one in charge of the country and making the decisions. Empress Cixi received Tjong Yong Hian with curiosity and eagerness to learn about the conditions in Nanyang. The Empress first inquired about the conditions in Guangdong,

[11] In 1908, coolies exported to Hongkong 12,876, to the Straits Settlements 52,678, to Sumatra 8,971, to Siam 46,246 and to Saigon 5,786 (Wright 1908: 829).

[12] https://kknews.cc/history/e8m484n.html.

[13] Nield 2015: 220.

[14] https://www.thepaper.cn/newsDetail_forward_9477671.

Fig. 12.2 A photo of Empress Dowager Cixi in the 30th year of Guangxu (1904) given to Tjong Yong Hian as a souvenir (photo courtesy of Rebecca Chandra)

but then she began asking a series of questions to learn about Tjong Yong Hian's business in Nanyang, his donations, and the geographical and political situation. She was especially interested in the conditions of the overseas Chinese people. During the meeting, Cixi also asked for his opinion on the newly established Ministry of Commerce and whether he could speak English.[15]

After the meeting, Tjong Yong Hian got the go-ahead and started planning the Chaozhou-Shantou Railway project. First, he went to Tianjin to meet a railway engineer and then went to Shanghai to discuss construction with the minister of railways Sheng Xuanhuai, and finally went to Guangdong to discuss the implementation with Cen Chunxuan, the governor of Guangdong and Guangxi.

Empress Cixi summoned Tjong Yong Hian a second time on December 14, a month and a half after the first meeting. Tjong Yong Hian reported his progress in securing funding and expertise for the railway project. Cixi expressed her approval, calling it beneficial to the nation and its people, and even issued an edict ordering local officials to protect the project, shielding it from bureaucratic interference. This was rare, as most private enterprises faced Qing suspicion, merchants were traditionally viewed as profit-driven.

Tjong Yong Hian moved carefully. He was aware of the political manoeuvrings of local officials, such as Beiyang Army General Yuan Shikai, who had become increasingly powerful in the region. He was also aware that some officials were trying to undermine his efforts and divert the railway project to other provinces. Empress Cixi finally hoped that Tjong Yong Hian would use his reputation in Nanyang to recruit more Chinese business people to invest in China. Tjong Yong Hian reassured Empress Cixi that his investment in constructing the railway was not for personal profit but to address the issues of food import and agricultural product export in Chaozhou and even Jiaying prefectures. Empress Cixi was very satisfied with Tjong Yong Hian's thoroughness and said:

> *This is what benefits the country and the people, so you should hurry up and take it seriously.*

[15] Rao Ganzhong, *Kai fan chui fen yao qianqiu. Yinni Zhang Rongxuan xian xian shishi yibai zhounian jinian wenji.* 2011:136–151.

Before dismissing him, she urged him again to mobilise Nanyang capital for China's development. Empress Cixi awarded him paintings and her calligraphy, a symbolic reward aligning him with loyalist elites.[16]

12.2 Building the Railway

Tjong Yong Hian's trip to Beijing was a great success. He realised that the construction plan could only be executed with strong support from the highest level. The Grand Council supported the proposal, and Empress Cixi handed the decree in late December 1903. An imperial order was passed to the governor of Guangdong to clear the way for the construction of the railroad (Fig. 12.3).

In early 1904, Tjong Yong Hian was appointed by the Ministry of Commerce to supervise the railway. Originally, the project was planned to raise 1 million taels of silver, but due to rising costs, Tjong Yong Hian proposed increasing the capital to 2 million taels, which was approved by

Fig. 12.3 The Chao-Chow & Swatow RY (Chaozhou–Shantou railway) train (photo courtesy of Rebecca Chandra)

[16] Rao 2011:136–151.

the Ministry. Tjong Yong Hian sought capital from his Penang business partner, Hsieh Jungkuang (also known as Cheah Choon Seng), to raise a capital of one million taels. A Hong Kong millionaire, Wu (Ng Li Hing), invested 500,000 taels, Lin Lisheng, a leading merchant from Taiwan, provided 300,000 taels, and Zhang (Cheong Chong Hong) from Siam contributed 200,000 taels. The initial fund raised was 2,000,000 taels.[17] The Chao-Chow & Swatow Railway Co. Ltd. was registered with the newly formed Chamber of Commerce in Beijing with 10,000 shares and a capital investment of 2,000,000 taels. It was the first railway company registered at the Chamber of Commerce of Peking.[18]

In April 1904, the shareholders appointed Tjong Yong Hian as managing director-general. Lin Lisheng was the managing director and the rest were members of the board of directors. Given the limited number of qualified Chinese engineers at the time, Tjong sought to recruit Zhan Tianyou, the chief engineer of the Tianjin–Yingkou Railway, who was already renowned for his accomplishments. Tjong Yong Hian travelled to Tianjin and consulted Yuan Shikai, the Viceroy of Zhili and Minister of Railways, who agreed to release temporarily Zhan for the railway project. On February 6, 1904, Zhan was officially dispatched by the Shanhaiguan Railway Administration to Shantou, accompanied by six engineering students.

At the same time, Lin Lisheng suggested engaging the Japanese company Mitsui Bussan Kaisha to oversee the construction of the railway.[19] Lin was, in fact, working for the Japanese, but he argued that they did not want European firms to be involved and could not find qualified Chinese engineers.[20] Tjong Yong Hian met Aikuzawa Naozai, a Japanese businessman who proposed reasonable prices for surveying and construction. But

[17] *The Hong Kong Daily Press Office* 1910:1004.

[18] Wright 1908:680.

[19] Godley contended that Lin Lisheng was working for Japanese and his shares were bought out by Tjong A Fie in 1908. SCMP reported that Thio Siau Siat bought out the capital of Lin at $800,000 (SCMP 22-09-1909). The Directory & Chronicle 1910 edition still listed Lin (pronounced Lim La Sang) as the managing director of the Company. Lin was born at Fujian in 1868, and educated at Hongkong. Before the China-Japan War he was one of the largest tea merchants in Taiwan (Formosa). After that he was in banking and commercial enterprises in Amoy and Hongkong (Wright 1908: 680).

[20] *Straits Echo* 06-11-1906.

there was a negative sentiment, as Japan had just defeated the Qing empire in 1895.[21]

The Ministry of Commerce stressed that the Japanese engineer was only approved to handle material procurement, not to lead engineering or construction. The engineering responsibilities must remain with Zhan Tianyou. However, Zhan Tianyou's salary was very high (900 taels), and when combined with that of his assistants, totalled over 1400 taels/month. Additionally, Zhan's cost estimates for the project were triple the price. In contrast, the Japanese engineer's salary was only 400 yuan, and his proposed costs for construction and procurement were far lower than Zhan's or other Western (British, German, French) firms. Tjong Yong Hian proposed to outsource all aspects of the project, track laying, station construction, materials procurement and transport, to the Japanese engineer via a bundled contract.

The Ministry insisted that the engineering responsibilities be retained by Zhan Tianyou, Tjong Yong Hian repeatedly argued that China's engineering capacity was still limited and that separating supply and construction could create confusion and conflict, especially with competing foreign interests. Facing operational redundancy and cost concerns, Zhan Tianyou resigned and returned to Tianjin. The Ministry eventually approved hiring the Japanese engineer.[22]

Tjong Yong Hian and Tjong A Fie were skilful businessmen and had lots of experience dealing with the Sultans, Dutch officials, and Chinese merchants and coolies in Deli. Former Dutch military officer and editor of *Deli Courant*, P.B. van Staden ten Brink, described the Tjong brothers as:

> *champion chess players of the abacus. The innate level-headed and clear mind, aided by an excellent memory and unparalleled dexterity, makes them as first-class sharp men, who make money in Deli a pleasant, animating sport.*[23]

Tjong Yong Hian's experience in Deli and diplomatic skills proved useful in dealing with the gentry, foreign forces, and local residents. First, Tjong needed to get the support of the local gentry. The local government of Shantou was entrusted to the *Daotai*, a high Chinese official, who resided in the courthouse at Chaozhou. He courted an influential member

[21] Yen 1984:130.
[22] Xiao Wenping & Rao Ganzhong 2021: 17–177.
[23] SP 06-09-1906.

of the gentry named Hsiao Chih Shan and awarded him a position on the Railway Company's managerial board. Tjong Yong Hian reasoned to Hsiao that the railway would resist the foreign imperialists and convinced him that it would also benefit local merchants and people.[24] Tjong Yong Hian further demonstrated his devotion through his philanthropy in Guangdong. In 1902, the Tjong brothers donated 80,000 taels to fund a high school in Guangdong. In 1903, they built a charity temple for the Teochew people in Shantou.[25] Tjong requested county magistrates in Haiyang and Chenghai to issue proclamations urging villagers not to remove survey markers or obstruct construction. Gentry and elders were tasked with restraining clansmen and mediating land purchases.

To deal with the foreign powers, Tjong Yong Hian held a dinner party for foreign consuls and consuls general in Shantou on May 20, 1904. These included Austria-Hungary, Belgium, France, Germany, Great Britain, Italy, Japan, the Netherlands, Norway, and the United States. Tjong Yong Hian was used to dealing with the Dutch in Deli, and parleyed with the foreign consuls about the railway and assured them it wouldn't undercut their influence and the economy.[26]

Finally, the project started. Preliminary surveys were completed in August 1904, and the construction was about to commence. However, a conflict arose between the locals and the Japanese construction team in early 1905. At the village of Anbu (Ampow), about 10 km north of Shantou, the residents refused to allow the railway to pass through their village. Some residents were wealthy merchants who had made a fortune in Singapore, Malaya, Siam, and Saigon. The railway was going to run through a cemetery with about 2000 graves. They refused to move the sacred family graves; some had paid a lot for the best *feng shui* locations. The railway company offered only $50 per acre in compensation for the land, though local valuation placed it at $300 per acre. There was also a report that some Japanese workers were being rude to the women in the village.[27] A rumour was that the Japanese were trying to control the railway through overseas Chinese merchants.

On January 21, the villagers attacked the Japanese workers; twelve Japanese overseers took shelter in a house guarded by Chinese guards.

[24] Yen 1984: 131–132.
[25] Yau 2021: 125; https://kknews.cc/history/nbx2lq5.html.
[26] Idem.
[27] SCMP 27-01-1905.

However, three other Japanese workers arrived at the village without knowing the situation. The mob killed two of them and set fire to a workshed.[28] The Japanese government was upset and demanded punishment for the murderers and compensation for the victims' families. If not fulfilled, the Japanese threatened a national crisis.[29] A group of 200 Chinese soldiers was dispatched to Anbu so that the railway construction could continue.[30] The Japanese representatives demanded heavy compensation of 385,000 taels from the railway company. After a bargain, the settlement was reduced to 175,000 taels. Following the company's contractual liability agreement, Tjong Yong Hian offered 10,000 taels to compensate the two workmen. The compensation was duly accepted as Japan was preoccupied with the Russo-Japanese war. However, the locals' dislike of the Japanese continued throughout the project. Some members of the gentry even remarked that Tjong Yong Hian was a traitor and profiteering from the project, demanded that he be expelled and that railroad rights be cancelled. Tjong Yong Hian carefully resolved these issues.[31]

After two years of complex negotiations and engineering challenges, the Chaozhou–Shantou railway was finally completed. It extended 24 miles (39 km) of standard gauge. The total costs exceeded 3,000,000 taels. However, the question of a Japanese engineer appeared again. Chinese engineers were supposed to be in charge and were sent to Europe and America, but none returned. Thus, Tjong Yong Hian asked Viceroy Shum to allow a Japanese engineer to be in charge. The Viceroy ordered the Magistrate at Swatow to investigate and agreed to engage the Japanese engineer solely to superintend the railway engineering work.[32]

The line was officially opened on November 25, 1906 with Ng Li Hing as the director. A band from the German cruiser Jaguar played on the train's first journey. The opening ceremony guests included Chinese officials, Consuls of various foreign powers, the commissioner, and railway staff (Fig. 12.4).[33] The community was treated to a banquet.[34]

The railroad started from the west gate of Chaozhou city and terminated at Hsialing of Shantou, crossing six stations: Feng Chi, Fou Yang,

[28] SCMP 20-03-1905.
[29] Wright 1908: 680; Godley 1981:153.
[30] SCMP 07-05-1905.
[31] Yen 1984: 132–133.
[32] *Straits Echo* 6-11-1906.
[33] Godley 1981: 154.
[34] *The Singapore Free Press and Mercantile Advertiser* 05-12-1906.

Fig. 12.4 The opening of the Chaozhou and Shantou Railway on November 25, 1906 with Tjong Yong Hian and dignitaries. (Photo courtesy of Rebecca Chandra, used with permission)

Kuan Chow, Tsai Tang, E-bue, and Ampow.[35] The train ran three times a day. It carried around 2000 passengers daily with a fare of 67 cents gold for first class and 27 cents for second class.[36]

It was the first railway line that was entirely financed and managed by Chinese merchants. All existing railways in China had been built by Europeans. This success meant a lot. It showed that the Chinese could finance and build their own railway and bring economic development. Historian Yen Ching Wang remarked that:

It brought self-confidence and national pride to all Chinese.[37]

Tjong Yong Hian was received by Empress Cixi again and awarded the Third-Order Mandarin and Titular Vice-President of the Department of Agriculture, Industries, and Business in Beijing.[38] Empress Cixi gifted a

[35] Fengxi, Fuyang, Guanchao, Caotang, Huamei, and Anbu in Pinyin.
[36] *The Far Eastern Review* November 1909.
[37] Yen 1984: 134.
[38] Godley 1981: 154; SP 10-03-1911.

calligraphic scroll with the character *Shou* (long life) and a drawing of a peony for his birthday. But some shareholders, especially Huang Daojingtang, grew resentful for not receiving recognition and spread rumours, and obstructed company affairs. Tjong Yong Hian, again, had to ask the ministry to resolve the problem).

Tjong Yong Hian's reputation soared in China and over Southeast Asia. When Tjong visited his village Songkou in Meixian, a forerunner announced his arrival with gongs, and villagers had to kneel by the roadside as he passed in a red-topped sedan chair carried by eight uniformed men. He proudly brought glory to the village of his ancestors.[39] When he returned to Medan, the Chinese celebrated his homecoming by hoisting Dutch flags.[40]

Due to this success, another private railroad, the Fukien Railway Co. followed suit in 1905, with a railway line from Amoy (Xiamen).[41] Tjong Yong Hian commissioned the Dutch engineer Martens who worked for the Dutch Indies railway, to conduct a survey for possible railway expansion.[42] In March 1907, the Board of Agriculture, Industry, and Commerce awarded Tjong Yong Hian South China's railroad degree. His name was listed in Cantonese as "His Excellency Cheong Yuk Nam" in the *Twentieth Century Impressions of Hongkong, Shanghai, and other Treaty Ports of China* (1908).[43]

The success brought confidence and was marked by increased interest in Chinese private companies investing in building railways.[44] A proposal from a company to construct a railway from Shantou to Chenghai insisted that no foreigner was allowed to be a shareholder.[45]

The 1911 Revolution in China, which overthrew the Qing Dynasty, began in the summer of 1911. Tjong Yong Hian passed away due to illness in Medan on September 10, 1911. Subsequently, the Republic of China was established on January 1, 1912, four months after Tjong Yong Hian's death. This marked the end of 2132 years of imperial rule in China and concluded the 276-year reign of the Qing Dynasty.

[39] Chang 1984: 73–74.
[40] SP 17-4-1905.
[41] Godley 1981:155.
[42] SCMP 16-04-1907
[43] Wright 1908: 833
[44] *Straits Echo* 8-07-1907
[45] *The Singapore Free Press and Mercantile Advertiser* 03-11-1910.

12.3 The Demise of the Railway

The railway manager position was passed to Tjong Yong Hian's eldest son, Chang Pu Ching (Zhang Buqing). Initially, the railway's senior operations staff were Japanese, including the drivers and guards. The Chinese eventually replaced them in the 1920s.[46] After his father's death, Chang Pu Ching returned to Medan and took over his father's business.[47] The railway management was passed to his brother, Tjong Seng Liong.

At the completion of the railway, the region's economy was growing, and in 1915 the railway carried more than 1 million passengers and about 24,000 tons of goods, with gross earnings of about USD $160,000, boosted the local econmoy, further accelerated Shantou as a modern city.[48] However, by the 1920s, China experienced significant economic and political instability, which affected the value of its currency. Additionally, the demand for railways was declining as the dredging of the local Han River made it navigable for transport, with boats offering a more cost-effective alternative.[49]

After Tjong A Fie's death in 1921, his business affairs were managed by Dolf Kamerlingh Onnes, who in 1923 travelled to Shantou to inspect the struggling Swatow Railway company and invited his nephew, the artist Harm Kamerlingh Onnes, to accompany him. The railway faced financial strain with high maintenance costs and military requisition without payment. Recurrent flooding from the Han river further damaged part of the tracts and operational accidents added to its decline. Harm's illustrated letters from April–May 1923 reveal a line plagued by typhoon damage, poor management, and suspected embezzlement. Though the railway appeared active, Dolf believed large sums were being siphoned off by family members. A visit to Tjong Seng Liong's once-grand mansion exposed decaying opulence and financial ruin, mirroring the state of the enterprise. Dolf spent his days uncovering "tampering" and sending detailed reports to Medan, convinced the Tjong estate was being systematically drained (Fig. 12.5).

Fig. 12.5 *The train of the major* (Buiskool, *De reis van Harm Kamerlingh Onnes* 1999:151,154)

[46] Yen 1984.

[47] Feldwick 1917: 1195.

[48] Hannon 1916: 2.

[49] The Chinese Economic Bulletin Vo. VII No. 228. July 4, 1925: 27.

In 1935, Tjong A Fie's daughter, Queeny Chang (Zhang Fuyin) took over the management. In 1938, the Japanese started bombing Shantou, aiming to capture it, and the railway was bombed in March 1939.[50] Anticipating the Japanese landing in early June 1939, the Kuomintang army ordered part of the tracks to be destroyed. The irony is that the Japanese engineers built the railway line, and 35 years later, it was dismantled to prevent the Japanese from using it. The Japanese landed in Shantou in late June, and in July 1939, the railway line became a battleground between the Chinese and Japanese armies.[51] Soon, Shantou was captured by the Japanese.

Although the railway spanned a modest distance of 40 km, was not integrated with other lines, and had a brief operational lifespan of 33 years, this endeavour highlights Tjong Yong Hian's leadership in introducing modern enterprise. As a businessman from Medan, his efforts set a precedent for national pride and confidence at a time when the Chinese were often perceived as outdated, contributing to a transformation in societal attitudes.[52]

[50] *The Singapore Free Press and Mercantile Advertiser* 23 -06-1938; *Malaya Tribune* 10-03-1939.(There is a report from 1935 about the railway from the KPM. In that year Mr. van Riet of the KPM travelled from Hong Kong to the Mui Yuen district. For the Chaochowfu-Swatow part of his journey he took the train. Mr. Van Riet: "The first class compartments were leather furnished, at least this was our impression we got from the remnants. The seats were very narrow. This was probably caused by the fact that these wagons were built in Osaka (1905). The locomotive dated from 1906 and was American made. All wagons were connected by bridges (overflows) so that one could step easy from one wagon into the other [...] I forgot to inform, that the Chaochowfu – Swatow railway has been established by a Belawan Deli Chinese, who nowadays however has only a part of the shares". (Extract from letter, pa. no. 1021 d.d. 28.5.35. No. 142. ARA tweede afdeling, archief KPM, 387; KPM or Koninklijke Paketvaart Maatschappij (Royal Dutch Package Company) for the sea transport within the Indonesian archipelago.) (Buiskool 2025:126). Mrs. Lemye-Tjong, the younger sister of Queeny Chang, still saw shares of the Swatow railway in 1957, after that no more. (Interview Mrs. Lemye-Tjong in Brussels at 13-03-1992)

[51] *The China Critic* 27-07-1939.

[52] Godley 1981: 155.

CHAPTER 13

Law Ah Yok, the Father of Medan's Chinatown

Kampong Law Ah Yok, now known as Sukaramai, which translates to "pleasantly busy," forms the core of Medan's Chinatown on the eastern side. Developed in the 1910s under the pioneering efforts of Law Ah Yok, it began as a marginal settlement amid neighbouring *kampongs* and plantations. Over the past century, the area has transformed from a notorious slum into a dense commercial and culinary hub (Fig. 13.1).

At the beginning of the twentieth century, Medan was known as a trading centre on the East Coast of Sumatra. It had a large population of Chinese. The 1905 census recorded 13,205 people, comprising 48% Chinese, 28% Indigenous, 7% European. The Chinese dominated retail and trade. However, not all Chinese were wealthy merchants, a misconception that still lingers today. The 1905 survey of the East Coast of Sumatra revealed that among the Chinese, 44% were merchants, 22% had small industries and crafts, and the remainder were underprivileged.[1] That survey did not include more than 20,000 Chinese working as coolies in tobacco plantations. The impoverished Chinese worked as labourers, servants, and rickshaw pullers.

A significant portion of the Chinese population in Medan, estimated at least one-third, could not afford to live in the Chinese quarter and had to settle in *kampongs* on the city's outskirts. As a community that cared for its own, someone needed to step up to assist these individuals. Law Ah

[1] Buiskool 2025: 307.

B. Minasny, D. A. Buiskool, *Stories from Medan, Volume 1*,
https://doi.org/10.1007/978-981-95-7707-1_13

Fig. 13.1 Law Ah Yok (photo courtesy of Suriadi Lau)

Yok emerged as a champion for the poor Chinese. He was a businessman, construction developer, and contractor who resided in Medan from 1900 to the 1930s. Law Ah Yok was responsible for constructing a village called Kampong Law Ah Yok to provide affordable houses to support these underserved individuals. Unfortunately, he had been forgotten with time, and little was known about him. Here is a brief glimpse into his life, compiled from Dutch newspaper articles and his family's traditions.

13.1 A Brief Story of Law Ah Yok

Law Ah Yok or Lau A Yok or Liu Ayu (劉阿煜) or Liu Zengyi (劉增煜) was born around 1870 in Taishan, southwest of Guangdong province in China. His early life is unknown, but he appeared in Medan in the early 1900s as an architect, construction developer, and contractor (Fig. 13.2).[2] As the town of Medan was being constructed, Law Ah Yok and other businessmen, such as Khoe Tjin Tek, found prosperity in building houses.

[2] DC 13-06-1907.

Fig. 13.2 Law Ah Yok (photo courtesy of Suriadi Lau)

His office and warehouse were located on Djalan Kling (now Jl. Irian Barat) near the race track, where he built and renovated houses and sold supplies such as timber and cement.

Law Ah Yok was a successful contractor, and in 1910, he was invited to a discussion with members of the Medan city council and Tjong A Fie regarding the construction of the first cinema in Medan. Law Ah Yok was in negotiation with the Deli company for the lease of land near the race track. Unfortunately, after conducting a thorough investigation, it was discovered that the land was unsuitable for the permanent construction of the cinema.

Because of his successful business, the road where his shop was located was called Djalan Law Ah Yok. It was next to the race track, and later renamed Hailokhongstraat (now Jl. Pandan) (Figs. 13.3 and 13.4). Djalan Law Ah Yok served as the hub for the local Chinese and Indigenous population, and it featured Malay theatres at night. The street was especially

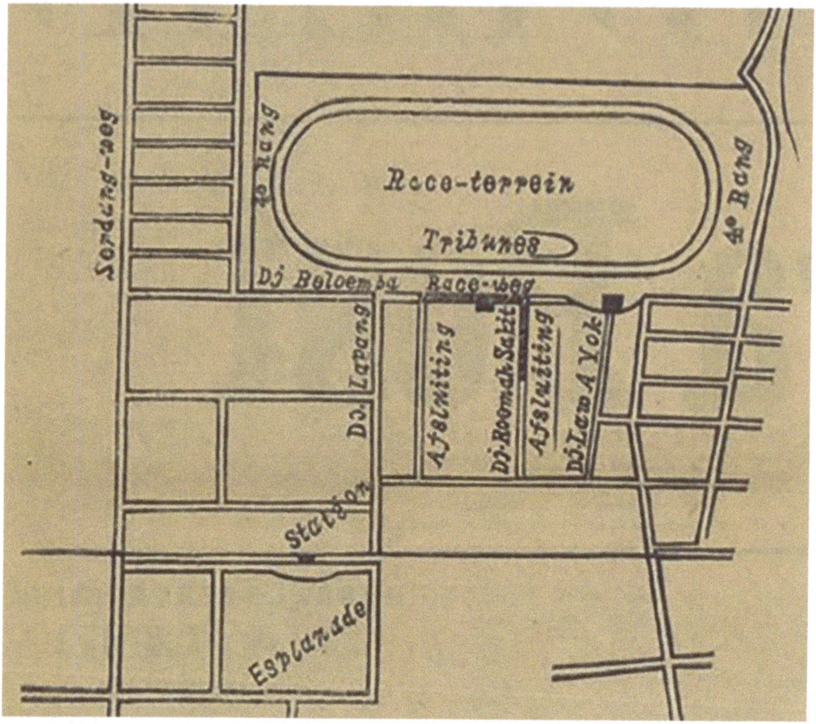

Fig. 13.3 Djalan Law A yok, named for the street where Law Ah Yok's business was located (SP 15-05-1911). It was renamed to Hailokhongstraat in 1911 and currently known as Jl. Pandan

popular for hosting *bangsawan* shows performed in tents in the evening. *Bangsawan* is a Malay theatrical performance often featuring European-themed plays, complete with songs and dances. For example, in July 1911, Law Ah Yok Street hosted a performance of Shylock, the Merchant of Venice. In August of the same year, the Indra Mahnikam Theatre Company of the Federated Malay States presented Aladin Lampoe Adjaib (Aladdin and the magic lamp). Djalan Law A Yok was renamed to Hailokhongstraat in 1911.

Law Ah Yok's first marriage resulted in no children, leading him to adopt a son and a daughter. His adopted son later moved to Bandjarmasin and became a navy officer, known as Kapten Lau. Subsequently, he had a

Fig. 13.4 Law Ah Yok's construction and builder company on the right on Kwanteebiostraat (Jl. Irian Barat) in 1913 (Fujisaki, Geheugen Delpher)

second marriage to a girl from his village. On June 7, 1912, Law Hien Khoen, his first son, was born, bringing immense joy. Overflowing with happiness, he announced a grand celebration at the *Deli Courant*, inviting all his friends.[3] In the years that followed, Law Ah Yok had three more daughters.

Besides being a contractor, Law Ah Yok also had several businesses, including a trading company N.V. Handel Mij Seew Nam Kongsie, established in November 1918 in Kesawan with a capital of *f*50,000.[4] The company traded gold, jewellery and watches.[5]

Law Ah Yok was known for his charitable work, particularly for the homeless. In 1921, a newspaper article noted that his house, located on the corner of Hakka and Wilhelmina street, was dilapidated and had been repeatedly condemned for demolition. Nonetheless, it was repeatedly patched and served as a shelter for new arrivals in Medan who needed a place to stay.[6] Law Ah Yok was president of the Cantonese Society of

[3] DC 06-06-1912.
[4] *Indische Mercuur* 15-11-1918.
[5] SP 23-08-1921.
[6] SP 02-03-1921.

Medan, Kwong Tong Kong Soh (Guangdong Gongsuo). The organisation helped and organised charity and funerals for the Cantonese people, with the Cantonese cemetery at Kampong Doerian. The organisation had existed for a long time but was only registered with the government in 1922.

Around 1915, he acquired a piece of land at the end of Julianastraat (now Jalan Asia), on the outskirts of the city, building houses for the poor Chinese. This new area was called Djalan Law Ah Yok.

Over time, the business of Law Ah Yok did not go well. The family tradition says that Law Ah Yok was involved as a guarantor for a friend who proved to be dishonest and lost his money in court.[7] At an occasion, Law Ah Yok had to borrow money from a Chetty or Indian moneylender by mortgaging 22,900 m^2 of land at Kampong Soekaramai. As Law Ah Yok failed to pay the interest, the property was sold by the moneylender.[8]

His company N.V. Handel Mij Seew Nam Kongsie was declared bankrupt in September 1924.[9] Law A Yok himself declared bankruptcy in Medan in 1923, and in 1930, the Council of Justice at Batavia declared his bankruptcy while residing in Pontianak. N.V. Handel Mij Law Ah Yok was declared bankrupt in May 1935. In 1931, he established Lai Kwong Siong Giep & Co. at Laboeanweg in Gloegoer, a small village on the outskirts of town. He became a second-hand car dealer and acted as a traditional Chinese medicine doctor. His failure seemed to affect the Cantonese society, with Vereeniging Kwang Tong Kong Soh declared bankrupt in 1936.[10] In the end, he lost most of his wealth. He died around 1941 at the age of 70, and the Japanese occupation plunged the family into hardship).

13.2 Kampong Law Ah Yok and Soekaramai

Around 1915, Law Ah Yok bought a large area located at the end of Julianastraat (current Jl. Asia). The *kampong*, named after its founder, Law Ah Yok, was located on the outskirts of the Medan municipality. At the end of Julianastraat, a gate with a sign "N.V. Law Ah Yok" marked the entrance to the Law Ah Yok village.[11] Law Ah Yok established his large

[7] Information from Suriadi Lau.

[8] *Indisch tijdschrift van het recht; orgaan der Nederlandsch-Indische Juristen-Vereeniging*, 1931, Deel: Deel honderd drie en dertig, 01-01-1931: 498–502.

[9] SP 22-08-1924.

[10] SP 15-08-1936.

[11] N.V. is Naamloze Vennootschap, literaly means "nameless partnership," refers to a public limited company.

Fig. 13.5 Law Ah Yok gate (photo from Chang Yoh Shen, *A Memorandum for Thirty Year's Cultivation in Nanyang* of Dr. Chang Yoh Shen, Special volume prepared on the occasion of Zhang Hongnan being an official of the Dutch administration for 30 years in 1916)

home in this area. In addition, simple wooden houses were constructed and rented out for a reasonable fee (Fig. 13.5).

Next to Law Ah Yok Street was Kampong Soekaramai, which was under the Sultan's governance. This *kampong* was created when the Deli Railway Company required land for its workshops in Poeloe Brajan in the 1910s. To acquire the land in Poeloe Brajan, the company offered a new plot to the local residents in exchange for their existing property. A strip of land 250 m wide, next to Medan Estate, adjacent to Soengei Rengas and Kota Ma'soem (Matsoem, the Sultan's *kampong* on lands which were owned by the Sultan of Deli) was selected for this purpose. An agreement was reached in January 1917 with the Sultan to acquire the 40-hectare land. The Deli Company, which had a concession of the land, returned it to the Sultan for the settlement of the Indigenous people and it was calles Soekaramai.[12]

[12] Gemeente Medan 1924: 30–31.

In March 1917, Law Ah Yok requested an extension of his land to Kampong Soekaramai. An additional agreement was added to the contract, granting Law Ah Yok permission to settle on the northern section of Soekaramai. The governor subsequently approved this agreement on May 21, 1917 (Fig. 13.6).

A few years later, Law Ah Yok expressed interest in acquiring a larger plot of land in Soekaramai by purchasing the rights of his indigenous neighbours. The Deli Company did not object to the transfer of superficies rights. However, no consultation was held with the municipality of Medan, despite the land being close to the municipal boundaries.[13]

Law Ah Yok established a coconut plantation and also provided houses to the less privileged Chinese, and to newcomers to Medan seeking work. He was known for his generosity and also provided Chinese medicine to those who were sick. Later in his life, he became a traditional Chinese medicine practitioner.[14]

Sultan's *kampongs*, including Soekaramai, Soengei Kerah-Pertjoet, Soengei Rengas, Kota Ma'soem, and Sukaradja, were located within the

Fig. 13.6 Law Ah Yok's plantation around 1911 (photo courtesy of Suriadi Lau)

[13] Gemeente Medan 1924: 30–31.
[14] SP 25-01-1940.

limits of the Medan municipality and were governed by the Sultan, not the municipality of Medan. Kampong Soekaramai had a dirt road stretching about 1.5 km, with a little village square in the middle. The primary road connected to the city via two entry points: the extended Julianastraat and Djalan Antara. As a result, the residents of Soekaramai had to pass through the Law Ah Yok gate to reach the city. When the gate was closed, residents of Soekaramai had to take the long way to Djalan Antara to reach the city.

The houses in the *kampong* were densely populated and were referred to as *petakhuis* (rumah petak), small square-shaped dwellings that accommodated a single household with no paved roads, only muddy paths. The *kampong* was densely populated and frequently reported incidents of fights, theft, drunkenness, and even murder. While some Chinese lived in Soekarame, the relationship could turn tense. In 1932, the Sultan issued a regulation barring Chinese and Arab residents from living or opening businesses in Soekaramai and Kota Matsoem, aiming to shield indigenous traders from competition.[15]

After Law Ah Yok's bankruptcy, the ownership of the houses in Kampong Law Ah Yok passed on to other Chinese individuals who rented them out at affordable rates.[16] The Dutch referred to the area as Law Ah Yok *nederzetting* or settlement. It became a notorious slum plagued by frequent outbreaks of violence. The residents lived in small *petak* houses, which also served as home-based industries such as coconut oil pressing, bakeries, and *es lilin* (ice lolly) production, enabling them to make a livelihood. A report in *De Sumatra Post* described the settlement as a breeding ground for injustice and unsanitary conditions.[17] Beyond the confines of the settlement, one could find vast coffee and rubber plantations.

The wooden houses in Kampong Law Ah Yok made them highly susceptible to fires. Half an hour before midnight in July 1937, a large fire blazed through Law Ah Yok street. The fire was so huge that it was visible in the Medan city centre. Fire engines rushed through, but the fire had already consumed 12 houses. *De Sumatra Post* reported:

> *A wooden pondok (simple cottage) covered with zinc plating, housing twenty "pintoes", providing housing for many Chinese families and a hearth of uncleanness and poverty, - the settlement falls short of urban hygiene regula-*

[15] SP 25-04-1932.
[16] SP 16-07-1937.
[17] SP 16-07-1937.

> *tions and is an eyesore- appeared to be ablaze. There was no stopping it, the flames rose high. It was fortunate that the wind was favourable, so that with little difficulty the remaining three pondoks of the same structure as the now burnt down ones could be saved.*[18]

A man called Kou A San, who ran a bread bakery on the corner of the *pondok*[19] started the fire through gross carelessness. He spilled some burning charcoal while baking biscuits, causing the wooden shack to catch fire.

Despite being a slum area with frequent violence and fire hazards, the Chinese community in Kampong Law Ah Yok maintained a strong spirit of mutual aid. Many charitable foundations and schools were established to help the community. With assistance from the Chinese Consul Huang Tienmai, an asylum for impoverished Chinese individuals was established at Djalan Law Ah Yok in 1934.[20] The association received financial support from Singaporean millionaire Aw Boon Haw and provided temporary lodging for physically challenged individuals while also facilitating the repatriation of Chinese people. In 1940, the association offered shelter to 300 destitute Chinese individuals from Belawan.[21]

In 1934, Ng Ho Hian, a prosperous merchant involved in duckling rearing, constructed a housing complex for the poor and a public swimming pool in Kampong Law Ah Yok, intended specifically for Chinese and indigenous communities. These facilities were created in response to indirect racial segregation, which barred non-Europeans from using the European swimming pool, while bathing in the nearby Gedong Djohore River posed safety risks. The swimming school attached to the pool offered affordable lessons. Despite these intentions, the pool attracted few users and was forced to close in 1935. Ng Ho Hian also established several charitable foundations and schools serving the Chinese and their children in Kampong Law Ah Yok. He later proposed the construction of a second swimming pool on Avroslaan, but this plan was abandoned following the failure of the first facility.[22]

[18] SP 16-07-1937.
[19] A small wooden house
[20] SP 16-05-1934.
[21] SP 10-01-1934.
[22] Buiskool 2025: 232; SP 05-01-1935.

13.3 Law Ah Yok Village and Chinese Settlement

After the war, the revolutionary fighting between Indonesians and the Dutch caused many Chinese living outside Medan to lose their homes and businesses. During the Dutch police action in 1947, Indonesian fighters conducted a scorch and burn operation in the town of Pangkalan Berandan, the centre of the oil industry. Many Chinese refugees fled to Medan and they were temporarily housed in two large warehouses in *kampong* Law Ah Yok, between current Jalan Emas, Suasa, and Kuningan. These warehouses were made of red zinc panels and were known as Hong Niu Lang, or the Red Warehouses. This boosted the population in the Kampong Law Ah Yok. Most of the refugees were from Guangdong, and spoke the Huizhou dialect. The residents included carpenters, cement workers, and food sellers. The area was still largely agricultural land with rubber and coconut trees. Some Chinese settled and grew vegetables.

In 1952, a storm struck Kampong Soekarame, leaving roughly 1500 people homeless, with the Chinese-inhabited area being the hardest hit.[23] The refugees had to move to various locations. Some had saved enough money to find their own settlements, while others had to rely on aid and were relocated to other areas. As the population increased, people began small businesses and constructed simple houses, despite the lack of formal ownership.

Kampong Law Ah Yok expanded with residential alleys, which connected with neighbouring alleys, creating an inter-connected area. Soon, the *kampong* extended eastwards to the Galeng Galeng ditch area, forming a complex of alleys, most of which were lined with simple wooden houses. It eventually merged with Kampong Sukarame, and was administratively called Kelurahan Sukaramai II, covering an area from current Jalan Besi up to Jalan AR Hakim (*kereta api*), which marks the border with the old Medan Estate. The original Sukarame is now known as Kelurahan Sukaramai I. Despite the name change, Kampong Law Ah Yok continued to be referred to as Kampong Cina or Chinese village and remained a slum with landmarks such as the big sewer, Kebon Pisang, and the railway line. The area became home to Chinese settlements and expanded eastwards, forming a complex network of alleyways with simple wooden houses. The inhabitants established a market, Pasar Sukaramai, selling vegetables, fruits, meats, clothing, and other necessities. A school was also established in 1952 for poor migrant children.[24] Living

[23] *Het Nieuwsblad voor Sumatra* 13-06-1952.

[24] Yizhibi 2015: 106–109.

conditions were harsh, with people struggling to make a living. Nevertheless, the community remained resilient, and a charitable mutual aid organisation was formed to protect residents from extortion and harassment.

Frequent fires still plagued the densely populated area of Kampong Law A Yok. In 1979, a massive fire destroyed half of the wooden homes with *atap* roofs, leaving an estimated 13,000 people homeless. Later, more permanent brick houses called "barack" were built, and in 1986, public housing in the form of apartments was constructed. The solidarity of the Chinese people living in the area is very strong, and in the spirit of Law Ah Yok, people help each other. Despite this setback, the village continued to grow, and as time passed, Sukaramai was transformed from a simple settlement to a bustling commercial area. In the past 20 years, the area has emerged from poverty and is now known as Asia Mega Mas, a bustling Chinatown with multi-story buildings and new shophouses. It has become a thriving commercial hub with various businesses and is also known as a culinary hub.[25]

Law Ah Yok was a pioneer in building a settlement for poor Chinese. As an *aanemer*, builder, and contractor, he paved the way for his Cantonese compatriots in Medan to become builders of many important structures. The Medan's Warenhuis was built by contractor Ng Ah Tan; the Rex cinema by Liew A Pho; Derikanpark was constructed by one of his former employees, Li Ah Kui; and St. Elizabeth Hospital was built by Li Ngan Chiong through his company, Kong Tong Seng.

Today, his legacy lives on as the area he founded has become a vibrant and thriving community. Though largely forgotten, Law Ah Yok's contributions to the community deserve recognition. He is to be celebrated as a champion of the poor, with his impact on par with other notable figures like Tjong A Fie.

In recent times, the youth residing in the area have established the "Law Ah Yok Brotherhood" group.[26] They appreciate Law Ah Yok for his altruism in helping fellow countrymen and his strong emphasis on friendship and loyalty. The group has taken to TikTok to honour Law Ah Yok's spirit and to promote inspiring stories. Suriadi Lau, Law Ah Yok's great-grandson and a current resident of Jakarta, is grateful that his ancestor's legacy is now receiving recognition and can be shared with the world.[27]

[25] Yizhibi 2015: 99–101.

[26] https://www.tiktok.com/@lauahyok.

[27] The initial publication of this story on the web led Suriadi Lau to reconnect with his long-lost cousin, the great-grandson of Law Ah Yok's brother in Canada. They later reunited and travelled to Thai San to visit their ancestral hometown.

CHAPTER 14

Rickshaws in Medan

In January 1947, the Pao An Tui (Chinese Security Corps) of Medan burned the remaining man-pulled rickshaws of around a hundred vehicles in a ceremonial bonfire, ending their existence. Tan Wee Beng, the vice president of Pao An Tui, said that the bonfire was a landmark in the local history and a symbol of a new spirit.[1] Man-pulled rickshaws were once a common mode of transport in Medan, serving the city for over 60 years before eventually disappearing (Fig. 14.1).

In the early 1900s, transportation options in Medan were limited, making rickshaws and *sado* carts the most popular means of getting around. Automobiles began appearing around 1906, but they were expensive and primarily used for tourism rather than daily transport. [2] The Hokkien community referred to the rickshaw as *angkong*, a hand-pulled cart operated by Chinese coolies. Dutch residents misheard the term and referred to it as *Hongkong*. The *sado*, derived from the French *dos-à-dos* and known locally as *kereta sewa*, was a hired horse-drawn carriage driven by a *koesir* (from the Dutch *koetsier*, meaning a coachman).

The man-pulled cart had been around for a long time; it originated from Japan in 1869, called *jin rikisha* (*jin* = human, *riki* = power, *sha* = vehicle), or human-powered vehicle.[3] Rickshaws emerged in Japan in the

[1] *Sunday Tribune* (Singapore) 09-02-1947.
[2] SP 16-01-1906.
[3] Warren 2003:14–15.

B. Minasny, D. A. Buiskool, *Stories from Medan, Volume 1*,
https://doi.org/10.1007/978-981-95-7707-1_14

Fig. 14.1 A rickshaw in Medan (Tropenmuseum 10013834)

late 1860s (often dated to 1869) and were quickly commercialised in Tokyo in the early 1870s. They were introduced to Singapore in 1880 and subsequently made their way to Medan in the early 1880s. Rickshaws were also found in China, the French colony in Indo-China (called *pousse-pousse*), the British colonies of the Straits (Penang and Singapore), Ceylon (Colombo), and India. They were even found in Durban, Natal, South Africa.[4]

In the Dutch Indies, rickshaws could only be found in Medan, Koeta Radja (current Banda Aceh), and Palembang,[5] but not in Java or other islands. The rickshaw was a popular mode of transport for the citizens of Medan, often featured in Dutch colonial literature describing encounters with Chinese rickshaw drivers.

> *The rickshaw was a high two-wheeled cart, a kind of wheeled chair with two long poles, between which a Chinese puller moved, half-naked with a small dirty towel around his neck. When it rained, there were sails stretched around it so*

[4] SP 15-12-1930.

[5] In Palembang, rickshaw was called betja (Poortenaar and Poortenaar-van Vladeracken, 1925: 38).

that one could only stick one's head out of it for a moment. The rickshaw puller threw a goni sack or a furry cloak about his skinny shoulders. Click-clack-click--clack got you where you needed to be in the cracking beast weather... it usually only started after an endless debate about the price, a fierce tawar (bargaining)...[6]

Initially, rickshaws were mostly used in the evenings because horse--drawn carriages were used during the day. In the 1910s, the fee of *f*0.10–0.20 would take one from Hotel de Boer to home. On rural roads, the fee was *f*0.10–0.20 per kilometre.[7]

14.1 Inhumane Profession

Many Chinese considered rickshaw pulling as a demeaning and inhumane profession. The pullers were Chinese coolies who came from poor villages in China or were ex-plantation coolies.

The Dutch female author Carry van Bruggen, who lived in Medan from 1904 to 1907, wrote about the inhumane profession of the rick-shaw coolie:

They moved like beasts and the people who sat in the carts looked indifferent, accustomed to the crooked, sweating bodies before them ... Henriet had felt a physical sorrow, like a painful throbbing in the lower part of her chest, and she had told her husband, then told her, that she would never, ever want to sit in such a terrible cart ... don't you think it's awfully cruel to sit in such a cart and be pulled by such a poor Chinese?[8]

A visitor from Batavia in 1932 wrote:

Medan is the only town in Indonesia where we can see Chinese people "horses". As ones who love sports, we admire the human vehicle puller the way they run and their tenacity, as fellow human beings we feel sorry for them, as fellow Chinese we feel the pain.[9]

[6] *Het Nieuwsblad voor Sumatra* 18-05-1949.

[7] Langereis 1918: 27.

[8] Carry van Bruggen (1881–1932), Jan Fontijn and Diny Schouten De Engelbewaarder 92-98 Amsterdam Oktober 1987.

[9] "*Medan ada satoe-satoenja kota di Indonesia dimana orang bisa liat "koeda-koeda" Tionghoa. Sebagi orang jang soeka sport kita kagoemin itoe toekang langtjia poenja tjara lari*

The Hokkien people also called it *lang chia* (meaning human vehicle), and the Malay called it *kereta koeda kaki doea*,[10] the two-legged horse cart.

In 1896, the Deli Race Club held a rickshaw race as part of the equestrian event to amuse the audience:

> *it took off as fast as the legs of a Hong Kong Chinese dragging through the mud can run, the shattered hoods of the shaws banged melodically on the barges, the grateful passengers hissed and made all kinds of noises to cheer their pulling friends, who sometimes roared along to this end. It was a strange noise and sight. Three were declared winners, but all the rest also received a grateful reward and grinned more than satisfied. The end of the day could be regarded as a good health cure, many a liver was shaken vigorously, everyone had a good laugh.*[11]

The rickshaw race event in 1900 was cancelled and replaced with a *sado* race.[12] Most probably, the Chinese did not want their fellow countrymen to be humiliated.

14.1.1 Rickshaw Coolies and Europeans

Rickshaw pullers frequently waited outside hotels to offer services to European guests visiting Medan. Planters going to a party on *hari besar* found them to be a useful means of transport to wander around at night. The noise caused by rickshaw riders at 1–2 AM prompted complaints from local residents.[13]

Their lives and interactions were often portrayed in literary works. László Szèkely portrayed a rickshaw puller as both hardworking and cunning. In the short story titled *Career of Chaw A Hjong*, Szèkely depicted:

> *...he trotted for a day, sweating and panting for a rickshaw. In a run, he drew on countrymen born under a happier star as well as the rulers of the world, the whites. At the end of the day, he returned the rickshaw to its owner, counted ninety percent of his earnings as rent, and, with the few pennies left, crawled*

dan kaoeletan, sebagi sesama manoesia, kita merasa kasian, sebagi sesama Tionghoa kita merasa perih" (*Sin Po* 12-11-1932).

[10] *Pertja Timoer* 26-11-1927.

[11] DC 29-08-1896.

[12] SP 01-10-1900.

[13] DC 28-03-1894.

back to his twisty, maze-like neighbourhood; or he would sit on a street corner begging, his wounded feet sticking out.[14]

Dutch author Annie Salomons wrote a more empathetic narrative in *Verhalen uit het Verre Oosten* (1930), or Stories from the Far East, about the relationship between a rickshaw puller and his Dutch customer. Every Saturday night at seven, Ah Lim came to pick up the Dutchman to go to the club. Five hours later, he returned to bring his customer home. They formed a friendship. One day, the Dutchman paid Ah Lim one guilder, and Ah Lim had no change. The Dutchman said to keep the change and went away on holiday for five months. After his return, one night at 7 o'clock, he heard the familiar shuffling of bare feet and a small cough at the front porch. There was Ah Lim, grinning under his large straw hat. Ah Lim said he visited the house regularly to see if the *toean* had returned. The Dutchman was moved. When they arrived at the club, the Dutchman wanted to pay him half a guilder, but Ah Lim refused because he had already given him a guilder five months ago. He told the story of the rickshaw driver to his mates at the club, but no one cared. After that, the friendship between the rickshaw driver and the Dutchman became closer than ever. Rain or sun, Ah Lim was always ready to take the Dutchman to a concert, to the office, or home.[15]

In the novel *Piong Pan Ho* (1894) by J. Dermoût, Ah Lim was described as an honest rickshaw puller. He only accepted as much money as he deemed appropriate, and if he had no change, he would return it at the next ride. He formed a friendship with his Dutch customer, and when Ah Lim's "driver's licence" was taken away, he visited the Dutchman and begged him for help. The Dutchman sympathetically helped him. He saw Ah Lim as a stranger in a foreign land, exactly like himself.[16]

H. Tscherning Petersen, a Danish planter who was in Deli in the 1930s, described his friendship with a rickshaw coolie called Chang. As Petersen got on the rickshaw, Chang dashed and ran through the streets of Medan with great energy. Finally, Chang stopped and said sorry, *Minta ampoen Toean* (I am sorry, Sir). He was so energetic because he was losing face with other rickshaw pullers who looked down on him as his vehicle was in such a dilapidated state that no white man would ride in it. Now that he

[14] *Indische Letteren* 10, 1995:207.
[15] Dharmowijono 2009: 256–258.
[16] Dharmowijono 2009: 259.

had a white man riding his rickshaw, he was proud and ran around showing off. The coolie offered a free ride, but Petersen could not accept it and handed him a silver piece. Petersen learned that even a wretched coolie could lose face, and such a loss could be as hard on him as it would be on any other man.[17]

In reality, rickshaw pullers were poor Chinese who had to work hard to support their families. They usually did not own the rickshaws but rented them from rickshaw bosses (*taukeh*) from Henghua and Hokchia clans, who charged a daily fee. In 1921, there were 30 rickshaw *taukeh*s in Medan.[18] Many pullers were often trapped in gambling debts and opium addiction. In Singapore, rickshaws were widely used but also heavily criticised, and rickshaw pulling was even called a murderous vocation as many pullers only lived to half the lifespan of an average person. Heart attacks, diseases, and traffic accidents or crimes were common causes of death of rickshaw pullers.[19]

14.1.2 Regulations

Initially unregulated, the rickshaw system drew Dutch complaints over its safety and cleanliness.

> *Broken axles held with a piece of wood or wheels with broken or torn spokes can sometimes have fatal consequences .... Also very fatal is the smearing of the hong kongs with shoe polish or other black substance, because in rainy weather, when the hood is closed, one comes out like a chimney sweep .... Yesterday evening in the vicinity of the Medan Hotel, two hongkongs lost their lives....*[20]

One reporter wrote that the rickshaw was used for transporting both goods and passengers; fish was transported in the morning, and a European would sit on the seat at night.[21]

Soon, the municipality of Medan established a regulation that rickshaws needed to be registered and inspected twice a year. Rickshaws could only carry one person and travel within the boundary of the city of Medan. Upon inspection, rickshaws deemed unsafe were rejected and marked with

[17] Petersen 1948: 41–42.
[18] *Verslag Betreffende de Gemeente Medan* Over het Jaar 1921.
[19] Warren 2003: 258–282.
[20] SP 29-05-1899.
[21] SP 15-04-1902.

rejection marks. However, the rickshaw drivers and owners came up with various ways to tamper with the registration, such as covering the rejection marks with paint, using fake number plates, showing up for inspection with new vehicles but later taking the numbers off them to put them on old rickshaws, or replacing new parts with old ones after the inspection.

The regulator then invented a new way; instead of marking rejected vehicles, they would mark the approved ones with an official stamp with the letters PK (*Politie Keur* or police approved). The rickshaw bosses were unhappy with this new form of registration, and the rickshaw pullers staged a strike, resulting in no rickshaws being available on the streets. The chief of local government ordered the commissioner of police to deny the unwilling bosses their licences.[22] Soon, the strike was called off as people were choosing to take the *sado*.[23]

In 1922, another regulation was made that the rickshaw puller should not have any skin or infectious disease, and while he was working, he had to wear clean clothes.[24] And the police set another rule for rickshaws that waited outside the Hotel de Boer and at the Medan Hotel. The pullers used to race each other to reach a customer who hailed a rickshaw. The regulation said that rickshaws had to stay in a line in front of the hotel to prevent disorder. Those who wished to use a rickshaw could choose one themselves or send a "boy" from the hotel to fetch one.[25] In 1921, there was a complaint about the low rate of hiring rickshaws, which was just 20 cents per hour, and thus the *sado* and rickshaw rate was fixed at 90 cents per hour.[26]

14.2 The Rickshaw Issue in the Municipality Council

The status of the rickshaw became a contentious issue within the Chinese community and was frequently debated in the Medan municipal council.[27] Since the beginning of the twentieth century, which marked the Chinese revolution, rickshaw pulling was seen as a degrading job, inhumane, and

[22] DC 16-10-1914.
[23] *Het Nieuws van den dag voor Nederlandsch-Indië* 16-10-1914.
[24] *Javasche Courant* 18-11-1922.
[25] SP 25-01-1927.
[26] DC 05-09-1921.
[27] Buiskool 2025: 256–258.

humiliating to the Chinese national self-esteem.[28] The Chinese-Malay--language newspaper *Andalas* wrote:

> *If the Chinese in Medan do not like to see their own race walk like a horse with a carriage, the Chinese organisations should protest against this humiliating business. The twentieth century is the age of nationalism; look at the Japanese, they are self assured and proud of themselves. The Chinese should also be that way, we should take an example of the Japanese.*[29]

Some Dutch, however, did not see anything wrong with it; an editorial wrote:

> *Why pulling a light wagon with a man in it is dishonourable and humiliating, and pulling a barge with people in it is not, has never been explained by the proponents of the movement.*[30]

In 1914, at the Medan Municipal Council meeting, the Major of the Chinese, Tjong A Fie, requested the Assistant Resident to ban rickshaws. Tjong A Fie considered pulling a cart in which people were seated as an unworthy profession. Moreover, it was harmful to the health of the puller. However, the Assistant Resident had found it was impossible to ban all the rickshaws at once, as it would create 800 unemployed people.[31]

In May 1916, council members Tjong A Fie and van den Brand proposed that the Town Council establish a special commission to study the prohibition of rickshaws in Medan.[32] Two years later, in 1918, councillor van den Brand recalled Major Tjong A Fie's proposal and that rickshaws should be banned on moral grounds. However, the proposal was rejected; as a compromise, the council set a rule to ensure that only physically fit people could pull the rickshaw.[33]

The topic of rickshaws was regularly re-discussed in Medan city council meetings. In 1918, Tan Boen An, a newly chosen council member representing

[28] SP 04-05-1916, 09-05-1916, 10-5-1916, 11-05-1916, 16-05-1916.

[29] *Andalas* 13-08-1918.

[30] SP 15-12-1930. The writer compared the rickshaw puller with the old style of sail- and horse-drawn boat specific to the Netherlands, where it was used for centuries as a means of passenger traffic between cities along trekvaarten, or tow-canals. However, these barges were in general pulled by a horse and not by a man.

[31] *Algemeen Handelsblad* 19-12-1914.

[32] SP 04-05-1916, 09-05-1916, 10-05-1916, 11-05-1916, 16-05-1916.

[33] SP 16-05-1918.

the Chinese community, pleaded for the abolition of the rickshaw business, but it was defeated.[34] The debate exposed a recurring colonial tension: European comfort depended on Chinese labour, yet Europeans could simultaneously condemn the practice as inhumane while insisting it remain available.

There was one anecdote, however, though it was not clear in what year and which council members were involved, where it was the other way round. The Chinese councillor defended the rickshaw profession. At this city council session, a European protested against the "inhumanity" and said that the heavy work caused rickshaw men's unhealthy appearance. Then a Chinese councillor stood up and smiled, saying that he found the humanity of the Western councillors very moving. The Chinese councillor argued that rickshaw was in fact a very lucrative profession, that the work was not that bad in practice, and that the driver's skinniness was caused by opium addiction. To support his argument, a rickshaw was brought to the town hall. The Chinese member sat on it, and a Dutchman trotted him around the Esplanade. It went well, and so the rickshaws were saved again from abolition.[35]

In September 1919, the Chinese of Koeta Radja in Atjeh burned all the rickshaws.[36] But rickshaws remained in Medan and Palembang. In Medan, the rickshaw number even increased. In 1916, it was 669, and the number was boosted to 873 by 1923.[37] Finally, at the council meeting of the municipality of Medan on October 27, 1926, Medan council member Gan Hoat Soei proposed the gradual abolition of the rickshaws. The council accepted the proposal, but not without a fight.[38] Gan Hoat Soei argued that the profession of rickshaw pullers also had a degenerating influence on their children. It would be unjust and disrespectful of the Westerners to go against this wish of the Easterners. But council member W. Jaski defended the profession of a rickshaw puller and argued that it was similar to that of a Venetian gondolier. Alderman de Waard called it absurd to make such a comparison, adding that the rickshaw profession was not idyllic, only repellent. It was undignified and should be abolished. Member J.W. Duys said that Gan Hoat Soei's view was not representative of the Chinese citizens, as two Chinese members of the council represented only a small part of the Chinese voters. Indonesian council member Mohamad Thahar disagreed

[34] *Andalas* 13-08-1918; Andalas 17-08-1918.
[35] *Het Nieuwsblad voor Sumatra* 18-05-1949.
[36] *Het nieuws van den dag voor Nederlandsch-Indië* 12-09-191.
[37] *Verslag Betreffende de Gemeente Medan* Over het Jaar 1923.
[38] SP 28-10-1926.

with Duys, and said that they indeed had been chosen by a small group of voters, but that this group was not larger was not the fault of the Chinese but of the voting system. As they were the only candidates, they represented the Chinese population as a whole. Council member Abdullah Loebis further said that all the Indigenous newspapers wrote in favour of abolition.[39] Finally, the council approved the proposal for the gradual abolition of the rickshaws, by nine to five votes.[40]

One year later, the Hongkong Ordinance or *Hongkongverordening* of November 16, 1927, was passed, and it was decided that from January 1, 1928, no new licences or registration certificates would be issued to rickshaw pullers.[41] As a result, the number of rickshaws started to decline. In 1925, there were 800; in 1926, 705; in 1927, 573; and in 1928, 549. Meanwhile, the number of *sados* increased; it was around 600 at the end of 1925, and by the end of 1928, their number had risen to 885.[42] The following anecdote was posted in *De Sumatra Post* in 1930:

> *For three years I have the same hongkong puller. He is a phenomenon among the Chinese and a jewel of his guild. I present him as Gap Gau Wang. […] Gap Gau Wang walks with long paces and those who are driving with him forgets that it is immoral that one person pulls the other. By the way, Gap Gau Wang does not think at all that his profession is immoral and said 'manah boleh' (that's not possible) when I told him about the decision of the Town Council (to gradually abolish the hongkong in Medan). My hongkong puller is a phenomenon: he can read! … He does not use opium and does not smoke Chinese pipes. 'Tjap Gadja' is his brand. His safe is built in under the seat…[then I did not see him for long time]… these days he was suddenly, smiling, in front of me again…. he told that he had gone on leave to China for 8 months …. And with longer strides than usual he drove me resiliently along Medan's peaceful lanes.*[43]

By 1935, the number of rickshaws had declined to 170; a European councillor wanted to eliminate them completely, but they persisted until the war.[44]

[39] *Pertja Timoer* on 27-11-1928 wrote that, because of humanity, rickshaws should be abolished. Those who do not agree are inhumane.

[40] Buiskool 2025: 257; Gemeenteblad 16-11-1927.

[41] *Algemeen Handelsblad* 15-11-1927.

[42] SP 14-02-1929.

[43] SP 11-07-1930.

[44] *De Locomotief* 04-04-1935.

14.2.1 The End of Rickshaws

After the war, only about 100 rickshaws remained in Medan. In January 1947, the Pao An Tui decided to buy them up and ceremonially destroyed them by fire. The Chinese community raised 100,000 guilders, providing each rickshaw puller a compensation of 1000 guilders. Most of the pullers were over 60 years old and were given the option to either return to China or find other jobs. Out of 100 pullers, 80 chose to return to China (Fig. 14.2).[45]

Fig. 14.2 Chinese leaders rounded up rickshaws in Medan and destroyed them in January 1947 (Djabatan Penerangan R.I. 1950). The person on the right is Tan Boen Djin, the youngest son of Tan Tang Ho of Seng Hap

[45] *Sunday Tribune* (Singapore) 09-02-1947.

Soon, other modes of mass transport emerged; *betja* or *becak* (derived from Hokkien *be chia* or horse vehicle) was introduced as a bicycle-powered trishaw. The *becak* in Medan, with the driver seated beside the passenger, originated from Singapore—unlike the Javanese version, where the driver sat at the back. The Chinese jokingly said that workers who turned to *becak* driving became *bo ciak* (Hokkien for no food). By the end of 1952, nearly 3500 *becak* were operating in Medan.[46] In 1955, motorised becak with a top speed of 40 km per hour were introduced in Medan.[47] This marked the beginning of another *becak* problem: traffic congestion in Medan.

[46] HNvS 07-11-1952; Djawatan Penerangan R.I. Propinsi Tapanuli - Sumatra Timur 1950.
[47] HNvS 07-06-1955.

CHAPTER 15

Streets of Commerce and Memory

Medan's story can be told through its markets and streets—living spaces where commerce, culture, and community met and mingled. From the nightly bustle of Cantonstraat to the intimate family life along Jalan Hakka, these places formed the city's social heart. Cantonstraat carried the rhythm of trade and nocturnal life; Jalan Hakka carried that spirit into the postcolonial years through the quiet endurance of Chinese-Indonesian households. Together, they show how Medan grew not only through architecture and commerce, but through everyday lives that filled its streets with sound, colour, and memory.

15.1 A Night at Cantonstraat

Cantonstraat, located in the Chinese quarter, evolved from a modest street of hotels and gambling dens into the most vibrant commercial strip of the 1930s. By night, it came alive with lights, aromas, and sounds: tinkling bells, clattering woks, the hum of bargaining voices. Cantonstraat (Jl. Surabaya), situated in the Chinese quarter of Medan, was once the city's busiest and most vibrant street, with retail stalls operated by Malay and Indigenous communities and shops run by the Chinese community (Fig. 15.1).

Originally called Djalan Tengah (Middle Street), the street was renamed Cantonstraat in 1911. The area became a new Chinese quarter, with

B. Minasny, D. A. Buiskool, *Stories from Medan, Volume 1*, https://doi.org/10.1007/978-981-95-7707-1_15

Fig. 15.1 Photo taken from the Hakkastraat towards Cantonstraat and the water tower in the background. (Nationaal Archief 505045_012)

gutters installed in 1912 and the road paved in 1916.[1] Originally, Cantonstraat was not very busy, home to a few Japanese hotels and gambling places, and theft was common. Slowly, starting in the 1920s, it became a shopping destination. By the 1930s, Cantonstraat had transformed into a lively shopping street, offering a range of products, from *kelontong*[2] and wine to tobacco and cigars, leather goods, iron wares, rice and food products, clothing and yarns, *sarong*[3] and *tenunan*[4]; there were photographers, tailors, shoemakers, watch retailers and repairers, and more.

Shops along Cantonstraat were operated by both Chinese and Indigenous business people, and in the 1930s, the street boasted several notable establishments, such as the Thai Sin toko *kelontong*, Asia bread and bakery, Fan Hua bookshop and artist's tools, Shanghai laundrette or *wasscherij*, and Wai Yat hotel. There was a unique shop called Tjan Tjauw Kie (Chen Jiuji), a taxidermist and leather goods store, which specialised in making and selling preserved animal specimens, including tigers, bears, monkeys, snakes, civets, and deer! Surrounding streets were equally lively. On the stretch of Hongkongstraat, between Luitenantsweg and Tjong Yong Hianstraat, food stalls and bicycle repairmen set up alongside the road.

At night, Cantonstraat transformed into a lively *pasar malam* (night market), lined with rows of brightly lit Chinese- and Indigenous-owned shops, their façades bathed in the glow of electric lamps. In front of these shops, street stalls crouched like small kiosks, displaying goods under strong lights: everything from *kain*, bicycles, and chocolates to soaps and bottles of imported-sounding perfume with French names.[5]

Minangkabau and Indian vendors from nearby Luitenantsweg came to sell their wares, and the area was packed with people. However, this caused some shopkeepers to find the entrances to their *tokos* or shops blocked. Additionally, the same goods were often sold in these stalls as in the *tokos*.[6] Despite repeated protests by shop owners against street vendors, Malay shopkeepers believed that prohibiting them would harm the area's vitality

[1] SP 17-10-1911; 30-01-1912; 19-01-1916.

[2] *Kelontong* Chinese, originally a peddler with two baskets over his shoulder, selling threads, needles, buttons, etc.

[3] *Sarong* is a garment consisting of a long piece of cloth worn wrapped round the body and tucked at the waist or under the armpits, traditionally worn in Southeast Asia.

[4] *Tenun* is an artful Indonesian technique of making a fabric by weaving different colours of threads.

[5] DC 23-09-1936.

[6] SP 21-04-1937.

and business. Although some Chinese shop owners were unhappy with the street vendors, who often blocked traffic and prevented customers from accessing their stores, the Malay shopkeepers saw it as a way to maintain the area's liveliness.[7] Despite attempts to ban street vendors, the issue persisted until the city council made a decision. The street vendors were then relocated to the centre of the road, which satisfied shop owners who were no longer obstructed by the vendors (Fig. 15.2).[8]

15.1.1 Culinary Paradise

In a culinary paradise. Kitchens lining the street. Where gourmets and food lovers rule. And the ting-ting and tik-tok men make their rounds.[9]

Fig 15.2 Riding along Cantonstraat around the 1930s (Tropenmuseum TM-ALB-2442-315).

[7] SP 21-04-1937.
[8] SP 12-04-1939.
[9] SP 31-03-1936.

Cantonstraat was a haven for food lovers. It was also home to two cinemas: Orion and Tjong Koeng Tat. Just a short distance away from Luitenantsweg was the Royal cinema. Chinese cuisine was abundant, with food vendors selling meals late into the night. The air was a mingling of enticing and pungent scents: the aroma of food hawkers, the sweet notes of perfumes from street vendors, and the sharp, herbal smells of traditional remedies. Street healers set up stands selling "miracle cures," touted as an all-healing medicine, displaying collections of animal bones, horns, and roots to impress customers. The market atmosphere was alive with bargaining, laughter, the calls of vendors, and the ebb and flow of strollers, flâneurs, and young people out for entertainment (Fig. 15.3).[10]

Fig. 15.3 A Chinese food stall in Medan (Nationaal Archief 505018)

[10] DC 23-09-1936.

There were also hotels for pleasure. The Tjong Jong Hianstraat, close by, was crowded at night with secret clubs and hotels that were frequented by young men. Writer Kho An Kim described the vibrant night scene in *Boenga Berhajat*:

> *As the night falls at Tjong Jong Hianstraat, it is crowded. Many clubs hold clandestine gambling. Hotels are also found there, and young men go in and out. One famous hotel at that time was the Tay Tong Hotel, where night butterflies (prostitutes) hang out. Various Chinese foods are sold along that street, so we can call it "Chinatown Street!" If we stay up until 2 or 3 in the morning, we could also buy food.*[11]

Chinatown has long been—and remains—a culinary paradise. The streets are alive with sounds: the clang of "teng-teng," the rhythmic knock of "tok-tok," ringing bells, and scissors snapping, as food vendors roam, selling delicacies to eager customers.

A journalist from *De Sumatra Post* described the nightlife in Chinatown in 1936 in a tone that mixes fascination with disdain for local foodways. The article, published on March 31, 1936, offers a vivid look at the street's colourful ambience (Figs. 15.4 and 15.5).[12]

> *We weave our way through some smoking nasi goreng and satay skewers.... We cross the street, where taxi drivers and motorcycle riders reign supreme, seemingly playing tag with pedestrians.*
>
> *At a pickle cart, which announces itself from afar with its monotonous ting-ting on a copper bell, we have a stomach-settling snack. In the glass case on wheels lies everything that Indies possess in unripe fruits and fruit peels soaked in vinegar. Black seeds like bat shit, taste deliciously savoury. One must set aside the somewhat unappetizing character of these delicacies and then enjoy sour mangga and sour chilli djamboes.*[13] *What you don't see doesn't hurt you is a popular saying everywhere here...*
>
> *The coffee is poured from a long coffee filter, which looks a lot like a half-cut lady's stocking, onto the white glazed tiles of the counter. The "koppie soesoe" (milk coffee) tastes excellent, whether it's due to the stocking, we don't know...*

[11] *Sinar Deli* 20-07-1933. Tjong Yong Hian street in 1960 was renamed Jalan Bogor, and in 2013 was renamed back to Jalan Tjong Yong Hian.

[12] SP 31-03-1936.

[13] *Mangga* is mango and *djamboe* is guava; *teng-teng* is a name for a street vendor selling fruits with chilli sauce.

Fig. 15.4 A food stall in Medan Chinatown (based on drawings from SP 31-03-1936)

Fig. 15.5 Chinese smoking waterpipes in a coffee shop (SP 31-03-1936)

Across the street is a food stall, where they are roasting and baking small, spindly, browned chickens. In the middle of the stall lies a suckling pig, surrounded by meatballs, lobsters, shrimp, sea cucumbers (tripang), diced pork, chicken livers, and a dish of bamy-slangetje[14] *and all sorts of vegetables.*

We got hungry, and after careful consideration from one of the restaurant staff, we decided to order from Jah Fan. Our order was promptly taken to the restaurant owner. The restaurants work closely with the eateries. The former provides drinks, while the latter provides food, and in return, they are given the right to tap into the electricity from the shop using a power outlet. Hence, the bright lights under the brown-grey tent cover. A blue porcelain bowl of steaming rice is already here, served by a chubby Chinese server, dressed in traditional calf-length pants and a brown-stained apron. He wears a cloth over his shoulder, which must have been white, and uses it to wipe everything clean, from plates and bowls to chopsticks, even his nose and fat neck.

Then comes the Jah Fan, a dish with a cocktail of meat types. We're amazed: a short chopped pork rib surrounded by some meat, a solidly filled chicken leg, then ear mushroom, and pork skin with fat. All of this is fried dry and has a spicy taste, some chili pepper and vinegar make the dry rice delicious to consume. It's simple food, but tasty and nutritious.

To try something else, we switch to Tjap Tjhai goreng,[15] *vegetables, shrimp, and pork. To soak up the atmosphere, we move to the café across the street after a friendly grin from our café boss. We sit on the low bamboo stool and try hard to feel at home, as if we were sitting on a bar stool at the Medan Hotel.*

We watch with interest as our cook prepares our dinner. With a large chopping knife and the skill of an executioner, he quickly chops vegetables and pork, adds roasted shrimp, and serves it all on a plate, which he inspects briefly before giving us a fork and a spoon.

We decided to continue our wanderings through the camp. After a friendly goodbye to the café owner, his large mirrors, and the portrait of Dr. Sun Yat Sen, we move on.

A Chinese man with a checkered sports cap and a duffle coat is sitting in a corner smoking a water pipe. Over there, another man, thin and sinewy, with one knee raised and the other foot gripping a clog. These water pipes are standing in an empty petroleum can in a corner, waiting for renters. Further on, an old man sits with a bottle of Chinese beer. He makes a disgusted face, smacks his lips, looks into his glass, and drinks slowly. Someone shouts something to the man at the counter, and he grumbles back. Above his head, bottles of medicinal wine

[14] *Bamy* refers to *bakmie* or noodle, and *slangetje* means snakes; *bamy-slangetje* refers to the long winding noodles.

[15] *Capcai* is a mixed vegetables stir-fry.

dangle from a steel rack. They hang everywhere in the cafés and have become part of the decor.

We can no longer eat, it is impossible, yet there is still so much to enjoy from the Chinese cuisine, we can still hear the voice of our cook, counting on his thick fingers the many dishes that we can get from him. Loempia goreng, rissoles with meat and vegetable filling. Mie swa koewa, shrimp with bacon and vermicelli, ordinary nasi goreng and bami goreng, but with lots of fat and bacon.[16] *Everything here is greasy and fatty and delicious. Woh Tiap, fried shrimp with bacon and ham covered with a sauce that could make one choke, fried lobster and so the menu continues.*

15.2 Lives on Jalan Hakka

A short walk from Cantonstraat, Jalan Hakka carried this legacy into the postcolonial era. After independence, as Medan's urban fabric evolved, Chinese-Indonesian families continued to live and trade in these same quarters. The story of the Khoe family reflects the endurance and adaptation of this community through economic hardship and social change (Fig. 15.6).

Khoe Hok Tiong and his wife Lim Kiam Sui purchased property number two on Jalan Hakka (current Jl. Nusantara) in 1968 when they relocated from Sibolga to Medan.[17] Jalan Hakka is situated in the bustling commercial centre of Medan and is predominantly occupied by rice wholesalers who sell their products to retailers in the city. However, at number two, there was a transport company that was established by the late Khoe Hok Tiong. This company provided transport services for a diverse range of goods that were delivered by bicycle rickshaws, including kitchen racks, bottles of soy sauce, plastic baskets, and live chickens. Various companies brought their merchandise to Jalan Hakka, and the transport company fetched and delivered them to their designated stores.

In addition to the rice trade, several buildings along Jalan Hakka served different purposes. One such building was number six, where the owner earned his living through gambling. On the other side of the street, there was an eatery for porters, which did not have a house number. This shop was owned by Koentil and his 17 children. One of Koentil's children was always available to prepare meals for the customers.

[16] *Lumpia* is a spring roll; *mie swa koewa* is a rice vermicelli soup.

[17] The original version of this story by Dirk A. Buiskool was published in Dutch in *Archipel* magazine, spring 2006.

Fig. 15.6 Medan Chinese house (photo by Dirk A. Buiskool)

After Khoe Hok Tiong and Lim Sui Kiam moved into their new home on Jalan Hakka, Khoe Hok Tiong established his transportation company. As the economy worsened over the years, the family considered selling the house. However, they were able to prevent this and keep a roof over their heads. In addition to their own children, some cousins who came to Medan to study or look for work also lived with them. The house was always full; cousins arrived to study or find work, and five people might share a bedroom without complaint.

They described it as "suka ramai," meaning the more people the merrier. If this means ten people live in a house with only two bedrooms, this is no problem. In the household, noise was also not important, as they were accustomed to it. As with all Chinese "ruko" (*rumah toko*, shophouse), the business was on the ground floor, and the family lived upstairs. The kitchen, bedrooms, and the living room were located on the first floor. Right next to the small bedroom, the television was turned on at a loud volume, and the family slept through it.

This is a story of a family's rise and fall. Prior to World War II, Lim Kiam Sui's father owned a transportation company in Sibolga that included dozens of cars, an ice cream factory, and cinemas. However, during World War II, their cars were confiscated by the Japanese army, and all economic activities ceased. The next generation was unable to continue the business, and the family spent all their money, eventually falling into poverty.

To escape their difficult circumstances, they left Sibolga and tried again in Medan. However, it was not an easy journey, and poverty remained prevalent in their new home on Jalan Hakka number two throughout the 1970s. The family struggled to pay for school fees, and they only had enough money to make ends meet and feed everyone.

Despite their lack of wealth, there was always food on the table. Cooking was a full-time job for the women in the house, and the smell of sambal oelek and garlic filled the air from 9 am onwards. Mother Lim Kiam Sui cooked for the whole family and anyone who came to visit.

During *Imlek*, or Chinese New Year, the family would come together to pray for deceased relatives, and elaborate meals would be prepared for the occasion. Even though some of the children had become Catholic, it was not a problem; two beliefs in one house were accepted.

After the passing of Khoe Hok Tiong in 1985, his children were able to achieve financial independence. The oldest son went to the United States, self-funded his education, and later returned to Medan to become a computer science lecturer in 1995. The eldest daughter, Ai Hap, established a travel agency with the assistance of her sister, A Guek. The youngest son, Si Siong, initially worked with his sisters before starting his own trading company. He resided with his wife and daughter at Jalan Hakka number two.

Following the passing of their mother, Sui Lim Kiam, the family put their house in Jalan Hakka up for sale. Seeking guidance, Si Siong's wife consulted the temple, where the *biksu* (monk) advised against the sale due to the unfavourable location according to the teachings of *feng shui*, the doctrine of air and water. From a *feng shui* perspective, the proximity of a Methodist church was seen as further inauspicious. Nonetheless, due to its central location, the property remains attractive to many in the Medan Chinese community.

Si Siong's family holds the temple's opinions in high regard and consults the priest for a variety of matters, such as adoption dates, weddings, school choices, business decisions, and social relationships. However, the temple's opinions are not always accurate. For instance, when a ferry sank years ago and there were fears that an acquaintance had drowned on the boat, the mother showed the priest a photo of the person and asked if they were still alive. The priest bluntly replied, "*No, he drowned.*" Fortunately, it turned out to be a bad prediction, for that same evening it was reported that the person had miraculously survived.

While the family residing in Medan values the advice of the temple, those who have lived abroad do not. Despite seeking guidance from the temple, the house in Jalan Hakka remains unsold. Perhaps the priest's caution will ultimately prove to be justified.

15.3 Where the Streets Got Their Name

In the early days, the street names in Medan were in Malay, based on local landmarks, such as Djalan Passar for a street with a market, Djalan Blakang (back street), Djalan Tengah (middle street), and Djalan Roemah Makan for the street with a restaurant (or hotel) (Fig. 15.7). The street where the Sultan's palace was located was called Djalan Astana (palace street). Official street signs were introduced at major road intersections in 1888. European names, such as Demmeni, Cremer, and Nienhuys, were introduced. There

Fig. 15.7 A street in Medan (Wereldmuseum, TM-ALB-0277-41)

were names related to buildings, such as Kerkstraat, Hotelweg, and Societeitsstraat.[18] The street where the Hüttenbach firm operated was called Djalan Hüttenbach and Djalan Law Ah Yok was where Law Ah Yok had his construction business. This led to an awkward situation, as other building contractors on the street had to include their competitor's name in their address.

In 1911, assistant resident Van der Plas attempted to rationalise and unify the street names of the municipality of Medan.[19] Street names were changed to Dutch, typically ending in -straat (street) or -weg (road). Djalan Padjak became Pachtstraat (current Jl. Kumango), Marktstraat (Jl. Perdagangan) for Djalan Pasar, and Nieuwmarktstraat (Jl. Perniagaan) for Pasar Baroe. Djalan Astana became Paleisweg, Djalan Roemah Makan became Nienhuysweg (current Jl. Pulau Pinang), and Djalan Mesjid became Moskeestraat (only to be changed back in 1942).

Street names in the Chinese and Indian quarters were named accordingly. In the Indian quarter, names were given as Calcuttastraat, Madrasstraat, Bombaystraat, Ceylonstraat, and Colombostraat. In the Chinese district, the streets were renamed after Chinese cities or regions, Pekingstraat (used to be Djalan Pematang), Hongkongstraat, Cantonstraat (Djalan Tengah), Shanghaistraat (Djalan Club), Swatowstraat (Djalan Kosong), Tjong Yong Hianstraat (Djalan Majoor), Kwanteebiostraat (Djalan Keling), etc. Adjacent to the Chinese quarter, street names were named after regions across the Indies archipelago, such as Riouwstraat, Bankastraat, Balistraat, Javastraat, Madoerastraat, and Timorstraat. Streets near Petisah were named after fruits and plants, such as Djalan Pepaja, Nangka, etc. In the European quarter, the so-called Oranje buurt (Orange quarter), streets were given names after members of the Dutch royal family (House of Orange), such as Prins Hendrikstraat, Julianastraat, Emmastraat, and Oranje Nassaustraat.[20] Kartinilaan was named after the Javanese feminist Raden Adjeng Kartini, and Max Havelaarlaan was named after the novel *Max Havelaar* by Multatuli (Eduard Douwes Dekker). Nevertheless, the locals still prefer to use local names, for example, in the 1930s, Sportlaan was called Djalan Boelan after Hiu Ngi Fen's company Anggoer Tjap Boelan.

[18] *Bataviaasch handelsblad* 28-04-1888.

[19] Medan got a mayor in 1918, Daniel Baron Mackay. Van der Plas later became the governor of East Sumatra (Buiskool 2025: 48).

[20] SP 17-10-1911.

In 1917, Tjong A Fie, as a town council member, proposed that the streets and alleys in Medan be named in both Malay and Chinese, but the request was rejected.[21] When the Japanese occupied Sumatra in 1942, all Dutch names were changed to Indonesian. Wilhelminastraat became Djalan Soetomo, Daendelstraat became Djalan Hajam Woeroek, Idenburgstraat became Djalan Erlangga, Sportlaan became Djalan Boelan, etc.[22] After 1950, most street names were replaced with Indonesian names. Following 1966, all Chinese street names were banned.

[21] Buiskool 2025: 184.

[22] *Kita Sumatora Sinbun* 29-10-1943.

CHAPTER 16

The Centrale Pasar and Pasar Malam of Medan

The Centrale Pasar, known locally as Pusat Pasar, stood as the pride of Medan when it opened in 1933. Built in the heart of the new Chinese district, it was considered the most modern and the largest and cleanest market in the Dutch East Indies. It covered 12 hectares, housing 179 shops and four massive sheds for meat, fish, vegetables, and general foodstuffs—each equipped with ventilation, tiled floors, and cold rooms. The opening ceremony on February 24, 1933 blended modern spectacle and local ritual, a Dutch ceremony, a buffalo sacrifice (*slametan*), and a festive night market (*pasar malam*) that drew thousands.

The *pasar malam*, or night fair, became an annual highlight in Medan, merging trade, entertainment, and multicultural celebration. Initially linked to royal holidays, it soon evolved into large-scale fairs showcasing local crafts, foods, and industry alongside European technology and amusement. The 1933 pasar malam, held on the new Centrale Pasar grounds, featured music, theatre, boxing, dragon dances, and exhibitions from across the Indies.

The Centrale Pasar and *pasar malam* embodied the cultural and economic dynamism of pre-war Medan. Centrale Pasar symbolised Medan's rise as a cosmopolitan hub, while the *pasar malam* expressed the city's multicultural vibrancy (Fig. 16.1).

B. Minasny, D. A. Buiskool, *Stories from Medan, Volume 1*,
https://doi.org/10.1007/978-981-95-7707-1_16

Fig. 16.1 Aerial photo of the newly built Centrale Pasar (*Officieele Pasarmalam en Centrale Pasar Gids* 1933)

16.1 The Central Market

Our pride: the Central Pasar. An architecture, a space and hygiene like anywhere else.[1]

Among the white neat buildings and historical landmarks, the Medanese are proudest of is the municipal central market. Clean, attractive, constructed in 1931, it is Indeed one of the best constructed and finest buildings in the Indies. Inside the market there is nothing of the Oriental hustle and bustle, dirt and misery, so typical of similar centres all over the world. Native shopkeepers and customers enter the place with solemn devotion.[2]

De Centrale Pasar or the Central Market of Medan, also known as *Pusat Pasar* or *Tua Pa Sat* in Hokkien, opened in 1933 and was the pride of Medan. Located in the new Chinese district, it was considered the most modern with the largest and cleanest market in the Dutch Indies.

The markets in Medan had been in the hands of the Tjong family since 1886. On January 18, 1886, H.C. van den Honert, an administrator for the Deli Company, signed a lease agreement with Tjong Yong Hian, who

[1] SP 28-03-1936.
[2] *The Age* (Melbourne) 24-01-1942.

was then the Lieutenant of the Chinese community. The contract was for a plot of land approximately 3600 m^2 in size, intended for the construction of a market. The lease was set at a nominal rent of just 1 guilder annually. The local authorities proposed to the Tjong brothers that they could utilise the profits generated from this market to fund the Chinese hospital, known as Tjie On. In 1886, the Tjong brothers built a meat market on Nieuwemarkt straat (Jl. Perdagangan). A year later, a fish market was built on Spoorstraat (known now as Pajak Ikan Lama). In 1906, a vegetable market was established with sheds between Pekingstraat, Tjong Yong Hian straat and Kapiteinsweg.[3]

In Medan, a unique local term for market is *padjak* rather than *pasar*. *Padjak* means tax, but it was commonly referring to a place where tax is collected or a revenue farm, such as *padjak joedi* (gambling shop), *padjak gadei* (pawn shop). Thus, *padjak sajoer* means vegetable market, *padjak daging* is a meat market and *padjak ikan* is a fish market.

The markets persisted for more than 30 years. No new markets were developed in Medan between 1905 and 1933. Only in 1915, a small market called Pasar Petisah was established. As the population of Medan increased, the established markets became too crowded. In addition, there were complaints about hygiene. Traffic along the fish and meat market was chaotic, and there was a joke (Figs. 16.2 and 16.3):

> *whoever can ride or walk through Spoorstraat, Niewmarkt, and the streets in between, has earned his spurs as a brave man.*[4]

In 1919, the Town Council of Medan discussed new regulations concerning the control, management, and use of private markets with the intention of replacing them with municipal markets. After several negotiations, an agreement was reached between the Town Council and the Tjong family, whereby the old markets would be closed in 1933, after a new market was established.

A new large market was proposed to be located in the heart of the town. The old racing ground called Pasar Loemba[5] was chosen as the location. This area lay within the new Chinese district and the *kampongs* of

[3] Buiskool 2025:129, 130, 222.

[4] DC 24-02-1933.

[5] Pasar in Medan means road, thus pasar loemba means racing track.

Fig. 16.2 The traffic chaos at Marktstraat (*rapport omtrent den toestand der pasars te Medan eerste gedeelte 1927*)

Fig. 16.3 A market for clothing materials in Medan (Wereldmuseum, TM-FV-3100-5207)

East Medan, which were not heavily populated at that time. Existing football fields near the racing ground were moved to Keboen Boenga. And to make it attractive, part of the area was made into parks and the roads were widened.

Architect J. H. Valk designed the market, and the plans were completed in 1928 and approved by the council in 1929, costing two and a quarter million guilders.[6] However, the global economic crisis hit in 1930. Although it struggled financially, Medan's greatest public work was initiated in April 1931 and completed within 21 months at the end of 1932, during the height of the economic crisis. It took about 600 workers to complete a 12-hectare area, using about 6100 tons of cement, 3.87 million concrete tiles, 1 million bricks and 2.25 tons of steel, etc.[7]

The entire *pasar* complex housed 179 shops in five blocks, along with four huge sheds. The sheds were for selling food. Each shed was 155 m in length and 36 m wide, with tile floors; each was designed for a specific product, following health regulations. Roof vents kept the interior cool while narrow frosted glass panes provided soft natural light. Shed no. 1 was on Hakkastraat (jl. Nusantara) on the corner of Wilheminastraat (jl. Sutomo), selling vegetables from Brastagi and other areas. Shed 2 was on Hakkastraat, where pork was sold. Chicken, noodles and other foods were also available. Shed 3 on Balistraat (jl. Veteran) and Sportlaan (jl. Bulan) was mainly for fish, either fresh or salted. Finally, Shed 4 on Balistraat was for beef. There were cold rooms in the meat and fish sections. Food stands were not allowed inside the sheds, and other products were to be sold in shops surrounding the market, ensuring a distinction between fresh foods and market sales areas.[8]

Sheds 2 and 4 served the early-morning small traders from *kampong*. Shed 4 was for the indigenous and Shed 2 was for the Chinese. All warehouses were cleaned three times a day with rubber hoses. The market was also impressed with its diverse selection of goods, ranging from local fruits and vegetables to imported items such as Australian apples and Chinese pears. There was even a special section for Chinese pickles.

[6] DC 27-01-1931.
[7] Officieele Pasarmalam en Centrale Pasar Gids 1933.
[8] DC 27-01-1931; SP 24-02-1933.

Shop allocation followed practical considerations, for example, the lot selling pork would be near Chinese shops, not Muslim shops. The silk shops (called *toko Bombay*) were not located near shops with unpleasant odours, such as those selling dried fish or kerosene, or those with a lot of dust, like charcoal. Thus, clothing stores were allocated on Wilhelminastraat. Glassware and foodstuffs were put together. Rice and dried fish were next to Sportlaan near the fish and pork stores. At each block, there were *kedai kopi* and *kedai nasi* (coffee and food stalls).

The market's cleanliness was maintained through efficient waste disposal and the availability of clean, water-supplied restrooms. The market's administration was attentive to maintaining cleanliness and order. Flowering *boengoer* trees[9] were among the stalls, adding to its unique charm (Fig. 16.4).[10]

Centrale Pasar was officially opened by the Mayor of Medan, J. M. Wesselink, on February 24, 1933 with a bustling atmosphere, vivid colours, and a range of activities. Shop fronts were adorned with brightly

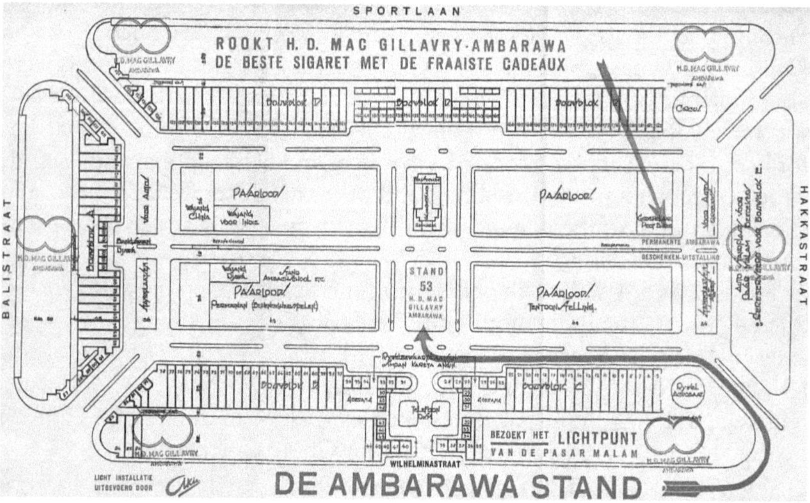

Fig. 16.4 The Centrale Pasar plan in 1933. (Officieele Pasarmalam en Centrale Pasar Gids 1933)

[9] Bungur (*Lagerstroemia indica*), a deciduous tree with bright pink to light purple flowers.
[10] SP 24-02-1933.

painted signs, Dutch flags, and orange pennants, welcoming visitors during a tour of Medan's new market. A restaurant was serving tap beer, a large table displayed a model of the Central Pasar, and various commercial stands showcased products ranging from machinery, tiles, and cigarettes to automobiles. Tradition was honoured with a *slamaten* ritual which included burying a buffalo head, and offering prayers for prosperity, providing good omens for the market's future.[11] That night, the *pasar malam* (night market) opened on the grounds.[12]

It was the pride of Medan, but the local people preferred a local name. And thus the name "Medan Baroe," or the New Medan, a city within a city, was proposed (Fig. 16.5).[13] Some even called it the heart of Medan. In terms of architecture, hygiene, and organisation, the Centrale Pasar stood unparalleled, not just in the Dutch Indies but even when compared to markets in British India, earning it the distinction of being *hors de concours* (in a class of its own). This market successfully combined Western hygiene and order with Eastern vibrancy. A notable and exceptional

JAARGANG — ZATERDAG 28 MAART 1936 — DIT NUMMER BESTAAT UIT VIER BLADEN — No. 75

De Sumatra Post

Verschijnt dagelijks, Zon- en Feestdagen uitgezonderd. Abonnementsprijs per kwartaal (Medan) f 6.25—, (Ned.-Indië) f 7.50, (Buitenland) f 11.25—. Men abonneert zich voor volle kwartalen. Abonnementsgelden zijn bij vooruitbetaling te voldoen.

Uitgegeven en gedrukt door: N. V. BOEKHANDEL EN DRUKKERIJ v/h VAREKAMP & Co., MEDAN. Hoofdredacteur: A. P. A. A. BESNARD. Tel. Nos.: Redactie 1600, Huis Hoofdredacteur 293, Administratie 1600, Huis 470. Kantoor te Amsterdam (C): Singel 389, Telefoon No. 32303.

ADVERTENTIE-TARIEF. Prijs per regel f 0.35, met een minimum van 10 regels. Plaatsing binnenzijde eerste blad f 0.70 per regel. Advertentiën moeten vooruit betaald worden.

AANTEEKENINGEN

Weer wat meer licht.

Onze trots: de Centrale Pasar.

Afslag bij fluisteling!

Fig. 16.5 Medan Baroe (SP 28-03-1936)

[11] SP 24-02-1933.
[12] Idem.
[13] *Sinar Deli* 01-03-1933.

feature was its remarkable absence of flies, a typical nuisance in traditional markets.[14]

However, this beacon of market excellence had a transient glory. With the advent of the Japanese occupation and the subsequent emergence of Indonesian independence, the once illustrious Centrale Pasar gradually succumbed to decline. It lost its unique charm and order, eventually transforming into a more typical, chaotic *pasar.* Two of the large sheds were destroyed by fire in 1971. In 1978, the remaining two sheds burned down, leading vendors to set up their businesses on the streets surrounding the area. Subsequently, in the 1990s, the government constructed a central market and Medan Mall.

16.2 Pasar Malam

On August 31, 1927, hundreds of people had been flocking to the grounds since the afternoon. By six o'clock, a dense crowd was waiting in front of the gate for the opening of *Pasar Malam* (night fair), which coincided with the Dutch Queen, Wilhelmina's birthday. The mayor, the Sultan of Deli with a few *tengkoes*, the heads of local government, Chinese and Indigenous officials had arrived. Finally, the mayor declared Medan's pasar malam officially open. And the children from the girls' schools sang both in Dutch and in Malay (Fig. 16.6)[15]:

> *Sri Ratoe Wilhelmina Di negeri Belanda Memerintahkan tanah Hindia Dengan sentosanja.... (Queen Wilhelmina in the land of Holland Governing the land of Indies with peace ...)*
>
> *Stands with bright lights shine through the night encircling the ground. People were crowded viewing various stands on display, including Velodrome's car booth with Dodge and Fiat cars. The highlight was the stand with bright electric lights, a shining Osram advertisement of the Nederland Indies Gas company. The Kwong Ban Leong company had a stand with bright lights promoting its ketjap. This is rivalled by Weng Seng ketjap and Poo Thai Foo Seng Kie Dispensary known for its anggoerTjap Boelan. There was also a stand of stuffed animals from the Tjan Tjauw Kie company which attracted much attention, and a showroom of the Ultraphone. Various shows also attract the*

[14] SP 28-03-1936.
[15] SP 01-09-1927.

Fig. 16.6 A depiction of *pasar malam* in Medan

> *European and the indigenous people, two ronggengs, wayang kulit for the Javanese, wayang orang, open cinema, and a bangsawan.*[16]

The *pasar malam* was traditionally a night market held in towns across the Dutch East Indies. Once a year, however, many towns hosted a large-scale *pasar malam*, an evening market and fair that combined entertainment with a showcase for trade, industry, and handicrafts. These events featured exhibitions by both European companies and local artisans, with stalls set up in the town square offering goods for sale, live craft demonstrations, traditional performances, games, fireworks, and lotteries, often with government support.

The tradition began in Batavia in the early 1900s, later spreading to Soerabaja and other towns in Java. Medan had hosted smaller pasar malams since the 1910s, but a large-scale version was first staged in 1923 to mark the 25th anniversary of Queen Wilhelmina's inauguration. Held at the Esplanade, it served as a cultural showcase of local arts and crafts, featuring a Year Fair (*Jaarbeurs*) gallery, agricultural and school exhibits, cinema,

[16] Idem.

bangsawan theatre, *Si gale-gale*, *wajang China*, *wajang wong* with *gamelan*, *koeda kepang*, and *ronggeng* dances, along with food stalls, craft kiosks, and games.[17]

The annual *pasar malam* in Medan drew tens of thousands of visitors and generated tens of thousands of guilders, commonly organised by a committee of European business leaders. In 1933, the greatest pasar malam to date was held on the grounds of the newly built Centrale Pasar, with the organising committee members represented by the European, Indonesian, Chinese, and Indian communities. Officially opened on October 31 by the Governor of the East Coast of Sumatra with seven cannon shots, the event embodied multicultural collaboration with a charitable purpose—to fund the establishment of a private school following government budget cuts, and to assist victims of a recent earthquake in South Sumatra. The fair featured a major exhibition of indigenous industries, crafts, agricultural products, and cultural artefacts from across the Dutch East Indies. Entertainment included performances by the Moonlight Opera, boxing champions, Chinese dragon dance, Batak mask performers, Javanese dancers, and a row of Indian children singing and dancing.[18] The organising committee, led by businessman A. Soeleiman, faced controversy. They budgeted for about 230,000 paying visitors, expecting *f*23,000 in gate receipts plus substantial rental income from stands, yet around 40% of the stands went unrented. The final accounting showed that the event brought in *f*9451.84, mainly from entrance fees (*f*6,668.50) and stand rentals/advertising (*f*2312). After expenses of *f*6393.71—covering stands, publicity, lighting, entertainment, exhibitions, staff, and even a rain charmer (*doekoen*) —the net profit was *f*3058.13, of which *f*1058.13 was donated to the South Sumatra disaster fund.[19]

Subsequently, the 1936 Pasar Malam marked the first organised by the Chinese community, with proceeds benefiting Chinese, European, and

[17] DC 21-03-1905, 26-08-1913, 01-02-1923; SP 30-04-1912, 18-05-1923. *Si gale-gale* is a wooden puppet of the Batak people, *wajang China* is a Chinese opera, *wajang wong* is human wayang or a Javanese theatrical performance, *koeda kepang* also called kuda lumping is a traditional Javanese dance involving flat woven bamboo horses and *ronggeng* is a traditional social dance performed by female dancers (ronggeng) who invite men from the audience to join in.

[18] SP 29-07-1933, 19-10-1933; 01-11-1933 ; DC 01-11-1933; De Indische courant 09-11-1933.

[19] SP 14-11-1933, 17-11-1933; 30-11-1933.

Indigenous charities, as well as the Su Tung School. It offered a wide range of attractions, from Chinese goods and handicraft exhibits to operas, ronggeng dances, gamelan, krontjong music, martial arts, boxing, carnival rides, skill games, and plentiful food stalls, creating a lively spectacle for all audiences.[20] This was followed in 1938, when the Chinese Pasar Malam Committee in Medan held a two-week event to support the Red Cross in China during the ongoing war with Japan, raising a total of *f*32,361.76.[21]

In 1941, the pasar malam was organised under the auspices of the British War Relief Fund, transforming Medan's Esplanade into a lively festival ground filled with stands, restaurants, music, games, and exhibitions. Highlights included the Churchill Bar, shooting games with effigies of Hitler and Mussolini, boxing, opera performances, Chinese theatre, and cultural displays. Speeches urged support for Britain and the Allied cause, emphasising that proceeds would help purchase Spitfire aircraft. Few anticipated that Japan would attack eight months later.[22]

16.3 The History of *Ketjap*

One of the standout features of pasar malam was *ketjap*, or kecap, or soy sauce —the main ingredient of Chinese and Indonesian cuisine. It was a big business in Medan and the Dutch Indies. The Dutch were also addicted to *ketjap* and other soy products. *Ketjap* became a main ingredient in Dutch Indo food, with one of its famous dishes is *babi ketjap*.

Legend has it that *ketjap* came from the Chinese word *guizhi* or *ke ciap* in Hokkien, meaning "fish sauce." According to popular folklore, fish sauce was invented by an imperial chef during the reign of King Jing of Zhou in 544 BC. However, in China, soy sauce is generally known as *jiangyou* and in Hokkien, known as *tao yu* or bean oil. According to an article in *Sin Po*, the legend was that in 1621, Souw Beng Kong from Fujian went to Batavia and was appointed Captain of the Chinese by Governor-General Jan Pieterszoon Coen. Souw Beng Kong brought his family and friends from Fujian to Batavia. Subsequently, they introduced

[20] SP 01-02-1936.
[21] SP 08-12-1937, 16-02-1938.
[22] SP 03-06-1941.

Chinese food to the community in Java, and *ke ciap* was known as *ketjap*.[23] The tradition was later introduced throughout the Dutch Indies.

Soy sauce, known as "shoyu" in Japan, had been imported to Europe by the Dutch East India Company since the mid-1600s. Thus, the Dutch referred to the soybean as "soja" and later introduced it to the United States in 1750, where it became known as soy. Since Europeans had limited access to soybeans at the time, they attempted to create their own version of soy sauce using vinegar with mushrooms or walnuts. Additionally, the Javanese-style soy sauce called *ketjap* was imported to America and Europe, where it eventually became known as ketchup, catchup, or catsup. It wasn't until the 1800s that tomato ketchup, as we know it today, was invented in America.[24]

Dutchman P.A. Boorsma, who lived in Java in the 1900s, was captivated by soy food and tempeh, and as a naturalist, he conducted laboratory tests on the chemical composition of indigenous soybeans and their products. He published a report in 1900 describing the indigenous and Chinese preparations of soybean, including *tempe kedeleh* (soybean tempeh), *ketjap,* which he called Batavian soy (*Bataviasche soja*), *Tao hoe en Tao koan* (soft and hard tofu) and *Tao-tjo en Tao-dji* (fermented black soybeans).[25]

16.3.1 Ketjap competition

At the *pasar malam* in Medan, the two largest *ketjap* companies from Medan competed: Kwong Ban Long promoted its *ketjap*, called Batavia Globe or Bolah Doenia, while Weng Seng promoted its ketjap, called Ketjap tjap Mata Hari. The same scene was repeated in 1928 (Fig. 16.7):

> *Among the Chinese stands that stood out were Kwong Ban Long and Lee Mun, which produced ketjap brand Bola Doenia and Ajam. Ketjap Weng Seng also had an important role because the advertisement lamps show that if you eat grilled chicken with its soy sauce, you will certainly salivate.*[26]

[23] *Sin Po Wekelijksche Editie* 12-10-1940.

[24] Shurtleff and Aoyagi 2015: 33–34.

[25] Idem, but he missed tauge or bean sprout, but that was unprocessed soy.

[26] *Pertja Timoer* 10-11-1928.

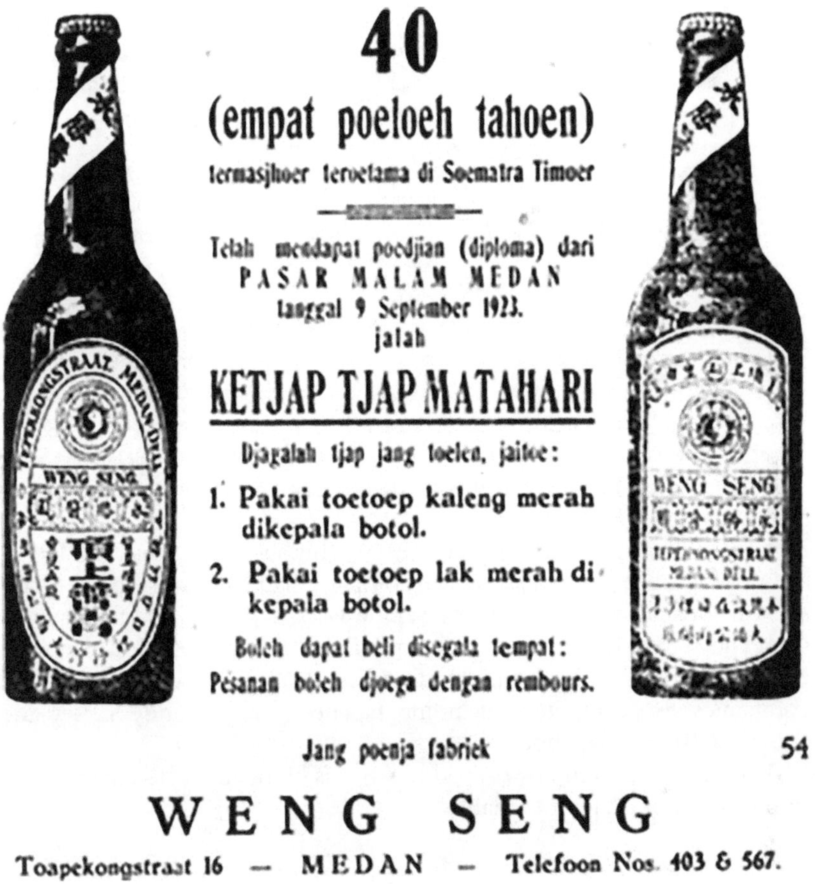

Fig. 16.7 Weng Seng's Ketjap Tjap Matahari used to be the best in Medan (*Sinar Deli* 18-04-1930)

There are also many versions of *ketjap*, including *ketjap hitam*.[27]

> *In Atjeh, the ketjap preparation is of great interest, based on black kedelee (soy bean), in contrast to the white kedelee, which produces the salty ketjap according to the Chinese (fermentation) method. The black kedelee provides the sweet soy sauce, which is often popular in Java.*

[27] SP 08-05-1935.

That was *kecap manis* as we know it today, originally from Java.

Unfortunately, *ketjap* was so popular that it became a source of misdeeds. In Soerabaja, the factory was a cover to make illegal alcohol.[28] Some producers also attempted to manufacture counterfeit *ketjap*:

> *The police discovered a batch of 93 kg of salt in a kedeh on Julianastraat Medan, which was smuggled from Atjeh.... The fake soy sauce was made by just dissolving the salt and cooked to brown-colour, and the excess salt was then removed.*[29]

Real soy sauce is more expensive and requires skill to ferment soy into a delicious sauce rather than just pure salt. Many *ketjap* companies emerged in Java, mostly set up by *totok* Chinese as the *peranakan* considered it a dirty job.[30] There was a street in Batavia known as "gang ketjap" (kecap lane) as it was a centre for *ketjap* production. The name *ketjap Batavia* referred to the sauce, which was made with equal amounts of wheat and soybeans.

Nevertheless, the real *ketjap* business was highly competitive. In Medan, Weng Seng, 永勝, a Chinese-owned company, had been in the business for 40 years or since the 1890s. Weng Seng was located in Topekongstraat (Jl. Topekong). Not that far from that company, at Pachtstraat (Jl. Kumango), another company, Lee Mun, produced its Tjap Ajam soy sauce. Other companies also competed, including Japanese kecap brands Sansey and San Yin Chan from Laboean Deli.

The competition in *ketjap* production was high, and it became an issue in the board of trade in Medan:

> *Manufacturers complained about the heavy competition from the soy sauce factories. The board is now investigating to what extent the soy sauce, soy and taotjo quota can be used to protect the local industry.*[31]

These *ketjap* companies seemed to disappear after World War II. In 1948, Chu Sam Yak and Chu Sok Sam, Teochew businessmen from Medan, embarked on a venture to produce a Chinese wine known as Anggur Tjap Orang Toea. As their business grew, they expanded into the

[28] *Soerabaijasch Handelsblad* 09-10-1935.
[29] SP 10-04-1941.
[30] *Sin Po* 24-08-1929.
[31] SP 13-03-1934.

HET COMITÉ VAN DE
PASAR MALAM TE MEDAN
heeft na ingewonnen advies van de daartoe gekozen Jury, ter beoordeeling der inzending op de Pasar Malam te Medan, van 31 Januari tot en met 11 Februari 1936·

Aan N.V. IJSFABRIEK
„SIANTAR"

toegekend een

DIPLOMA

LIMONADE "JAP"
„KEPALA BADAK"

棉蘭華僑主辦
首屆一九三六年
夜市場獎狀

Fig. 16.8 The certificate for Kepala Badak lemodate at Pasar Malam in 1936 (Su Hwa Trade Journal, Issued by the Associated Chinese Chamber of Commerce of Sumatra Medan, Vol. 4, Issue 1. January 1937) battery industry and established the ABC battery in Medan. Their success led them to venture into Jakarta, where in 1975, they introduced the internationally renowned kecap manis ABC, a sweet soy sauce.

While there are many ketjap brands in Indonesia, not all ketjap tastes the same; each has its own secret traditional recipe. As *kecap* was added to any food to add flavour, and all kecap brands claimed to be number one, a person could be called kecap for overstating his story, and *ngecap* was a term used to describe gossip or adding tales to stories (Fig. 16.8).

PART III

Colonial Business and Trade

Medan, a city of white and fresh buildings nestled within its green, manicured lawns owes its emergence to the bustling life of plantations that surround it. It is truly unique in all of our Indies archipelago, and one will find no other place like it, neither on the island of Sumatra nor on the island of Java. Modern and European in style, Medan bears a slight English touch, undoubtedly influenced by its proximity to Singapore. The White Society, rightly named, the Post Office, Town Hall, and the Javanese Bank, Hotel de Boer, and Medan Hotel, as well as the imposing offices of various companies such as Harrisons and Crosfield, Deli-Maatschappij, Deli-Proefstation, Deli-Spoorweg-Maatschappij, and Firma Van Nie & Co., all stand majestically amidst the remarkably fresh greenery of the palms, ficus, and tjemara trees that have been drenched by the rain. These buildings symbolise prosperity, hard work, and remarkable Western efforts.[1]

[1] Couperus, L. *Oostwaarts*, 1924:42.

CHAPTER 17

Early Entrepreneurs and Merchants of Medan

Long before its shophouses, cafés, department stores, and tramlines became the defining symbols of Medan's urban life, Kesawan served as the crossroads where global ambitions met. On this dirt-road commercial artery, European planter capital intersected with Chinese trading networks, Indian traders, Arab merchants, and a small but influential community of Jewish entrepreneurs brought subtle changes to the region's economy. They recognised the greater fortunes to be made in supplying the booming estates with everything they required—from machinery, spirits, rifles, and textiles to canned foods and the latest European technologies (Fig. 17.1).

17.1 The Jewish Merchants

When Medan was founded as a trading centre of Deli in the 1880s, several Jewish merchants established businesses supplying merchandise and various needs to the Dutch government and growing European companies. They became prominent early entrepreneurs to control the region's supply economy. [1]

Like the Chinese, the Jewish merchants were well-connected to the Straits Settlements in Penang and Singapore. German and Jewish

[1] This chapter was originally published in *Inside Indonesia* 146: Oct-Dec 2021, modified and updated.

B. Minasny, D. A. Buiskool, *Stories from Medan, Volume 1*,
https://doi.org/10.1007/978-981-95-7707-1_17

Fig. 17.1 Merchants standing in front of Goldenberg & Zeitlin at Kesawan (KITLV 154472)

merchants had already formed early communities in Penang and Singapore, including the Katz Brothers, Behn Meyer & Co, Behr & Co, etc.[2] These traders established trading houses importing and selling new German and other European technologies, alcohol, and equipment.

During the "brown gold rush" (1870–1890) period of tobacco production, some Europeans travelled to Deli not specifically for the tobacco itself but to profit from the "prospectors." The European colonies were a convenient place for Jews to escape prejudices and assimilate.[3] They included Ashkenazi Jews mainly from Central and Eastern Europe (including Austria, Germany, and Poland), Sephardic Jews whose ancestors lived in Southern European countries like Spain, Portugal and the Middle East, and others who relocated from existing Baghdadi Jewish communities in Penang and Singapore. There is also scattered evidence of Jews in the KNIL (Koninklijk Nederlands Indisch Leger) or Royal Netherlands Indies Army, serving in Sumatra.

Among the first Europeans who came to Deli were members of the Hüttenbach family, an established merchant family from the German Rhineland city of Worms. The eldest son, August Hüttenbach, began

[2] Nasution 2006: 8–9, 61–65.

[3] Kowner 2011.

working for the Katz Brothers in Penang in 1872. The Katzes invested in a variety of businesses, including shipping. When the Dutch-Atjeh war broke out in 1873, the Katz Brothers secured the provision of logistics and supplies to the Dutch military.[4] August Hüttenbach followed with a shipping business that ran a regular service to the Atjeh ports and was a major player in pepper trading.

While August became a prominent merchant in Penang, his younger brother, Jacob Hüttenbach, went to Deli and opened the first European store in the harbour settlement of Laboean Deli in 1875, catering to the needs and requirements of the Dutch government, plantations, and industrial groups. Gradually, the family firm grew into a general merchandise company, supplying a wide range of goods from Europe and even founding offices in London and Amsterdam. With their own shipping lines at their disposal, they were, for a time, the only importer in Deli. The Hüttenbach enterprise supplied all kinds of goods and services, ranging from live water buffaloes and Brazil nuts to Bordeaux wines, machinery, and the Ford motorcar. In the 1910s, its annual imports totalled 1,200,000 guilders, and these were distributed throughout Sumatra. At the turn of the twentieth century, Jacob retired to Europe and left Heinrich Hüttenbach (1859–1922), the youngest of the brothers, in charge of the company.

Medan's growth attracted other Jewish merchants, who also opened stores selling European consumer goods such as clothing and luxury items. Jacques Deen, a Jew from Amsterdam, saw the economic growth in Deli and launched the first newspaper in the region, *Deli Courant,* in 1885. Two German Jews, Louis Kellermann of Leipzig and Max Goldenberg of Hamburg, opened the S. Katz & Co. shop in the Kesawan shopping street in 1887.[5] It may be that Kellermann and Goldenberg used the well-known Katz name to capitalise on their business. The Katz brothers, prominent in London, Frankfurt, Penang, and Singapore, were annoyed with S. Katz & Co., and advertised in the *Deli Courant* that they were unrelated.[6] The Katz brothers from Penang eventually established their branch in Medan in 1922, supplying English food products such as hams, jams, White Label whiskey, and Jon Dewar & sons Scotch whiskey.[7]

[4] Wright 1908: 684.
[5] DC 13-07-1887, 01-11-1893.
[6] DC 21-11-1888.
[7] *Het nieuws van den dag voor Nederlandsch-Indië* 21-10-1922.

The bookkeeper at S. Katz was Russian-born Alfred Aron Arnold Zeitlin, based in Leipzig (1863–1938). Partnering with Max Goldenberg, they opened a new store, Goldenberg & Zeitlin, in November 1898, with a majestic storefront on the main shopping street, Kesawan. This attractive building, designed by the firm Langereis & Co., featured "bay windows" that added charm. Some viewed the windows humorously, likening them to a booth for a Jewish holiday, the Feast of Tabernacles, or a signal post for judging people entering the building. Inside, the shop displayed beautiful, modern trinkets (Fig. 17.2). They had luxury items such as jewellery, music boxes, typewriters, hunting rifles, glassware, curtains, suitcases, cigars, etc.[8] Later, Goldenberg & Zeitlin expanded its branches in Penang,

Fig. 17.2 The majestic Goldenberg & Zeitlin building at Kesawan around 1900 (Stafhell & Kleingrothe, KITLV 154472). The company later became M. Goldenberg & Co. and was acquired by a German company. Ironically, it was seized by the Dutch when Germany invaded the Netherlands in 1940. The building has been demolished and turned into shophouses

[8] Wright and Cartwright 1908: 806, DC 09-11-1898, *Bataviaasch nieuwsblad* 14-12-1898.

Hamburg and the Hague. It seems the Jewish population was large enough that, in *De Sumatra Post* in 1899, we read:

> *the Israelite Feast of Tabernacles will be celebrated later than usual in Medan this year.*[9]

Unrelated to Max Goldenberg, Eduard Goldenberg (1868–1945) came from Zutphen in the Netherlands to Medan as one of the directors of a German company, Handel Maatschappij Güntzel & Schumacher.[10] He was also the director of the European Chamber of Commerce of Medan with an investment in the rubber and coconut plantation Boekit Pajong Cultuur.

Other competitors were not far behind. An English-language travel guide to Sumatra in 1912 wrote:

> *A visit should also be paid to the establishment of Messrs. Cornfield. The firm are the official suppliers to the various sultans, and make a specialty of superior diamond jewellery of every description, although their stock includes well selected continental fancy goods, pictures and also the latest modes.*[11]

Wilhelm Cornfield, an Austrian Jew, came to Deli as a tailor at the S. Katz shop. In 1893, Cornfield started his own business, offering European clothing with imported fabrics. Prospering, the business soon expanded into a store with a complete range of clothes and luxury items from London and Paris.

The first generation of merchants eventually left or passed away and were replaced by their children. When Wilhelm Cornfield passed away in 1908, his children continued and expanded their father's business. In particular, his son, Isidore (1885–1923), was an investor in many luxury stores and plantations in North Sumatra.

Jewish merchants competed to import European consumer goods, merging, dividing, and clashing. In 1915, the Hüttenbach company split into a wholesaler and retail business. Isidore Cornfield managed the retail business, while Heinrich Hüttenbach maintained its import business. This split, however, caused a dispute between Heinrich Hüttenbach and Isidore Cornfield about who should manage the new department store. In the

[9] SP 06-10-1899.
[10] SP 01-04-1901.
[11] Lorck 1912: 236.

end, Isidore Cornfield won the case and rebuilt Medan's Warenhuis in 1920, the largest department store in Sumatra. The Hüttenbach firm, on the other hand, was declared bankrupt in December 1921, after 46 years of business, due to the financial crisis and mismanagement.

The debacle resulted in Heinrich Hüttenbach's departure. A few months later, he went missing on a passage from Amsterdam to London and was declared dead five years later. Nor did things end well for the Cornfields. Isidore returned to Vienna and died in October 1923 at the age of 38, due to heart disease. By 1939, the Cornfield fashion store, run by his brother Adolf, was in financial trouble and was liquidated. The shop closed its doors in July 1939 after trading for over 50 years.[12] Like many German and Dutch Jews, these merchants were assimilated and identified with their national societies (e.g. the Deutscher Verein) in Medan.

17.1.1 Dutch Jews and World War II

At the end of World War I, there was a high demand for expatriates to come to the Deli region to manage plantations and serve the colony. Some Dutch Jews responded and worked for plantations, Dutch companies or the government, and there are also a few examples of Jewish doctors. However, newspaper archives suggest that numbers remained tiny, and community activities were only recorded from the mid-1920s.

László Székely, born to a Jewish family in what is now eastern Hungary, arrived in Sumatra in 1914 as a planter, escaping poverty in Europe. His work was overshadowed by an affair with a Dutch planter's wife, Madelon Lulofs, that scandalised Deli's colonial society. After divorce and remarriage to Székely, Lulofs, in works such as *Rubber* (1931), became one of the principal literary voices critical of Dutch colonial power. Székely also wrote literary sketches of his own.

When Germany invaded the Netherlands in May 1940, the Jewish community of Medan raised funds for relief, but by March 1942, Sumatra, too, had fallen to the Japanese. Some Jewish families were threatened on either end of the world: persecuted in Europe as Jews and in the Indies as Dutch enemies of the Japanese. Adolf Cornfield died in a Japanese internment camp. Dr. Hans Koperberg, a Dutch Jewish physician who worked on the East coast of Sumatra, was captured and imprisoned by the Japanese. He wrote about his bitter experience, being moved from one camp to

[12] DC 04-04-1939.

another, in his poetry book *Bittere pillen en scherpe pijlen* (Bitter Pills and Sharp Arrows), which he

> *dedicated to my two Sisters murdered by the Huns, Uncle Dr. Felix Catz and Aunt Brama and to all the friends murdered by the Japs.*[13]

We have found little record of Jews in Sumatra after the war. Survivors left for the Netherlands or other countries, and by 1958, Soekarno had expelled all Dutch citizens from Indonesia.

17.2 The Saga of the Silver Coins: From Mexican Dollar to Roepiah

The guilder, or *gulden* or *florijn* (florin) with a symbol *f* or fl. was the official currency in the Netherlands for centuries, dating back to the Florentine florin gold coin in the thirteenth century. In the Dutch Indies, the guilder was also referred to as the *roepiah*.

An article in *Java Bode* in 1895 wrote (Fig. 17.3):

> *Due to the proximity of the Straits, Dutch currency is rarely used by the locals. A thin, flat dime holds little or no value in their eyes. Dollars are preferred, and although I, like most Europeans, prefer our much lighter and more compact Dutch currency (never mind the many counterfeit rijksdaalders that circulate and cause much trouble), the locals still refuse to use it. A significant advantage for Europeans is the low dollar exchange rate. Although some native*

Fig. 17.3 Coins used in the Dutch Indies, from left: Spanish pilaar dollar, Mexican dollar (ringgit boeroeng), rijksdaalder (ringgit kepala) and Straits dollar (pictures from Wikimedia)

[13] Koperberg, Hans. 1946. *Bittere pillen en scherpe pijlen.*

> *merchants have begun to understand that one ringgit blanda (Dutch guilder) is worth almost two regular ringgits and have raised their prices accordingly, the market prices have remained roughly the same, and as a result, wages for native servants have not increased significantly.*[14]

In the early stages of the development of Deli, the currency in use was aligned with the trading practices of the Straits. The Spanish dollar or piaster emerged as the dominant currency in international trade since the 1500s. The Spanish dollar or Spanish mat in the form of a silver coin was called *peso*, *peso fuerte*, or *peso duro* in Spanish, but was called *ringgit* in Malay. Spain and its colonies in Spanish America and Mexico were among the world's leading producers of silver. It was also known as the *pilaar* dollar, named for the depiction of the pillars of Hercules on the coin. In Malay, it was known as *ringgit mariam* (*mariam* means cannon, as the pillars were mistaken for cannons), sometimes also called *ringgit tiang.*[15]

In the early eighteenth century, the Spanish silver coin contained 25.5 grams of fine silver and was valued at *f*2.70. The Spanish dollar gained popularity in Asia, particularly in China, from 1759 to 1833. This coin was also used in the Dutch Indies, including Deli. The Batak Karo people traded peppers for the Spanish silver coins. The coin was highly valued as it could be made into *padung padung*, the traditional earrings. However, as time progressed, its value gradually declined to around *f*2.50 by the mid-nineteenth century.[16]

The late nineteenth century saw the Spanish dollar facing new contenders. Mexico, with its abundant silver resources, introduced the Mexican dollar. This currency closely resembled the Spanish dollar but slightly differed in weight and composition. The Mexican dollar gained considerable traction in East Asia and emerged as a significant export commodity, especially to China and the Straits Settlements. Similarly, the United States introduced the Trade dollar, Japan issued the Silver Yen, and England issued the Hong Kong dollar and Straits dollar. The Dutch also introduced their silver coin, the *rijksdaalder*, valued at *f*2.50. Nevertheless, the Mexican dollar was a popular currency in Southeast Asia and China, and was locally known as *ringgit boeroeng* due to the eagle motif on the coin.

[14] *Java Bode* 29-08-1895.
[15] Eong 1974: 58–65.
[16] DC 09-07-1890; information from Uli Kozok's blog.

Around 1861, the Mexican dollar was worth *f*2.70.[17] However, this value gradually decreased to around *f*1.86 to *f*1.90 by 1887[18] and declined to *f*1.1 to *f*1.25 after 1900.[19]

In Medan, several currencies were traded: Straits currencies, Spanish mats, Mexican, Japanese, Hong Kong dollars, and British trade dollars. The Mexican dollar was the most widely used, while the rijksdaalder was more common in Java. As the Mexican silver coin was called a *ringgit*, Javanese coolies working in plantations in Deli often were cheated. Coolies recruiters in Java were promised wages in silver dollars or *rijksdaalders* (worth *f*2.50). However, when the coolies reached Deli, they were paid with Mexican dollars or *ringgit boeroeng*, which was about three-quarters of the value of a *rijksdaalder* (also called *ringgit kepala* due to the head of King Willem of the Netherlands on the coin).[20]

In 1888, the British Chartered Bank opened an office in Medan, which strengthened the use of the Straits dollar in Medan and Deli. The silver dollar fluctuated because its value depended on the unstable global silver price, which fell as major economies adopted the gold standard and silver supply increased. However, planters preferred silver dollars, since they could pay wages and expenses in cheap silver while selling tobacco for gold abroad, securing large profits. However, importers suffered as they paid in gold for imports but were forced to accept fluctuating silver in return. Over time, merchants and salaried Europeans increasingly turned to the Dutch guilder, which was more stable as tied to the Dutch gold-based system, especially in areas dominated by the Royal Dutch Petroleum Company, where it became the sole medium of exchange.[21]

A major shift came in 1903, when the Straits Settlements adopted the gold standard, introduced the King Edward VII dollar, and banned the import of Mexican dollars. Deli's economy was compelled to follow, and significant losses were incurred when old silver coins had to be withdrawn. From then on, Sumatra's money supply became dependent on monetary decisions made in Singapore. Planters continued to favour the dollar for wage payments, while importers, bankers, and officials preferred expanding the role of the guilder to reduce risks from silver volatility and foreign

[17] *Java bode* 15-06-1861.

[18] DC 29-06-1887.

[19] *Het vaderland* 07-03-1900.

[20] *Rijksdaalder* was called "head coin" after the image of Dutch King Willem I on the coin or *ringgit nonna* for the coin had the head of Queen Wilhelmina; (DC 29-06-1887).

[21] DC 09-11-1906.

policy. Chinese merchants remained largely indifferent, concerned mainly with liquidity and cheap remittance facilities. [22] In September 1905, about 65 residents of Medan met at Hotel de Boer to oppose the continued circulation of the dollar, which they believed harmed the local economy. After a heated debate, lawyer van den Brand passed a motion calling for a definitive monetary reform, making the guilder the sole legal tender, and telegraphed to the colonial government.[23]

To resolve the uncertainty, the Dutch Indies government dispatched O. Vissering, the president of the Java Bank, in 1906 to investigate the state of currency circulation, assess whether the guilder could serve as the standard currency, and consider establishing a branch of the Java Bank in Medan. Two years later, in 1908, the guilder was declared the official currency in Deli, pegged at *f*2.50 to US$1, and the Java Bank inaugurated its Medan branch on the Esplanade. This decision unsettled the Straits Settlements, where August Hüttenbach of Penang warned that withdrawing the Straits dollar from Sumatra could release some 10 million coins back into circulation, creating oversupply, depreciation, and instability in the Straits' monetary system.[24]

The local populace, accustomed to a medley of foreign currencies, watched as ship after ship delivered gold pieces and coins from the Netherlands to Belawan. Under heavy guard, these treasures were transported by rail and stored in the local prison in Medan, lacking a bank vault, where they were vigilantly watched by a dedicated police force.[25]

The journey to distribute the coins further inland presented fresh challenges. The roads were rough, under construction, and fraught with dangers from both the terrain and the disgruntled local populations. Each leg of the journey required meticulous planning and brute strength, as oxen carts strained under their precious burdens. When the path grew too narrow or steep for the oxen, the task fell to local Bataks, who were coerced into carrying the crates on their backs.[26]

As the new currency took root, resistance flared, notably in Bagan Si Api-Api, where local fishermen clung to the British pounds. Tensions escalated until the Dutch authorities, led by a police commander, displayed

[22] Andrew 1904: 321-356; DC 09-11-1906.

[23] SP 02-10-1905.

[24] SP 14-10-1907.

[25] SP 15-04-1916.

[26] SP 17-04-1916, 18-04-1916.

Table 17.1 The average exchange rate of currencies used in the Dutch Indies (expressed as USD per one unit of currency) and its equivalent value in 2020

Period	*Dutch guilders f*	*Mexican dollar*	*Straits dollar*	*Hong Kong dollar*	*Chinese yuan*	*Approximate value of US$1 in 2020*[a]
1880–1910	0.400	0.46	0.56			
1914–1921	0.402	0.46		0.47		21
1922–1928	0.402	0.46	0.57	0.46		16
1929–1932	0.402	0.22	0.52	0.25	0.22	17
1933–1936	0.628		0.56	0.37	0.32	20
1937–1940	0.550		0.52	0.28	0.17	19

[a] Evaluated based on the consumer price index inflation value. Data from US Federal Reserve Bulletin (1900–1940)

their military might, marching through the village with drums beating and horns sounding, compelling the fishermen to exchange their cherished foreign coins for the new Dutch guilders (Table 17.1).[27]

17.2.1 *Plantation Tokens*

In the early establishment of the Deli plantations, the plantation companies created their own coins or tokens to pay the coolies. Plantation owners on the East Coast of Sumatra used these tokens as a means of exchange or payment within their plantations. The plantation owners argued that they had to create their own money due to the shortage of smaller currency in the region. However, the main reason was that the tokens could only be used within the plantation or for buying goods in the shops or *kedehs* within the plantation. The coolies were required to purchase and settle their food expenses using these plantation tokens. This also meant that the coolies had no real money if they deserted the plantation. The payment was made once a month, encompassing all the previous month's expenditures, including expenses for food, opium, and gambling debts.[28]

The *kedeh* was usually run by the head foreman or *tandil* of the Chinese coolies, who controlled it through family members. Coolies were compelled to buy their necessities there, especially rice. The plantation

[27] SP 19-04-1916.
[28] http://plantagegeld.nl/.

Fig. 17.4 Plantation token of Asahan Tabak Maatschappij Silau (National Museum of World Cultures, TM-3747-1)

administrator argued that this prevented coolies from gambling or using money for opium. However, they conveniently did not mention the large price markup by the *kedeh*. The *kedeh* extended credit but charged high prices.[29]

These plantation tokens were also common in English colonies and used in the West Indies and Ceylon, even in the United States. The tokens were mainly made from copper and usually came in the shape of a coin, but other shapes could also be found. The tokens had the company's name and nominal dollar value in English or Dutch, Chinese and sometimes Arabic. Some early tokens in Deli include the ones issued by de Guigné Fres, with tokens for buckets of rice *gantang bras* (1 gantang is about 2 litres or 1.5 kg of rice). There were also tokens issued by companies such as Hüttenbach & Co, for use in their plantations in Bobongan. Today, these plantation tokens, with their dark history, have become highly sought-after collector's items, each fetching a value of over US$200 (Fig. 17.4).

[29] Breman 1989: 109–111.

CHAPTER 18

The Rise and Fall of the Hüttenbach Family of Deli

Hüttenbach & Co. was a prominent business in Medan from the city's founding until the 1930s. A street near Kesawan was named Hüttenbachstraat (now known as Jl. Jend. A. Yani VII) in recognition of the company (Fig. 18.1).

18.1 The Hüttenbach Family

The Hüttenbach family originated from a well-known Jewish merchant family in Worms in the Upper Rhine in Germany.[1] The head of the family, Salomon Hüttenbach, and his wife, Jeanette Lorch, had six sons and two daughters.[2] The family's eldest son August, was born in 1850 and served in the Franco-Prussian war in 1870. In 1872, at the age of 22, August tried his fortune in Penang, where he found work at Katz Brothers, a well--known Jewish family company. The Katz brothers invested in nearly every business in Malaya, including fuelling ships for freight. When the Dutch waged war against the Atjehnese in 1873, the Katz Brothers provided logistics and supplies to the Dutch army. It was during this time that August Hüttenbach learned the art of trade. Eventually, his brothers Jacob and Ludwig joined him in Malaya, and together, they started a shipping

[1] Warnk 2011, 2012.

[2] Information from Laura Lee Hüttenbach, the Hüttenbach family members were Luise, Rosalie, August, Adolf, Jacob, Ludwig, Emil, and Heinrich.

B. Minasny, D. A. Buiskool, *Stories from Medan, Volume 1*,
https://doi.org/10.1007/978-981-95-7707-1_18

Fig. 18.1 Hüttenbach shop in Laboean Deli in 1876 (postcard produced by Hüttenbach, KITLV 1402038)

business to serve the Dutch troops. They became a contractor and ran regular services from Malaya to the Atjeh port, supplying food, forage, and fuel for the Dutch army.[3]

In 1885, August and Ludwig established Hüttenbach Brothers and Co., headquartered in Penang with a branch in Singapore. Ludwig set up an office in London called Hüttenbach & Co.[4] Additionally, they ran a shipping company called Hüttenbach & Liebert Co. that operated in the Straits. August, in particular, was instrumental in opening new steamship communications between Penang, Selangor, and the Coromandel Coast, in the southeast of India. August also established the British Mail line from Europe via Bombay-Negapatam-Straits Settlements. Furthermore, August was involved in shipping coolies from South India to Penang. His company was able to compete with other companies by providing a unique offering to coolies. In addition to providing a free ride, they also included an added attraction by taking the coolies around town in bullock carts

[3] Wright 747.
[4] DC 11-11-1885.

adorned with flags and a brass band.[5] August had a stable of racehorses in Singapore and even sent horses to the Saigon races, where they won prizes.

These endeavours proved that he was a successful and respected businessman, and August was appointed as a member of the Legislative Council of Penang in 1894–1896 and 1905–1906. August was considered an authority in business and currency matters.

After observing the development of the new land in Deli, Jacob Hüttenbach decided to venture there. In 1875, Jacob opened the first European store in Laboean Deli to cater to the requirements and needs of the Dutch government, the plantations, and industrial groups (Fig. 18.1). They exported agricultural products from the indigenous people to Penang and supplied Europeans with canned goods, beverages, helmets, shoes, perfumes, jewellery, lamps, hardware, etc. With their own shipping lines, in the early period, Hüttenbach was the sole importer in Deli, including supplying cattle from Singapore and Penang to Deli.[6] From 1877, they also operated the Sumatra hotel, a small hut catering to travelling Europeans.[7] The hotel closed in 1883 due to a lack of clients.[8]

In the early days, the import of goods to Deli relied on shipment to Penang and Singapore via Hüttenbach. An illustration of this process can be seen in the kerosene trade from America to Sumatra in 1885. Meyer Bros. & Co. purchased 5000 cases of Chester brand kerosene from the Chester Refining Co. in America. The kerosene was shipped on the chartered Italian bark Paolina from a dock on the Delaware River to Hüttenbach Bros. in Penang. Hüttenbach Bros. Co. then shipped the kerosene via inter-island steamer to Laboean Deli. From there, it was transported by railway to Medan, where it was distributed to one of the tobacco plantation companies or to a Chinese dealer who sold it to retail stores in smaller towns and villages.[9]

To facilitate trade and movement, in 1893, August Hüttenbach bought the steamship Ho Kwei and provided a Penang-Belawan route that operated every five days.[10] Ho Kwei became the main transport from Belawan to Penang for the next ten years.

[5] *The Straits Times* 23-02-1900.

[6] *Straits Times Weekly Issue*, 07-11-1893.

[7] De Saint-Pol Lias 1884: 297.

[8] *De locomotief* 20-01-1883.

[9] Gould 1961: 44.

[10] Ho Kwei was a 209 ton steamship, operated from 1893 to 1904 Penang to Medan, and in 1905 sold to E. C. Pearce, Hong Kong and to Kin Chong & Co., Shanghai in 1908. In

As time passed, Hüttenbach transformed into a general merchandise company that supplied all sorts of goods from Europe. They also acted as commission agents for various European companies. Management was entrusted to Europeans, and it had diverse employees, including Ung Beng Seing, a Chinese from Malaya, who had served as a clerk since 1878, and Mandailing clerk Shech Ibrahim, who had worked for the company since the 1880s.[11]

With the blooming of Deli tobacco as a precious commodity, the brothers also invested in tobacco plantations.[12] Since 1883, the Hüttenbach & Co. company in Deli had started cultivating tobacco. They established Fortuna estates, Augustburg, and Ludwigsburg in Langkat. The latter was later renamed Djohor Lama, and some of the estates were closed due to poor results. In 1886, Hüttenbach established the Frankfurt and Adolina estates in Bobongan.[13] In 1889, Hüttenbach & Co. transferred their plantations to a newly established company. The Netherlands India Sumatra Tobacco Company, incorporated in London with a capital of £125,000. The directors included Ludwig in Singapore, Jacob in Deli, together with British tobacco brokers and the Standard Chartered bank.[14] The company sought investors on the London Stock Exchange. In 1894, the company was replaced by the Serdang Tabak Maatschappij, incorporated under Dutch law with a capital of 1.7 million guilders.[15]

During the 1880s, Hüttenbach relocated its headquarters to Medan (Fig. 18.4). The street where the new premise was located was called Djalan Hüttenbach, later named Hüttenbachstraat, which is now known as Jalan Ahmad Yani VII. Initially, the company, Handel Maatschappij Hüttenbach, was a wooden warehouse. Over time, it expanded and occupied an expansive 1800 square meter premise (Fig. 18.5).[16]

1916, it was wrecked 50 miles from Shanghai enroute to Hainan (https://www.clydeships.co.uk/).

[11] Shech Ibrahim later became the head of a village (penghulu pekan) and co-founder of the Sjarikat Tapanoeli which published *Pewarta Deli* newspaper (SP 21-04-1933).

[12] *Bataviaasch Handelsblad* 18-04-1891.

[13] Adolina or Adalina or Adeline refers to a girl's name of German origin meaning noble. Frankfurt plantation later split into Bobongan and Batang Trap. Adolina plantation is still a well-known landmark near Perbaungan, North Sumatra.

[14] *Investors Chronicle and Money Market Review* 1889: 573, DC 05-06-1889.

[15] Stock exchange 1916: 1124. Serdang Tabak Mij was dissolved in 1917 and reorganised to Serdang Cultuurmaatschappij under NHM.

[16] Feldwick 1917: 1185.

Hüttenbach in Medan was a vast empire that provided a wide range of merchandise and services, from a needle to an engine. They offered machinery, tools, motors, electrical goods, harnesses, saddlery, guns, ammunition, watches, and even water buffalos during the Islamic New Year to cater to plantation needs. The company was also an agent for various prominent brands such as Ford, Cadbury, Heineken, Guinness Stout, Bear Brand milk, whiskey, and many others. Hüttenbach also supplied everyday needs such as clothing, typewriters, and food from Europe, including canned goods like soup, corned beef, tongue sausage, anchovy sausage, "Wienerwurstel," beans, carrots, cauliflower, asparagus, among others. The company served as an agent for several famous European trading, insurance, and manufacturing companies. Hüttenbach was a registered supplier for the Dutch Indies government. Hüttenbach also produced an early postcard series of Deli, 35 sepia cards depicting the plantation life and Europeans in the region in the 1860s-1890s (Fig. 18.3).

In 1920, Hüttenbach had an annual import worth *f*1,200,000[17] and had an extensive network throughout Sumatra.[18] It had offices in London and Amsterdam and also operated the Sumatra Tobacco Syndicate in London and Hüttenbach's Automobiel in Medan (Fig. 18.2).[19]

Planters often purchased items using a credit system, and trust was built up within the community. There was an anecdote involving the Hüttenbach company, which sold a saddle to a planter but then forgot who the planter was. In an attempt to retrieve payment, Hüttenbach issued bills for the saddle and charged six customers, one of whom might be the buyer. They believed that the real buyer would eventually come forward and pay, and the others would recognise the mistake. However, to their surprise, five out of the six bills were paid for the same saddle (Figs. 18.3, 18.4 and 18.5).[20]

[17] 1.2 million guilders were equivalent to 480,000 USD in 1920s, or worth 7.7 million USD in 2020 (Based on inflation rate, 1 USD in 1920 has the buying power of $16 in 2020).

[18] Wright, 1909: 572.

[19] Sumatra Tobacco Syndicate was established in 1893 with L. Hüttenbach as the director. Hüttenbach's Automobiel was established in 1919 (Colonial Business Indonesia).

[20] DC 02-11-1938.

Fig. 18.2 Hüttenbach lotteries with a permit from the Resident of the East Coast, selling 500 tickets at 2 Roepiah each. The lottery offered 26 prizes, with a top prize of a bicycle worth *f*165, followed by a singing machine valued at *f*50, Pewarta Deli 08-10-1918. (Picture courtesy of Dr. Surjadi https://niadilova.wordpress.com/)

18.2 Heinrich Hüttenbach

Born on December 14th, 1859, in Worms, Heinrich Hüttenbach was the youngest of the family. While his father hoped that he would study medicine or law, Heinrich was interested in travelling. As a young man, he left school and joined the military service. Upon his return from the army, his brothers asked for his assistance in Deli. He first went to Deli in 1876, first as a salesman and then as a bill collector. His memoirs also reveal the paternalism and violence of the plantation society:

> *There were then no roads in Deli to speak of, and the whole Government consisted of an Assistant Resident and Controleur. In those days people could die and their bodies lie about until devoured by tigers or carried away by floods. I myself have seen bodies floating up and down with the tide. Occasionally the*

HÜTTENBACH & Co.

Bekroond met Gouden Medaille en Eere-Diploma's Tentoonstelling Medan 1908.

HÜTTENBACH & Co.

Opgericht 1875.

Leveranciers aan het Nederlandsch-Indische Gouvernement.

Kleermakerij.	Mecaniciens.	Horlogerie.	Lederafdeeling.	Wijnhandel.
Landbouw-Werktuigen	Wapens	Jachtartikelen	Manufacturen	Zijde
Langkat Lampen	Gasoline Lampen	Spiritus Lampen	Porcelein	Meubelen
Gramophoons	Motorcars	Fietsen	Naaimachines	Boussoles
Sigaren	Sigaretten	Champagne	Paardentuigen	Bascules
Odeon Records	Pathé Platen	Hymnophons	Schrijfmachines	Rolschaatsen
Fietsen	Bellen	City-bags	Lantarens	Zadels
Lijm	Banden	Carbid	Zilverlak	Assen
Pompen	Rijwielen	Dranken	Vrijbuiter-Jenever	Sherry
Whisky	Stout	Havana Sigaren	Deli M. Sigaren	Peterhof Sigaretten
Kremlin Sigaretten	Peerless Sigaretten	Pijpen	Koffers	Paardentuigen
Provisiën	Chocolade	Toffee	Biscuits	Jam
Suikerwerk	Zalm	Boter	Melk	Kaas
Odeurs	Zeep	Haarwater	Eau de Chinine	Tennisnetten
Pistolen	Revolvers	Tijgervallen	Tennisrackets	Tennisballen
Voetballen	Diabolo Spellen	Zweepen	Halters	Speelgoed
Pistaches	Kerstboomen	Wagens	Bioscopen	Meubelen
Kinderwagens	Kinderbascules	Uurwerken	Wekkers	Scheepsklokken
Regulateurs	Wandklokken	Koekoekklokken	Horloges	Waltham Horloges
Roskopf	Zenith Horloges	Rouletten	Spelen	Waschstellen
Fonteintjes	Waschtafels	Waterclosets	Badkuipen	Kinderbaden
Zitbaden	Ligbaden	Filters	Berkefeld Filters	Fornuizen
Bascules	Weegschalen	Poetsmachines	Vleeschmachines	IJsmachines
Family Scales	Sieraden	Ringen	Broches	Armbanden
Tooneelkijkers	Waaiers	Messen	Scheermessen	Tondeuses
Gillettes	Zakmessen	Dinéretuis	Vorken	Lepels
Rozenscharen	Meubelen	Rustbanken	Stoelen	Etagères
Tafels	Spiegels	Kasten	Ledikanten	Veldbedden
Schoenen	Parapluies	Hoeden	Manufacturen	Sokken
Singlets	Onderbroeken	Jaegers Ondergoed	Drill	Shirtings
Handdoeken	Buikbanden	Manchetten	Potten	Boorden
Kantoorbehoeften	Slijpmachines	Copieerpersen	Brievenmappen	Theographen
Dagstempels	Waaiers	Ploegen	Kebon Bellen	Parangs
Tjankols	Harken	Kapmessen	IJzergaas	Verf
Olie	Controleklokken	Kompassen	Pedometers	Meetlint

BOVENSTAANDE ALLES VERKRIJGBAAR

Fig. 18.3 List of items provided by Hüttenbach & Co. as a supplier to the Dutch Indies government, from lamp, cigar, champagne, to cuckoo clock (from Laura Lee Hüttenbach)

Fig. 18.4 Hüttenbach in Medan in the 1880s (from KITLV Album Or. 27.377)

Fig. 18.5 Hüttenbach in Medan in 1909 (Wright 1909)

> *Battaks and Gaiooks (Gayos) came down from the hills and attacked and murdered the planters. I once saw seven Battaks hanged in one day.*[21]

Heinrich was not content with his trading job and continued to move around until his brother August offered him a role in the shipping

[21] *The Selangor Journal* vol.3, 1895:143.

business. August needed Heinrich's help to supply goods to the Dutch troops who were fighting in Atjeh.

> *My duties now were to weigh the pigs, take delivery of the poultry, look after some 200 coolies who were handling the rice, etc. and see to the loading of the steamers, of which we would sometimes have as many as eight large ones in the harbour at one time...*[22]

Then Heinrich got a job purchasing pepper from Atjeh:

> *I made great friends with the Achinese, and had many opportunities of studying their customs: I have witnessed the death penalty inflicted for adultery, and death by burning for theft --and, at the finish, was very near being put to death myself, because I refused to pay for the pepper I had on board before the full quantity contracted for was supplied.*[23]

After exploring various businesses, including shipping, he finally returned to Deli in 1883 to oversee Hüttenbach's newly established plantation in Deli at Bobongan. In 1885, he managed the Bengabing concession of 4500 acres.[24] Heinrich explained the authority of a planter:

> *... he now has to walk back and forth in the shed like a schoolteacher with his stick, checking the bundled tobacco to see if it is properly sorted and monitoring the fermentation of the tobacco. He must be the first in the barn in the morning, and the last to leave her in the evening. When I say, as a schoolmaster, I am quite right, for just as naughty boys do all kinds of mischief at school to annoy the master for their own pleasure, so do the coolies, and ventriloquists and similar artists celebrate triumphs. If one discovers the culprit who has barked or meowed, one punishes him as a naughty boy, because in fact they are just big children and not people of character and education. Sense of honour, for example, is completely unknown to them.*[25]

Heinrich served as the head administrator of the plantation until 1887.

> *Shortly before I left Deli there was a riot on the estate: about 100 armed Chinese attacked me, and in self-defence I shot three of them; with the assistance of my*

[22] *The Selangor Journal* vol.3, 1895:144.
[23] idem.
[24] *Investors Chronicle and Money Market Review* 1889: 573.
[25] *Soerabaijasch Handelsblad* 29-02-1888.

> *Sikhs and some Malays the remainder were overpowered and handed over to the Dutch Government for punishment.*[26]

After returning to Germany for a few years, Heinrich moved to Selangor, Malaya, where he managed the Selangor Trading and Coffee Curing Company in 1890, and later the Selangor Plantation Syndicate. Heinrich became actively involved in the planters' society, first as secretary and later as chair of the Selangor Planters Association. He was known for his active and confident demeanour and held various social positions, such as the honorary secretary of the Selangor club, lieutenant of the Selangor Fire Brigade, and treasurer of the Gymkhana club.[27] As chair of the Selangor Planters Association, he actively participated in discussions about coolies recruitment and treatment. One notable discussion involved revoking the pass system in favour of granting freedom to the coolies' movement. An employer should be compelled to provide certificates of discharge or *soerat lepas* when the worker had paid off his debts; without one, a coolie could not find other employment.[28] Heinrich pledged to allow Tamil coolies, who had repaid all their passage fees and expenses, to seek employment elsewhere without facing obstacles from influential Europeans.[29] He also advocated the payment of coolies via the yield system of Deli.[30]

Heinrich returned to Europe via America in 1900, still in search of adventure. He planned to visit Peking and travelled via the S.S. Apenrade. However, while sailing between Chefoo (now Yantai) and Weihaiwei (Weihai), the ship encountered a severe gale, causing the engines to fail. After three days of being battered by the storm, the ship anchored near a deserted shore, with everything on deck washed overboard, and the passengers and crew suffering from injuries and frostbite. Fortunately, they were rescued by a German cruiser. Following this ordeal, Heinrich was forced to return to Shanghai.[31] Nevertheless, he visited the German-leased territory in China, Kiautschou (Jiaozhou) Bay and wrote:

[26] *The Selangor Journal* vol.3, 1895:145.

[27] Gymkhana derived from British India term meaning a social and sporting club. *Straits Mail* 15-01-1895.

[28] *The Straits Budget* 25-09-1894.

[29] *Pinang Gazette and Straits Chronicle* 09-10-1899.

[30] *The Straits Budget* 17-12-1895.

[31] *Pinang Gazette and Straits Chronicle* 28-02-1901.

It is a most pleasant sensation for a German, to land in China at a place where the German flag flies, signaling that one is in German territory; to have tangible proof that Germany as a power no longer stands in the background but is assuming its rank in the world. You, Englishmen, have always known this feeling, but we Germans remember very well that the rest of the world could treat us as it pleased.[32]

18.2.1 *Hüttenbach in Medan*

In 1895, Jacob Hüttenbach left Medan for Frankfurt am Main, while his brother Ludwig was in charge of the company in London and the headquarters in Amsterdam. Jacob passed away in Europe in 1897.[33] Later, in 1913, Ludwig also passed away in London. [34]

Thus, in 1902, Heinrich went to Medan to manage the Hüttenbach company. He was active in the community, including as the treasurer of the German association of Medan.[35] David Sandel, the German consul in Medan and from the well-known company Firma Sandel of Tandjoeng Poera in Langkat, introduced Heinrich to his sister, Gunda Sandel.[36] Heinrich ended his bachelor life and married Dorothea Kunigunde (Gunda) Sandel in Penang in 1905 (Fig. 18.6).[37] Three years later, in 1908, Heinrich became a Dutch citizen (Fig. 18.8).[38]

Heinrich developed an interest in the Malay language and wrote a German book titled *Anleitung zur Erlernung der Malayischen zum Studium während der Reise nach Ost-Indien* or Guide to learning the Malay for Study during your trip to East India (Fig. 18.7). The book, first published in Worms, Germany, in 1885, was designed to serve as a practical guide for newcomers to the Dutch Indies and Malaya, as he wrote:

This is not an academic book. You will search in vain for these words in Malay grammar; I have compiled this, however, because academic works are useless for newcomers. Good, correct Malay is not needed in communication, just as little use of High German in Switzerland.[39]

[32] *Soerabaijasch Handelsblad* 28-03-1901.
[33] DC 13-11-1897.
[34] SCMP 11-12-1913.
[35] SP 17-03-1904.
[36] Information from Laura Lee Hüttenbach.
[37] SP 01-05-1905.
[38] *Nederlandsche Staatscourant* 12-06-1908.
[39] Warnk 2015.

Fig. 18.6 Heinrich and Gunda's wedding in Penang 28-05-1905. Front row, from left: August Hüttenbach and his wife Clara, Gunda and Heinrich, Luise Sandel (wife of Paul Sandel), Ernst von Beeren, Frau Maieir from Rantau Pandjang. Back row: Paul Sandel, unknown guest, sister of Clara, David Sandel, and Mr. Jones, the best man (Photo courtesy of Laura Lee Hüttenbach)

After its initial publication, the book underwent revisions and was expanded into a second edition published in Medan in 1909. Subsequently, a third revised edition was published in 1921. Interestingly, the conversational situations in the book were influenced by Heinrich's experience managing plantation workers.[40] Holger Warnk, a librarian from Frankfurt University, called this "coolie talk," with an example conversation in the plantation (*kebon*):

[40] Warnk 2011, 2012.

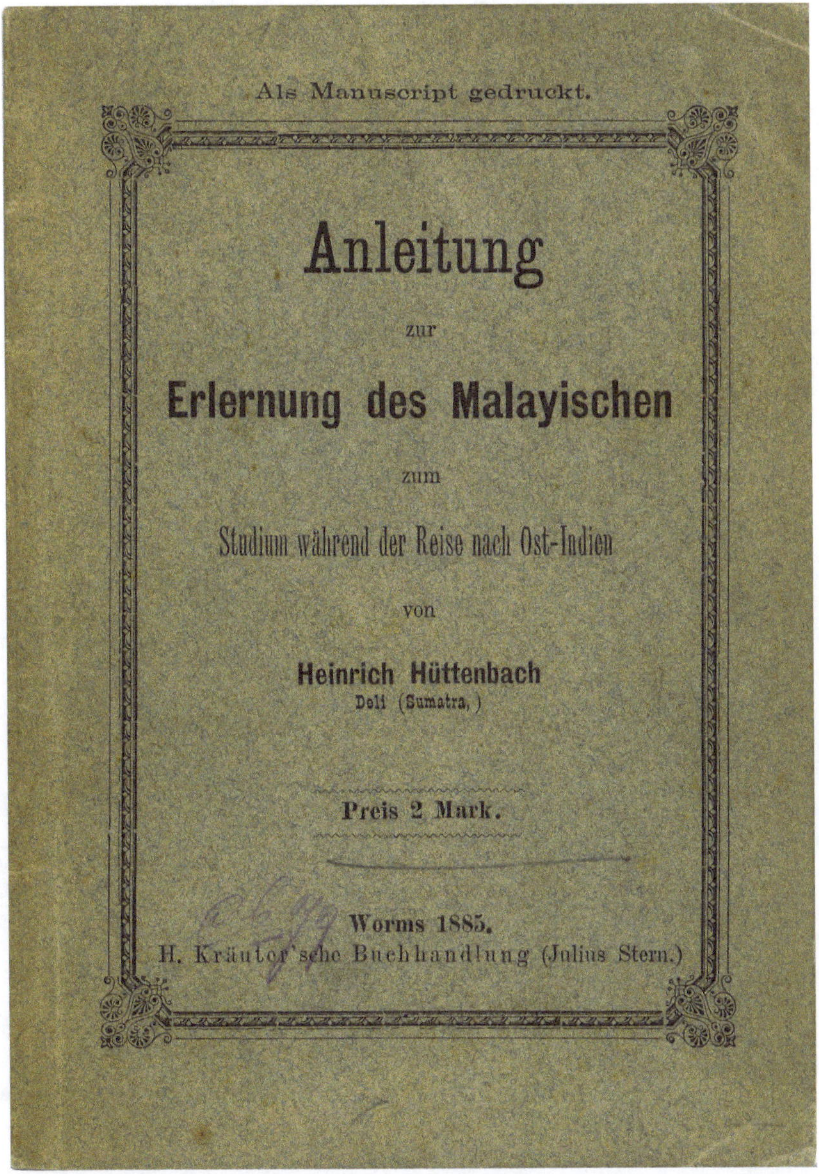

Fig. 18.7 Heinrich Hüttenbach's guide to learning the Malay language, published in 1885 (photo courtesy of Holger Warnk)

Fig. 18.8 Heinrich Hüttenbach, Gunda Sandel and their firstborn child, Greta, in Medan with a maid in 1906 (Photo courtesy of Laura Lee Hüttenbach)

Kenapa lu tida kerdja? Saya sakit. Apa kurang? Saja sakit kepala. Lu orang bôhong. Lu bukan sakit. Lu malas sadja. Saja mau kassi pukul sama lu. ... Ampun Tuan, djangan marah sama saja, tida bohong saja sakit betul-betul.[41]

(Why are you not working? I am sick. What's wrong. I have a headache. You lied, you're not sick. You are just lazy. I hit you. ... Forgive me sir, don't get angry, I am not lying, I am really sick).

Despite his hard stance, Heinrich also contributed to philanthropy by establishing the Hüttenbach study fund for Sumatra's East Coast in 1916, with a starting capital of *f*20,000. The fund was specifically created to provide financial assistance to gifted children from underprivileged families, enabling them to attend secondary or higher secondary schools in Java. The fund was available for Europeans and Indigenous children. The fund also supported a limited number of Indigenous children from the East coast of Sumatra with financial allowances to support their education and housing needs.[42]

Heinrich and Gunda had three children - Greta, William, and Erik. While still managing the business in Medan, the family relocated to London in late 1906 and stayed there until just before the outbreak of World War I, when they moved to Amsterdam.[43]

18.3 The Split and Demise

In 1915, the Hüttenbach company underwent a division, separating its import and wholesale business from its retail business. [44] The retail arm was branded as N.V. Medan's Warenhuis, with Isidore Cornfield appointed director. Meanwhile, Heinrich in London continued to oversee the import business under Hüttenbach & Co. However, this split resulted in a disagreement between Hüttenbach and Cornfield over who should manage Medan's Warenhuis. After a legal battle, Cornfield emerged victorious and assumed control of the retail business.

World War I started in 1914, and the Dutch economy suffered. The war officially ended in 1918. However, the commodity markets crashed in 1920 due to an overflow of stocks accumulated during the war. Industry

[41] Idem.

[42] SP 06-07-1916; SP 23-04-1920.

[43] Information from Laura Lee Hüttenbach.

[44] *De Indische mercuur* 31-12-1915.

increased production, expecting a post-war surge in demand, but supplies ended up exceeding demand, causing prices to collapse. This situation hit banks and merchant houses particularly hard, as they had supplied finance for the expansion of production during and after the war. Manufacturing and trading companies experienced reduced capital and losses, while international traders faced severe stock losses.[45]

Hüttenbach overstocked at peak prices, then suffered sharp depreciation. The unsold goods ultimately resulted in large overdrawn funds.[46] To make matters worse, Hüttenbach could not get further credit from companies in Amsterdam. A similar situation also hit another Dutch Indies company, Kerkhoff & Co., which faced liquidation due to the bank's refusal to provide further credit.[47] In August 1921, Hüttenbach & Co. obtained a loan of one million guilders from Nederlandsch-Indische Escompto Maatschappij by pledging all its goods as security.[48]

Unable to pay the loan, in March 1922, the remaining goods of Hüttenbach company were auctioned. The company accumulated a debt of *f*240,683.55.[49] As a result, its building was taken over by Borneo-Sumatra Handels Maatschappij (Borsumij or Borneo Sumatra Trading Company).[50]

Heinrich was distressed by the bankruptcy of the large family business. He subsequently returned to Amsterdam. On March 8th, 1922, he left for London aboard the St. George steamship to visit the company. However, when the ship arrived at its destination the following day, Heinrich was nowhere to be found. The exact cause was unknown, *De Sumatra Post* reported that he fell overboard and drowned.[51] Despite extensive efforts, Heinrich's body was never recovered.[52] Gunda had to wait five years before filing for her husband's formal death on November 24th, 1928.[53] She and her two remaining children, Greta and William, moved to

[45] Jonker and Sluyterman 2001: 227–228.

[46] SP 07-03-1922.

[47] Jonker and Sluyterman 2001: 228.

[48] Weekblad voor privaatrecht, notaris-ambt en registratie 03-10-1931.

[49] Worth US$1.45 million in 2020.

[50] SP 30-03-1922.

[51] SP 20-04-1922.

[52] A police report described a body that was likely Heinrich that washed ashore near Staveren (Stavoren), Friesland, The Netherlands, however, the family didn't claim the body (info from Laura Lee Hüttenbach).

[53] *Nederlandsche Staatscourant* 28-11-1928.

Stuttgart, Germany, to live with her mother. Unfortunately, their third son, Erik, died during the Spanish flu epidemic of 1918.[54]

That was the end of Hüttenbach in Medan. Despite that, Heinrich's legacy continued. Sixteen years later, in 1938, the book publisher Varekamp in Medan advertised that Heinrich's book *Erlernung der Malaysischen Sprache* was available for sale.[55] The scholarship he founded, Hüttenbach studiefonds, continued to be managed by a committee and awarded until the end of the 1930s.[56]

[54] Information from Laura Lee Hüttenbach, 04-02-2023.
[55] SP 24-08-1938.
[56] DC 16-02-1924; SP 24-05-1934.

CHAPTER 19

The Legend of Medan's Warenhuis

The grand opening of Medan's Warenhuis on November 15, 1920, marked the debut of the largest department store in Sumatra at the time (Fig. 19.1).

> *You will find everything there, in this first East Coast department store, literally... an extensive emporium, with the largest retailer in the Far East.*[1] *Medan's Warenhuis was opened on a late night attracting enormous public interest.*
>
> *At first, there was a huge disappointment, as the electricity company announced at the time of the opening at 7 pm, that it could not supply sufficient power to ignite all the lights. However, half an hour later, the gigantic building was bathed in a sea of electric lights. The rooms were full, and when Mayor Mackay spoke, it was estimated that at least 600 people were in the building. The mayor cut the ribbon, and the Warenhuis was declared open to everyone. Visitors wandered through the countless neat display windows and display cases, and all congratulated Mr. and Mrs. Cornfield.*[2]

The construction of the building was estimated to cost *f*300,000.[3] Coming out of economic trouble post World War I, Medan was a thriving colonial plantation town and Medan's Warenhuis had an extensive range

[1] Feldwick 1917: 1187.
[2] SP 16-11-1920.
[3] Equivalent to US$ 1.9 million in 2020.

B. Minasny, D. A. Buiskool, *Stories from Medan, Volume 1*,
https://doi.org/10.1007/978-981-95-7707-1_19

Fig. 19.1 Medan's Warenhuis

of products to offer, from perfume to glassware. The furniture department boasted the most extensive European collection. There were hosiery, haberdashery, provision, perfumery, jewellery, sporting, and confectionery departments. You could find hand-painted Bohemian glassware, from the everyday glasses to the most expensive crystal. A European tailor was available in the men's department, while a French modiste served the ladies of Medan. There was also a restaurant serving luncheons, cakes, and afternoon teas (Fig. 19.2).[4]

[4] Feldwick ibid.

Fig. 19.2 Medan's Warenhuis was advertised as the largest department store in the Dutch Indies (DC 14-12-1926)

The story of Medan's Warenhuis is intertwined with the histories of two families, the Hüttenbachs and the Cornfields. The Hüttenbach family was discussed in the previous chapter.

19.1 The Cornfields

The best customers in the town go to Cornfield's, and among the firm's patrons are the members of the family of the Sultan of Deli.[5]

Wilhelm Cornfield (1862–1908), an Austrian Jew, arrived in Deli in the 1890s and began working as a "cutter" (master cloth-cutter) at the S. Katz company. Following a dispute with his employer, he decided to open his own tailoring and outfitting shop, Cornfield Tailleur, in 1893. Unhappy with the competition, S. Katz published advertisements in the *Deli Courant* to announce that W. Cornfield was no longer employed by them. [6] Furthermore, S. Katz offered discounts of 25–30% on its clothing to

[5] Feldwick 1907:1192.
[6] DC 19-04-1893.

undercut its new rival.[7] Undeterred, Cornfield persisted, regularly placing his own advertisements in the *Deli Courant*:

> *W. CORNFIELD TAILOR, MEDAN, formerly a seamster at the firm of S. KATZ & Co., recommends himself to receive orders. He has the best fabrics in stock at very reasonable prices.*[8]

Over time, Cornfield's business grew and, in 1896, became W. Cornfield Merchant. Two years later, in 1898, Cornfield built a two-storey shop at Kesawan, located next to Goldenberg & Zeitlin. The store offered a complete range of clothes, including flannels, worsted vicuna cheviot, serges, tweeds, felt hats for the gentlemen, and leather handbags for the ladies. It had a European tailor and chief cutter. Luxury items from London and Paris were imported, and the store also supplied gold, silver, and bronze goods, household furniture, lamps, pictures, and other luxury items (Fig. 19.3).[9]

Wilhelm Cornfield, originally bearing the Austrian surname Schwartz, hailed from a merchant family in Vienna. [10] His wife, Esther Kalinhoff, also came from Vienna.[11] Together, they had four children: Isidore, Adolf, Edith, and Louis. Cornfield also invested in plantations in the growing region.

After achieving great success in Medan, Wilhelm Cornfield expanded his business by opening a branch in Penang in early 1901. The tailor and outfitter's shop was located at the Whiteways Arcade, Beach Street, which was considered the finest and newest block of offices in Penang. However, in March 1904, a fire broke out at the Cornfield store and quickly spread throughout the building, causing significant damage to the arcade.

Undeterred by this setback, Cornfield established the International Hotel at Leith Street in Penang and continued to explore new opportunities and ventured further to Colombo, Ceylon (now Sri Lanka). Unfortunately, during a business trip to Colombo with his wife and daughter in 1908, Wilhelm Cornfield died at the age of 46. His body was then transported back to Singapore, where he was laid to rest.[12]

[7] *Pinang Gazette and Straits Chronicle* 31-05-1893.

[8] DC 29-04-1893.

[9] Feldwick 1907:1192.

[10] The father F. Cornfield (1894-1903) died in Constantinople age 79 years (DC 05-08-1903).

[11] The father H. Kalinfoff died in Vienna in 1913 (DC 15-12-1913).

[12] *The Straits Times* 02-01-1909; DC 09-06-1905.

Fig. 19.3 Cornfield advertisement in *Isles of the East: an illustrated guide* by Lorck, W. Royal Packet Steam Navigation Co. (K.P.M. 1912)

After the passing of Wilhelm Cornfield, his children, Isidore, Adolf, and Edith, took over their father's business. They reorganised it into a company called Cornfield Magazijn, which was involved in import and export trade, commission agencies, plantations, and other commercial activities. The company had a capital of 500,000 guilders,[13] divided into 100 shares,

[13] Equivalent to US$5.4 million in 2020.

with the majority owned by Isidore Cornfield, Mrs. Cornfield in Vienna, and Adolf Cornfield.[14]

Isidore Cornfield, known as Is. or Dory, was a highly successful businessman and the director of Cornfield Magazijn. In the 1910s, he was a shareholder in several luxury stores in Medan and North Sumatra, including Medan's Warenhuis, Cornfield's Stores in Medan and Pematang Siantar, Maison Mesters in Medan, Sijpestijn & Co. in Medan, Tebing Tinggi, and Palembang, and E. Ter Meulen & Co. in Medan (capital *f*100,000). He was also the director of Deli Handel Maatschappij (capital *f*100,000), engaged in import and export, insurance, and shipping. Isidore was an investor in the Rajabosi Tea Estate Company in Simalungun, with 800 acres under cultivation, the Aloeritam coconut plantation, with 900 acres under cultivation, timber harvesting at Birem Rayeu Cultuur in Langsa, Atjeh (capital *f*500,000), and Sungei Moesam Rubber Syndicate (capital *f*150,000).[15]

Isidore was an avid footballer and was regarded as a shrewd businessman. He observed that many stores were struggling to achieve satisfactory returns for their capital outlay in Medan's growing community. Isidore saw an opportunity in this and was quick to capitalise on it. By combining various retail establishments, including some that were losing money, and leveraging his knowledge of the local retail trade, gained through years of experience, he revitalised the industry and ushered in a period of prosperity.[16]

After wandering as a bachelor in Penang and Singapore for some time, Isidore finally tied the knot with Henriette (Henny) Zerkowitz, an opera singer and member of a Viennese Industrial family. In a letter dated April 11, 1920, Henny described her journey to Medan:

> *We reached Belawan on February 24. Had about thirty people greeted me, I got two rose bouquets. We were just about to go to the car when a wagon trotted by four splendidly full horses: out jumped a black man, the Crown Prince of Deli, who presented me with a beautiful orchid bouquet. At the same time, he invited me to visit his first wife, the sultana (he has fifty concubines), in the harem, which I will do soon. Last week he sent us a golden coffee service.*
>
> *Now we drove to Medan, an hour away. I will never forget this journey. In front of our decorated car, behind it, the Crown Prince and then all the others.*

[14] SP 24-06-1914.

[15] Colonial Business Indonesia; *Indische Mercuur* 28-02-1919.

[16] Feldwick 1917: 1187.

At the end of Medan, my husband had built a villa, which was just being finished in a rush. The villa is located in a vast garden with bananas, coconuts, pineapples and oranges. Inside it was a sea of flowers of rare splendour and preciousness. Medan is a villa town with which the most beautiful cottage district cannot be compared.

At Easter, we were in our villa in the mountains. The road leads across the jungle. A giant snake lay down the road and tore the head off our car. The howling of the wild elephants, buffalos, and monkeys sounded discordant in the glaring sunlight. We rested to avoid an unpleasant encounter.

My husband received a congratulatory note scribbled on an ivory dagger from the chief of a cannibal tribe. We had to visit the human-eating tribe. At the entrance to the village, we were given rice as a sign that we were ready to come. We would find half-naked savages who, although not strangers, are supposed to eat their own parents.[17]

19.2 Hüttenbach vs. Cornfield

In 1915, the Hüttenbach company decided to establish a separate retail store under the name N.V. Medan's Warenhuis. Hüttenbach & Co. was a wholesaler under the directorship of M. Enthoven and Heinrich Hüttenbach, while Medan's Warenhuis was managed by Isidore Cornfield. Cornfield was a major shareholder at Hüttenbach & Co. A new department store was planned to be built on Hindoestraat.[18] However, the relationship between Medan's Warenhuis and Hüttenbach & Co. soured, and the building did not go ahead.

In 1916, a dispute arose between Hüttenbach and Cornfield over Warenhuis. In June, during a shareholder meeting of Medan's Warenhuis, Heinrich Hüttenbach, acting as a commissioner (supervisory director) of Warenhuis, dismissed Isidore Cornfield as the director.[19] Cornfield disputed the legitimacy of the meeting's attendees who voted for his dismissal. He argued that these attendees had been previously dismissed as commissioners and hence lacked the authority to make decisions affecting the company's leadership. In addition, Heinrich Hüttenbach was mainly in London, while Cornfield demonstrated his dedication to the shareholders' interests and had greatly advanced the company's operations.[20]

[17] *Neues Wiener Tagblatt* 30-05-1920.
[18] *Pinang gazette and Straits chronicle* 15-12-1915; DC 13-12-1915.
[19] DC 17-06-1916.
[20] DC 24-06-1916.

Hüttenbach requested the court of justice of Medan to suspend Cornfield as director. He further requested the court to force Cornfield to hand over control of Warenhuis' assets. But, the court found that Hüttenbach could not legally prove his status as a *negotiorum gestor* (a voluntary interim manager of the company). While Hüttenbach was the sole commissioner (supervisory director) of the company, he did not have the authority to legally represent and manage the company, as such rights were not explicitly provided for in the company statutes.[21]

Cornfield did not take this lying down and convened an extraordinary general meeting of the shareholders of N.V. Handel Mij. Hüttenbach & Co. The two parties presented 50 shares each, but disputed the voting rights of the shares. Hüttenbach's faction declared the meeting illegal because Cornfield, the suspended director, was presiding over it. The Cornfield faction continued the meeting and decided to dismiss its commissioner, N.V. Handel Mij. Hüttenbach & Co., whose directors were Heinrich Hüttenbach and B. C. van Wingerden, on the grounds of misconduct and infringement. They considered the suspension of the director was invalid and appointed three new commissioners.[22]

At the same time, the public prosecutor investigated allegations of smuggling or tax fraud that surfaced during the Hüttenbach-Cornfield case. The inquiry concerned accusations that Hüttenbach submitted false invoices to customs officials in London, while his company in Medan received goods worth significantly more.[23] In another desperate attempt, Hüttenbach tried to seize control of the Warenhuis's books by forcing his way into the store and grabbed Cornfield by the neck. Meanwhile, van Wingerden tried to open the safe to get the books. Cornfield called the police and filed a lawsuit against Hüttenbach and van Wingerden for assault and attempted burglary.[24]

On August 3, 1916, a summons was issued by lawyer van den Brand on behalf of Medan's Warenhuis to enforce the transfer of management to van Wingerden, based on the decisions from the disputed meeting. However, just before the court session, Cornfield issued an order revoking van den Brand's authorisation to represent Warenhuis and appointed lawyer Gazan de la Meuse as the new representative. During the session, de la

[21] SP 26-06-1916.
[22] DC 15-07-1916.
[23] SP 15-07-1916.
[24] *De Indische mercuur* 11-08-1916.

Meuse requested the case be withdrawn as his principal, Medan's Warenhuis, had not authorised bringing the matter to court. The president of the court recognised de la Meuse as the legal representative of Medan's Warenhuis and withdrew the case accordingly. Thus, Cornfield remained the director of Warenhuis.[25]

Parallel to the management dispute, Cornfield was engaged in a financial transaction with notary Focquin de Grave. Focquin de Grave advertised soliciting shares in Hüttenbach & Co. at 110% of their value, and Cornfield responded by agreeing to sell 50 shares. However, the notary later retracted the immediate cash payment and proposed a deferred payment plan, which Cornfield refused. This led to another legal dispute where Cornfield sought damages for what he perceived as a breach of contract.[26] This dispute was widely covered in the local newspapers for several months. Finally, the shareholders of N.V. Medan's Warenhuis held a meeting in September and unanimously ratified Cornfield as director. [27]

19.3 Medan's Warenhuis

Cornfield decided to register Medan's Warenhuis as a company and construct a new building to become the largest department store in Sumatra. The construction project was tendered, and a young architect named Gerard Bos won the tender in 1918. The municipal beauty commission *Schoonheidscommissie* approved the design of the building in July of that year.

The first stone was laid on February 16, 1919, by the mayor of Medan, Daniel Baron Mackay, who made a speech:

> *Hüttenbach guarantees that the company will continue in the old, fresh way and paid tribute to the current director Mr. Cornfield. He hoped that the new building would be a jewel in Medan's and a picture of Medan's boom as a business city.*[28]

The facade along Hindoestraat was 29 meters long, and along Hüttenbachstraat, 60 meters, covering an area of 1740 square meters. The ground floor was 1400 square meters of shop space, and 1000 square

[25] SP 07-08-1916.
[26] SP 24-07-1916.
[27] SP 04-09-1916.
[28] SP 17-02-1919.

meters on the upper floor, a total of 2400 square meters. The building was free-standing on all four sides, with a wide, paved access road at the back for deliveries. It featured 10 display spaces with 4-meter-wide windows, covering a total area of 200 square meters with an underground safe. The upper floor included additional sales space, a lunchroom, a music room, and offices. A light hall with a stained glass roof and numerous windows ensured abundant light inside, and electric fans were also provided.[29]

A double staircase led from the main shop floor to the upper level and the lunchroom, with a view over Hüttenbachstraat. The building's exterior was designed to be shaded during the hottest part of the day. It featured a prominent corner entrance with a tower, a secondary tower entrance on Hüttenbachstraat, and a marble terrace surrounding the building, visually widening the street. Constructed from reinforced concrete with Java marble detailing, the building had a modern, large-scale design with a corner entrance and differing facade lengths. The design focused on the equal importance of the surrounding streets and future urban development.

After a construction period of one year and nine months, Medan's Warenhuis opened its doors. During the opening ceremony, architect Gerard Bos mentioned the numerous challenges that had to be overcome to bring the building to fruition, including working with his Chinese subcontractor, Ng A Tan. The mayor then cut the ribbon at the main entrance.

> *... the staircase ascending to the floors, has an overview of everything that can be found in the Warenhuis, all departments can be seen, but each department is individually arranged in an attractive way. ... the shop windows and cupboards are made using very thin (djatti) wooden frames, and one gets the feeling that only glass is used. A curious thing is that, even when the actual construction had only just started, all the details had been worked out so precisely by the architect, Mr. Bos, that Mr. Cornfield with the drawings in his pocket could order them in Europe. Thus the stained glass in the roof was supplied by a Dutch firm, according to the specification from here. The brown-yellow colour allows the light to pass through in a pleasant way for the eyes, but moreover it reflects the ultraviolet rays, so that the goods are not in danger of fading, etc.*[30]

[29] SP 06-07-1918.
[30] SP 12-11-1920.

It was even boasted as the largest department store in the Dutch Indies.[31] Its appeal was enhanced by the neighboring Empire Theatre, an art deco cinema. Warenhuis became the talk of the town, known for offering the latest and largest selection of goods. Medan had been dubbed the "Paris of Sumatra," and the *De Sumatra Post* went as far as referring Medan's Warenhuis as the "Paris in Medan" in recognition of Isidore, who travelled to Paris to source the latest clothing for his store.[32]

Tragically, Isidore's life was cut short by a heart attack during his time in Vienna in October 1923, when he was just 38 years old.[33] Following his death, Adolf Cornfield took over managing Warenhuis and Cornfield stores (Figs. 19.4 and 19.5).

Fig. 19.4 An impression of the interior of Medan's Warenhuis

[31] *Inter-ocean: A Dutch East Indian Magazine Covering Malaysia and Australasia*, Volume 3, 1922.

[32] SP 24-11-1919.

[33] DC 16-10-1923; *Neues Wiener Tagblatt* 17-10-1923.

Fig. 19.5 Medan's Warenhuis at night with lights, celebrating the wedding of princess Juliana and prince Bernhard in 1937 (Bouwes Bavinck 1937)

19.3.1 The Fall of Cornfield

After 35 years, the Cornfield shop which was described like a *gelosten huis* or closed house, resembling a bourgeois residence, which was deteriorating and needed an upgrade. In 1933, the old Cornfield building in Kesawan was demolished and replaced with a modern building despite difficult economic times. Constructed by architect Herman van den Heuvel of the Langereis company, the new building featured modern display windows with spacious interiors, offices, storage, and an in-house workshop for making men's suit.[34]

[34] SP 20-05-1933; Buiskool D.A. *Tours through historical Medan and its surroundings*, Medan, 2003: 28,59.

Fig. 19.6 An impression of Cornfield's Magazijn in the 1930s, now known as the Bata Shop in Kesawan

The Great Depression, which began in 1929, took its toll, and the Cornfield fashion store soon faced financial difficulties. Cornfield had to give up two of his shops in Kesawan, which were used as collateral for loans from the Chartered Bank of India, Australia, and China.[35] Ultimately, the business was liquidated. In July 1939, the store closed its doors after more than 40 years of operation in Kesawan. Subsequently, the building was taken over by the Chartered Bank. Later, it was occupied by the Bata shoe store and became better known as the Bata building (Fig. 19.6).

When the war broke out in Europe in 1939, Adolf mobilised funds to assist the Jewish community. However, in 1942, when the Japanese occupied Sumatra, Adolf was captured, interned, and eventually died in the camp.

The Warenhuis building suffered a similar fate. It was utilised as a prisoner camp during the Japanese period, causing significant damage to the structure. After the Japanese surrendered, it briefly served as the KNIL soldier camp and was later repurposed as a meeting point for Europeans searching for their families. In 1949, during the short-lived Negara Sumatra Timur, it functioned as an office for the Department of Cultural

[35] DC 04-04-1939.

Affairs. Later, it was used as the headquarters for the labour department office and a labour organisation. After years of neglect, the building was badly damaged by fire in 2013. Heritage interest revived in 2019, and restoration work began in 2023; today, the Warenhuis once again dominates the corner as one of Medan's most recognisable landmarks.

CHAPTER 20

From Tobacco to Oil: Aeilko Jans Zijlker and the Birth of Royal Dutch Shell

Few people realise that one half of Royal Dutch Shell's origin story began in Langkat, Sumatra. Aeilko Jans Zijlker, a former tobacco planter, triggered the chain of events that led to the creation of the Royal Dutch Petroleum Company in 1890, long before its later merger with the London-based Shell enterprise (Fig. 20.1).[1]

Aeilko Jans Zijlker was born on May 31, 1840, in a well-to-do farming family in Nieuw-Beerta in the Groningen province of the Netherlands. Zijlker's father was a member of the Dutch parliament around 1850 and one of the founders of the liberal party. Zijlker went to Eastern Java at age 20 to seek his fortune in a tobacco plantation.[2]

When the Deli tobacco industry was in its early boom in 1870, Zijlker went there to try his luck. Zijlker worked for the *Sumatra Tabakvereeniging* (Sumatra Tobacco Association) formed by investors from Batavia and Soerabaja. As large companies had already taken all good areas in Deli with fertile volcanic soils, the company could only obtain a concession in Lepan, a low-lying area in Langkat, about 90 km northwest of Medan. Zijlker became an administrator of the plantation called *Boeroeng Merak* in Lepan, with a large concession area of 2000 bouws (around 14 km^2) in 1870.[3]

[1] With thanks to information from Tammo Zijlker, great-grandson of Aeilko Jan's Zijlker brother, Hero Jan Zijlker.

[2] Gerretson, F.G., *History of the Royal Dutch* Vol I, 1958: 58–59.

[3] *Koloniaal Verslag* 1880.

B. Minasny, D. A. Buiskool, *Stories from Medan, Volume 1*,
https://doi.org/10.1007/978-981-95-7707-1_20

Fig. 20.1 Aeilko Jans Zijlker (*Leeuwarder Courant* 18-06-1990)

The soil in this area was not of good quality, derived from old sediments, and was also frequently flooded. In 1879, it produced 6 tons of tobacco, and there was a tenfold increase the next year (60 tonnes).[4]

Whale oil had been the primary source of lighting fuel since the 1700s, but it became increasingly expensive as whale populations began to decline by the mid-nineteenth century. People also discovered natural oil seeps, where petroleum seeped to the surface and collected in pools or along riverbanks. These oil seeps had been used by various civilisations for centuries for waterproofing, medicinal purposes, and as a rudimentary fuel source. However, the petroleum industry did not truly emerge until drilling technology enabled large-scale extraction to become commercially viable. In 1859, Edwin Drake successfully drilled the first oil well in Titusville, Pennsylvania. This marked the beginning of the modern oil industry, with kerosene, a refined product of crude oil, quickly replacing whale oil in lamps due to its lower cost and greater efficiency. In 1867,

[4] Idem.

Rockefeller formed the Standard Oil Company. For much of the late nineteenth century, America was the world's leading oil producer.[5]

The romanticised story goes that, on one afternoon in 1879, Zijlker was inspecting the tobacco field and was caught by a large storm. He and the *mandor* (local overseer) took shelter in a shed and had to spend the night there. The *mandor* lit a torch, and Zijlker was surprised by the unusually bright flame. He asked the *mandor* how he got the fuel, and the *mandor* told him that locally, this was called *minjak tanah*, the oil of the soil, commonly found in the area. They could be found in pools called *telaga*, in which the oil floated. The local Malays found these liquids on the banks of the Lepan, Balaban, and Besitang. They skimmed it and used it as fuel, for relief of joint stiffness, for wound healing, for boat caulking, and for many other uses. Zijlker wrote a more truthful account:

> *During my stay in Langkat, the natives there drew my attention to certain springs which they asserted had been yielding a plentiful supply of an inflammable sort of earth oil. At two places, shallow holes had been dug by them on the ground for getting the oil and these yielded oil so copiously that several of them (Telaga Tiga) were even abandoned because a single one (Telaga Tunggal) gave enough of it to supply with lamp oil... The oil is burned raw, in small bottles... I have often seen these primitive lamps burning, and must confess that they gave a very good light.*[6]

Zijlker went to inspect Telaga Tiga (which meant three pools) and Telaga Tunggal (single pool), which are located in the village of Telaga Said. The Malay coastal people had dug a hole there to obtain the oil. He cleared and dug the hole to 4 metres and oil gushed from the soil. Within 30 minutes, this simple dig could already draw 200 litres of oil, similar to an American oil field, making it a valuable well. Zijlker went further to Balaban, which was higher up the Lepan River, and also found sources of oil. He was convinced that the ground along the river contained an abundance of oil. Zijlker took some samples and sent them to Batavia for analysis. The analysis returned a good result: it had 59.2% flammability, a quality similar to American kerosene.[7]

Zijlker negotiated with the prince of Langkat, Pangeran Indra di Radja, to lease the land with the Telaga along Lepan. The area was called Sie

[5] https://ektinteractive.com/history-of-oil/.

[6] *The Straits Times* 25-09-1883.

[7] Idem.

Minjak (the oil). Unfortunately, the land had already been leased to a couple of Englishmen. Zijlker convinced the owner to let him have the land, since the tobacco production in that area was not that great. And in exchange, the Sultan provided another piece of land elsewhere.[8] Zijlker obtained a 75-year concession of Boeroeng Merak for 2000 bouws and Sie Minyak for 2000 bouws (Fig. 20.2).[9]

Zijlker went to the Netherlands in 1882 to seek investment but was met with scepticism. A year later, he was back in the Dutch Indies, and with Batavian bankers, he set up the *Voorlopige Sumatra Petroleum Maatschappij* (Preliminary Sumatra Petroleum Company) with a capital of *f*500,000 in 1000 shares.[10]

The prince of Langkat entered into an agreement with Zijlker to exploit petroleum resources, legalised by the Resident of the East Coast of Sumatra. He had to pay the sultan a fee of 30 guilders cents for every 100 litres of refined oil extracted, or 15 guilders cents for unrefined oil.[11] Zijlker wanted to ensure that the locals would not counteract his concession area.

The consortium provided 25,000 guilders for research; however, the initial exploration was not easy. The location was along the Lepan River, approximately 30 km from Alor Montayan, the nearest accessible river. The rough terrain posed a major challenge for drilling. Paths had to be built, and the cart road from Tandjung Poetoes to Telaga Said had to be rebuilt twice due to flooding. Some of the coolies did not want to stay and often ran away.

The sites were located in a remote and largely uninhabited area. The journey from the main town of Tandjoeng Poera to the drilling location took nearly 12 hours and was described as almost an "infernal" ordeal. It involved multiple river crossings by sampan, long marches across *alang-alang* grass plains, through pepper gardens and tobacco estates, notably Glen-Bervie, and into dense rainforests. The trek was physically exhausting, requiring passage over tangled roots, fallen timber, swampy ground, and steep forested hills. Only after this arduous route did travellers reach

[8] Gerretson 1958: 58–59.
[9] *Bataviaasch Handelsblad* 26-04-1880; a bouw is 0.7 hectares.
[10] Idem.
[11] *Straits Times Weekly Issue* 27-09-1883.

Fig. 20.2 An advertisement in April 1880 for investment in *Sie Minjak* (*Bataviaasch Handelsblad* 26-4-1880)

the Lepan River and Zijlker's modest establishment at Kapala Boekit Sintang.[12]

The Dutch Indies Government Department of Mines offered some help with the surveying. At Telaga Said, a skin of oil on the water could be found at a depth of 42 metres. When drilling resumed a month later, drill pipes were lowered up to 50 metres; gases rose from the borehole, exploded, and set the surroundings on fire. Adding to this disaster, the

[12] DC 17-10-1885.

workers were agitated by a rumour of an Atjehnese attack. Zijlker also could not convince investors to put in more capital.[13]

Between 1883 and 1889, seven drillings were carried out, three of which only reached a depth of 40–50 metres, and only a small amount of oil was obtained. Three other drillings to 95, 121, and 165 metres also yielded insignificant amounts. Telaga Tunggal, which was initially drilled in 1885, showed little oil and was left out. However, in 1887, another drill found an unexpectedly large flow of oil (Fig. 20.3).

Other tobacco companies in Langkat began exploring oil. The British-owned Sumatra Shanghai Tobacco Company successfully drilled and struck oil in Bulu Telang. Along the Lepan River, the Pelawi Lapan and Bombay Burma Trading Company also conducted drilling operations. Meanwhile, Hüttenbach's Augustburg estate in Lower Langkat sank a well in hopes of discovering oil. These companies aimed to utilise Langkat's four navigable rivers for transporting any oil they might find.[14]

Zijlker was convinced that the east coast of Sumatra had a great expanse of petroleum-bearing formation. The bank on the river Babalan, 10 kilometres from Telaga Said, could serve as a port to transport the oil. The oil could then be transported to Pangkalan Brandan, a port town, where ships would collect it for export. Large capital was needed for road construction, land acquisition, factory buildings, and more workers.

Zijlker's initial success finally convinced investors in the Netherlands. A public limited company, supported by King Willem III and thus called Koninklijke Nederlandsche Maatschappij (Royal Dutch Company), was formed. The company was established in The Hague and commenced on June 16, 1890. The registered capital was 1,300,000 guilders, divided into 1300 shares of a thousand guilders. Zijlker officially transferred the concession to the Royal Dutch Company (Fig. 20.4).[15]

However, Zijlker did not live to enjoy his hard work; he died unexpectedly in Singapore on December 27, 1890, at the age of 50. Some said he died of a "tropical disease,"[16] while others claimed that he was poisoned.

The wells' exploitation was delayed until 1891, when the leadership was taken by Jean Baptiste August Kessler. The job was still not easy, Kessler found:

[13] Broersma 1919: 208–209.
[14] *The Straits Budget* 25-08-1896.
[15] Poley, JPh. *Eroica: The Quest for Oil in Indonesia* (1850–1898), 2013: 93.
[16] Idem.

Fig. 20.3 Petroleum extraction in Telaga Said, 1900 (Tropenmuseum 60001640)

> *a hostile jungle and ineradicable lalang, local crews difficult to manage, equipment that did not fit, tropical diseases, operational setbacks such as fires, and absence of adequate geological know-how.*[17]

A refinery was set up in Pangkalan Brandan. On February 28, 1892, the first oil flowed from Telaga Said through the pipeline with a loud boom. It took another two years to get the production going, and from 1895 to 1897, the production was increased fivefold. The lamp oil product was branded Kroonolie or Crown oil.

In 1897, another port was completed in Pangkalan Soesoe, where tankers could collect kerosene. The crude oil was distilled for kerosene, used for oil lamps, by letting the volatiles (gases) escape through a 15 m tower. The by-product called petroleum or gasoline was initially discarded until automobiles were widely used in the early twentieth century. The flammable fumes easily caught fire and explosions were common. Kessler's

[17] Poley, 2013: 93.

NAAMLOOZE VENNOOTSCHAP
KONINKLIJKE NEDERLANDSCHE
MAATSCHAPPIJ
TOT EXPLOITATIE VAN PETROLEUMBRONNEN
IN NEDERLANDSCH-INDIË.
KAPITAAL f 1,300,000.-
verdeeld in 1300 aandeelen à f 1000.
BEWIJS VAN AANDEEL
AAN TOONDER
No 1268
groot DUIZEND GULDEN.
HOUDER dezes is gerechtigd tot een AANDEEL, groot Duizend Gulden, in bovengenoemde Naamlooze Vennootschap.

Fig. 20.4 The 1000 guilder share of the Ritak Dutch Company for the exploration of Petroleum in the Dutch Indies (from *Provinciale Zeeuwsche Courant*, 10-06-1965) hard work caused his death in 1898 on his way back to the Netherlands, just 46 years old.[18]

Henri Willem August Deterding took over and bought up competing companies such as Moeara Enim and the Dordtsche Petroleum Maatschappij. In 1903, Deterding contacted the Shell Transport and Trading Company, owned by the British Marcus Samuel, and the French banking and trading house Rothschild. To confront Rockefeller and his Standard Oil Company in the United States, Shell, Koninklijke, and Rothschild established a joint subsidiary in Asia under the name The Asiatic Petroleum Company.[19]

In 1907, Royal Dutch and Shell combined into the Royal Dutch/Shell Group. Two operating companies were established: De Bataafsche Petroleum Maatschappij (BPM, for exploration and exploitation), headquartered in The Hague, and The Anglo-Saxon Petroleum Company (for transport and storage), headquartered in London. The "Royal" acquired a 60% interest in the company while Shell had the remaining shares.[20]

Zijlker was almost forgotten. The directors of Royal Dutch in 1890 wrote:

> *That the government put down the money, so that its engineers might analyse and record more precisely what Zijlker had discovered, has its merit. But what is this in comparison with the sacrifices they made in earlier days for setting up of tea and indigo plantations in Java, for the breeding of silk worm and cochineal, and not long ago, for the cultivation of cinchona bark, not to mention what was done for the tin exploitation in Billiton.*[21]

In 1921, Royal Dutch Shell commissioned historian F.C. Gerretson[22] to write a book on the history of the Royal Dutch. The first volume *Geschiedenis der "Koninklijke"* or History of Royal Dutch was published in 1932, where Zijlker was credited as the pioneer of the petroleum industry in the Dutch Indies,

[18] Poley, 2013: 97.

[19] *De Telegraaf* 16-06-1990.

[20] *De Telegraaf* 16-06-1990.

[21] Gerretson, F.C. 1958: 89.

[22] Frederick Carel Gerretson (1884–1958) was a Dutch writer and historian. He was a professor of colonial history at the University of Utrecht at the time. He was a secretary of the Bataafsche Petroleum Maatschappij, a subsidiary of the Royal Dutch Company. He was also a right-wing politician.

a stubborn, tough, persistent Groningen farmer with a motto: what won't bend must break.[23]

Telaga Said started to dry up in the early 1900s and finally closed down in 1934. Millions of barrels of oil were sucked up by the world's richest company. By the end of the lease on August 8, 1958, the company had grown into a global corporation. Following Indonesia's nationalisation of Dutch-owned business in 1958, all Dutch companies had to leave Indonesia and the BPM facilities in Indonesia were nationalised.

In 1965, the Dutch newspaper *De Volkskrant* wrote that anyone who had subscribed to one share of Royal (1000 guilders) in 1890 could now have earned about 10 million guilders from it.[24] However, neither Zijlker nor his family received any money from the Royal Dutch Company.

In 1968, the PN Pertambangan Minyak dan Gas Bumi Negara (Pertamina), an Indonesian state-owned oil and natural gas corporation, was founded. In 1985, Shell was active in Indonesia again. Gijs Verspyck, General Representative for Shell in Indonesia, was quoted in *Shell World* in December 1985:

This is a crucial time for Shell in Indonesia. People say Shell came back in 1969 and what have they got to show for it? Well, we must find something worthwhile—within this decade—and get on a higher level of activity. The investment climate in Indonesia is very positive. Foreign companies are welcome, financial restrictions are few, and if you play by the rules, which are sometimes a bit complex, you can do business here. The next few years will count.[25]

The Netherlands has benefited from the growth of Koninklijke (Royal Dutch), from natural gas to petrol and a range of by-products.[26] It all started with Aeilko Jans Zijlker from Nieuw Beerta, Groningen province, the Netherlands. The *Algemeen Handelsblad* wrote in 1891 on the passing of Zijlker:

We pay tribute to the memory of the man who, with great financial sacrifice and to the detriment of his physical condition, continued with so much energy what he had once started, defying all difficulties and sometimes resistance

[23] Gerretson, F.C., 1958: 90.
[24] *De Volkskrant* 15-06-1965.
[25] Gijs Verspyck, General Representative, Shell, in Indonesia, in *Shell World* December 1985.
[26] *Trouw* 14-06-1965.

encountered. And once those inhospitable places at Lepan and Babelan have been transformed into a lively region, from where the petroleum produced spreads throughout our entire archipelago as a commodity, then remember that this is primarily due to the energetic Hollander, who, with rare willpower, managed to achieve success, which, it appears, will once again make a significant contribution to the development of these regions.[27]

[27] *Algemeen Handelsblad* 15-02-1891.

CHAPTER 21

The Making of the Deli Press

Two rival Dutch newspapers, *Deli Courant* and *De Sumatra Post*, didn't just report Deli's rise; they **shaped** it, acting as mouthpieces, marketplaces, and battlegrounds for colonial policy, labour politics, and speculative oil capital.

21.1 Jacques Deen, the Founder of *Deli Courant* and a Petroleum Entrepreneur

Jacques Deen (1855–1915) was an entrepreneur and the founder of the first newspaper in Medan, *Deli Courant.* Jacques Deen was born Jacob Mozes Deen in 1855 to a Dutch Jewish textile merchant in Tilburg, the Netherlands (Fig. 21.1). He grew up in Amsterdam, and around 1881, he went to Soerabaja to visit his elder brother Hendrik, a produce trader there. There, he learned about the excellent tobacco produced in Deli and the region's promising future. Intrigued by this, he travelled to Deli to explore possibilities. During 1885 and 1886, a significant number of land contracts were issued, with prospectors venturing into the hinterlands to lay the groundwork for future development. At the time, the European population in Deli was relatively small, and it wasn't until 1887 that the regional government moved its seat from Siak to Medan. Despite the scepticism and limited infrastructure, Jacques Deen's optimism led him to launch the *Deli Courant*, the first newspaper in the region in March 1885, aiming to serve over 500 families and unmarried individuals, including many Europeans who couldn't read Dutch.

B. Minasny, D. A. Buiskool, *Stories from Medan, Volume 1*,
https://doi.org/10.1007/978-981-95-7707-1_21

Fig. 21.1 Jacques Deen (1855–1915) (*Deli Courant* 18-03-1935)

21.1.1 Deli Courant

In the first issue of *Deli Courant*, Deen wrote an editorial on the aim of the newspaper (Fig. 21.2):

> *portraying the image of a powerful, progressive Dutch colony, which has grown out of its infancy, has come to ask for its rightful share of the benefits that it has been generating from the mother country for years, and from an industrious population, which, recognising the many good things that recent years have brought them, gives a "grateful but not satisfied" response.*[1]

[1] DC 18-03-1935.

Nº 1 Woensdag, 18 Maart 1885. 1ste Jaargang.

Deli Courant.

Dit blad verschijnt tweemaal 's weeks, Woensdag en Zaterdag.

Prijs der Advertentiën:

UITGEVER en wd. REDACTEUR: J. DEEN.

Abonnementsprijs:

Fig. 21.2 The first edition of *Deli Courant*

Deli Courant also aimed to introduce the *terra incognita* to the people and government in Java and Holland. The Deli community initially had to depend on newspapers from the Straits Settlements, like the *Pinang Gazette*, which were delivered by boat once a week. *Deli Courant* fulfilled the need for a local newspaper. The office was a small wooden building at Djalan Hüttenbach with a steam-powered printing machine (*stoomdrukkerij*), and the newspaper was published twice weekly with a circulation of 150 copies. The newspaper quickly garnered support and became a unifying force in a region with limited transportation and communication infrastructure. Roads were scarce, and the Deli Railway Company didn't open its first section until 1886. The newspaper played a crucial role in fostering a sense of community and served as a vital source of information. The Dutch Indies government in Java could now access information about East Sumatra directly rather than relying on news from the Straits.[2]

Jacques Deen assumed duties as the founder, publisher, editor, and administrator of *Deli Courant* until 1887. A few months after its inaugural issue, P.B. van Staden ten Brink, a retired major of the Dutch Indies Army, was hired as an editor and assumed administrative duties until 1888. The editorial position was succeeded by J.A. Naudin ten Cate.[3] The newspaper grew alongside the development of Deli. By 1894, it had grown so much that it was transformed into a public limited company with a capital of *f*200,000.[4]

[2] DC 18-03-1935.

[3] Naudin ten Cate resigned as manager to set up his own company Bank and Handelsvereeniging Naudin ten Cate in 1896.

[4] W. Cremer was appointed director. Jacques Deen had 50 shares, Frits Gransberg 7 shares, Jan Broos 7 shares, and W. Cremer 6 shares.

From its inception, the *Deli Courant* served as the mouthpiece of the tobacco plantation industry. When coolie riots erupted at the Tandjong Selamat plantation of the Deli Maatschappij in 1893, the paper remained conspicuously silent. On another occasion, it was criticised for underreporting a major arson attempt involving nine sheds on the Kuala Mentjirim Estate and for failing to promptly inform the public. The *Deli Courant* was accused of deliberately withholding reports of violent incidents in deference to powerful tobacco interests.[5]

While it took some time to become a daily newspaper, its growth accelerated in the early twentieth century when rubber cultivation began, followed by other crops like tea and oil palm. The company also provided the first printing service in the region. It expanded into printing and operated book and office supply stores in Medan and Koeta Radja. It even established a newspaper in Atjeh. In later years, it expanded its activities in Atjeh to include import businesses, handling the import of various goods, from baby carriages to beer.

The printing house in Medan grew into a large modern enterprise, from 10 to 400 employees. Jacques stayed in Medan for several years before returning to the Netherlands around 1893. He became active in the Dutch Journalists' Circle and served as secretary-treasurer from 1897 to 1905.

21.1.2 Jacques Deen on the Indirect Rule

Jacques Deen, writing in the *Deli Courant*, was critical of the administrative system on the East Coast of Sumatra but strongly supported the indirect governance (*indirecte bestuurswijze*) model used there. He argued that this system had proven effective, maintaining trust with local rulers who had welcomed the Dutch as friends and providing maximum benefits with minimal costs.[6]

Deen emphasised that effective governance on Sumatra's East Coast required a balance of firmness to maintain order (exemplified by Resident Michielsen) and diplomacy to ensure cooperation with local rulers (as demonstrated by Resident Kroesen). He compared this to the British system on the Malay Peninsula, which successfully balanced the interests of the colonial power with the rights and customs of the local population.[7]

[5] *Pinang Gazette and Straits Chronicle* 31-05-1893, 21-08-1893.
[6] DC 08-12-1897.
[7] SC 10-05-1899.

Deen criticised the Dutch for failing to engage and educate the local Malay rulers effectively, leading to slow progress and development in the region. He argued that the stagnation was not due to flaws in the Malay rulers themselves but rather the Dutch government's neglect in providing proper education and guidance.[8]

21.1.3 **Deli Courant** *on Van Den Brand*

Jacques Deen was a strong supporter of the Deli tobacco industry. When the Sultan of Serdang opened a tobacco plantation in Serdang, Deen wrote an editorial raising two questions: firstly, whether the Planters Association in Deli had lost its influence in government circles, allowing this break of tradition, and secondly, whether an Indigenous ruler could have opened a tobacco plantation in the past without resistance from Dutch authorities.[9]

In 1902, Johannes van den Brand, a lawyer from Medan, published an explosive booklet titled *De Millioenen uit Deli*, or *The Millions from Deli.* This exposé shed light on the deplorable working conditions of Chinese and Javanese labourers and the systematic exploitation perpetrated by Dutch plantation owners against the so-called contract coolies. *De Sumatra Post* immediately contested the booklet, while under editor W.E.J.H. Mulier, the *Deli Courant* remained silent for several days before delivering an assessment. *Deli Courant* challenged van den Brand's one-sided negative view and lack of details. However, the newspaper also acknowledged existing flaws and structural reform in administrative practices and legal enforcement to address corruption, exploitation, and violence. As a result, *Deli Courant* and its editor faced backlash for their perceived impartiality. Subscribers and investors, including Jacques Deen, criticised *Deli Courant*'s editor for not being more critical of van den Brand and for insufficiently defending planter interests. The editor's stance led to a loss of subscribers.[10] Jacques Deen wrote his commentary much later:

> *Mr. v.d. Brand attacked the Deli planters with the Bible.*[11]

[8] DC 19-11-1897.
[9] DC 16-07-1898.
[10] DC 26-11-1902, 27-11-1902, 21-07-1934.
[11] DC 06-10-1906.

Deen wrote from Amsterdam that van den Brand refrained from naming individuals when describing the prevailing abuses and misconduct by Europeans towards labourers in Deli, which he said:

> *Caution according to your opponents, discretion according to your claims.*[12]

Deen challenged van den Brand to reveal the names of officials and planters so that the defence could also be heard.

The case brought by van den Brand aroused debates in the House of Representatives, and the Dutch Indies government ordered an inquiry. J.L.T. Rhemrev, a public prosecutor in Batavia, was assigned to investigate the accusations in 1903.

In May 1903, Rhemrev published his report, which was made available only to a limited audience. Deen, who had access to the report, wrote a letter to Janssen, presumably C.W. Janssen, the director of the Senembah Company:

> *The Rhemrev report is bad, so bad, in fact, that it should not come under the eyes of the foreign press, because they would feast on it, not unjustifiably so. It proves beyond doubt that Van den Brand was right, but what is not in the report is perhaps even worse. I did not expect it to be so miserable on deeper and more thorough examination. The local administration has a lot on its plate, as is evident again. This report also proves that clearly enough.*[13]

The report was damning, and Deen preferred the report to be kept confidential, while *De Sumatra Post* wanted it to be made public.[14] But in public, Deen dismissed the report as unreliable, doubting its effectiveness and impartiality. Deen described it as mere speculation aimed at garnering public attention, characterising the Rhemrev investigation as “a mountain that produced a mouse.” He went on to criticise the Minister of Colonies, Idenburg, for failing to thoroughly assess the credibility of Rhemrev’s findings and conclusions and for neglecting to consult officials with expertise on the conditions in Deli.[15]

[12] Idem.

[13] Letter from Jacques Deen to Janssen, Amsterdam, 24-04-1904.

[14] DC 17-06-1904; SP 22-06-1904.

[15] DC 06-10-1906.

21.1.4 Deli Courant*'s Editors*

As noted above, the first editors of the *Deli Courant* were J. Deen and P.R. van Staden ten Brink.[16] W. Mulier served as the editor-in-chief from 1899 until 1904.[17] Mulier was characterised as conservative with a view of maintaining order and economic growth focused on structure, economic development, and a hierarchical societal order. While he acknowledged van den Brand's view and suggested improving labourers' condition, he criticised Rhemrev's investigation as intrusive.[18]

The *Deli Courant* had social aspirations: it supported the idea of giving the Chinese and Javanese coolies and Indigenous people a pension so that they would feel more attached to the region.[19] However, the paper generally supported the interests of the plantation companies, and in instances of labour disputes, it often blamed the coolies. The *Deli Courant* was widely regarded as the mouthpiece of the plantation industry (Fig. 21.3). This was particularly evident in 1907 when a progressive editor-in-chief,

Fig. 21.3 Newspaper composing room of *Deli Courant* around 1920 (Rijksmuseum NG-1990-14-4)

[16] DC 12-03-1898.
[17] SP 13-04-1899.
[18] DC 21-07-1934.
[19] DC 08-06-1895.

Kees van Bruggen, was forced to leave Medan due to a conflict with the management of the plantations.[20]

Van Bruggen's successors, A.W. Naudin ten Cate and W.A.Th. Burger, who were in charge from 1907 until 1910, expressed highly discriminatory views. They claimed that the coolies were drawn from the "scum" of the Javanese and Chinese populations and argued that they should be treated accordingly. This meant that the standards applied to Europeans and educated Indigenous individuals should not be extended to the coolies.[21] Although conservative in their view, these editors were often well-informed. Naudin ten Cate, for instance, authored *Deli in Woord en Beeld*, a richly illustrated and well-documented overview of the social-economic history of Deli from 1860 to 1909.[22]

J.J. van der Laan assumed the role of the editor-in-chief in 1910. Van der Laan, who was also a member of the Town Council for the European group, sympathised with the Vaderlandsche Club, a conservative political organisation that advocated for the preservation of Dutch colonial interests in the Dutch Indies. His alignment with the club reflected his support for maintaining the colonial status quo and resisting the growing calls for Indonesian autonomy.[23] Van der Laan and his successor, Willem Klooster, from 1936 until 1942, continued the conservative image of the *Deli Courant*. Klooster, a pro-colonial writer using the pseudonym Willem Brandt, was prolific in his output, writing numerous poems and authoring novels like *De aarde van Deli* (The Soil of Deli). This work explored the history and economic success of tobacco plantations in East Sumatra from the perspective of a white man.[24]

21.1.5 Petroleum Hunter and Entrepreneur

In the late 1880s, Aeilko Jans Zijlker discovered oil wells in Telaga Said in Langkat. Jacques Deen became aware of this and started to look for land concessions in the area. He was one of the so-called concession hunters, who were not interested in prospecting but looked for areas for speculative investment. In 1891, Jacques received a concession of Boekit Mas in

[20] Kees van Bruggen's wife was the author Carry van Bruggen (Termorshuizen 2011: 625).

[21] DC 22-5-1895, 28-9-191.0

[22] A.W. Naudin ten Cate, *Deli in Woord en Beeld*, Amsterdam, J.H. De Bussy, 1905.

[23] *Gemeenteblad* 6-4-1927; SP 15-6-1926; 28-10-1926; .Termorshuizen 2011: 632.

[24] Brandt, W. *De Aarde van Deli* N.V. Uitgeverij W. van Hoeve, Gravenhage 1948; DC 8-2-1936; Termorshuizen 2011: 634; Buiskool 2025: 266, 267.

Langkat, adjacent to Telaga Said. He had no interest in the exploration; rather, he went to the Netherlands and leased it to the Royal Dutch Company.[25] He and his brothers in Soerabaja, Henri and Emile, set up Oostersche Exploratie en Exploitatie Maatschappij in 1895. His youngest brother, Emile, was the most active, and they obtained the Peureula concession near Perlak in Atjeh in 1898.

The Deen brothers founded the Perlak Petroleum Company in Amsterdam in 1902 as a limited company with a capital of *f*10 million. The company leased the exploration to the Royal Dutch Company. In 1906, Emile founded Zuid Perlak with a capital of *f*3 million. They also established various petroleum exploration companies in Sumatra, ventured to the United States, and bought the Oklahoma and other companies. Jacques and Emile became super rich, and in 1905, Jacques was on the list of the most highly regarded people in the province of North Holland. Emile was known in The Hague as a philanthropist and was even elected as the city's council member.[26]

Jacques Deen married Marssim, a Javanese woman, and they had a son, Tino Alexander, who was born in Medan in 1886. Jacques Deen was the director of the Central Israeli Children's, Orphans and Transit Home in Leiden. He was a philanthropist, a candidate member of parliament for the liberals, assisted refugees from Belgium with money during World War I, and was appointed Knight in the Order of Orange-Nassau.[27]

However, the Deen brothers were rocked by a corporate scandal called "Perlak-bloodletting" in 1910, alleged misconduct by Emile Deen during his tenure as the director of the Perlak Petroleum Company. The company's board sued Emile Deen for compensation for damages. The Perlak bloodletting refers to a transaction in 1909, in which Perlak acquired ordinary shares of the Perlak Zuid Company (owned by the Deen brothers) at an elevated price. The acquisition was made by Perlak's board, which included three members of the Deen family, while Emile Deen himself was the seller of these shares. There were also accusations of insufficient geological information regarding oil reserves.[28] These Zuid-Perlak shares had not paid any dividends and were perceived as potentially worthless. This case resulted in a protracted legal battle spanning more than ten years, and

[25] Van Gorsel 2022: 63.

[26] *Het nieuws van den dag voor Nederlandsch-Indië* 08-01-1913.

[27] https://www.joodsamsterdam.nl/jacques-deen/.

[28] SP 14-01-1916.

culminating in Deen being ordered to pay 4.3 million guilders plus interest of 5% per year.

Jacques Deen, after battling with a long illness and being severely affected by the court case, died in Amsterdam on December 23, 1915. His brother Emile fought the court unsuccessfully for another ten years, with Perlak company seizing a portion of his annual royalties. Emile joined Jacques exactly ten years later.[29]

Despite their philanthropic reputations in the Netherlands, the Deen brothers, like many colonial investors, accumulated their wealth through exploitative extraction in Sumatra, where little concern was shown for the people or environments from which that wealth was drawn.

21.2 Hallermann and *De Sumatra Post*

While the *Deli Courant* became the official voice of Deli's plantation elite, its dominance also invited competition and dissent. The early press in Medan mirrored the social order it reported on, hierarchical, partisan, and deeply entangled with commercial and political interests. Yet as the city expanded and its public sphere grew more complex, there emerged a demand for an alternative voice. Into this environment stepped Joseph Hallermann (1863–1928), a German entrepreneur whose vision for an independent newspaper would challenge the monopoly of the *Deli Courant* (Fig. 21.4).

Like most Europeans, Hallermann was initially a planter who worked in the tobacco culture in British North Borneo before moving to Deli. While working, Hallermann was attacked on the plantation, forcing him to stay in Medan to recuperate. Then he thought of opening a bookshop as the city had no bookstore. In 1895, Hallermann opened a bookshop in Medan. Three years later, in December 1898, his bookshop moved to a wooden house next to Tjong A Fie's mansion in Kesawan, and at the same time, he published *De Sumatra Post*, which initially appeared twice a week. Hallermann claimed the newspaper would be "independent and detached from any specific interests in the region, and tried to the best of his knowledge, to serve the ideal interests of all residents of the East Coast, regardless of their nationality, rank or status."[30] To make it more attractive, Hallermann made its subscription fee much cheaper than *Deli Courant*.

[29] SP 31-12-1925.

[30] *Nieuwsblad voor den boekhandel* 11-07-1924.

Fig. 21.4 Joseph Hallermann (*De Sumatra Post* 1924) (*De Sumatra Post 1898–1923,* 1924)

The paper was distributed free of charge for a month in Deli to gain traction.[31]

Hallermann also founded the first Malay newspaper in Medan, *Pertja Timor*, in 1902 (Fig. 21.5).[32] He also issued an annual address book for the entire East Coast of Sumatra. In 1914, *De Sumatra Post*'s office and bookshop were rebuilt as a modern building in Kesawan.[33]

The first editor-in-chief of *De Sumatra Post* was the well-known lawyer Johannes van den Brand.[34] In the inaugural edition, van den Brand wrote:

[31] *Bataviaasch nieuwsblad* 14-12-1898.

[32] *Pertja Timor* ended in December 1912.

[33] The bookshop and printing office were separated. In 1922 the company Varekamp & Co. and *De Sumatra Post* moved to Manggalaan (Termorshuizen 2011: 657).

[34] SP 24-05-1899; 03-08-1899.

Fig. 21.5 Staff of *De Sumatra Post* and *Pertja Timor* in front of Hallermann's office (KITLV 86073)

> *It is the aim of the Sumatra Post to discuss public events and interests in an honest manner. Anyone who thinks he has something to say in the interest of public affairs has opened his columns. Personalities will be avoided as much as possible. …*
>
> *It will be the aim of De Sumatra Post to stand up for the interests of everyone who seeks a livelihood in our region, for everyone who contributes to the great goal, whether through trade, agriculture or industry: to make the colony more prosperous. …*
>
> *De Sumatra Post will not have a political orientation, which does not rule out that the editors will not hide their own opinions when dealing with political events.*[35]

Three months later, from April 1, 1899, it became a daily paper.[36] On the occasion of the first anniversary of *De Sumatra Post*, the paper wrote

[35] SP 02-12-1898.
[36] SP 06-01-1928.

that it wanted to be an open medium and not a *doofpot*, a "cover-up" medium.[37]

Karel Wybrands succeeded van den Brand as the editor in 1899. Wybrands was known for his conservative stylistic talent and later became one of the most well-known journalists in the Dutch Indies. *De Sumatra Post* had several rubrics, foreign correspondents, a weekly political overview and serials, adaptations of Arthur Conan Doyle and Rudyard Kipling, and book reviews, all written by Wybrands. *De Sumatra Post* became very popular within a short span of time.[38] In 1901, Wybrands moved to *Het Nieuws van den Dag* in Batavia.

Wybrands and the subsequent editor A.J.C.M. Tervooren transformed *De Sumatra Post* into a conservative newspaper. Following the release of van den Brand's publication, *De Millionen uit Deli*, the newspaper's editors responded with a series of articles attacking van den Brand, such as:

> *But let us not forget that here in Deli we only get the scum from Java and China, let us not forget that the word freedom has a completely different meaning for such people than for us Europeans, than for the educated in general. Freedom means for a coolie, as we know him here in Deli, doing nothing, or in any case, only doing what he himself finds necessary.*[39]

From 1904 to 1914, under the editorship of Anton Lievegoed, an enlightened ethicist, *De Sumatra Post* adopted a progressive image stressing the importance of a free press, openness, and a "healthy" western economy. His successor, M. Vierhout, continued this course until his resignation in 1924, after which the paper reverted to conservatism.[40]

Initially, the subscribers to *De Sumatra Post* were primarily the assistants on the plantations. By 1910, it had the largest distribution in Sumatra, maintaining its dominance until World War II. Its articles generally supported colonial policies and often reflected the perspectives and interests of the colonial administration.[41]

[37] SP 01-12-1899; Buiskool 2025: 267–270.

[38] Termorshuizen 2011: 116; 'De journalist in Indië', *Bataviaasch Handelsblad* (11) 28-11-1911.

[39] SP 05-04-1902.

[40] Buiskool 2025: 268–269.

[41] (SP 2-3-1909; SP 31-1-1942) The subscription fee in the 1930s for *De Sumatra Post* was *f*5 per quarter (Medan) and *f*6.25 per quarter in the Netherlands Indies (SP 15-12-1933).

At the onset of World War I, Hallermann left for Germany in 1914. He had to withdraw from the company and eventually, in 1916, he sold his business to his trusted colleague, Ant. P. Varekamp. The company became Dutch-owned, Varekamp and Co. The company was then restructured as Naamlooze Vennootschap Boekhandel en Drukkerij with a separate bookstore and stationery store housed in a wing of the main building at Kesawan.

After returning to Germany, Hallermann continued to follow the company's further development. Hallermann passed away in 1928 at the age of 65 in the villa Haus Insulinde in Rhöndorf.[42]

De Sumatra Post was known to be more independent and progressive than the *Deli Courant*. From the start, there was a tense competition between the two newspapers.[43] By 1940, *De Sumatra Post* and the *Deli Courant* together had between 1500 and 3000 paying subscribers.[44] The rivalry lasted until 1942 when the Japanese invaded Sumatra and both papers had to stop publication. In 1948, they merged into *Het Nieuwsblad voor Sumatra*, with the first issue published on July 1 with an editorial[45]:

> *As a Dutch daily newspaper, it will naturally represent Dutch interests and advocate and promote Dutch culture. But not in such a way that it places one-sided emphasis on these aspects. We have an open eye for the necessity to bring the Indonesian and Western elements closer together than before. We do not hesitate to openly state one of our most important objectives, which is that we wish to contribute to achieving mutual understanding and cooperation in the belief that both culturally and economically, there is a need to strengthen these ties—with full respect for and recognition of the high national ideals of those born and raised here.*
>
> *May these bonds unite us all, white and brown, for the prosperity of the Negara and Indonesia in general, for the well-being of everyone privileged to work here, regardless of religion or colour.*[46]

Het Nieuwsblad voor Sumatra lasted 10 years.

[42] *Het nieuws van den dag voor Nederlandsch-Indië* 10-01-1928.
[43] DC 3-12-1898, DC 31-12-1898, SP 3-1-1899, SP 18-4-1899.
[44] Termorshuizen 2011: 81.
[45] Dootjes 1952: 97; HNvS 01-07-1948.
[46] Het Nieuwsblad voor Sumatra (HNvS) 01-07-1948.

CHAPTER 22

Kehding, Haas, and the Making of a Colonial Enterprise in East Sumatra

The making of a colonial enterprise in East Sumatra was driven by successive generations of merchants, adventurers, and financiers who turned a remote frontier into a thriving economic zone. Franz Kehding belonged to the first wave of solitary traders who braved fever, floods, and uncertainty to connect Deli's plantations with global markets. A few decades later, Jacob Herman Haas represented a new era of organisation and capital, when commerce evolved from individual enterprise into corporate structure. The journeys of Kehding and Haas illustrate how East Sumatra's trade transformed from personal ventures of survival and opportunity into the systematic machinery of colonial capitalism.

22.1 Franz Kehding's Journey in Sumatra

In 1875, a young German named Franz Karl Eduard Kehding arrived in Singapore, sent by an export company to oversee its struggling operations. He was no stranger to trade, having worked for a British firm in London years before, but the company he now served was on the brink of collapse. By 1880, after the death of a key partner, the business folded, leaving Kehding unemployed and adrift in a foreign land (Fig. 22.1).

With little left for him in Singapore, he prepared to return to Germany. But fate had other plans. Before departing, he visited an old compatriot, Dr Arnold, who ran a business in Langkat, a remote region on the East

B. Minasny, D. A. Buiskool, *Stories from Medan, Volume 1*,
https://doi.org/10.1007/978-981-95-7707-1_22

Fig. 22.1 Kehding's office on the Esplanade (Aangeboden door den. V. Handelsvereeniging v. H. F. Kehding ter gelegenheid van haar 50-jarig bestaan 1880–1930) (F. Kehding on the occasion of its 50th anniversary 1880–1930)

Coast of Sumatra. What Kehding found there astonished him: vast, newly established tobacco plantations, cheap land leases, and almost no competition. It was a land of opportunity—a hidden gold mine (Fig. 22.2).[1]

Returning to Singapore, Kehding sought out Mansfield, Bogaardt & Co., agents for the Holt shipping line. The Alfred Holt Line from Liverpool, which held the monopoly in the Straits of Malacca, was already eyeing Sumatra's tobacco trade and needed a man on the ground. They had been negotiating with a local Lieutenant of the Chinese, Tjia Djoe Djin, to establish a branch in Klambir, a rundown port village in Langkat. Kehding seized the chance.[2]

On October 18, 1880, F. Kehding & Co. opened its doors in Klambir. The settlement was little more than a collection of ramshackle huts, but

[1] Veersema, 1930: 11–16.
[2] DC 11-10-1930.

Fig. 22.2 Franz Kehding. (*Aangeboden Door de N. V. Handelsvereeniging V.H. F. Kehding. Ter Gelegenheid Van Haar 50-Jarig Bestaan 1880–1930.* Medan 18 October 1930)

the Dutch *controleur*, Heymans van Anrooy, assured him that Langkat was destined for growth. Soon, Bogaardt urged Kehding to relocate to Laboean Deli, the region's emerging commercial hub.[3]

In April 1881, Kehding moved to Laboean Deli and became an agent of the Chartered Bank, where planters could get their cash. His building was one of the few built of bricks, with a safe for books and money, and was equipped with an iron vault door. Kehding also sold various items for planters, including the German Beck's beer, locally known as *Koentji*

[3] Idem.

beer.[4] Kehding initially imported all sorts of goods from Penang and Singapore for the planters and, later, direct imports from Europe. Kehding also made a fortune by selling granulated sugar imported from Java.

But Laboean Deli was no paradise. It was a swamp, flooded periodically and almost cut off from the surroundings in the rainy season. It was even regarded as "the most unhealthy spot in the island," as described in a poem by an Englishman:

Now the vapour, hot and damp,
Shed by day's expiring lamp,
Through the misty ether spreads
Every ill the white man dreads;
Fiery Fever's thirsty thrill,
Fitful ague's shivering chill![5]

In the first half of the 1880s, a cholera epidemic ravaged Deli, with little medical assistance. The primitive conditions took a toll. Kehding's two children died at a young age and were buried at Kampong Besar.

However, Kehding persisted, his business expanded, and a branch was established in Bindjei in the 1880s. The railway line from Medan to Belawan opened in 1885, and Kehding opened a branch office in Belawan. Eight years later, the head office moved to Kesawan in Medan.[6]

Kehding was more than a merchant; he was a collector, a diplomat, and a naturalist. He sent botanical specimens to Italian botanist Odoardo Beccari, earning a fern species named in his honour: *Luerssenia kehdingiana*. He was a member of the Royal Asiatic Society.[7] He served as the German consul in Sumatra from 1885 to 1897, with his company doubling as the consulate.[8]

Deli and the East Coast of Sumatra expanded and grew; the government invested in this new region with roads. With the expanding tobacco culture, Europeans flocked to Deli as planters, investors, and civil servants. Tea, coffee, and rubber were grown, and Kehding also expanded. Branches

[4] Koentji means key, the symbol of Beck's beer.

[5] Eastwick 1893; *Fortnightly Review* 54: 323.

[6] In 1895, Gustav Adolph Julius Kehding, Franz's brother, joined the company and hired their first clerk, a Chinese, Ng Hok Yauw. *De Locomotief* 17-07-1895.

[7] The finding was published in *Botanisches Centralblatt* 11:77 in 1882 https://plants.jstor.org/stable/10.5555/al.ap.person.bm000325489.

[8] Wright, 1909: 573.

sprang up in Tebing Tinggi, Pematang Siantar, Tandjung Balei, Bagan Siapiapi, and Langsa. Kehding stocked Peruvian Guano for fertiliser, crushed horse feed, lawnmowers, nails, asbestos, ring lubricator, blocks for building and plantation operations. Kehding also owned Sungei Rawa sawmills, furnishing cut wood and timber for building purposes and *ataps*. It also imported Victoria Water, Hultkamp Genever, Dry Pale Sherry, Champagne Pommery and Greno, and Bourgogne Wines.[9]

In 1906, Kehding expanded to Handelsvereeniging F. Kehding and shifted operations to Dresden, leaving day-to-day management to his partner, Cornelis Siegmund.[10] As the region grew, the English started to establish their own companies on the East Coast of Sumatra, and the Holt Line decided to end its partnership with Kehding in 1913. The incident upset Kehding, who had a 33-year relationship with Holt. However, Kehding managed to build relationships with other shipping lines. World War I strained his German ties, and in 1925, his company was absorbed by the Dutch firm Internatio.[11]

Franz Kehding died in Dresden in 1926 at 76, but his legacy endured. His collections of Batak artefacts found homes in museums in Dresden and Hamburg.[12] The man who had arrived in Sumatra as a failed clerk built an empire from the swamps, only for time to erase nearly all trace of it. The jungles of Langkat have long been cleared, Klambir remains a desolate village, and the name Kehding has faded into history.

[9] Kehding was later joined by his fellow countrymen Gustav Güntzel and F. A. Schumacher, who founded the Güntzel and Schumacher company, as a general import and estate agency business. In 1892, Güntzel and Schumacher sold their business to Carl Hick and Aug. Jaenichen, who, at that time, were assistants on Deli plantations. In 1905 the company Güntzel and Schumacher became a limited liability company with branches in Belawan, Loeboek Pakam, and Hamburg. Wright, 1909: 572.

[10] SP 18-09-1906; *De Indische Courant* 02-04-1940.

[11] The International Credit and Trade Association "Rotterdam," also known as Internatio, is the name of a cultural bank and trading house that existed from 1863 to 1970.

[12] Kehding's family donated the collection to the Museum of Ethnology in 1938; https://skd-online-collection.skd.museum/Home/Index?page=1&pId=12831079; Friedrich 2020, *Manuscript Cultures* 14, 83; SP 09-09-1926.

22.2 Nolte & Haas and Handel Maatschappij Deli: Atjeh

The commercial world Kehding helped found became the stage for younger Europeans such as Jacob Herman Haas (1863–1932). Haas' trajectory, like Kehding's, began in the Netherlands' provincial towns and led to the feverish plantations of Deli. Born in 1863, Jacob Herman Haas began his education at the local HBS (Higher Secondary School) in Wageningen, but left in his third year to apprentice at a notary's office in Everdingen, encouraged by his father, H.J. Haas, the town's municipal secretary. Yet Jacob soon diverged from this trajectory, drawn instead to opportunities in the Dutch East Indies.[13]

With support from his uncle, Batavia-based lawyer S.M.A. du Mosch, Jacob arrived in the colony in 1881. His first role was as an unpaid assistant at the Goenoeng Melatti tea plantation in Buitenzorg (Bogor). Within six months, he moved to the Bajabang tea and cinchona estate near Bandung, earning a modest 25 guilders monthly under owner Mr Bosch.

His multilingual skills (French, German, and English) and basic accounting knowledge soon secured him a position at Reiss & Co., a Batavia trading firm, through his uncle's connections. But Java was only a stepping stone. By 1883, Jacob ventured to Deli, Sumatra's booming tobacco frontier, where he joined Friederichs & Co. as an assistant on the Selajang plantation in Langkat—a German-managed estate under the umbrella of the Deli Company.

At a tobacco plantation in Deli in the 1880s, the European assistant had to supervise a large number of mainly Chinese coolies, and one assistant had to supervise around 100 workers. The Chinese coolies worked in groups of 20–40 people in *kongsis* (work-gangs), under the supervision of a foreman or *tandil.* Two to four *kongsies* formed one *afdeling* (department) under the supervision of a head *tandil* and a European assistant. Few assistants spoke Chinese; the assistant conversed with the head *tandil* in a kind of Malay, and communication was improvised but functional. Usually, there were two to four *afdelingen* on a tobacco plantation. The head *tandil* was the mediator between the Chinese and the European personnel and was supposed to solve problems between them.[14]

[13] This article is based on the family chronicle *Haas, planter en handelsman op Deli* (Haas, planter and trader at Deli) by the grandson of Jacob Herman Haas, Dr B.J. Kam.

[14] Buiskool 2025: 35, 36.

In the European hierarchy, the assistant was at the bottom of the ladder. It took a long time before he was able to get a better position, such as, perhaps eventually, an administrator (6 buttons on the coat; an assistant had 5), or could earn enough to get married. The salary ratio was as high as 10 (administrator) to 1 (youngest assistant).[15] At that time, there was a marriage ban for assistants. Thus, the planters employed a housekeeper or *njai* with whom they lived without being married.

Jacob Herman Haas moved to another tobacco company, Batang Kwis of the Senembah Company, where he became an assistant with a salary of 200 dollars per month. The administrator was a German named Frey. At Batang Kwis, he experienced a coolie row, where the coolies fought among themselves and Haas was tasked to intervene and defuse the situation.[16]

The daily wage at the Senembah Company for coolies in 1889 was 20 dollar-cents for men and 10 dollar-cents for (Javanese) women, and there were no Chinese women on the plantation. By 1914, this had increased from 35 to 38 cents for men and 28 cents for women.[17] This meant that male coolies received a monthly salary of 6 dollars. In the 1880s, the Straits Dollar was the common payment method. Jacob Herman Haas received a monthly salary of $200, which was more than 30 times the salary of a coolie. The administrator, in contrast, earned a salary approximately ten times greater than that of the assistant, around $2000 per month. This sum amounted to more than 300 times the salary of a coolie. The administrator and assistants would receive a bonus if the sale was profitable. For example, in the 1910 season, substantial bonuses were paid to administrators and assistants. Notably, Deli Maatschappij paid *f*1000–3750 to assistants and *f*24,000–68,000 to administrators, while Senembah paid *f*2730–5725 to assistants and *f*28,000 to administrators.[18]

The Senembah Company was founded in 1889 with J. Nienhuys and C.W. Janssen as directors, and commissioners J.T. Cremer, H. Nacher, G.E. Haarsma, A.L. Wurfbain, and R. Von Seutter. Senembah also owned the tobacco plantation Tanjong Morawa, previously owned by the company Näher and Grob. Näher and Grob were a German and a Swiss who first worked as merchants in Sicily. Näher and Grob employed many compatriots and they continued to work for the company after it was taken

[15] Kam 195: 29.
[16] Kam 1995:18.
[17] Senembah 1914: 31.
[18] *Pinang Gazette and Straits Chronicle* 29-06-1912.

over by Senembah in 1889. This was one of the reasons why so many Germans worked in Deli.[19] In 1914, the land contracts of all the Senembah Company plantations covered more than 36,000 hectares.[20]

Haas lived with a Javanese *njai* called Roekima and had a daughter Jetty, born in Batang Kwis in 1888.[21] After Batang Kwis, he moved to the tobacco company Tandjong Morawa Kiri, also owned by Senembah, with a salary rise to $400. The administrator was a German, Zimmermann.

In 1889, Haas went on leave to Europe, paid by the Senembah Company. In the Netherlands, he remained active and, together with G.J. Pieters from Amsterdam, whom he knew from Deli, founded Pietersburg, a tobacco company in Asahan in June 1891 with a capital of 500,000 guilders. This amount was raised by various shareholders, including Leendert Ankersmit from Arnhem, a former tobacco planter; H.P. Haas (a cousin of Jacob Herman Haas), who was a securities broker in Amsterdam; and six other shareholders. Jacob Herman would then become the administrator. However, the Pietersburg company was short-lived and was dissolved in December 1891 due to a disagreement between the shareholders during a meeting in Amsterdam.[22] Disappointed, Jacob Herman Haas took the boat back to Deli and worked as a planter.

When Jetty was three years old, Haas officially recognised her as his daughter (Fig. 22.3). Unfortunately, not long after this, Roekima passed away. At age six, Jetty was sent to the Netherlands in 1894 to live with her grandmother, who warmly embraced the girl as her family. In 1902, when Jacob Herman Haas married a Dutch woman named Fenna Wieringa, Fenna also embraced Jetty as her own daughter.[23]

In 1891, there was a tobacco crisis due to overproduction and prices fell. Haas was again looking for work and got a job at the German trading firm F. Kehding in Medan. Jobs were few and far between, and he was happy to work at Kehding with a reduced salary of 125 guilders per month. Jacob Herman became head of the Belawan office, representing the Holt line between Singapore, Deli, and Penang.[24]

[19] Senembah 1914: 38.

[20] Kam 1995: 31, 32; Senembah 1914: 9,12, 21.

[21] Kam 1995: 93.

[22] Verlofregeling (leave regulations) Senembah Maatschappij, Senembah 1914: 40; Kam 1995: 36, 37.

[23] Jetty Haas was the grandmother of Benjamin Kam, author of *Haas, planter en handelsman op Deli* (Kam 1995: 17, 47, 93).

[24] The Holt Line of Holt & Company was founded by Alfred Holt from Liverpool. The Holt Line owned 14 ships in 1875, all sailing on the Far East. She operated a regular service

Fig. 22.3 An impression of Jacob Herman Haas and Emma Roekima with their daughter Jetty Haas (based on pictures in Kam 1995: 73)

Kehding had agencies, sold various products such as building materials, provisions, and drinks, and took out insurance. Haas worked his way up in the company and earned up to 300 guilders per month. Nevertheless, he was always looking for something better and switched to the competitor, Nolte, where he became a partner in the firm Nolte & Co in 1897. The company became Nolte & Haas, with an office in Belawan. The partner

to China even before the opening of the Suez Canal. They brought cotton there, among other things, and returned with tea, so they also visited Belawan. The ships sailed via the Suez Canal for 55 days out and 60 home journey days. They also transported pilgrims to Jeddah. A branch office in Penang was established in 1878 by a Dutch partner, Mansfield and Bogaardt & Co. This created two companies: Blue Funnel (the original Holt) and the Ocean Steam Ship Cy trading from Singapore to Deli, Western Australia, Bangkok, and Borneo. The Norddeutsche Lloyd also sailed between Sumatra and Penang and Singapore and the Dutch company Van Nie sailed from 1889 onwards, later taken over by the KPM (Koninklijke Paketvaart Maatschappij) (Kam 1995: 43,44). The "Blue Funnel Steamers" of the Holt line had an excellent reputation. One of Sir Alred Holt's famous slogans was: *Please look after my Chinese crew and keep my funnels painted blue* (Lindeboom 1993: 22).

Hendrik Jan Nolte (1856–1922) had logging rights in Langsa in Atjeh. Haas contributed $2000 to the company, while Nolte put in $34,000. In the beginning, Haas received 30% of the profit, and after three years, Haas received half of the earnings.[25]

Nolte supervised the tree felling, and Haas sold the timber in Belawan. The timber was transported down the Belawan River using *tongkangs*. These logging concessions were very lucrative; the profits were as high as 700–800%.

The tobacco plantations operated in an eight-year rotation, with a new area being planted each year while others remained unused for seven years. Thus, it became necessary to construct new sheds in different locations within the plantation to facilitate the storage and processing of the harvest. This was the reason for the high demand for sturdy beams and roofing.

However, the logging area near Bajan was more than 200 kilometres away from the port of Belawan. Initially, *tongkangs* (small boats) were used for transport. However, these boats were too slow and depended on the weather, sometimes taking weeks to reach Belawan. In 1901, the Nolte & Haas company purchased its first steam-powered boat, the Henriëtte, named after Jacob Herman's grandmother Henriëtte Haas-du Mosch.[26]

To boost revenues, Nolte travelled to Europe and successfully attracted additional agencies to Medan, including those of Dobbelman's Tobacco and Boldoot. Once Nolte and Haas joined forces, the business experienced rapid growth. Both were skilled businessmen, with Haas being exceptional in accounting and marketing.

Nolte & Haas, later became Deli-Atjeh company, with offices in Medan and Belawan.[27] From 1905, offices were also opened in Amsterdam at Keizersgracht 126 and at Muntplein 2.[28] Its initial capital in 1910 was *f*500,000, and by 1925 it had increased to *f*2,500,000 and became *f*5,000,000 in 1940 (Fig. 22.4).[29,30]

[25] Kam 1995: 93.

[26] Letter B.J. Kam, Zwolle 1997.

[27] Schadee, 1918 II: 244.

[28] Kam 1995: 18.

[29] Colonial business https://www.colonialbusinessindonesia.nl/.

[30] Wright (1909) wrote about Deli-Atjeh: *General store for all kinds of commodities as well as a representative for insurance companies, the company also held oil concessions. Trading Company Deli – Atjeh. Sold matches from Sweden, tobacco, mineral water, Nestle and Milkmaid*

Fig. 22.4 An impression of Jacob Herman Haas on the left and Gerard di Gazar around 1905 (based on the picture in Kam 1995: 81)

Jacob Herman Haas and his wife Fenna Wieringa left for the Netherlands in 1904, where their daughter Fenna was born in Arnhem in 1905. Later, they settled in Amsterdam. Deli-Atjeh remained active as a trading company, even though the partners had been repatriated. In the years that followed, Nolte went back and forth from Amsterdam to Medan several times when problems arose with the Deli-Atjeh company. He visited Medan for the last time in 1919. Hendrik Jan Nolte died in 1922 in Amsterdam.[31]

dairy products, Huntley & Palmer's and Patria biscuits and Van Houten cacao, vinegar, eau de cologne, earthenware, crockery and glass, nails, candles and soap, confectionery from John Gray & Co. from Liverpool. The firm represented the Algemeene Verzekering Maatschappij (Insurance Company) Providentia, the Netherlands Insurance Company and the Noord en Zuid Hollandsche Transport Verzekering Maatschappij (North and South Holland Transport Insurance Company). It also had concessions for oil mining. The firm established by H.J. Nolte and J.H. Haas had branches in Medan, Belawan and Atjeh. Nolte & Haas was also agent for the Manchester Fire Insurance Company and the Insurance Company Arnhem. Wright 1909: 573; Schadee, 1918 II: 244.

[31] Kam 1995: 58.

Jacob Herman Haas outlived him by a decade and still held the company director's position until he passed away in Amsterdam in 1932. He had accumulated a substantial fortune through his business ventures in Deli and Atjeh. Upon his death, his estate was valued at 225,000 guilders.[32] The company continued to expand under the directorship of J.A. Zeeuw van der Laan.[33]

The archives of the Deli-Atjeh company were largely destroyed during World War II.[34] Dr B.J. Kam, the grandson of Jacob Herman Haas and Roekima, wrote his family's chronicle in 1995: *Haas, planter en handelsman* (Haas, planter and trader at Deli).

The legacies of Kehding and Haas capture the transformation of Deli from an isolated frontier into one of the Dutch Indies' most dynamic colonial economies. What began as scattered trading posts along the Deli River evolved into a network of plantations, ports, and commercial houses linking Sumatra to the world. Yet beneath this progress lay the silent labour of thousands of coolies, the environmental costs of relentless expansion, and the balance between profit and human endurance.

[32] Kam 1995: 134.

[33] Colonial Business Indonesia https://www.colonialbusinessindonesia.nl.

[34] Kam 1995: 79.

CHAPTER 23

Seng Hap and the Chinese Entrepreneurs

During the late 1880s, amidst the thriving expansion of Medan, in addition to European enterprises, three large Chinese companies were among the key suppliers to European demand: Seng Hap, Chong Lee, and Soey Tek Bie. In this new urban landscape, commerce was no longer limited to trade; it was about presentation and persuasion. Tan Tang Ho's Parisian-style Seng Hap turned shopping into a spectacle. It represented the beginning of modern advertising and brand identity in Sumatra. This spirit of innovation would later be taken to unprecedented heights by figures such as Auw Pit Seng, the self-made "King of Advertising," who mastered the art of publicity and transformed marketing across the Dutch Indies (Fig. 23.1).

23.1 Seng Hap

In 1900, Tan Tang Ho, a Chinese businessman and proprietor of the Seng Hap, unveiled a fresh building at the Kesawan entrance. This striking new building was fashioned in the Parisian style, adding a touch of elegance to the city of Medan. *De Sumatra Post* wrote:

B. Minasny, D. A. Buiskool, *Stories from Medan, Volume 1*,
https://doi.org/10.1007/978-981-95-7707-1_23

Fig. 23.1 Seng Hap and Tan Tang Ho (Tan Tang Ho photo by Dirk Buiskool, Seng Hap from Indië, jrg 2, 1918, 38:597)

> *Seng Hap has almost finished his building and we have to inform Baedeker that it is a construction, designed after drawings of the Madeleine in Paris, a jewel for the municipality.*[1]

Citizens of East Sumatra were invited to the grand opening of Toko Seng Hap on Sunday, March 25, 1900. The Manilla Band played high above at the gallery.[2] Visitors were

> *admiring all the treasures stacked up and displayed in glass showcases along the walls and on the shop windows between the columns of the temple building.*"[3]

Tan Tang Ho personally offered cigars to his guests, along with *koude split* or whisky soda.

[1] SP 2-12-1899; SP 23-12-1899; SP 24-3-1900. Baedeker is a travel book. The Madeleine Church with Roman pillars in Paris was constructed from 1698 to 1777.

[2] SP 2-12-1899, SP 10-03-1900; SP 21-03-1900; SP 24-3-1900, DC 17-03-1900; SP 26-03-1900; Buiskool 1999: 95.

[3] SP 26-03-1900.

What can you find for sale at Seng Hap? Everyone probably knows, we believe, but in case there might be someone in Medan who doesn't know, let it be mentioned here that at the Batavia shop, you can find the simplest mustard pot and the most precious luxury item, and everything in between. Seng Hap took pleasure in his guests' enjoyment; for him, we hope that the Batavia shop will often be as busy as it was last night, but not with mere onlookers, but rather with buyers.

Deli Courant wrote:

The whole is in the Corinthian style, the capitals of the outer pillars are crowned with acanthus leaf decorations, and the pillars that support the interior structure end in Etruscan motifs, which can very well be paired with the late Corinthian style. Upon entering the building, it is divided by columns into three sections, each approximately 24 meters long, with the middle forming the corridor that leads to the storage rooms for provisions and drinks. These, too, are built spaciously. Stairs lead in the main building to the two floors, while the pillars on the upper floor resolve into arches. Everything is kept in a distinguished white, while the ceiling plane is decorated by a few rosettes.[4]

Inside the store were a Mercury statue, a replica of a creation by Giovanni Bologna, and sphinx statues on either side of the store. The Roman pillars were the only ones in town, and the front of the shop, Seng Hap, was used as a set for a performance of the second act of Shakespeare's *Julius Caesar*, which was supposed to take place at the Capitol in Rome.[5]

Tan Tang Ho was a Hokkien born in Batavia, with little formal education. He arrived in Medan at the age of 14 as a peddler or *kelontong*, selling needles, buttons, thread, and other items in two baskets carried over his shoulder. Tan was so frugal that sometimes he did not eat in the evening to save his hard-earned money. A Dutch employee of the Deli Railway Company became his regular customer and helped him. In 1881, he established his store, Seng Hap, at the forefront of Kesawan as a *kedeh*, offering diverse merchandise. Over time, it evolved into a primary source of imported goods for European planters' needs. Tan Tang Ho ventured into a revenue farm for spirits in 1897, controlling spirits sales throughout the East Coast of Sumatra.[6] He expanded as a contractor, supplying food

[4] DC 24-03-1900.
[5] SP 17-10-1899.
[6] DC 23-12-1896.

to the garrison Deli from 1890 to 1892.[7] He also had a business in *atap* palm roofs, which were in great demand in Medan during its development period.

The business was so successful that in 1900, Tan Tang Ho constructed a new building in the style of Parisian architecture as the most luxurious shop in town. The shop at the entrance of Kesawan covered an area of about 710 square metres and was lit by electricity. His business was incorporated as the Seng Hap Trading Company Ltd. with a capital of *f*200,000 in 1000 shares to take over different ventures. Five years later, Seng Hap sold provisions and liquors, and the following year, a branch was established in Bindjey, followed by Pangkalan Brandan in 1904. Besides being a department store, Seng Hap traded in sugar, tobacco, Java and Chinese tea, mats, and gambier.

A travel guide in 1912 wrote:

> *The largest wholesale and retail store in Medan. The visitor is impressed with the line proportions of the building occupied by the Company, which will bear favourable comparison with the largest emporiums of Java, and the well-worn phrase, "from a needle to an anchor"*[8]

Seng Hap, known as Toko Batavia, advertised a large variety of products in the newspapers and on advertisement boards. Imagine walking through a captivating shop filled with a world of commodities. Products from around the globe were available to diverse ethnic groups—Malay, Chinese, Indian, and European. Seng Hap imported goods directly from the United States, the Netherlands, England, South Africa, and Australia.[9] It specialised in food products, dairy products, meat, and fish. There was cheese from the Netherlands, caviar from Russia and tinned marmalades from Great Britain.[10] In the 1890s, the wines, sherries, and champagnes were imported via Dutch firms like Hoogewerff Chabot & van Hoorn in Rotterdam. Red port wine was sold under Seng Hap's trade name *Tjap*

[7] DC 25-05-1899, *For the delivery of foodstuffs, fuel and light materials, etc. for the purpose of the War Department in Delian for 1890, 1891 and 1892: IJo Tiang Hoat f439,927.50, Tan Tang Ho f446,661.75, Thio Tiauw Siat f565,649.10, Hüttenbach and C° f476,732.70, Brown and Co. f540,097.35, Bawadji f545,283.36, De Heer f442,429.80, Deli Handel Mij f459,206.85, E. v. Angelbeek f465,419.85.*

[8] Lorck 1912:240.

[9] SP 14-10-1912.

[10] Buiskool 2025: 173–176.

Ajam. It had the Dutch liquor *oude jenever* (old gin), *Oude Bols*, a favourite drink in the colonial society.[11] Household products were also offered in large quantities: spoons and forks, knives and scissors from the firm F. Herder & Sohn from Solingen, Germany, as well as cucumber slicers, champagne tongs, complete dining services, money safes, leather travel suitcases, and Fongers bicycles from the Netherlands.[12]

Every year, Seng Hap celebrated the feast of Sinterklaas with the St Nicolaas Etalage or window decoration featuring various gifts and children's toys. There were Christmas tree decorations, candles, and the elegant "lametta" (angel hair) in gold, silver, and various other colours. It offered a selection of "Papier en Guirlandes" (paper and garlands), delicate paper flowers, international flags, and "Lampions" (lanterns) shaped like flowers and birds. Masks, beards, wigs, confetti bombs, and more. There were toys of serpentine, boats, and trains, as well as the thrilling "Looping the Loop." Fashionable items, including Japanese silk fabrics in a spectrum of colours, carefully tailored dresses and blouses, and luxurious materials like "Crêpe de Chine," "Mousseline de Soie," and "Gaze de Sole." The jewellery collection featured gold and silver pieces, children's bracelets and necklaces, as well as watch and fan chains, medallions, earrings, hoops, hat pins, and more.[13]

Tan Tang Ho was known for his philanthropy. He was the president of *the Hoa Siang Hak Tong* association of Medan, which was devoted to providing educational facilities for the Chinese in Medan. He contributed to the Hokkien society of Medan in terms of burial funds and social work to help the poor. In 1897, one of the members of the Stamboel Comedy Group, who was conducting a performance at the Esplanade, passed away. Tan Tang Ho covered the entire funeral expenses for the artist.[14]

Tan Tang Ho died suddenly in 1918 and the business was continued by his sons Tan Boen An, Tan Boen Hok, and Tan Boen Djin. The youngest brother, Tan Boen Djin, went to the Netherlands to study. After graduating, he sailed back to Medan in 1937 to manage the Seng Hap Company with his brothers. After the war, Seng Hap was run by Tan Boen Djin. However, he eventually had to sell the company as he had no successor. Tan Boen Djin passed away in 2009, at 95 years old.

[11] Idem.
[12] Idem.
[13] SP 12-12-1907.
[14] Buiskool 2025: 178.

23.2 Soey Tek Bie

Soey Tek Bie was one of the first department stores in Medan, founded by Oei Soei Boe (also known as Wee Swee Boo in Malaya, or Huang Ruiwu) in 1887, located in Kesawan. While Seng Hap was called Toko Batavia, Soey Tek Bie was popularly referred to as Toko Weltevreden, named after Weltevreden, a prosperous district in Batavia (now Sawah Besar), renowned for its elegant European-style houses and shops. The store specialised in imported goods catering to European tastes, offering items such as ham, sausages, cheese, chocolate, beer, and wine. It was an agent for the Standard Oil Company of New York and the New Zealand Fire Insurance Company. In 1898, a new brick building was constructed for the store, occupying a prominent space on Kesawan, between Tjong Yong Hian's residence and the corner of Marktstraat (now Jl. Perdagangan) (Figs. 23.2 and 23.3).[15]

Fig. 23.2 An impression of Firma Soey Tek Bie at the intersection of Kesawan and Nieuw Markt (Jl. Perdagangan)

[15] *Bataviaasch nieuwsblaad* 11-08-1898.

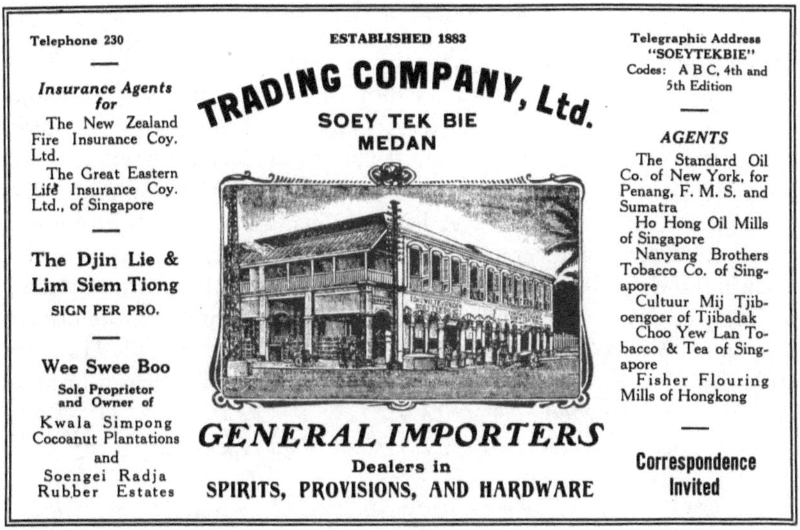

Fig. 23.3 An advertisement of Soey Tek Bie Ltd. (International Trade Developer, Propagador de Comercio Internacional. Propagateur de Commerce International, Volume 17, 1920: 599)

Oei Soei Boe began his career as a head foreman for coolies in Deli and later became a successful businessman. He entered into partnerships with Tjong A Fie, venturing into revenue farms for salt and liquor. He established the firm Soey Tek Bie, which also had rubber plantations Soengai Radja Kiri and a coconut plantation Kwala Simpang. He had real estate in Medan and businesses in Penang and Singapore. In Penang, he established Tiang Lee & Co. as a general merchant with export and import services in 1898.[16] His house in Penang was called "Medan House" located at Logan Street, Penang.[17] After the death of its founder, Oei Soei Boe, the business was continued by his son Wee Gim Puay. The shop lasted until 1922.[18]

[16] *The Singapore and Straits Directory* 1918: 428.
[17] *The Straits Times* 15-07-1935.
[18] Buiskool 2025: 136,174; SP 31-12-1915.

23.3 Chong Lee & Co.

Chong Lee & Co. was a general trading company established by Tjong Yong Hian in 1890. It opened its shop in Kesawan in 1897, providing various goods for European needs. It imported European food, spirits, wines, and various products from Penang and Singapore. After Tjong Yong Hian's death, Chong Lee at Kesawan No. 103 became a general company for managing Tjong A Fie and Chang Pu Ching's business. It was an importer and general merchant of food products, whisky and wine, hardware and steel safes. It was an agent for W & R Jacob of Dublin, Fingel's Ice Waters of Holland, The Austral Canning of Melbourne, Campanhia Vinicola of Oporto, etc. It also managed the Medan brickworks and Zun Ciat laundry in Medan.[19] The business survived until the Japanese occupied Medan (Fig. 23.4).

On St Nicolaas day in 1900, *De Sumatra Post* reported:[20]

> *Katz & Co. have acquired many new goods, especially porcelain; Goldenberg & Zeitlin are now great in jewellery, bronze vases, phonographs; Cornfield now also has silver cloisonné in beautiful and artistic designs. Soey Tek Bie offers toys for sale, as does Chong Lee; Seng Hap filled his temple halls with treasures from East and West. Hallermann has a choice of picture books.*

Fig. 23.4 Kesawan with Cornfield and Chong Lee shops (on the right) around 1900; on the left-hand side is Tjong A Fie's house, and the empty land was to be built for Tjong Yong Hian's house (Mazaraki KITLV 36153)

[19] *The Singapore and Straits Directory* 1918: 598.

[20] SP 04-12-1900.

Fig. 23.5 Chong Lee in the 1930s (photo courtesy of Rebecca Chandra)

Despite their rivalry, the three Chinese stores frequently collaborated and fulfilled the growing demand for fine foods and beverages in the booming tobacco city. As Medan grew, Tan Tang Ho left an indelible mark on the city's landscape. Their firms' legacies reflect the dynamic and interconnected nature of commerce, culture, and progress in shaping the city's identity (Fig. 23.5).

23.4 Auw Pit Seng, the King of Advertising

By the 1920s, Medan's commercial world was shifting from grand architecture and imported luxuries to the growing power of branding and advertisement. The success of companies like Seng Hap and Soey Tek Bie had opened a new era in consumer culture, where persuasion mattered as much as product. Health tonics, cosmetics, and imported medicines began to dominate shop windows and newspaper pages, reflecting new anxieties of modern life and new opportunities for entrepreneurs who understood the language of promotion. It was in this changing environment that Auw Pit Seng rose to prominence, an innovator who turned advertising into an art form and transformed the trade of medicated wines into a regional empire (Fig. 23.6).

The *Lancet*, a leading British medical journal, published a laboratory analysis of a widely promoted Serravallo's bark and tonic wine from Trieste

Fig. 23.6 Toko Auw Pit Seng at Kesawan in 1930 (Nationaal Archief 823_15)

in Italy in the July 3, 1897, issue.[21] It reported a chemical analysis of the wine, confirmed the two main ingredients of iron and cinchona, and commented that

> *this wine would appear to be of distinct value in chlorosis and anaemia... It is a sweet, somewhat syrupy liquid of peculiar purplish colour, with a slightly bitter taste. ... The wine affords an agreeable way of presenting two valuable tonic agents.*

Medical practitioners and doctors in Europe and their colonies widely promoted it to treat anaemia.[22]

Many medicinal wines and tonics were produced and promoted in Medan. Hard-working people needed a boost of energy, and the wines were promoted as a potion that could replenish strength and cure most ailments. Chinese companies produced medicinal wine using Korean red

[21] Analytical records from the Lancet Laboratory. Serravallo's Bark and Tonic Wine. *The Lancet* July 3, 1897, p. 26.

[22] *Indian Medical Gazette* July 1935: 420.

ginseng, known in Hokkien as *kolesom*. Entrepreneur Hiu Ngi Fen, the last chairman of the Chinese Chamber of Commerce of Medan, produced Anggoer Tjap Boelan, advertised as a tonic drink to replenish energy. Hiu hired an aeroplane to drop leaflets promoting his wine.[23]

But one man conquered the sales of tonic wine, not just in Medan but throughout the Dutch Indies, the whole of Southeast Asia, and Hong Kong. Auw Pit Seng succeeded in promoting the sale of the Italian Chinese wine, Serravallo, as a tonic for regaining strength and an elixir for women after giving birth. Auw also introduced Chiclets chewing gum, and Aladdin kerosene lamps to the Dutch Indies. Serravallo is still highly regarded in East Asia to this day, thanks to the efforts of Auw Pit Seng.

Like many early Chinese entrepreneurs, Auw had a humble beginning. Auw Pit Seng (Mandarin: Ou Picheng) was born in 1901 in the Zhenjiang village on the bank of the Yellow River in Jiangsu province, China. He was the eldest of five children, and his father sold him to a Chinese merchant because the family was poverty-stricken. His stepfather brought him to Atjeh to help with the business.[24]

His daughter, Dr Emily Ruth Auw, wrote that Auw did not receive a proper education, but only tuition at home for several years. His stepfather treated him poorly and made him work from a young age. By the age of ten, he was already helping his stepfather forage for pepper and herbs in the jungle to sell. He was made to do all kinds of manual labour.

When he reached 18, he ran away from home and moved to Medan. To support himself, he served tea to morning walkers by the hillside. At night, he studied on his own, reading books and newspapers by the flickering light of a candle. Eventually, he got a job as a bookkeeper in an import-and-export firm in Medan. The firm offered free food and lodging and paid him 15 guilders per month. Because he was a hardworking and smart worker, he got a raise from 20 guilders to 35 guilders, a considerable increase.

Auw had an interest in writing articles and submitted them to local Chinese newspapers. He didn't expect any payment; he just wanted the opportunity to publish and to receive a copy of the newspaper. He got to know many of the people in the press in Medan. At that time, many Chinese who could write and speak English could get a job as a clerk in European companies, earning a reasonable salary of about 75 guilders per

[23] Buiskool 2025: 184–186.

[24] Information from Dr Emily Ruth Auw, the daughter of Auw Pit Seng.

month.[25] The European-owned printing companies, such as *Deli Courant* and Varekamp, employed several Chinese clerks and workers. Several Chinese newspapers emerged in Medan in the early 1920s, including *Sumatra Bin Poh*, *Sumatra Times*, *Sumatra News*, and *New China Times*. There was also *Nan Yang Jit Pao*, *The Daily Morning News*, *Sin To Djit Po*,[26] and *Pelita Andalas*, a Malay-Chinese newspaper. Besides news, these papers had a large section of advertisements.

Auw loved writing so much that he gave up his job at the trading firm. His employer persuaded him to stay by offering him a salary raise, but he had made up his mind. He kept studying English and Dutch by himself, using a dictionary. Any new words he encountered on the streets, shop signs, or brochures, he would memorise and later check in the dictionary at home for their correct pronunciation and meaning. As a result, he could almost understand Dutch and was also comfortable with English usage (Fig. 23.7).

As Auw approached the age of 20, a time traditionally seen as ripe for marriage, his stepfather asked him to marry. In 1922, Auw married Kim Lan Toh and took on the responsibility of supporting a family. That same year, he opened a shop at No. 12 Luitenantsweg (now Jl. Bandung), where he sold lottery tickets, books, and newspapers. He installed his first telephone line in 1923.

At the age of 24, Auw already had a shop in Kesawan No. 122, a small emporium selling foods, children's clothing, general clothing, smoking pipes, ties, violins, mandolins, sporting equipment, and many other products. He was ahead of his time, offering new products across the Dutch Indies. He advertised in papers in Batavia (*Sin Po* and *Keng Po*), offering a "must-have" pen that was delivered from Medan.[27]

Auw kept looking for new products and ideas. When his first daughter was born, he sought a nourishing tonic for his wife. The Chinese had a tradition of keeping the mother well-nourished after giving birth, and usually a tonic wine was given. Auw came across Serravallo tonic wine from Trieste, Italy. It was advertised as a Chinese wine, a tonic made from cinchona and iron that treats anaemia, strengthens weak bodies, and cures malaria and influenza.

[25] Said 1976: 765.
[26] Said 1976: 79.
[27] *Sin Po* 30-05-1925.

Fig. 23.7 Young Auw Pit Seng (photo courtesy of Emily Ruth Auw)

He was so impressed with the wine that he started drinking it himself, buying it by the case and recommending it to his friends and relatives. He sold them so well at his shop that the Dutch agent N.V. Handel Mij Holland Deli appointed him its main sales agent (*Hoofddepot*) in Sumatra. Auw successfully distributed the wine throughout large towns on the East Coast of Sumatra. Within a year, in 1928, he became the sole agent in the Dutch Indies. He was on the money.

Auw still had an interest in publishing. He published a Malay weekly magazine called *Internationaal* in September 1924, but it did not last long.[28] In 1930, Auw started another twice-monthly Malayan periodical, *Reclame via sport dan film*, promoting advertisements on sport and film.[29] He had a publishing company and published a Malay book titled *Nona Bessy* in 1925.[30]

By the age of 30, he was already an established entrepreneur. His interest in publishing led him to design his own advertisements. The Dutch would only advertise in the Dutch newspapers, targeting Europeans or the upper class, which would only be a small market share. Indeed, in the 1930s, no European company published an ad in *Pertja Timoer*, a Malay newspaper. Only Medan's Warenhuis and Toko Van Der Pol published ads in *Sinar Deli*. Thus, Auw launched his own advertising campaign, publishing in both Malay and Chinese newspapers, not just in Medan but across Sumatra and Java. He was very creative as well.

He advertised on a full page in *Pertja Timoer* on December 29, 1928, promoting Serravallo for health and women's well-being. Selling at 3 guilders a bottle, the ad included a testament from a *mandor* (foreman) of a plantation[31] and even Dr A. Rivai, a nationalist physician in Batavia, endorsed it. Rivai wrote *that it was the best wine for everyone, including postnatal women and children.*[32]

Miss Riboet, a famous travelling theatrical troupe from Java, also provided a commendation that the wine helped them recover from their busy schedule and travel.[33] During the fasting month, the ad recommended a drink at the break of the fast to promote appetite and that would not cause intoxication.

Auw was also very generous in promoting the tonic wine. He advertised in various newspapers throughout the Dutch Indies. In 1931, he sent a case of twelve bottles of Serravallo to *De Sumatra Post*, which was accepted by the editor, who wrote: *We immediately started a Serravallo cure, the results of which we eagerly await.*[34] Although this imported wine cost two to three times more than the local wine, the wine's sales figures shot through the roof within a short time; as a result, his friend and competitors regarded him with awe.

[28] DC 20-09-1924.

[29] SP 16-09-1930; Han 2017: 361.

[30] Overzicht van de Inlandsche en Maleisisch-Chineesche pers, 1925, no 19, 07-05-1925. The book is now considered an example of classical Malay literature from Medan, although it was a translation from an English novel.

[31] A plantation overseer.

[32] *Sinar Deli* 25-07-1933; *Han Po* 8-10-1932.

[33] *Sinar Deli* 13-02-1933.

[34] SP 30-01-1931.

Auw befriended Walter A. Foote, an American consul who was stationed in Medan from 1927 until 1931.[35] Foote introduced him to American products, and he became representative for the whole Dutch Indies for many items, including Tempters Candy Coated Gum, and products by the American Chiclet Company in New York: Adams Chiclets chewing gum, Sen Sen aromatic tablets, and Crawford's cough candy. He also represented Aladdin petroleum lamps from Tennessee,[36] Mitchum soaps, vacuum flasks, etc.

Soon, Auw decided to leave retail, sold off his stock, and focused on wholesale.[37] He became Serravallo's sole agent for the Far East or East Asia. In 1934, he auctioned all his belongings in Medan, including a 1931 Willys Knight Sedan. He moved to Hong Kong to open Auw Pit Seng Trading Company and expanded his business into Singapore, Malaysia, Thailand, the Philippines, Burma, and other Southeast Asian countries at the young age of 33.

Auw, who started as a humble worker in Medan, became a successful multinational entrepreneur. His iconic look was dark sunglasses—as he had sensitive eyes—and a white suit. His daughter Emily Ruth Auw proudly showed pictures of Auw with Lee Kuan Yew in Singapore and Tun Ku Abdul Rahman in Malaysia.

Despite being busy with his business and travelling throughout Asia, he was health-conscious and a family man with 16 children. He treasured family reunions and kept the elders company as much as possible, especially during the Chinese New Year. Emily Auw remarked that he had no affluent upbringing, big inheritance, or formal education, yet could turn every obstacle into an opportunity, and was blessed with a Midas touch. He lived a whole life of 93 years with a spirit: "Where there is a will, there is a way!"

From the grand arcades of Kesawan to the crowded pages of Malay and Chinese newspapers, the story of Medan's commerce was one of imagination as much as enterprise. Figures like Tan Tang Ho, Oei Soei Boe, Tjong Yong Hian, and later Auw Pit Seng turned trade into a stage of modernity, ambition, and identity. Their shops, advertisements, and imported goods connected East Sumatra not only to Batavia and Singapore but to Europe and North America. What began with the sale of tobacco and spirits evolved into a new consumer culture.

[35] https://politicalgraveyard.com/geo/ZZ/ID-consuls.html.
[36] *The Tennessean* 24-05-1959.
[37] *Sinar Deli* 30-03-1930.

CHAPTER 24

Kamerlingh Onnes Family Journey: From Tobacco Plantations to Nobel Prize

The Kamerlingh Onnes family bridged two worlds: plantation capitalism in Deli and experimental physics in Leiden. While Heike Kamerlingh Onnes became a Nobel laureate for low-temperature physics, his relative Dolf Kamerlingh Onnes rose as a powerful administrator in Medan, managing major enterprises associated with Tjong A Fie. Less visibly, philanthropic money linked to Deli's tobacco fortunes helped finance the skilled laboratory assistants who made Heike's research machine possible.

24.1 The Kamerlingh Onnes Family

Heike Kamerlingh Onnes (1853–1926) was a Dutch physicist and Nobel Prize winner, best known for his pioneering work in cryogenics (the study of extremely low temperatures) and for being the first to successfully liquefy helium. Born in Groningen, the Netherlands, he made significant contributions to understanding the behaviour of materials at extremely low temperatures. When substances are cooled to extremely low temperatures, they undergo significant transformations. In 1908, Heike Kamerlingh Onnes developed an apparatus to liquefy helium. In 1911, Kamerlingh Onnes made a groundbreaking discovery when he observed that the electrical resistance of mercury vanished completely at temperatures just a few degrees above absolute zero. This extraordinary phenomenon came to be known as superconductivity. This scientific achievement

B. Minasny, D. A. Buiskool, *Stories from Medan, Volume 1*,
https://doi.org/10.1007/978-981-95-7707-1_24

led Heike Kamerlingh Onnes to be awarded the Nobel Prize in Physics in 1913.[1]

The father of the family was Harm Kamerlingh Onnes, a wealthy roof tile manufacturer living in Groningen with his wife, Anna Gerdina Coers. They had five sons and two daughters: Heike (1853–1926), Albert (1855–1886), Meisina (1858–1860), Menso (1860–1925), Onno (1861–1935), Jenny (1863–1926), and Adolf (1864–1933).

The surname "Kamerlingh Onnes" was coined by Heike, whose original name was written as H.K. Onnes. While studying at the Groningen HBS (Hogere Burger School) or Secondary Higher Civic School, he adopted the name "H. Kamerlingh Onnes," combining his middle and last names as the family's surname.[2]

After the passing of his father in 1880, Heike assumed the responsibility of managing the family. In particular, he made significant efforts to support his brother, Menso. In 1881, Heike took Menso to Delft, where he received instruction in ornament painting from A. le Comte. During this time, Heike worked as an assistant at the Polytechnic School.

Heike obtained his doctorate in Groningen in 1879, and in 1882, he applied for the position of professor of experimental physics at Leiden University. However, he faced competition from Wilhelm Röntgen, who later discovered X-rays. With the support of his friend Hendrik Lorentz, a professor of theoretical physics at Leiden, Heike eventually secured his professorship at Leiden.

Heike's brothers achieved successful careers in business and art. His second brother, Albert, travelled to Java, where he achieved success by inventing a centrifuge, and then lived a lavish life in Soerabaja. He later settled down as an architect in Central America. However, he tragically died from a heart attack while working in a mine in Mexico. Menso became a famous artist and painter. Menso's son Harm (1893–1991), like his father, was a gifted painter. Onno settled in Amsterdam and became the director of the Office of Trade and Information in Amsterdam, providing advice on international business and trade. He was a member of the Amsterdam city council (1897–1909). He was also a painter and poet and occasionally exhibited paintings and published a collection of poetry.[3]

[1] https://www.nobelprize.org/prizes/physics/1913/onnes/biographical/.

[2] There is a school in Groningen named after Heike Kamerlingh Onnes, known as the Kamerlingh Onnes School.

[3] van Delft 2002: 945–952.

Finally, the youngest of the family, Adolf Johan Kamerlingh Onnes or Dolf, was an *enfant terrible*, the black sheep of the family. He did not wish to continue his schooling, so in the late 1870s, he embarked on a journey to America, where he worked as a cowboy. However, he found that this lifestyle didn't suit him. Like many Dutch who couldn't find their path in the Netherlands, he chose to seek his fortune in the Dutch Indies.

24.2 Dolf Kamerlingh Onnes

Dolf Kamerlingh Onnes arrived in Deli around 1885 and, like other Europeans, found employment as an assistant in tobacco plantations, including a stint at Rotterdam Deli Maatschappij in 1896 (Fig. 24.1).[4]

Within a few years, he ascended the ranks to become an administrator of the Soengei Sikassim plantation of De Nederland Asahan Tabak Maatschappij. However, his volatile temper often led to job losses, ultimately prompting his resignation from Sikassim in 1900.[5] Then, he moved to Soengei Biroeng tobacco plantation in Padang Bedagai. In 1903, he had to face the court in Batavia, accused of destroying a pigsty.[6] Following the incident, he moved to Soengei Bedjankar and Tanah Datar plantation in Laboean Roekoe, a location further south in Batu Bara.[7]

Eventually, he found himself unemployed. Around 1906, he sat alone in despair, sipping a drink at Medan Hotel, when he crossed paths with Tjong A Fie. Tjong A Fie, moved by his predicament and recognising his sincerity, extended a job offer to manage his recently acquired rubber plantation, Si Boelan. Tjong A Fie's estate became the first Chinese company in Sumatra to employ a European as its manager. Dolf Kamerlingh Onnes excelled in this role, earning the trust of Tjong A Fie, who later entrusted him with managing his businesses.

In the 1910s, as global rubber demand surged, the Kamerlingh Onnes Administratiekantoor shipped rubber directly to America, which led to regular telephone orders from the United States. As a result, rubber prices on the East Coast surged, exceeding both the latest London quotations and Singapore prices. Additionally, this region supplied rubber to Japan at

[4] *The Singapore and Straits Directory* 1896; DC 09-09-1933; Chang 2016: 60–62.
[5] SP 13-02-1900.
[6] SP 04-02-1903.
[7] *Nieuw adresboek van geheel Nederlandsch-Indië* 1903, 1904, 1905.

Fig. 24.1 Dolf Kamerlingh Onnes in 1920 (Buiskool 1999: backcover)

competitive prices, whereas English companies in Malaya were obliged to sell their product in London. This brought newfound prosperity to rubber planters on the East Coast, turning their fortunes around from the difficult times during the war. Medan emerged as a prominent rubber market with the highest prices in the industry, leaving rubber planters in a favourable position.[8]

Dolf managed various enterprises owned by Tjong A Fie, including the Rubber Company Si Boelan, the Soekaradja Cultivation Company, China

[8] SP 02-12-1914.

Fig. 24.2 Dolf (right) with Tjong A Fie and Khouw An Kim (left), Chinese Major of Batavia in 1918 (photo from Tjong A Fie museum)

Kasih Cultuur, Algemeene Cultuur Maatschappij, and other smaller firms, some 20 in total, with combined investments of millions of guilders. Many of the plantations under his administration covered roughly 400–700 hectares and employed several hundred coolies (often 300–800). In April 1912, Tjong A Fie Landen was founded to oversee Tjong A Fie's expansive business ventures, solidifying Dolf's position as Tjong A Fie's closest confidant and advisor (Fig. 24.2).[9]

In 1912, Dolf established his own enterprise, the Administration Office Kamerlingh Onnes, serving as an agent and manager for various businesses and companies. As his ventures prospered, the firm underwent incorporation in 1917, becoming N.V. Administratiekantoor Kamerlingh Onnes. The firm became a respected establishment and assumed the role of administrator for numerous enterprises in Medan and along the east coast of Sumatra. These included Medan Hotel (owned by Tjong A Fie)

[9] Buiskool 1999: 21–25; Colonial Business https://www.colonialbusinessindonesia.nl/.

and Hotel de Boer. Additionally, he managed Medansche Belegging Maatschappij, a real estate investment and leasing company with a capital of 3 million guilders; Mulder & Co. Tegel en Beton, specialising in concrete with a capital of *f*150,000; Medansche Drukkerij, a printing business with *f*150,000 in capital; and Unitas Apotheek, a pharmacy with a capital of *f*125,000.[10]

Dolf was a prosperous businessman who not only achieved success but also took good care of his workers, and he refrained from resorting to *poenale sanctie* or punitive measures. The *Indische Gids* from 1919 wrote:

> *It is certainly very striking that the well-known Major of the Chinese, Tjong A Fie (he has 23 enterprises on Sumatra's East coast or is one of their major shareholders) has been excluded in the matter of the poenale sanction commission. Could it be that his Superintendent, Mr. Kamerlingh Onnes, must represent him amongst the leaders of the planters as he is no longer seen as being on their side? Mr. K.O. has conducted a trial at one of his enterprises to award the coolies with 5% of the profits.*[11]

In 1917, under the leadership of Kamerlingh Onnes, the Algemeene Cultuur Maatschappij made a significant decision to allocate 5% of the gross profit as a bonus for the coolies, to be distributed based on the number of days they worked at the company during the year. With a profit of *f*150,000 in 1916, this amounted to *f*7500 guilders which were shared among the 472 coolies employed by the company.[12] On average, each coolie received about 16 guilders as a bonus for their hard work. This move was considered an act of fairness, recognising that the coolies' labour was a crucial factor contributing to the company's profits. *De Sumatra Post* quoted a French expression, *Les idées marchent!* (Ideas Work!).[13]

In August 1922, faced with a decline in rubber prices, the company had to implement significant cost-cutting measures, including reducing coolie wages to align with the rates adopted by AVROS or the General Association of Rubber Companies on the East Coast of Sumatra-affiliated companies. However, as the economy improved, the management reinstated higher wages.[14]

[10] Idem.
[11] *Indische Gids* I, 1919: 648.
[12] Buiskool 1999: 116.
[13] SP 27-02-1917.
[14] SP 17-03-1923.

Fig. 24.3 Office of the Administration Office Kamerlingh Onnes at Hüttenbachstraat with Medan's Warenhuis on the far right (photo collection of Dirk Buiskool)

Business thrived until the 1920s, when rubber prices plummeted. In 1921, another turning point occurred with the passing of Tjong A Fie. During this challenging period, Dolf Kamerlingh Onnes again played a crucial role in assisting the Tjong family in settling the company's debts and managing their investments. He collaborated with the Javasche Bank to gradually liquidate and salvage the invested capital. Despite the setbacks in the rubber industry, Kamerlingh Onnes' real estate and other ventures continued to prosper. The business remained in operation in Medan until the 1950s (Fig. 24.3).

In August 1920, Dolf invited his nephew Harm Kamerlingh Onnes, the son of his artistic brother Menso, to travel to the East. Harm, like his father, was a painter. He sent several paintings to Dolf, which led Dolf to invite him to travel to the Indies. Harm went to Medan in 1923, and with Dolf, they met Tjong A Fie's widow and visited the late entrepreneur's plantations. Harm described his uncle as a kind of business tycoon who won all his cases. During the journey, Harm wrote beautifully illustrated letters home, giving vivid descriptions of his time in Sumatra, China, and Japan.

In 1923, Dolf decided to return to the Netherlands and established the Administration office "Vastgoed Holland-Indie" in Den Haag. He settled in Warmond, near Leiden, where he spent the remainder of his life. He continued to serve as a director of the Administration Office until his resignation in 1931. Dolf Kamerlingh Onnes eventually passed away in 1933.[15] After his death, his firm in the Netherlands continued under Hollands Administratiekantoor Kamerlingh Onnes. In the 1970s, the firm became Makelaarskantoor Makko, which is still operating. The business in Medan thrived until the 1950s, including managing the leases of 246 houses. It was taken over by the Indonesian government in 1958 and renamed P.D. Obor.[16]

24.3 The Deli Connection to the Nobel Prize

The link between Deli and Leiden ran not through experiments, but through money and labour. Although Indonesia has not produced a Nobel Prize winner, it's worth noting that the wealth generated from Deli tobacco played a role in supporting the research of Heike Kamerlingh Onnes, ultimately leading to his Nobel Prize achievement (Fig. 24.4).[17]

Heike Kamerlingh Onnes began working as a professor of experimental physics in Leiden in 1882. One of his goals was to conduct research to test the theory put forward by Johannes Diderik van der Waals on the behaviour of gases and liquids. Van der Waals formulated a theory that describes the behaviour of molecules in terms of attraction and volume. It introduced the concept of a "critical temperature" above which a substance exists only in the gaseous phase. Heike aimed to study molecular

[15] DC 09-09-1933.

[16] Pemerintah Daerah Sumatera Utara, Sumatera Utara Membangun 1976: 135.

[17] A Dutch Nobel Prize winner for his work in Indonesia was Christiaan Eijkman, who shared the award in 1929 "for his discovery of the antineuritic vitamin." His research in Java on beriberi in the 1890s showed that chickens and prison inmates fed polished rice developed the disease, while switching to unpolished rice cured it. Eijkman's findings laid the foundation for understanding vitamin deficiency diseases.

Fig. 24.4 Leading physicists at Leiden. Standing, left to right: Paul Ehrenfest (Austria, later Leiden), Paul Langevin (France), Albert Einstein (Germany, later the United States), Edmond Bauer (France). Sitting: Heike Kamerlingh Onnes and his wife (Buiskool 1999: 17)

phenomena by precisely measuring gases and gas mixtures, focusing on simple substances like oxygen, neon, argon, nitrogen, and hydrogen.

However, these simple substances had extremely low critical temperatures, making it difficult to condense them into liquids. To tackle this challenge, Heike had to establish a cryogenic laboratory capable of reaching extremely low temperatures, approaching absolute zero or -273 degrees Celsius.

Initially, he started with one technician, but soon recruited a group of boys aged 14–18. These young apprentices were known as "blue boys" due to their work attire. The apprenticeship system was advantageous for his laboratory in supplying skilled yet low-paid labour. Heike relied heavily on these young trainees to conduct his experiments and thus needed financial support to secure a continuing apprenticeship system for his laboratory.[18]

This is where P.W. Janssen came into play as Heike Kamerlingh Onnes sought Janssen to secure financial support for the training of instrument makers. P.W. Janssen from the Deli Maatschappij made a lot of money from the Deli tobacco and was known as a philanthropist, supporting the Dutch. Janssen supported the Ons Huis association in Amsterdam, which opened the first Dutch people's house in 1892, and a school in Leusden where boys learned the basket-making trade. In 1894, Janssen founded the Dutch Housing Foundation. He was particularly concerned about the education of the Dutch of the lower social class.

It is unknown how Heike Kamerlingh Onnes got to know P.W. Janssen, perhaps through the connection with his brother Dolf, who was working in Deli. Heike Kamerlingh Onnes wrote a letter to C.W. Janssen, the son of P.W. Janssen and director of the Senembah Company, outlining a proposal for financial support. He proposed scholarships to cover the school fees and educational materials and to compensate the family for the income lost while the boy attended school. If the boy showed talent, he could become an apprentice instrument maker in the laboratory after vocational school. Heike calculated these costs until the age of 18, which was around 550 guilders per apprentice.

He suggested establishing a fund for talented boys from less privileged backgrounds. In a letter to Janssen, Heike Kamerlingh Onnes outlined the detailed costs for students aged 12–18 and proposed a sum of *f*6541 to initiate the system, with an annual *f*1653 to sustain it. He emphasised the importance of having bright young assistants available for his experiments.[19]

P.W. Janssen accepted Heike's proposal and established a foundation in 1897. The *Janssenfonds* provided allowances to almost all students at the physics laboratory, continuing even after the initial six-year trial period.

[18] Van Delft 2005: 298–313.

[19] Idem.

The Janssen Fund for Vocational Training Scholarships was a success and later received funding from the Dutch government and the municipality of Leiden.[20] The Janssen family's descendants managed the fund until the 1950s.

Heike Kamerlingh Onnes utilised this workforce of affordable technicians, gradually expanding their numbers to 16 in 1898 and 32 six years later, for constructing and operating his laboratory. To ensure the sustainability of this system, which was vital for his expansive cryogenic laboratory, Heike formalised the workshop training by establishing the Leiden School of Instrument Makers in 1901. This school was fully integrated into his laboratory. The collaboration was highly successful, with the students contributing to the laboratory's research efforts. The internal training initiative produced not only errand boys and skilled technicians but also invaluable contributors such as "measuring slaves" and glass artisans.

Fig. 24.5 Drawing by Marijke Kamerlingh Onnes of Paul Ehrenfest (professor of theoretical physics at Leiden University), Albert Einstein, and Harm Kamerlingh Onnes, in Leiden, circa 1920. (Buiskool 1999:18)

[20] *Algemeen Handelsblad* 06-04-1927.

Without their presence, the level of precision and the scale of operations at Heike's Physics Laboratory would have been inconceivable.[21]

Heike Kamerlingh Onnes was renowned for his exceptional organisational talent, in addition to his brilliance as an experimental physicist. In 1908, he made history by liquefying helium, and three years later, he discovered superconductivity. Heike Kamerlingh Onnes was awarded the Nobel Prize in Physics in 1913 for his work on the properties of matter at low temperatures and the discovery of superconductivity. His laboratory was well known and attracted world-renowned scientists, including Albert Einstein in 1911 and Julius Robert Oppenheimer in 1927.[22]

It is not a long stretch, but it can be said that Heike Kamerlingh Onnes' research was financially supported by the proceeds generated from the soils of Deli (Fig. 24.5).

[21] Idem.

[22] See: https://en.m.wikipedia.org/wiki/File:Leiden_Kamerlingh-Onnes_Lab.jpg.

CHAPTER 25

Colonial Businesses in Medan

Medan emerged as a major colonial business centre in the early twentieth century, drawing European capital, migrant labour, and regional trade into a fast-growing urban hub. Contemporary guides noted that, for Europeans, daily routines could feel "somewhat" familiar:

> *...life somewhat resembles that in Europe. Offices open at half-past seven in the morning and work continuously until noon, followed by lunch and a rest period. They reopen at two in the afternoon and close at five. In Java, offices usually remain open during lunch hours, with meals brought to the office by servants.*
>
> *After work, sports enthusiasts head to the football or tennis field until dusk. By half-past seven, they enjoy a social evening with a drink at the club. The lifestyle is distinct from that in the Netherlands, with many recreational options such as music, theatre, and even opera performances, visiting the main towns.*
>
> *The social life among residents is generally pleasant and cordial. Since the European population is relatively small, people know each other well and quickly form close connections, aided by regular club visits. Improved travel facilities now make it easier to get home on time, further enhancing life in the Indies.*[1]

This chapter traces several prominent colonial businesses and the afterlives of their buildings, brands, and institutions, beyond those already

[1] Langereis 1917: 527.

B. Minasny, D. A. Buiskool, *Stories from Medan, Volume 1*,
https://doi.org/10.1007/978-981-95-7707-1_25

discussed in earlier chapters. Because the surviving sources are overwhelmingly European, these narratives often marginalise Indigenous lives and perspectives. Where possible, we therefore focus on institutional legacy and material continuities while acknowledging the limits and exclusions of the archive.

25.1 Hotels

25.1.1 Medan Hotel

The oldest hotel in Medan was the Medan Hotel. Mr Vink established this hotel in the 1880s, known as Hotel de Vink, located between the Esplanade and the railway station. In 1884, it suffered a fire but was rebuilt, becoming the Medan Hotel in 1890. Eventually, it was owned by a limited liability company with prominent commercial figures in Deli, including Tjong A Fie. This company had shareholder meetings like the one held on June 16, 1896 (Fig. 25.1):

> *At the annual general meeting of shareholders held in Medan on June 15, the profit distribution to shareholders for the financial year 1895–1896 was set at*

Fig. 25.1 Medan Hotel (KITLV 182256)

7% of the registered capital, being Dutch guilders 70 per share, payable from July 1. At the office of the Medan Hotel against the withdrawal of dividend certificate no. 6. The Board. Medan, June 16, 1896.[2]

Wright's *Twentieth Century Impressions* in 1909 described the Medan Hotel:

The two-storey building with sixty two lofty, well ventilated rooms is the oldest hotel in Medan. It is here that people bid the traveller feast him and bid him farewell, and this is also the place where on the first and sixteenth of every month the planters come to enjoy their 'hari besar'. The Medan hotel is also a supplier of iced beer for the estates. Besides the main building is a private dining room for more than a hundred guests. There is the public dining room with over seventy tables, a billiard room and a reading room with English, French, Dutch and German newspapers. The chef is Mr. Rohr from Switzerland who worked before in the Trocadero Restaurant in London. The hotel was established in 1888 by Mr. Vinck and was in 1909 a limited liability company directed by several of the most prominent commercial men in Deli. The hotel is fully electrically lit with over 500 lamps.[3]

Locally called "*roemah makan*" or a house of food, Medan Hotel was a popular venue for various events, including farewell parties for those going on leave or retiring. On the 1st and 16th of each month, it became a favourite destination for planters, who could enjoy European beer. The hotel specialised in providing iced beer to nearby plantations, ensuring it stayed fresh and cool during transport. Dancing evenings were regularly advertised in the newspapers, scheduled for Tuesday nights at Hotel de Boer and Wednesdays at the Medan Hotel.[4]

In 1915, the hotel was bought by Tjong A Fie, leading to the demolition of the old building and the construction of a modern hotel. The hotel featured numerous amenities, including electric lighting and advanced sanitary facilities. It became a hub for planters and a renowned dining destination known for its excellent service and cuisine.

H.H. Ottersberg began his career as a pastry chef and cook in various prestigious hotels across Europe. In 1922, after returning to the Netherlands, he received two job offers as a chef, one in Rio de Janeiro

[2] DC 17-6-1896; DC 20-6-1896.

[3] Wright, 1909: 576.

[4] SP 27-02-1930. *Het nieuws van den dag voor Nederlandsch-Indië* 19-10-1915.

and the other in Medan. He chose Medan, and in December 1922, at the age of 31, he arrived as head chef of the Grand Hotel Medan, earning a salary of *f*500 per month. The hotel was in poor condition, but Ottersberg gradually transformed its restaurant into a renowned culinary establishment, achieving notable milestones, including winning a gold medal at an international cooking competition.[5]

By 1930, the Medan Hotel underwent extensive renovations, including adding an American bar and constructing a Trianon hall,[6] featuring the region's first sprung dance floor. The hotel was subsequently rebranded as the Grand Hotel Medan. Ottersberg's expertly curated dishes quickly gained popularity, with the hotel serving up to 300–400 guests on busy days. He also introduced the *tussen neus en lippen* dishes[7]—a precursor to modern snack bars—which were a huge success. In 1935, the hotel merged with Hotel de Boer, and in 1937, Ottersberg was appointed manager of the hotel.

After the war, on November 4, 1945, the Medan Hotel resumed operations, though initially only for British and Dutch military personnel. The hotel was fully reopened to the public in May 1947. In the 1950s, the hotel was nationalised and renamed Hotel Granada. The building was eventually demolished in the 1980s (Fig. 25.2).

25.1.2 Hotel de Boer

Aeint Herman de Boer (1867–1931) arrived in Java from Workum, Friesland, the Netherlands, in 1897. Initially working as a ship's cook and later at Stam and Weyns in Soerabaja, he soon shifted his focus to Medan by 1898, attracted by the flourishing tobacco industry. At the time, Medan only had a few establishments for Europeans, including the Medan Hotel and Oranje Hotel. Interestingly, these establishments were Chinese-owned, prompting tobacco managers to call for more European influence in the local hospitality industry. Recognising this demand, the Deli Company allotted a piece of land to Herman de Boer. He began with a modest eatery with timber walls and *atap* roofs, along with some guest

[5] *Het nieuwsblad voor Sumatra* 14-01-1953.

[6] Trianon hall refers to a large, elegant ballroom or banquet hall. The name "Trianon" is inspired by the Grand Trianon and Petit Trianon, which are opulent palaces located within the grounds of the Palace of Versailles in France.

[7] Dutch meaning between nose and lips, referring to small, easy-to-prepare snacks or light dishes that could be quickly served, or finger foods.

Fig. 25.2 Grand Hotel Medan, dining room (Uitgeverij Köhler & Co. Medan circa 1920)

rooms for planters. The business quickly prospered, allowing him to upgrade to a brick building named "Herman de Boer" with a restaurant, a patisserie, and six rooms. An advertisement in 1898 in the *Deli Courant:*

> *H.A. de Boer. Cuisinier, patissier, glacier. Medan. Can be subscribed from 15-8 for lunch and dinner. In stock: All types of chocolates… fine chocolate works… fruits crystals… fine dessert items… Dutch and French liqueurs… fine French comestibles… fine German comestibles… Havannas and various cigarettes… orders for cakes, jellies, ice cream, dishes, dinners, suppers… everything that belongs to the profession is carried out with the utmost care…*[8]

By 1907, this establishment had morphed into a hotel with an expanded dining area and bar. De Boer's establishment became renowned for its offerings of wine, caviar, Leiden cheese, ham from York, herring, Japanese soy, Frankfurt sausage, and other delicacies.[9] In 1909, he further amplified

[8] DC 13-08-1898.
[9] SP 08-12-1908.

the hotel's capacity by adding 40 rooms. In 1912, there was further expansion. *De Sumatra Post* wrote:

> *Hotel de Boer continues to grow. The building complex will now be expanded again by adding a large new taproom in front of and annexed to the existing one, and a new dining room next to it, after which the current dining room will be given a different purpose. The new premises will take up most of the lawn in front of the hotel. Tasteful, modern furnishings will be strived for. The dining room will have a few nice round tables for intimate dinners, the tap room will have a few German-style beer corners. The expansion of the number of hotel rooms is still being studied. Mr De Boer will soon visit Java to see the latest in this field.*[10]

Over time, De Boer expanded his business footprint with modern architecture, with compact and separate bungalow-style rooms equipped with showers and splash baths, using insect-proof gauze wireframes instead of mosquito curtains. Herman de Boer and his wife, Louise Carolina de Boer-Rood, managed the hotel. Two of their six children settled on the East Coast of Sumatra, while the rest pursued careers in the Netherlands. In 1926, De Boer hired a famous hotelier Johan Martinus Gantvoort, who was the director of Hotel du Papillon in Semarang and Hotel Des Indes in Batavia, as the director of Hotel de Boer.[11]

The hotel's ambience, offering a buffet, iced drinks and live music, attracted planters on *hari besar*. Hotel de Boer became the icon of Medan and was referenced in many novels and travelogues as the place in Medan:

> *Everyone Sunday evening dinner music at Huize (House) de Boer.* [12]

Mrs. H.L. Burgerhardt-De Boer, daughter of the owner, wrote an article about her father's hotel. The hotel was renowned for its real old Dutch "*speculaas,*" a traditional spiced biscuit. In the months before St Nicholas' day (December 5), orders for this special treat came from all over the Dutch Indies and as far abroad as Singapore, Bangkok, and Hong Kong.

[10] SP 26-08-1912.

[11] Johan Martinus Gantvoort (1864–1944) was the director of Hotel De Boer from February 1, 1926, to November 24, 1927 (SP 30-1-1926).

[12] SP 04-06-1912.

The speculaas were packed in square tins, which were soldered to keep the contents fresh and crisp.[13]

German traveller Martin Borrmann in *Soenda, Een reis door Sumatra*, described the dining room:

> *The large dining room at the "Hotel de Boer" in Medan is two stories high. European ingenuity has done everything possible here to keep the tropical heat at bay. The height of this gigantic space—larger than the entire hotel in Lho Seumawè with all its outbuildings—the four large whirring propellers, the narrow slits more than a man's length long, directly beneath the ceiling, in the walls, the light green paint—all of this makes it possible to momentarily forget the less pleasant aspects of life in the Indies. …*
>
> *It truly takes a lot of effort to go from the Surprise de Turquie, the appetiser, to lobster soup, omelette, fish, poultry, and meat, and finally to the dessert, pineapple pudding and white wine. But that's not the end of it, because there's also Glace indienne, soursop with ice, and finally, coffee, the delightful extract of Sumatra coffee, which cannot be surpassed by anything else. One must truly be a gastronomic diplomat to navigate one's stomach through such a minefield every day. Everything I despise is here, everything I fled Europe for: real bon-vivant faces, as if straight out of a Balzac novel, as well as typical Americans with carefully massaged wrinkles, as befits true sportsmen.*[14]

The hotel was not just a place to stay or dine but a convergence point for various social and professional activities, housing long-term residents, hosting lavish dinners, and accommodating the eccentricities of a diverse set of guests. European lifestyle and customs were transplanted into a tropical setting, often resulting in a blend of grandeur and absurdity. The menu could range from consommé tortue Claire and Mignon Rossini to simple ham sandwiches. Occasionally, peculiar orders appeared, such as *hors d'oeuvre riche bien soignè*[15] with horses in gold, which turned out to be decorative wax horses on a gold-rimmed dish for a special occasion (Figs. 25.3 and 25.4).[16]

Hotel de Boer also introduced a "mosquito-free room" with wire gauze windows that replaced mosquito netting around the beds. This was

[13] Letter H.L. Burghardt-de Boer, 17-06-1969.

[14] Borrmann 1926: 43-44.

[15] "Hors d'oeuvre riche bien soigné" is a French phrase used to describe a type of elegant appetiser or starter.

[16] SP 18-01-1938.

Fig. 25.3 Hotel de Boer around 1900 (KITLV 26912)

mentioned in Arnold Wright's *Twentieth Century Impressions of the Netherlands Indies* published in 1909 (Fig. 25.5):

> *These bedrooms are a novelty in Eastern hotel life, quite unlike anything to be found either at Batavia, Singapore or Colombo. The old fashioned mosquito curtains give place to a wire gauze frame, which is perfectly insect proof, and makes sleep the comfort it ought to be.*[17]

Dutch writer Madelon Lulofs, in her novel *Rubber*, published in 1935, wrote about plantation life in the 1920s:

> *The principal hotel of Medan, hotel De Boer, was situated at a wide grass field round which went a broad asphalt promenade. The main building had two stories. Downstairs was the dance hall and the dining room, with a large terrace. Upstairs were bedrooms. On either side of the main building stood a pavilion, two long rows of bedrooms each with its veranda and its bathroom. The annexes were joined to the main building by a roofed cement path. Between the main building and the pavilions lay a strip of garden, a path, and a strip of grass.*[18]

[17] Wright 1909: 576.
[18] Lulofs 1931: 31.

Fig. 25.4 Hotel de Boer in the 1920s (KITLV 19744)

By 1930, Hotel de Boer grew further, adding 120 rooms and a grand hall. The rooms were connected by telephone, and the hotel hosted illustrious guests, including Crown Prince Leopold III of Belgium, the Prince of Siam, and author Rabindranath Tagore from India. Sutan Sjahrir, Indonesia's first Prime Minister, played the violin there during his school days.[19]

Australian performer Billy Heaton wrote:

> *At the Hotel de Boer, where we appeared last night, they have the orchestra mounted on a turntable. This table is half in the hotel and half in the beer garden. Most of the dancing is done in the beer garden, which is open, and the floor concrete. Should it suddenly commence to rain, the orchestra retain their seats and the whole orchestral arrangement is pushed around, holus bolus, per medium of the turntable, and they find themselves playing into the ballroom of the hotel instead of the garden. The dancing at the Grand Hotel is also done in the garden.*[20]

[19] Mrazek 2018: 25–26; SP 17-08-1927; SP 26-07-1932.
[20] *Kalgoorlie Miner* 12-02-1937.

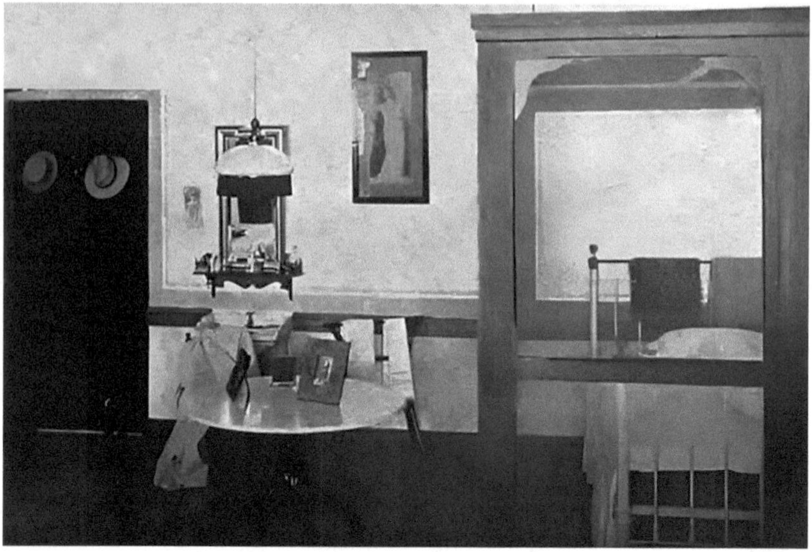

Fig. 25.5 A room within the room of De Boer Hotel (Wright 1909)

In January 1938, when Princess Juliana gave birth, aviatrix Helen Skinner, who visited Medan, wrote in her diary:

> *Lunch at Hotel de Boer. Excellent German beer, veal liver in paper thin slices — very good.*
>
> *Blanc mange with orange sauce in honor of the House of Orange, stood up for the Dutch National Anthem, heard other Dutch airs. The public buildings decked with bunting, Dutch flags, orange streamers - the stork with crown and infant princess on the hotel top. Orange flowers on the tables, an orange streamer on the cloth.*[21]

Yet, the hotel industry in Medan was not without challenges. After the death of Tjong A Fie, who also owned Medan Hotel, the Kamerlingh Administration upgraded and rebranded the hotel as Grand Hotel Medan, igniting fierce competition. De Boer resisted merger proposals and fought to retain primacy. The two hotels fiercely competed for European patrons with orchestras, parties, balls, and extravagant dinners featuring the most

[21] https://flyingundertheradar.blog/2024/09/18/33-chinese-new-year-and-the-house-of-orange-dutch-east-indies-jan-31-feb-2-1938/.

expensive cold-storage items, all sustained by a culture of deferred payment, as guests charged their expenses to ongoing credit accounts. Serious buyers twice offered to buy Hotel de Boer to incorporate it into a large hotel group in the Dutch Indies. However, De Boer refused the offer. The looming economic crisis and the unpaid credit led to the hotel's bankruptcy amidst stiff competition (Fig. 25.6).[22]

Mrs de Boer tried to keep the business afloat. However, as times changed and Deli became more subdued, the vibrant ambience of yesteryear faded. Eventually, in 1935, the bank took over the hotel, placing its management under the Kamerlingh Onnes firm, which also oversaw Grand Hotel Medan.

Later, Mrs de Boer initiated another venture in Bandar Baroe, a cooler region near Brastagi that was more conducive for her ailing husband. Herman de Boer passed away in Bandar Baroe in 1937 at 71.

Like a dance on the volcano, in January 1942, a few months before the Japanese invasion, Hotel de Boer still advertised in *De Sumatra Post:*

Fig. 25.6 Hotel de Boer's dining room (Wright 1909)

[22] DC 10-11-1937; SP 30-10-1937.

Hotel de Boer Matinee 12-2 Rijstaffel in the evening Concert Music Additional dinners from f2.50 per cover.[23]

On March 13, the Japanese entered Medan.

25.2 Banking

The Chartered Bank of India, Australia and China was founded in London by a Scotsman, James Wilson, in 1853. The booming businesses of Deli and the East Coast of Sumatra initially managed their finances and loans through the bank's branches in Penang and Singapore. The banks in Penang and Singapore attracted the largest agricultural businesses and provided services such as buying and selling goods and facilitating the recruitment of Chinese labourers. Seeing this potential in the "Wild East," the Chartered Bank established a branch in Medan in 1880 but had to close its doors in 1886 due to financial viability issues.[24] It reopened in June 1889, with Herbert C. Gulland at the helm.

The Nederlandsche Handel-Maatschappij (NHM), or the Netherlands Trading Society, a financial entity, has played an instrumental role in shaping the Dutch East Indies. With its roots stretching back to the VOC (Vereenigde Oost-Indische Compagnie, or United East India Company), it was rebranded as NHM in 1824 in Batavia. It financed the Deli Maatschappij. By 1888, business activities in Deli and Medan had drawn its attention, and an agency was set up as a small lodge at the Medan Hotel. It issued cash orders (in dollars and Straits dollars) that could be exchanged for silver dollars, as currency circulation was limited. The agency provided credit facilities for the plantation companies and was also active in consignment contracts, financing a significant portion of the tobacco harvest, buying and selling.[25] From 1888, the NHM had its office on the corner of the Esplanade and Hüttenbachstraat; in 1929, it moved to a new, impressive office building opposite the town hall. [26]

The turn of the century heralded transformative policies for the Dutch Indies. In 1906, the council "*Afdeelingsraad van Deli*" was established, and Medan achieved municipality status in 1909. Simultaneously, currency reforms swept across the East Coast of Sumatra. This shift was

[23] SP 31-01-1942.
[24] De Graaf 2012: 21–22, 108.
[25] Idem.
[26] Loderichs, Buiskool 1997: 109.

marked by the entry of De Javasche Bank in Medan, with a new building erected next to the town hall, completed in 1909.

At the same time, NHM was financing 20% of the total tobacco harvest on the East Coast. After 1913, when tea and rubber cultivation began, the Nederlandsch-Indische Handelsbank (NIHB) and Nederlandsch-Indische Escompto Maatschappij (NIEM) also set up branches on the East Coast.[27] NIEM established its new office in Medan in 1928, on the corner of Kesawan, opposite the AVROS building (now known as Bank Mandiri, previously Bank Dagang Negara), designed by architect Ed Cuypers.

Market segmentation emerged, with NHM, Javasche Bank, and Standard Chartered Bank serving large enterprises, while NIHB, NIEM, and the newcomer Koloniale Cultuur-en Handelsbank catered to different market segments. The NHM agency also became more active in mediating the sale of agricultural products, receiving 20% of the tobacco harvest on consignment and 10% of rubber due to British and American ownership.[28]

Adding more threads to Medan's banking was Naudin ten Cate & Co., founded by Isaac Albert Naudin ten Cate (1838–1908), a German businessman from Wiesbaden. His journey to Sumatra began in 1887 at Deli Handel Maatschappij. When the company was dissolved in 1889, he shifted careers, becoming co-editor of the *Deli Courant* until 1896, but his ambitions lay elsewhere.

In 1892, he established a trading company, Naudin ten Cate & Co., in Medan. The firm grew rapidly, becoming a limited partnership in 1901 with a capital of 1 million guilders. By 1909, it had evolved into the Bank en Handelsvereeniging (Banking and Trading Association) Naudin ten Cate & Co., serving as an agent for major shipping lines like Lloyds, the Nederlandsche Lloyd, and the Samarangsche Insurance Companies, while also managing tobacco, coffee, and rubber plantations across Sumatra. Beyond business, Naudin ten Cate served on various committees and boards and was a member of the Negorij and Church Council. Later in life, he moved to Garoet (Garut) in Java before returning to Germany, where he died in Wiesbaden in 1908.[29]

His son, Albert William (Willem) Naudin ten Cate, took over the family's legacy, first as editor of the *Deli Courant* and later as a businessman in Medan. Albert Willem embodied the colonial mindset of the time, once writing that coolies were "the scum of the Javanese and Chinese

[27] De Graaf 2012: 21–22.
[28] Idem.
[29] Wright 1909: 571; DC 09-03-1908.

population" and should be treated as such.[30] The firm's fortunes declined with the upheavals of World War I. After settling all debts, Naudin ten Cate & Co. closed its doors in 1916.[31]

In 1907, Tjong Yong Hian and Tjong A Fie established the Deli Bank, Medan's first Chinese bank, addressing the difficulties Chinese merchants faced in securing credit from European banks due to language and cultural barriers. Backed by revenue farmers in Medan and Penang, and supported by the Java Bank as a development financier for East Sumatra, Deli Bank quickly became vital to the local Chinese business community. Starting with 650,000 guilders in capital, the bank grew rapidly, reaching 5 million guilders by 1918. It offered loans, savings accounts, consignment contracts, and trade financing, while also facilitating remittances between Medan and China.[32]

The financial landscape of Medan saw another major development in 1913, when Khoe Tjin Tek and a group of Hokkien merchants established the Chung Hwa Shang Yeh Chinese Bank with an initial capital of 1 million guilders. Unlike traditional banks, it also provided fire and marine insurance, catering to the growing commercial needs of the Chinese business community. The bank's fortunes took a significant turn in 1921 when it acquired most of the shares of the struggling Deli Bank, absorbing its operations and expanding its influence. With an extensive network of agents and correspondents across Asia—including Amoy, Hong Kong, Penang, Singapore, Batavia, Shanghai, and Kuala Lumpur—the bank became a key player in regional trade and finance. In 1925, the company constructed a new headquarters in bustling Kesawan. Decades later, in 1962, it rebranded as Bank Kesawan.[33]

25.3 The Rens Brothers Carriage and Automotive Workshops

Frederik Johannes Fuchs started a business with a modest livery stable and farrier's shop in Batavia. In 1876, he established a repair shop for carriages, followed by the addition of a workshop for saddle and harness

[30] DC 22-5-1895; DC 28-09-1910.
[31] *Straits Echo* 08-01-1914.
[32] Buiskool 2025: 123,124.
[33] Buiskool 2025: 156,157.

production in Tanah Abang. The business was further expanded to include importing horses (Fig. 25.7).[34]

Fuchs' efforts turned to fortune, and by 1885, his enterprise had flourished to such an extent that it was transformed into a limited company. Collaborating with partners, the company was called N.V. Maatschappij tot Exploitatie der Rijtuigfabriek en van den Handel in Paarden, known as F.J. Fuchs.[35]

Despite the success of Deli's tobacco cultivation, the journey from Batavia to Belawan demanded a voyage of five to six days by steamship. The influence of the English-controlled ports of Penang and Singapore played a more important role in Deli's society. Deli residents turned to Penang and Singapore for most of their needs. Recognising this need, Fuchs dispatched carriages on consignment to a Medan-based company.

Fig. 25.7 Rens Rijtuigfabriek (carriage factory) at Kesawan in the 1900s (KITLV 377186). The street next to the shop was called Rensstraat (now Jl. Ahmad Yani I)

[34] Lorck 1912: 175.
[35] Rens 1936: 7–8.

In 1889, Fuchs sent L.M. van Breukelen from Batavia and entrusted him with the task of conveying assorted goods and horses to Deli while managing consigned goods in Medan. Over time, van Breukelen settled in Medan and established his own business.[36]

In the same year, Johannes Willem Rens (1867–1927) from Amsterdam initiated a business in Medan called J.W. Rens, crafting carriages and wagons, supplying upholstery, producing saddles, harnesses, selling horse foods, and more. Fuchs perceived the young businessman as a promising entrepreneur who shared a similar beginning to his experiences. He had an active business connection with Rens (Fig. 25.8).

The company J.W. Rens proved popular in the Deli region, as it was one of the few companies that sold carriages as a means of transport in the growing tobacco industry. J.W. Rens occupied a shop on Kesawan called Rens' Rijtuigfabriek. The corner street of the shop was called Rensstraat (current Jl. Jendral Ahmad Yani I). J.W. Rens was helped by his industrious brother Daniël Rens (1873–1948).

Fig. 25.8 Rens Rijtuigfabriek (carriage factory) in Deli, circa 1890 (KITLV 154117)

[36] Rens 1936: 18–19.

Fuchs, the steward of the Fuchs Company in Batavia, served as managing director until 1895, when he decided to retire due to health concerns. Fuchs trusted J.W. Rens from Medan as his successor. Thus, J.W. Rens moved to Batavia and served as managing director of the Fuchs company, while the Medan business was handed over to his brother. The company in Medan became D. Rens Carriage and Garage, still occupying the shop at Kesawan.[37]

After leading the company for seven years, J.W. Rens retired in 1902 and, in turn, handed the directorship to his brother, D. Rens. Under Daniël Rens' astute leadership, the company expanded its operations to include the sale of carriages and motor cars, as well as the importation of Australian horses (Fig. 25.9).

The Fuchs Company established its presence across two structures in Batavia, specifically in Tanah Abang and Parapatan. The workshop had an area of 32,580 m^2, with about half occupied by buildings, stables with 90–110 horses daily, and with about 160 people.[38]

With the emergence of automobiles around 1910, Daniël Rens realised that the horse and carriage would soon have to make way for the automobile. He revamped the company into Rijtuig- en Automobiel Maatschappij F. J. Fuchs, or Carriage and Automobile Company. D. Rens still maintained his business in Medan as D. Rens Garage and Carriage Factory, managed by H. Feringa, with a massive annual turnover of *f*300,000.[39] It was famous for manufacturing and repairing vehicles, importing leatherwork, automobiles, and other transport needs.

Rens recognised the need to set up branches in other large cities, and in 1910, an office in Soerabaia was opened, which quickly proved its viability and gave impetus to the establishment of a branch in Semarang in 1913. However, the war years of 1914 and subsequent years brought about important changes for the company.

New relations were established with America, and the company became a representative of automobile companies such as Hudson, Chrysler, Delaunay-Belleville, and Darracq. It also represented tyres such as Firestone. In 1917, the company absorbed the purchasing office in Amsterdam, while D. Rens Medan company eventually became an extension of the Fuchs company in 1918. The company finally closed down the

[37] Lorck 1912: 175.
[38] Wright 1909: 462–463.
[39] Feldwick 1917: 1028–1030.

Fig. 25.9 J.W. Rens (left) and D. Rens (photo by Kleingrothe KITLV 154177)

carriage factories. A plot of land was leased at Paleisweg for the garage and workshop.[40]

As the transition of business from carriage to automobile was completed, the company was reorganised in 1918. The name Fuchs was well known in Batavia, but in Medan, people only knew Rens; thus, the company became Fuchs & Rens Limited, or Maatschappij tot voortzetting der zaken voorheen Fuchs en Rens, with a capital of *f*1,200,000. A new

[40] Rens 1936: 69–71.

chapter began in 1920 with the establishment of an office at Bragaweg (Jalan Braga) in Bandoeng. In Medan, a new Fuchs and Rens showroom was built in front of the garage and workshops were established at Paleisweg. The new showroom with a modern look, designed by architect P. J. C van Kleeft, was opened in July 1926.[41]

The enterprise stopped during the war but resumed afterwards as a dealer for Mercedes-Benz, Chrysler, Plymouth, Packard, Renault, and the White Motor Company. Daniël Rens passed away in Amsterdam in 1948 at the age of 75. Fuchs & Rens became PT Fuchs & Rens Indonesia and flourished in the 1950s. It was later acquired by the Indonesian government, nationalised in 1957, and became P.T. Perusahaan Motor Indonesia (PT Permorin). Permorin was the car importer and dealer in Indonesia until the 2000s. Fuchs and Rens' legacy evolved from a humble horse carriage factory to being a renowned car dealer, marking a significant chapter in the history of the transportation industry in Indonesia.

25.4 Trading Companies

In the early twentieth century, Medan was a bustling hub of commerce. The Medan Chamber of Commerce (or Handelsvereeniging), established in 1912, had a substantial and highly representative membership, making it a prominent institution in the region. The following are a few examples of large Dutch companies with high mercantile stature in Medan and the East Coast of Sumatra (Fig. 25.10).

Naamlooze Vennootschap Deliveem, established in 1913, sought to replicate the success of Java's renowned Indische Veem and Batavia Veem. Deliveem was involved in stevedoring, shipping, and insurance ventures. The company set up warehouses across key locations from Belawan to Langsa with proximity to the railway, which gave it a strategic advantage.[42]

Van Nie & Co. was founded in 1885 by Jacob van Nie. Over the years, partners like W.H. van Breda Kolff, J.B. Cohen, and C.G. van Houten joined the venture. The company was managed by M. Chits (also the French Consular Agent in Medan) and thrived, adding prestigious agencies like N.I. Portland Cement Maatschappij to its portfolio. They were

[41] SP 03-08-1926.
[42] Feldwick 1917: 1187.

Fig. 25.10 Colonial businessmen in Medan: (1) J.L. Zeeuw van der Laan, Assistant Manager of Deli-Atjeh, (2) Th. C. Arensma, (3) A. Herman de Boer, (4) C.G. Van Houten, Managing Partner Van Nie & Co., (5) Emill Ott, Instructor, Deli Riding Club, (6) R.F.E. Ennema, Manager G.H. Slot & Co., (7) H. S. Haas, General Manager Deli-Atjeh (Wright 1909)

agents for major shipping lines and had a branch in Belawan that focused on shipping and tobacco exports. It even had its own football club.[43]

Handel-Maatschappij G.H. Slot & Co., originally from Penang, spread its wings in Sumatra and Java. Its business was primarily rubber, but also had a vast portfolio in trading goods and supplied shipping firms.[44]

The Deli-Atjeh Trading Company, as discussed in the previous chapter, offered a range of products from Swedish matches to Van Houten cocoa, Eau de Cologne, and cigarette papers. The company was listed in

[43] Feldwick 1917: 1192.
[44] Wright 1909: 573; Feldwick 1917: 1194.

Amsterdam, with branches in Medan, Belawan, and Bajan, established on January 2, 1905, with a capital of *f*400,000.[45]

Norwegian Thomas Konow Soeberg went to Tandjong Poera in the late 1890s and started a partnership with A. van Belkum Pieterszoon in 1896.[46] He was manager of the Güntzel and Schumacher branch and, in 1902, started his own business.[47] He was appointed the Norwegian vice consul for the East Coast of Sumatra in late 1909, but resigned eight months later.[48] He established Th. Konow Soeberg & Co. in 1910 as a general merchandise company of building materials, plantation tools, and insurance agents.[49] Konow Soeberg passed away in Christiania (Oslo), Norway, in 1917.[50] A year later, the company was incorporated as N.V. Medansche Handelsmaatschappij.

Toko van de Pol specialised in furniture, household items, luxury goods, etc. The business was founded in 1884 by G. A. van de Pol in Soerabaja. Van de Pol died in 1908, after which the company became a public limited company. The company expanded with a branch opened in Medan in 1912 at Paleisweg. This was followed by a branch in Semarang in 1916 and Batavia in 1930. It was known for its furniture designed by Dutch designers, with factories in Soerabaja, Semarang, and Medan.[51]

G.D. Langereis & Co. was a prominent company in the early development of Deli. G.D. Langereis, a construction employee of the Deli Spoorweg Mij, started his own business in 1890.[52] Three years later, he expanded with the inclusion of his brother Anton N. Langereis and W.J.G. Frohn, becoming G.D. Langereis & Co. It also had a concession for the supply of electric power in Medan, granted in 1897. The company's success grew as it completed several significant construction projects in Deli, Langkat, and neighbouring provinces, including the construction of mosques in Bindjey, Stabat, Tandjong Poera, and Laboean Deli (Al Osmani mosque), Sultan's palaces in Tandjong Poera and Tandjong Balei,

[45] Wright 1909: 573.

[46] *De Locomotief* 08-07-1896.

[47] DC 02-01-190.

[48] SP 17-08-1910.

[49] SP 05-03-1910.

[50] *De Locomotief* 11-01-1910 SP 31-07-1917.

[51] *Bataviaasch Nieuwsblad* 23-05-1939.

[52] Gerardus Diedericus Langereis (1866–1952), born in Medemblik 30-01-1866, established himself as a private architect in Bindjei on Sumatra on 01-08-1890 and retired in 1924. Wilhelmus Jacobus George Frohn (1864–1908), A.N. Langereis (1868–1937).

churches, residences, tobacco barns, hospitals, and various government buildings. They also built the Tjong A Fie office and AVROS building in 1919 in Medan. Recognising the need for timber, the company acquired a vast virgin forest area of over 3500 hectares in Langkat. It also had a coffee plantation and supplied electric installations and other infrastructure services such as water supply systems and ironworks, including bridges and buildings.[53] Langereis was also an avid writer who documented the development of Sumatra's East Coast and its diverse ethnic communities in the Indië illustrated magazine.[54]

After 36 years in Sumatra, G.D. Langereis retired in 1924 in the Netherlands. The business was split into G.D. Langereis and Co. in Medan and Langkat, and a sister company, A.N. Langereis and Co., serving Serdang and Asahan districts.[55] Its famous architects include W. Broekema, who designed the interior of the Varekamp bookshop at Kesawan.[56] The last director was Hermanus van den Heuvel, who took over the firm in the 1930s and worked in Medan till the 1950s. Van den Heuvel designed the BPM guesthouse (nowadays Bukit Kubu Hotel in Brastagi) which was completed in 1939, and the Roman Catholic church in Pematang Siantar.[57] J.W. Metz was another maestro in architecture, from public buildings to bridges, including several buildings and houses at Serdangweg.[58]

One of the most iconic buildings in Medan was the Harrisons & Crosfield office on the corner of Kesawan and the Esplanade. Founded in 1844 in Liverpool as a tea-trading partnership, Harrisons & Crosfield evolved into one of the most influential British plantation firms in Asia, with branches in Quilon, Calcutta, Colombo, Cochin, Melbourne, Batavia, Medan, Singapore, and Hong Kong.[59] Under the leadership of Arthur Lampard, the company expanded aggressively into the rubber industry during the early twentieth century. Drawing from his experience

[53] Wright 1909: 579–580.

[54] Indië; geïllustreerd weekblad voor Nederland en koloniën, 1918, nos. 1,2.

[55] *Algemeen Handelsblad* 26-07-1940. Anton Nicolaas Langereis (1868-1937) began his career with the Dutch Navy and arrived in Batavia in 1887. After joining his brother's architectural firm, he spent over 44 years in the region. Settling in Pematang Siantar in 1924, he served as a respected municipal council member (DC 16-04-1937).

[56] SP 16-11-1921; W. Broekema (1888-1956).

[57] Buiskool D.A. *Tours through historical Medan and its surroundings* 2025: 60.

[58] Feldwick 1917: 1192.

[59] Quilon is now Kollam and Cochin is now known as Kochi; both are coastal towns of India in the state of Kerala, southwestern India.

in British Malaya, Lampard recognised the potential of Sumatra's east coast for large-scale rubber cultivation. He envisioned replicating the organisational methods of the highly successful tobacco plantations. To navigate Dutch colonial restrictions on British enterprises, Lampard partnered with Victor Ris, a Swiss planter with tobacco experience and fluency in Dutch. In 1907, they bought the estate, which was managed by Ris, expanded it under rubber, and sold it to United Serdang Rubber Plantations. In 1910, Harrisons & Crosfield became one of the most visible British "agency houses" in Medan, combining plantation ownership with finance, supplies, and estate management. It provided credit, machinery, fertiliser, insurance and sales services, and helped channel East Sumatran commodities into global markets. It also founded local subsidiaries and managed 17 large plantations in East Sumatra and 5 plantations in West Java. Some of them include Bah Lias (5746 hectares), Rambong Sialang (4844 hectares), and Soengei Roembia (2920 hectares). Despite challenges during World War I, the Great Depression, and World War II, the company adapted by diversifying into timber, palm oil, and rubber-related technologies. Between 1936 and 1939, Medan became a highly profitable regional hub for Harrisons & Crosfield. The branch generated annual profits of around £100,000, with a profits-to-capital ratio of 70% in 1936, declining to 37% in 1939, still reflecting strong returns in a volatile era.[60] Other agency houses with offices in Medan providing services for rubber plantations include British Guthrie & Co. Ltd., the Anglo-Dutch Estates Agency Ltd., Dutch NHM, and Belgian Société Financière des Caoutchoucs (SOCFIN).

Giant Dutch companies also set foot in Medan, including the Big Five: N.V. Borneo Sumatra Maatschappij or Borsumij, N.V. Internationale Crediet- en Handelsvereeniging "Rotterdam" or Internatio, N.V. Jacobson van den Berg & Co, N.V. Lindeteves-Stokvis, and N.V. Geo Wehry & Co.

Lindeteves-Stokvis from Amsterdam expanded its operations, setting up bases from Java to New York. Initially, it was represented by Kerkhoff & Co. in Medan, but it set up its own office in 1914 at Kesawan and built and moved to a large showroom at Paleisweg in 1918.[61] Its vast portfolio encompassed everything from machinery and motor factories to coffee machines.[62]

[60] Brown 1994: 44:50; Kano 2008: 199–202.
[61] SP 29-12-1914.
[62] Feldwick 1917: 1185.

Borneo Sumatra Maatschappij, or Borsumij, was a Dutch trading company headquartered in The Hague. It was established in 1884 and initially traded forest products, but over time it expanded its operations to include the import of consumer goods and served as an agency for Ford motorcars. The director Luijt started a small branch in Wilhelminastraat in 1922 and in 1925 moved to Hindoestraat to a building that belonged to Hüttenbach & Co.[63]

Jacobson van den Berg was a major Dutch company founded in Den Haag in 1860, in trading, insurance services, and industry. It had offices all over the world. The Medan branch was started in 1928, and in 1937, a new building was established at Paleisweg with 68 employees.[64]

Geo Wehry dealt with general exports and imports, particularly of food and drink items, and established its office in Medan in 1927.[65] Finally, Internatio entered Medan in 1939 by taking over Kehding and Van Nie.[66]

25.5 Endnote

Medan's rise as a colonial commercial powerhouse was propelled by a dense network of banks, trading houses, and agency firms, largely controlled by European capital. Banks such as NHM and De Javasche Bank provided credit and handled international payments that sustained the expansion of tobacco, rubber, and palm oil; agency houses and trading companies organised shipping, warehousing, insurance, and global sales. These firms did not merely finance commerce; they shaped the city materially, building warehouses, offices, power systems, and transport infrastructure that still structure parts of Medan today. Yet this urban prosperity rested on extractive and racialised labour regimes, where capital accumulation was prioritised over Indigenous welfare and environmental limits. The institutions and streetscapes that remain are not neutral inheritances, but the residue of a colonial corporate order.

[63] SP 26-04-1938.

[64] SP 05-06-1937.

[65] *De Locomotief* 01-08-1927.

[66] *De Locomotief* 06-07-1939.

Summary: A Journey Through Medan

Our journey through Medan's past started with an introduction to the city's development. Medan's growth was anchored in the plantation economy—first tobacco, then rubber, and later oil palm. Fuelled by the extraordinary profits, the plantation companies built impressive offices and facilities in the city centre, and Medan became a plantation city.

From the outset, Medan and its plantations were multinational. Late nineteenth-century European industrialisation and periodic depressions pushed many to seek work overseas, and the plantation frontier drew migrants, investors, and adventurers from across Europe and Asia. The first planter to try tobacco cultivation in the region was Jacob Nienhuys. He was soon followed by the Swiss planter Albert Breker and the Polish planter Ludwig Michalsky, who founded the Polonia plantation. Medan's rise was inseparable from colonial capitalism: Nienhuys, together with financier P.W. Janssen, created the Deli Maatschappij, publicly listed on the Amsterdam Stock Exchange. Under the leadership of Jacob Cremer, the Deli Company grew into a powerful enterprise, generating substantial annual dividends for its shareholders. It became one of the most successful plantation companies in the Dutch East Indies and was a benchmark stock for colonial investors.

A significant economic and political development was the opening of the Suez Canal in 1869, along with the creation of new steam shipping lines. The new waterway accelerated colonial commerce and mobility in the European colonies in Southeast Asia, as journeys that used to take

B. Minasny, D. A. Buiskool, *Stories from Medan, Volume 1*,
https://doi.org/10.1007/978-981-95-7707-1

many months were reduced to less than a month. Exports rose spectacularly and were accompanied by infrastructure projects in East Sumatra, including roads and rail links.

The early planters were notably diverse, with one of the most influential groups being the Schweizer Verein (Swiss Association). Among its members was Swiss native Hermann Küng, who established the Saentis plantation. Cremer noted that in 1872, despite minimal administrative support, Deli saw an influx of 75 Europeans and 13 companies, along with 4000 Chinese and several hundred Javanese, Indians, and others. They managed to sell about 6400 packs of tobacco, generating roughly a million guilders. During this same period, the plantation Helvetia, named after the Latin word for Switzerland, was established. The Germans, Näher and Grob, were instrumental in founding Tandjong Morawa and Patoembah. Carl Grob amassed a fortune in Deli and built the grand villa Patumbah on Lake Zürich in Switzerland.

Late nineteenth-century China faced severe economic hardship and social unrest, with impoverished peasants, many of whom were tenant farmers, heavily dependent on landlords who extracted high rents. This exploitation and instability led to significant migration, with many Chinese travelling to Southeast Asia, including Deli, in search of better opportunities. The dark side of the plantation industry was evident from the beginning, as the recruited coolies were often mistreated. Their situation worsened with the introduction of the penal sanction, effectively turning them into slaves, as they were not permitted to leave the plantation during the three-year contract period. This led to numerous violent attacks by coolies against planters and assistants. One well-known incident involved the attack of a German assistant by five Chinese coolies who had sworn an oath of allegiance and were subsequently hanged together. In their memory, the Chinese community erected a temple known as the Five Ancestors, serving as both a monument to the violence of plantation history and a symbol of resistance against colonial exploitation.

Few realise that one of the key origins of the Royal Dutch Shell oil empire is in North Sumatra and was initiated by Aeilko Jans Zijlker, the son of a farmer from Groningen province. He started as a tobacco planter and discovered oil in Telaga Said in Langkat. He founded a company to extract and transport oil to the nearest waterway, securing the support of King Willem III. The Koninklijke Nederlandsche Maatschappij (Royal Dutch Company) was established in The Hague. Tragically, Zijlker died in 1890 in Singapore, not living to see his success. The Koninklijke Olie

Maatschappij (Royal Dutch Petroleum Company) and British Shell merged in 1907, combining oil extraction, processing, and transportation. Their subsidiary, Bataafsche Petroleum Maatschappij (BPM), eventually dominated the oil sector in the Dutch Indies until it was nationalised in 1958 and renamed Pertamina.

In the Dutch Indies, including the east coast of Sumatra, the Dutch government employed Indirect Rule by retaining sultans and traditional power structures. This strategy allowed the Dutch to control vast areas with minimal European officials by co-opting local elites to collect taxes, maintain order, and implement Dutch policies. Although these local leaders retained some authority, they were ultimately subordinated to Dutch control and were expected to follow Dutch directives, often under the supervision of Dutch residents or advisers.

However, the growth in Deli was without much support from the Dutch Indies government, especially in its early years. The early planters had to rely on their own resources to maintain order and infrastructure. Originally, Medan was concession land for a tobacco plantation owned by the Deli Company. This company set up its headquarters in Medan and began constructing facilities around the town centre, known as the Esplanade. By the 1880s, Medan had grown with the opening of the Medan–Belawan railway in 1884, and became the new residency capital in 1886. That year, Resident Kroesen established the *Negorijraad* (Municipal Fund Committee) to manage local affairs, which functioned for over 20 years before being replaced by Medan's official *Gemeenteraad* (Municipal Council) in 1909.

Following the 1903 Decentralisation Act of the Dutch Indies, the Deli District Council was established in 1906, alongside the existing *Negorijraad*. By 1906, Medan's population had reached about 15,000. In April 1909, the District Council was replaced by the *Cultuurraad* (for the East Coast plantation area) and Medan's Municipal Council. It wasn't until 1918 that the Sultan of Deli formally granted the land to the Medan municipality.

To facilitate the efficient export of agricultural products, the Deli Company established its own railway. The Dutch Indies government initially showed little interest in investing in the area. The Deli Railway Company provided telephone services. Street lighting was initiated by Langereis & Co. which obtained a concession in 1897 to supply electricity via the newly formed Electriciteits Maatschappij Medan (EMM). Lighting remained limited until the late 1910s, and gas lighting was introduced in

1920 by the Netherlands Indies Gas Company (NIGM). Even the provision of drinking water was headed by the Deli Company, which established the water company, Ajer Bersih, in 1905. The government's minimal involvement led to various issues, including inadequate policing and poor infrastructure. The city's sewerage system, planned in 1913, was delayed by the First World War and completed only in 1921.

Social life among the white population flourished in Medan, including the Witte Sociëteit. Once a month, there was *Hari Besar*, the day off, when the planters came from all over to Medan to celebrate, usually with lots of beer and spirits. Medan boasted two main hotels that became hubs of colonial leisure and sociability: the Medan Hotel (established in 1887) and the Hotel de Boer (opened in 1898). These establishments were more than luxurious accommodations; they were popular bars and restaurants where planters met to socialise and celebrate *Hari Besar*. Hotel de Boer gained international repute, welcoming foreign dignitaries and artists such as the Dutch writer Louis Couperus, author Carry van Bruggen, and noted cabaret performers Cor Ruys, Jean Louis Pisuisse, Koos, and Cesarine Speenhoff. Among its more sensational guests was the famed exotic dancer and later World War I spy, Margarethe Zelle, better known as Mata Hari. Royal visitors also graced the hotel, including Prince and Princess Schaumburg-Lippe, the latter being a niece of Queen Wilhelmina.

Religious and cultural life in Medan was equally diverse. For Europeans, both Protestant and Roman Catholic congregations were established, alongside institutions such as the Salvation Army, the Deli Masonic Lodge, and the Theosophical Society, all active in social and charitable works. The Malay and Javanese communities maintained their mosques, while the Chinese upheld their temples. Christian missionary organisations extended their efforts to the hinterlands: the Rhenish Mission Society operated in the Tapanoeli region, and the Netherlands Missionary Society worked among the Karo people.

Each ethnic population group was legally and administratively channelled into separate quarters, resulting in a division of the community into European, Chinese, Malay, and Indian quarters. Medan's economic development attracted many Chinese from the start, resulting in a lively Chinatown. This Chinatown remains largely intact today, as most Chinese shops are still located in this part of the city. However, about 1000 years earlier, Chinese adventurers had established Kota China near Laboean.

Tjong Yong Hian and Tjong A Fie were influential Chinese elites in Medan during the colonial period, amassing wealth through the control of key goods and real estate, and collaborating with Chinese entrepreneurs in ventures such as revenue farming and banking. In Medan, they left a lasting legacy, with Tjong A Fie becoming legendary due to his wealth and philanthropy. The growing Chinese community in Deli built temples to honour their gods, promoting unity and solidarity, while figures like Law Ah Yok, who was both wealthy and later impoverished, were remembered for their social contributions. To this day, Medan is renowned for its distinctive Chinese-Indonesian cuisine. The food centre around Canton Street (Jl. Surabaya) has been a long-standing node of this culture.

Another prominent ethnic group in Medan was the Indians. They contributed to Deli in roles ranging from plantation labour, milkman, and security work to trade and small business, and they left enduring cultural and culinary footprints in the city.

To communicate news in the region, Jacques Deen established the *Deli Courant*, the first Dutch-language paper in Medan. Deen was a strong supporter of the Deli tobacco industry and a conservative politician. When van den Brand published *De millioenen uit Deli*, *De Sumatra Post* contested it aggressively, followed by *Deli Courant* which responded more cautiously, defending planter interests. *De Sumatra Post* was established by a former German planter named Hallermann. From the start, there was a tense competition between the two newspapers. After the war, the two papers merged and became *Het Nieuwsblad voor Sumatra*.

As the plantation economy expanded, numerous companies were established in the region to support the industry, and capitalists gained a significant foothold in the economy. As in many capitalist cities, a few wealthy individuals controlled the economy. Other plantation crops were trialled. The first was coffee. However, since the lands were at low elevations, the Arabica coffee commonly grown on Java, which is usually cultivated at 1000 feet or higher, was not suitable. Instead, Liberica coffee was introduced. Unfortunately, the price of coffee dropped significantly in later years. The rubber boom in the early twentieth century was driven by rising demand, largely due to the growth of the automobile industry, which led to the establishment of large-scale rubber plantations in British Malaya and, around 1909, in Sumatra. This was followed by tea, oil palm and fibre. Additionally, these capitalists dominated the housing and real estate sectors. Virgin forests were cut down for timber, palm leaves were harvested to make *atap* roofs, and red clay was used for tiles and bricks.

Our book captures the development of Medan's vibrant commercial and social fabric through various influential enterprises and individuals from the late nineteenth and early twentieth centuries. In the early days of European business in Medan, several Jewish entrepreneurs, including Goldenberg & Zeitlin, Katz & Co., Hüttenbach, and Cornfield, established trading houses that imported and sold European goods. The street named Hüttenbachstraat existed until 1965, when it was renamed Jalan A. Yani VII.

Medan's Warenhuis, which opened in 1920, was heralded as the most beautiful, and possibly the largest, department store in the Netherlands Indies, reflecting Medan's image as the Paris of Sumatra through its luxurious architecture. The financial sector in Medan was anchored by the establishment of the first international bank, the British Chartered Bank, and the Nederlandse Handel Maatschappij (NHM), which facilitated payments in Straits Dollars. The Dutch Java Bank opened its doors in 1907, and the Dutch guilder was introduced as legal tender. In the same year, the first Chinese bank, Deli Bank, was established by Tjong Yong Hian and Tjong A Fie, promoting economic development in East Sumatra.

By the 1920s, the "big four" tobacco companies controlled the market in East Sumatra: Deli Maatschappij (capital *f*25.6 million), Senembah Maatschappij (*f*10.5 million), the Deli Batavia Maatschappij (*f*9.1 million), and Tabak Maatschappij Arendsburg (*f*4 million). These big four jointly bought up other smaller companies and formed the fifth largest company, the Cultuur Maatschappij De Oostkust (*f*12 million). The total tobacco industry was worth 120 million guilders or US$48 million in the 1920s.[1]

The city's economic landscape was further enriched by the presence of various trading companies and architectural firms, such as Deli Veem, van Nie & Co., and G.H. Slot & Co., alongside the Deli-Atjeh company. These companies contributed to the construction of iconic buildings throughout Medan. Additionally, prominent trading conglomerates, known as the "Big Five," including Borsumij and Internatio, cemented Medan's position as a central hub in the regional trade and economic network.

Then there were the Japanese who established themselves in Medan as merchants, hoteliers and photographers. Notably, there were more Japanese women than men in Deli, many of whom lived as housekeepers and mistresses. Following Japan's victory over Russia in 1905, which elevated Japan to the status of a world power, its imperialist ambitions

[1] Equivalent to 710 million US$ in 2020.

intensified. Japan aimed to achieve political and economic dominance over parts of China, aligning its goals with those of imperialist European nations.

While impressive as a modern city and trading hub, prosperity was unevenly shared. The colonial societal structure was demarcated along ethnic lines imposed by the Dutch, categorising individuals as "European," "Foreign Oriental," or "Native." These groupings ingrained a hierarchical social order in which the elite, predominantly European, followed by the Native nobility, enjoyed opulent lifestyles and significant privileges. In stark contrast, the vast majority of the population, especially those considered as "Native" or "Foreign Oriental," endured a social system that was racist and discriminatory. This segregation fostered profound disparities in wealth, status, and opportunity, perpetuating a cycle of inequality and marginalisation.

European planters and entrepreneurs, many celebrated in Europe for their philanthropy, built their fortunes through exploitative extraction in Deli, rarely showing concern for the people and lands from which their wealth was derived. This is in contrast to the Chinese brothers Tjong Yong Hian and Tjong A Fie, who donated generously to philanthropic projects and infrastructure in Sumatra. Few exceptions among the European entrepreneurs were P.W. Janssen, J. Nienhuys, and H.C. van den Honert of the Deli Maatschappij, who in 1899 donated 170,000 guilders to the construction of a school for the training of native physicians, known as *Dokter Djawa* in Batavia, which later became STOVIA (School tot Opleiding van Inlandsche Artsen).[2] This substantial investment, allocated through the Indies Budget of 1899, reflected not only their financial commitment to the Dutch Indies but also their vested interest in training doctors for their plantation hospitals. Ironically, through STOVIA, this initiative inadvertently helped educate a generation of Indonesian intellectuals who would go on to lead the nationalist movement.

As a metropolitan city, Medan was deeply connected to and influenced by global events. When World War I broke out, the region immediately felt its effects. The disruption of shipping routes to and from Europe further exacerbated the situation, resulting in significant food shortages. The Dutch colonial government's emphasis on producing plantation crops for European markets came at the expense of local food security. Little attention was given to cultivating staple crops, such as rice, and the high cost of

[2] *Haagsche courant* 28-04-1899.

Javanese rice made it inaccessible for local consumption. Instead, Medan relied heavily on rice imports from Siam (Thailand). This dependency on imports became a critical vulnerability during the outbreak of war, as global supply chains were severely disrupted. The potential crisis was mitigated through the Governor's intervention, which was carried out in collaboration with plantation owners to address the issue. Despite these efforts, rice cultivation remained underdeveloped.

The rubber crash occurred in the early 1920s. The crash was a result of overproduction and a subsequent collapse in rubber prices. This sharp decline in prices severely impacted the economies of Deli and the region. The crash led to widespread financial difficulties for rubber producers and contributed to economic instability in the affected regions.

The period from the 1930s was called the "low dishonest decade" by poet W.H. Auden, marked by uncertainty and conflict, shaped by the aftermath of the Wall Street Crash of 1929 and the Great Depression.[3] This period saw the discrediting of liberal capitalism, the rise of fascism, and the emergence of authoritarian regimes in Germany, Italy, and Japan. There was a lot of sympathy from the colonial society towards authoritarian fascist regimes like Germany and Italy, which coincided with Western racial superiority. However, not all colonials sided with the Nazi or the NSB, the Dutch equivalent, and there were also other voices like the Dutch intellectual Eduard DuPerron, who fiercely attacked the Dutch pro-fascist journalist Zentgraaff. Nazi Germany occupied the Netherlands in May 1940. While the Dutch homeland was under foreign control, the colonial authorities in the Dutch East Indies remained arrogant and continued to ignore the growing Indonesian nationalist movement, clinging to outdated notions of racial superiority and imperial entitlement, ignoring the imminent threat.

Simultaneously, Japan adopted an aggressive stance towards China during and after World War I, escalating in the 1930s and culminating in the Nanking Massacre in 1937. This series of actions fuelled strong anti-Japanese sentiments, particularly among the Chinese population in the region. During the same period, Japan's economy strengthened, and its international policy grew more assertive. In its pursuit of leadership in Asia, Japan

[3] Ekbladh, David. "No, the world isn't heading toward a new Cold War – it's closer to the grinding world order collapse of the 1930s." *The Conversation*. https://theconversation.com/no-the-world-isnt-heading-toward-a-new-cold-war-its-closer-to-the-grinding-world-order-collapse-of-the-1930s-234939.

waged war against other colonial powers and eyed the oil reserves in the Dutch Indies, including those in Langkat. These events ultimately led to its attack on several Southeast Asian countries, including Medan in March 1942.

As we have seen from this wide variety of stories about people and places in Medan, it appears to be a never-ending story. Every city has a story to tell. All those people—the common people, those who distinguished themselves in one way or another, and those who had lived in Medan from all backgrounds and ethnicities —are unique. If we record the history of the people who played a special role in the city, their stories will not be lost for future generations. Then, we can understand why Medan is as it is, who made it happen, and the story behind it.

We will explore more stories from Medan in Volume II, including plantation coolies, nationalist movements, social life, crimes and police, science, art, and literature.

Glossary

A	
Afdeeling [Dutch]	Division, in government, means a district or regency headed by an Assistant Resident.
AMS [Dutch]	Algemeene Middelbare School or the Dutch secondary school.
Andalas [Malay]	A local name for Sumatra island. Andalas is also a Malay newspaper published in Medan from 1912 to 1924.
Arak [Malay]	Locally brewed liquor made from palm trees.
Assistant-Resident [Dutch]	An administrative official in charge of a district (afdeeling).
Atap [Malay]	Roof, referring to a roof made out of palm leaves, in particular *nipah* palm.
AVROS [Dutch]	Algemeene Vereeniging van Rubber Ondernemers ter Oostkust van Sumatra, the General Association of Rubber Companies on East Sumatra.
B	
Bangsawan [Malay]	Meaning nobility, a form of Malay opera or theatre performed by a troupe accompanied by music and sometimes dances. The narratives are adapted from Malay, Indian, and Western stories.
Betja or Becak [Malay]	Three-wheeled, human-peddled, or sometimes motorised, cycle rickshaw. From Hokkien Be-chia (horse cart).
Borsumij [Dutch]	Borneo Sumatra Maatschappij, was a trade company established in 1884 for trading in Borneo and Sumatra, initially on forest products, and later all consumer goods.
Bouw [Dutch] or Bahoe or Bahu [Malay]	An area unit used during Dutch colonial rule, derived from an old Dutch term related to farming (bouwen = to cultivate). A bouw is equivalent to 7096.49 m^2 or 0.7 hectare.

B. Minasny, D. A. Buiskool, *Stories from Medan, Volume 1*,
https://doi.org/10.1007/978-981-95-7707-1

BPM [Dutch]	Bataafsche Petroleum Maatschappij (BPM), or Batavian Petroleum Company, a Dutch oil company established in 1907 as a subsidiary of Royal Dutch Shell.
C	
Commissaris [Dutch]	Commissioner or Member of the Supervisory Board. In Dutch companies (N.V.), a *commissaris* is a member of the Raad van Commissarissen (Supervisory Board). They supervise and advise the management board (*directie*).
Controleur [Dutch]	District officer, the lowest level of Dutch Indies civil administration with duties including police matters, taxes, cultivations, agrarian concerns, labour services, and public health.
Tjandoe or Candu [Malay]	Opium.
Tjenteng or Centeng [Malay]	A guard, or a man in charge of security, or a hired enforcer, worked in the plantation, shops, or in private houses.
Cultuurraad [Dutch]	Council of the Culture Area of East Sumatra. Established in 1909, the Council was responsible for plantation areas outside the municipality of Medan.
D	
Datoek or Datuk or Datu [Malay]	A local leader, a title used by Malay and Minangkabau people. In East Sumatra. Datuk is the leader of an area called *oerung* (in Karo) or *soekoe* (in Malay).
Deli Maatschappij [Dutch]	The Deli Company, founded in 1869 by Jacob Nienhuys and Peter Wilhelm Janssen as a tobacco culture company in Deli.
Djaksa or jaksa [Malay]	Prosecutor.
Djongos or jongos [Malay]	Referring to a male servant, particularly a low-ranking domestic worker. Derived from the Dutch word Jongen, or young man. A European family might had: A *kokki* (cook), a *baboe* or babu (maid), a *djongos* (young male to clean or run errands), a *sopir* (driver), a *toekang keboen* (gardener), and a *mandoer* (overseer of the household staff).
Doekoen or Dukun [Malay]	Traditional healer, spiritual practitioner, or shaman.
Doesoen or Dusun [Malay]	A village, in the East Coast referred to the Batak (Karo) villages.
Dokter Djawa [Malay]	Literally means Javanese doctor or Native physician.
DSM [Dutch]	Deli Spoorweg Maatschappij or Deli Railroad Company, was a private Dutch railway enterprise established in 1883 to serve the plantation economy of East Sumatra, particularly around Medan.
F	
f or fl. [Dutch]	Florijn (Florin) or Guilder, the Dutch currency, also called roepiah.

G

Gemeente Medan [Dutch]	The Municipality of Medan, established in 1909. Medan was a concession land to Deli Maatschappij, and an agreement was signed in January 1918, transferring the right to the land to the Municipality of Medan.
Gemeenteraad [Dutch]	The City Council of Medan was established in 1909, originally consisting of 15 members, with 12 Europeans or equivalents, 2 Indigenous, and 1 Foreign Oriental. In 1919, it was extended to 17, with 10 Europeans or equivalents, 5 Indigenous, and 2 Orientals.
Gouverneur-generaal van Nederlands Indië [Dutch] Or Goebernoer Djenderal [Malay]	The governor-general of the Dutch East Indies, the highest position representing the Dutch in the Dutch East Indies between 1610 and 1949.

H

Hailam or Hainan [Chinese]	People from Hainan island, south of China. They usually opened food stalls or worked as cooks, domestic servants, and hotel attendants. They brought with them the famous Hainan chicken rice.
Hailokhong or Hailufeng [Chinese]	Refers to Hai Hong and Lok Hong or Haifeng and Lufeng, two cities in the prefecture of Shanwei in Guangdong province, China. The two cities used to be part of Huizhou prefecture, where many peasants lived in poverty. They migrated to Deli as plantation workers or coolies and were preferred by the tobacco companies as they were used to farming in China.
Hakka [Chinese]	A Chinese clan originally from the North of China and migrated to the south of China. Since they were migrants, they were called *khejia* or guests. Hakka people who migrated to Indonesia were mostly from Meizhou prefecture in Guangdong province. The region has many subgroups, including Meixian as the largest group, where Tjong Yong Hian and Tjong A Fie came from. In Deli, the Hakkas were shoemakers, rattan furniture makers, tin makers, and shop owners.
Hari besar	In Malay meaning "big day," a payday of every two weeks, where all plantation workers had their day off.
Handel Maatschappij [Dutch]	Trading Company.
HBS	Hoogere Burger School or Dutch Secondary School, established by the Dutch Indies Government mostly for Dutch students.
HCK	Hollandsch Chineesche Kweekschool or Dutch-Chinese Teachers, College for HCS school teachers.
HCS	Hollandsch Chineesche School, Dutch Elementary School for the Chinese. In response to the THHK schools, the colonial Dutch government established HCS in Batavia in 1908. HCS in Medan was founded in 1914.

Hokkien or Hokkian or Fujian [Chinese]	The largest and earliest clan settled in Medan. Fujian is a province in southern China. There is a conflation of the term Hokkien people as they are diverse. Within the Fujian province, there are many clans, depending on where they come from. The main ones include: Xiamen (Amoy and Kinmen), Quanzhou (Tongan, Nan'an), Yongchun (Yongchun, Anxi), Zhangzhou or Chiangchew (Haicheng), and Longyan. The Hokkien Kongsi was established in 1904 and later became Hokkien Hwe Koan with a clubhouse at Kwanteebiostraat.
Hokchia [Chinese]	A clan originated from Fuqing, a county within Fuzhou in the Fujian province. They were usually involved in money lending businesses.
Hokchiu or Fuzhou [Chinese]	A clan from the prefecture in the north of the Fujian province, known to operate coffee shops (*kopi tiam*) in Medan. There were also people from Changle district in Fuzhou who came to Deli as coolies in tobacco plantations.
Henghua or Xinghua [Chinese]	A Chinese clan, also called Putian, as they originated from the Putian prefecture in the Fujian Province. They were known for operating bicycle shops in Deli.
Huizhou [Chinese]	Traditionally a prefecture in Guangdong, consisted of ten counties, including Haifeng and Lufeng. Huizhou is also known as E cheng, which literally means Goose City and is known as the capital of Hakka overseas Chinese. The association is called Medan Huizhou Huiguan established in 1895 by head foremen (head tandils) from tobacco plantations. It is now known as Yayasan Sosial Angsapura.
J	
Djalan or Jalan or Jl. [Malay, Indonesian]	Jl. or Jalan [Indonesian]: street.
Djawi or Jawi [Malay]	An Arabic-based script used to write the Malay language. Historically, Jawi was the primary script for Malay in Malaya and Malay kingdoms in Sumatra.
K	**K**
Kampong or Kampung [Malay]	Village. The English adopted the word *kampong* as "compound," referring to an enclosure or area surrounded by fences or walls that contains a group of buildings.
Kapala or kepala [Malay]	Head or leader, for example, *kapala toekang* is the head of workers or a contractor.
Kapitan system or Hoofden der Chinezen system [Dutch]	The Kapitan or heads of the Chinese system where the Dutch Indies government appointed Chinese officers to control the Chinese population. The first head of the Chinese in Batavia was appointed Kapitan (Kapitein). The Chinese Officers were given ranks according to military titles: Majoor (Major), Kapitein (Captain), Luitenant (Lieutenant). Below these officers were Chinese Wijkmeesters, or district wardens, who were in charge of local areas.

Kapitein [Dutch]	Or Captain of the Chinese, a middle-ranked Chinese officer. Kapitein mostly had external duties, including attending the regular meetings at the Resident's office to discuss matters regarding local government, representing the Chinese community, or sitting in the court to deal with conflicts between the Chinese and the indigenous or the Europeans.
Kedeh [Malay]	A shop selling most basic needs.
Kedeh kopi [Malay]	Coffee shop, usually operated by Chinese.
Kelontong [Malay]	Originally meaning a peddler or hawker. The word came from the sound made by a little drum carried by a Chinese peddler while the person was walking and selling his stuff. Toko Kelontong nowadays means a shop that sells basic needs.
Kenpeitai or Kempeitai [Japanese]	Military police corps, also secret police of the Japanese army. They carried out surveillance and used torture and cruelly repressive tactics to control the occupied territories.
Kerapatan [Malay]	The local court of justice for Sultan's subjects.
KMT or Kuomintang [Chinese]	The Chinese Nationalist Party, established by Dr Sun Yat-sen in 1912.
KNIL [Dutch]	Koninklijk Nederlands Indisch Leger, the Royal Dutch Indies Army which existed from 1814 to 1950.
KPM [Dutch]	Koninklijk Paketvaart-Maatschappij, The Royal Packet Navigation Company Ltd. The Dutch shipping company operating in the Netherlands Indies from 1891 to 1966. After that, it was taken by the Indonesian shipping company PELNI.
Kong Hu [Chinese]	Referring to the Cantonese people from the Guangzhou prefecture in Guangdong. The Cantonese in North Sumatra were known as gold and silversmiths, woodworkers, furniture makers, tailors, and merchants in silk fabrics. Cantonese in Medan were mostly from the Taishan region or Siyi (four counties).
Kongsi or Kongsie [Chinese]	From Hokkien. A syndicate or partnership can be in terms of a group of people or workers or forming a business or company.
Kota [Malay]	Town or city.
Krani [Malay]	Clerk
L	**L**
Landraad [Dutch]	Called *lanrat* by Indonesian, Lower or District court for indigenous and Chinese residents.
Laukeh [Chinese]	Old hand or experience worker, as opposed to sinkeh.
Leizhou [Chinese]	Referring to Luichow Peninsula, the southernmost part of Guangdong province bordering Hainan island in the south. They were recruited in a large group as coolies for tobacco plantations in Deli in the 1910s. They were sometimes grouped as Hainan. It had an association in Medan called Leizhou gongguan.
Luitenant [Dutch]	A Chinese officer who had the most contact with the Chinese community. He handled complaints and reports, any affairs were brought to these lieutenants through the district officers (*wijkmeester*). Called lui tin lan in Hokkien or leizhenlan 雷珍蘭 in Mandarin.

M	
Maatschappij or abbreviated Mij. [Dutch]	Company.
Macau [Chinese]	A term for *Kong Hu* or Cantonese, but they do not like that term, as it refers to Macau, the region which was occupied by the Portuguese known as a port of slave trading. There was Macaostraat (Jl. Garut), but the *Kong Hu* people felt the name insulting and requested it to be renamed Kongfoestraat. After a consultation, the Medan Council changed the name to Kongfoestraat in 1936.
Mandoer or Mandor or Mandur [Malay]	Overseer, in plantation it referred to an overseer of Javanese workers or coolies.
Majoor [Dutch]	Majoor der Chineezen or Chinese Major, the highest Chinese leader position. The Major was an *ex officio* member of the *Landraad* (district court). Chinese businesses often called for the assistance of the Major for matters relating to the government.
Mem [Malay]	From Madam, usually a respectful title for married women, usually of European or Indo-European background.
MULO [Dutch]	Meer Uitgebreid Lager Onderwijs or Junior High School.
N	
Nanyang [Chinese]	Meaning the South Seas. Referred broadly to Southeast Asia, including the Malay Peninsula, Indonesia, Singapore, Thailand, Vietnam, and the Philippines. Used by Chinese from southern provinces (like Fujian and Guangdong) to describe overseas migration to Southeast Asia.
Negorijraad [Dutch]	From *negorij* (settlement), the initial municipality of East Sumatra, established by the first Resident in 1886. The Negorij Council had no legal status, but it established a municipal fund that contributed greatly to the development of Medan. It was dissolved in 1909 as the Dutch Indies Government established the Municipality of Medan.
NHM [Dutch]	Nederlandsche Handel-Maatschappij N.V. or The Netherlands Trading Society, was a Dutch trading and financial company. It was established in 1824 in The Hague for trading, shipping and agriculture. In 1964, it merged with Twentsche Bank to form Algemene Bank Nederland (ABN), later joined with Amsterdam Rotterdam Bank (AMRO) and became ABN AMRO.
N.V. [Dutch]	Naamloze Vennootschap, a limited liability company.
NST [Indonesian]	Negara Sumatra Timur, an independent state established in 1947 with the head of state Tengkoe Mansoer. It was dissolved in 1950.
O	
Opas or Politieoppasser [Dutch]	An indigenous or Indian police assistant.

P

Pait or Pahit [Malay]	Meaning bitter, originally referring to bitters (aromatic alcohol) added to drinks. But most commonly referring to beer.
Pasar [Malay]	Market.
Pekong or Topekong [Chinese, Malay]	From Hokkien Pek kong, or Tua pek kong, refers to a local deity or deified local Chinese pioneers.
Peranakan [Malay]	Indonesian-born Chinese who were brought up in Malay or speak one of the indigenous dialects.
Pondok [Malay]	A shed or a roughly built hut.
PNI (Partai Nasional Indonesia) [Malay]	The Indonesian National Party was founded in 1927 by Soekarno and fellow nationalists to promote political consciousness and independence through non-cooperation with the Dutch colonial government. In 1929–1931, the Dutch authorities viewed PNI as a threat and arrested Soekarno and other leaders. The party was dissolved and later reorganised under different names (like Partindo and PNI-Baru).

R

Raad van Justitie [Dutch]	Court of Justice.
Regent [Dutch]	Highest-ranking office in the indigenous branch of Dutch Indies administration, or Bupati in Java.
Resident [Dutch]	Head of regional government.
Revenue farming or tax farming	A financial system in which the revenue of a particular product or service was leased to a party. In the Dutch Indies, the revenue farm includes opium, pawn shop, salt, liquor and other services. An auction was called and the highest bidder of the rent will be given the sole right or monopoly to sell or provide the service in a particular region.
Rp. or Roepiah [Malay]	The Indonesian currency.
Ronggeng [Malay]	A traditional social dance and musical performance associated with Javanese, and Malay traditions. It features dancing couples, often the female dancer inviting male audience to join her in interactive, playful, sometimes flirtatious manner.

S

Sado [Malay]	Horse-drawn cart with two wheels, from French *dos-a-dos*.
Schools in the Dutch Indies	Basic education started with an optional Frobel school (kindergarten) for Europeans. The next level was primary according to ethnicities: European school, Holland Chinese School and Holland Inlandse School. The next level was middle school. The Dutch school graduate can enter six years of HBS or MULO or Duitsche Cursus. An optional higher level was AMS, Algemene Middelbare School (Higher level Middle School) or Handelsschool (vocational merchants training school). For the Indigenous, the middle-level schools available were vocational training: Handelsschool (trading), Landbouwschool (agriculture), Ambachtsschool (craft and industry), Huishoudschool (household).

Siang Hwee or Zhonghua Shanghui [Chinese]	The Chinese Chamber of Commerce. The first Siang Hwee in the Dutch Indies was established in Batavia in 1907. In 1910, the Medan Chinese Chamber of Commerce (Chineesche Kamers van Koophandel) was established with the Chinese Major, Tjong Yong Hian as the president. A modern governance structure was established in 1930. Siang Hwee survived until the 1960s.
Singkeh [Chinese]	From Hokkien *sin khek* meaning new guest, or a new person or 'fresh off the boat' from China. The opposite is *Laukeh* or old guest, meaning person who had stayed for a longer period (in Deli).
Sinshe [Chinese]	From Hokkien, or mandarin xiansheng meaning Mister. Commonly referred to as a Chinese Medicine practitioner.
Soe Po Sia or Shubao she [Chinese]	Reading Club, established by Kuomintang in cities in Indonesia.
Soengei or Sungai or sei [Malay]	River.
T	
Tabeh or tabek or tabik [Malay]	Cortious greeting, excuse me, with your permission,
Tandil [Malay]	Or *kang tau* in Hokkien: Chinese workers overseer or supervisor in the Deli plantation. The word *tandil* has an Indian origin, A plantation usually had a head *tandil* (*babah tandil* or *tua kang tau* or *thai kung*), who was in charge of several tandils. Each *tandil* was in charge of a group of coolies.
Tiong Hoa Hwee Koan (THHK) [Chinese]	Meaning the Chinese Guildhall was first established in Batavia to unite the Chinese around Confucian ideology, and to finance schools for the Chinese community, funded by local merchants. In 1901, the first Chinese school was founded in Batavia. Medan never had a THHK, as each clan established their own schools.
Teochew or Chaozhou [Chinese]	A clan and a prefecture in Guangdong province. In Deli, Teochew people were known as farmers. Many were recruited as coolies in the tobacco farms in Deli. An early association was Hang Kang Kong Hwe, registered with the Dutch government in 1927. Another association is Teochew Hwe Koan.
Tengkoe or Tengku, Tunku [Malay]	An honorific title, used for members of the Malay aristocracy or royal families, equivalent to a prince. Tengkoe preceded the names of local aristocrats or rulers (e.g., Tengkoe Besar Deli = Grand Prince of Deli).
Titulair [Dutch]	Titular, in name or honorary, a title usually given as an honorary title to an officer of the Chinese as a helper of the official officer or as an honorary title of a retired officer.
Toean or Tuan [Malay]	Meaning Sir or Master, commonly used as a title of respect or deference, especially by native Indonesians when addressing European men. A plantation worker might say: *Toean besar* (the big/master lord—referring to the plantation owner), while a plantation assistant would be called *Toean kecil* (small master). A Dutch officer would be referred to as *Toean controleur*.

Toekang or Tukang [Malay]	A craftsperson or specialist who works with a specific material or performs a specific type of skilled manual labour, similar to a -smith in English. For example, *toekang roti* = breadmaker or breadseller, *toekang ajer* = a person carrying water, *toekang sajoer* = vegetable seller.
Toko [Malay]	Shop, e.g. *toko obat* = medicinal shop.
Topi [Malay]	Hat
Totok [Malay]	China-born Chinese residing in Indonesia who maintain Chinese dialect, as opposed to *peranakan*. The expression totok is also used for other ethnic groups, like totok Belanda, which means typical Dutch with all the physical characteristics, customs, and cultural habits.
Tongkang [Chinese]	From Hokkien meaning sailing vessel for about forty to fifty passengers.
Towkay or taukeh [Chinese]	From Hokkien, meaning Chinese businessman or boss.
U	
USU [Indonesian]	Universitas Sumatera Utara, the first university in Medan, established in Medan by Jajasan Universitas Sumatra Utara on June 4th, 1952.
V	**V**
Volksraad [Dutch]	People's Council, an advisory and later semi-legislative institution for the Dutch East Indies, established with Council members in 1918 in Batavia.
Vreemde Oosterlingen [Dutch]	Foreign Orientals, which include Chinese, Indians, Arabs, and other non-Indigenous.
W	**W**
Wajang or wayang [Malay]	Show or performance can be performed by people or puppet. *Wajang Tjina* is a Chinese opera, while *wajang wong* is human wayang from Javanese culture.
Wijkmeester [Dutch]	District-level Chinese warden, the lowest ranking Chinese officer in charge of the Chinese people in a local area under the Lieutenant of the Chinese.
Z	
Zaakwaarnemer [Dutch] or Pokrol [Malay]	Zaakwaarnemer means agent, caretaker, or administrator acting on behalf of another person or business. Pokrol was from *procuratiehouder* (proxy-holder), referring to a petty lawyer, legal fixer, or informal legal agent. Someone who acted on behalf of others in legal matters, often without formal legal training. Pokrols often operated in the native or lower courts, offering their services to Indigenous clients, Chinese, or Eurasians who could not afford or access formal legal representation.
Zelfbestuurders [Dutch]	Self-governing authorities, Indigenous leaders, such as sultans, rajas, or local princes, who retained nominal authority over their regions. In practice, they ruled under Dutch supervision and were often subordinate to a Dutch Resident or Controleur.

References

25 jaren decentralisatie in Nederlandsch-Indië 1905–1930. (1930). Uitgegeven door de Vereeniging voor Locale Belangen, Semarang.

Aardweg, van den H. P. (Ed.). (1938). *Persoonlijkheden in het Koninkrijk der Nederlanden in Woord en Beeld.* Nederlanders en hun werk, met een inleiding van H. Brugmans mede bevattende de biografieen van de leden van het koninklijk huis door N. Japikse. van Holkema & Warendorf n.v., Amsterdam. http://resources.huygens.knaw.nl/retroboeken/persoonlijkheden/#1:1444

Anderson, J. (1826). *Mission to the East Coast of Sumatra.* William Blackwood, Edinburgh.

Andrew, A. P. (1904, May). The End of the Mexican Dollar'. *The Quarterly Journal of Economics, 18*(3), 321–356.

Aoki, S. (2013). *Formation and Changes of Japanese Community in Medan until the 1910s under the Rule of Dutch East Indies.* オランダ領東インド(蘭印)時代のスマトラ島メダンにおける1910年代までの日本人社会の形成と変遷. Boekihu, April.

Aoki, S. (2017). *Indonesia di Mata Masyarakat Jepang di Hindia Belnda 100 Tahun yang Lalu dalam Kartu Pos Bergambar Foto.* PT Gramedia.

Behal, R. P. (2013). *Labour in the Making of a Global Economy.* De Gruyter Oldenbourg.

Berg Van den, E. J., & Neumann, J. (1907). De Batoe Kĕmang, Nabij Medan. *Bijdragen tot de Taal-, Land-en Volkenkunde van Nederlandsch-Indië, 1*(2), 89–92.

B. Minasny, D. A. Buiskool, *Stories from Medan, Volume 1*,
https://doi.org/10.1007/978-981-95-7707-1

Bevervoorde, van, K. Th. E. 1892. Een Bezoek aan de Bataksche Hoogvlakte. *Bijdragen tot de Taal-, Land- en Volkenkunde van Nederlandsch-Indië, 41*, 609–621.

Bool, H. J. (1918). *De Chineesche Immigratie naar Deli*, Koloniaal Instituut, Leiden.

Boom, M. (2005). Fotografie in de Sumatra-albums van Paul Sandel. *Bulletin van het Rijksmuseum*, Jaarg. 53, Nr. 3, pp. 243–269.

Bormann, M. (1926). *Soenda een reis door Sumatra*. W. De Haan, Utrecht.

Bouwes Bavinck, J. (1937). De huwelijksfeesten van H.K.H. prinses Juliana en Z.K.H. prins Bernhard. Gedenkboek voor de oostkust van Sumatra. Köhler, Medan.

Brand van den, J. (1902). *De millioenen uit Deli*. Höveker & Wormser, Amsterdam.

Brandt, W. (1948). *De aarde van Deli*. Van Hoeve, 's-Gravenhage.

Brau de Saint Pol Lias, X. (1884). *De France à Sumatra par Java, Singapour et Pinang: les anthropophages*. H. Oudin, libraire-éditeur.

Breman, J. (1989). *Taming the Coolie Beast: Plantation Society and the Colonial Order in Southeast Asia*. Oxford University Press.

Brink, L. (2020). Elke vakantie op ontdekkingsreis: De wonderlijke rol van Deli-planter Meissner in de ontsluiting van de Bataklanden. *Geografie, 29*(6), 34–38.

Broersma, R. (1922). De ontwikkeling van den handel in Oostkust van Sumatra. *Koloniaal Tijdschrift* II.

Broersma, R. (1919). *Oostkust van Sumatra: De ontluiking van Deli. Vol. 1*. De Javasche Boekhandel & Drukkerij.

Brown, R. A. (1994). *Capital and Entrepreneurship in South-east Asia*. Macmillan.

Bruin de, A. G (1918). *De Chineezen ter Oostkust van Sumatra*. Leiden.

Buiskool, D. A. (2019). *Prominent Chinese During The Rise of a Colonial City Medan 1890–1942*. PhD Dissertation Utrecht University, the Netherlands.

Buiskool, D. A. (1999). *De reis van Harm Kamerlingh Onnes*. Verloren, Hilversum, the Netherlands.

Buiskool, D. A. (2025). *Tours Through Historial Medan and Its Surroundings*. Medan.

Buiskool, D. A. (2005). Medan a Plantation City on the East Coast of Sumatra 1870–1942. In *Kota Lama Kota Baru, Sejarah Kota-Kota Di Indonesia Sebelum dan Setalah Kemerdekaan* (Old City, New City: The History of the Indonesian City Before and After Independence. Freek Colombijn and Others). Penerbit Ombak.

Buiskool, D. A. (2025). *Shaping Medan. The role and impact of prominent Chinese 1890–1942*. Brill, Leiden/Boston.

Cartwright, H. A. (1908). *Twentieth Century Impressions of British Malaya: Its History, People, Commerce, Industries, and Resources*. Lloyd's Greater Britain Publishing Company.

Cator, W. J. (1936). *The Economic Position of the Chinese in the Netherlands Indies*. Oxford.

Chang, J. (2013). *Empress Dowager Cixi*. Random House, New York.

Chang, Q. (1981). *Memories of a Nonya*. Eastern Universities Press, Singapore.

Claver, A. (2014). *Dutch Commerce and Chinese Merchants in Java.* Brill, Leiden/Boston.

Clemens, A. H. P., & Lindblad, J. Th. (1989). *Het belang van de Buitengewesten: Economische expansie en koloniale staatsvorming in de Buitengewesten van Nederlands Indië. 1870–1942.* Koninklijk Instituut voor de Tropen, Amsterdam.

Couperus, L. (1924). Eastward. In A. Reid (Ed.), *Witnesses to Sumatra: A Traveller's Anthology* (pp. 72–74). Oxford University Press.

Cremer, J. T. (1907, April). Per automobiel naar de Battakvlakte, met afbeeldingen. *Eigen Haard*, 16.

Cremer, J. T. (1885). Emigratie van Hindu's naar Sumatra's Oostkust. *Tijdschrift voor Nederlandsch Indië, II*, 205–231.

Cremer, J. T. (1924). *Jeugd en jongelingsjaren van Jacob Theodoor Cremer.* Leopold's Gravenhage.

Davis, W. (2024). I Will Burn Tuan's House: Tobacco, Opium, and the Villa Patumbah. *ABE Journal. Architecture beyond Europe* (24). https://doi.org/10.4000/13937

Dehne, P. (2019, June 28). How World War I Transformed Economic Warfare. *The Washington Post.*

Delft van, D. (2002). "Koude en kunst. Opkomst en ondergang van de familie Kamerlingh Onnes." *De Gids, 165*, 945–952.

Delft van, D. (2005). *Heike Kamerlingh Onnes. Een biografie. De man van het absolute nulpunt.* Uitgeverij Bert Bakker, Amsterdam.

Deli Gids. (1938). *Deli Gids.* Medan.

Deli Maatschappij. (1919). *Gedenkschrift bij gelegenheid van het Vijftigjarig Bestaan.* Amsterdam.

Deli-Data, 1863–1938. (1938). Mededeeling nr 26 van het Oostkust van Sumatra-Instituut.

Dharmowijono, W. W. (2009). *Van koelies, klontongs en kapiteins.* PhD dissertation. University of Amsterdam.

Dijk van, K. (2007). *The Netherlands Indies and The Great War 1914–1918.* KITLV Press, Leiden.

Dillon, M. (2010). *China: A Modern History.* Bloomsbury Publishing.

Djawatan Penerangan R.I. Propinsi Tapanuli - Sumatra Timur. (1950). *Perdjuangan Rakjat.*

Dootjes, F. J. J. (1950). *Oostkust van Sumatra Instituut, Kroniek 1948 en 1949.* Amsterdam.

Eastwick, R. W. E. (1893, November). Deli, in Sumatra. *Fortnightly Review, 54*, 323.

Encyclopaedie van Nederlandsch-Indië. (1917–1939). Vijfde deel, Nijhoff, Brill, Leiden.

Eong, S. E. (1974). Ringgit. *Journal of the Malaysian Branch of the Royal Asiatic Society, 47*(1), 58–65.

Feldwick, W. (1917). *Present Day Impressions of The Far East and Prominent & Progressive Chinese at Home and Abroad: The History, People, Commerce,*

Industries and Resources of China, Hongkong, Indo-China, Malaya and Netherlands India. The Globe Encyclopedia Company.
Florkowska-Frančić, H. (2009). Michalski, Ludwik. In *Historical Encyclopedia of Switzerland (HLS)*, version of 09/29/2009, translated from French. Online: https://hls-dhs-dss.ch/de/articles/028482/2009-09-29/.
Fowler, J. A. (1923). *Netherlands East Indies and British Malaya: A Commercial and Industrial Handbook*. U.S. Government Printing Office.
Franke, W. (1988). *Chinese Epigraphic Materials in Indonesia, Vol. 1. Sumatra*. South Seas Society.
Friedrich, M. (2020). The Power of Writing: The Manuscript Culture of the Toba Batak from North Sumatra. *Manuscript Cultures, 14*, 93–164.
Fusayama, T. (1993). *A Japanese Memoir of Sumatra, 1945–1946: Love and Hatred in the Liberation War*. Cornell Modern Indonesia Project, Monograph Series No. 71, 1993.
Fusayama, T. (2020). *Memoir of Takao Fusayama. A Japanese Soldier in Malaya and Sumatra*. Penerbit University Kebangsaan Malaysia.
Geerken, H. H. (2015). *A Gecko for Luck: 18 Years in Indonesia*. Books on Demand.
Gemeente Medan. (1924). *Kampoengrapport* (Samengesteld ingevolge gemeenteraadsbesluit 1922 no. 67). Varekamp, Medan.
Gemeente Medan. (1934). *Gemeente Medan 1909–1934*.
Gerretson, F. G. (1958). *History of the Royal Dutch Vol I*. Brill, Leiden.
Godley, M. R. (1975). The Late Ch'ing Courtship of the Chinese in Southeast Asia. *The Journal of Asian Studies, 34*(2), 361–385.
Godley, M. R. (1981). *The Mandarin-Capitalists from Nanyang: Overseas Chinese Enterprise in the Modernisation of China 1893–1911*. Cambridge University Press.
Gorsel, V. J. T. (2022). *Pioneers and Milestones of Indonesian Geology*. Part IV. ITB Press, Bandung.
Gorter, H. (1943). *Delianen*. Veen, Amsterdam.
Gould, W. (1961). *Americans in Deli*. Martinus Nijhoff's Gravenhage.
Graaf, de T. (2012). *Voor Handel en Maatschappij: Geschiedenis van de Nederlandsche Handel Maatschappij, 1824–1964*. Utrecht University.
Halewijn, E. A. (1876). *Geographische en ethnographische gegevens betreffende het rijk van Deli* (Oostkust van Sumatra), Leiden.
Han, S. T. (2017). Chinese Correspondence in Dutch East Indies, 1865–1949. *Wacana, 18*(2), 343–384.
Handboek van Cultuur- en Handelsondernemingen in Nederlandsch-Indië. (1940). Amsterdam, 1911, 1916, 1919.
Hannon, G. C. (1916). China. Swatow. *Supplement to Commerce Reports* No. 52a. Department of Commerce, Washington, D.C.
Heusser, C., & Mjöberg, E. M. (1920). De schelpheuvel van Boloe Tjina. *Teysmannia, 31*, 443–446.

Hongkong Daily Press Office. (1910). *The Directory & Chronicle for China, Japan, Korea, Indo-China, Straits Settlements, Malay States, Siam, Netherlands India, Borneo, the Philippines &c.*

Houben, V. (2013). The Indonesian Eurasian Community and Japan. *Internationales Asienforum, 44*(3–4), 227–237.

Itoh, T. (1914). Picture Book of the South Sea Islands (Nanyo Gunto Shashin Gacho). Nanyo Chosakai, Penang.

Jaelani, G. A. (2022). Preserving the Resources: Plantations and Mines Workers' Hygiene. *Archipel, 104*, 33–56.

Jagtiani, S. L. (2022). Foreign Armies are Functioning on Asian soil: India, Indonesian Decolonisation and the Onset of the Cold War (1945–1949). *Cold War History, 22*(3), 305–324.

Jansen, G. (1928). *Begraafplaatsrapport Gemeente Medan, 1928.* Gemeentelijk Bureau voor grondzaken. Medan.

Jansen, G. (1934). *De Andere Helft: Geloof en Gebruiken van onze Oostersche Stadgenooten.* Köhler & Co. Amsterdam.

Jansen, G. (1942). *Vreemde Oosterlingen.* Uitgever Van Hoeve's Gravenhage.

Janssen, C. W., & Bool, H. J. (1939). *Senembah Maatschappij, 1889–1939.* Senembah Maatschappij. Medan.

Jin, D. K., & Soo, and Kyoko Tanaka. (1984). Japanese Competition in the Trade of Malaya in the 1930s. *Japanese Journal of Southeast Asian Studies, 21*(4), 374–399.

Jonker, J., & Sluyterman, K. (2001). *At Home on the World Markets: Dutch International Trading Companies from the 16th Century until the Present.* McGill-Queen's University Press.

Kam, B. J. (1995). *Haas, planter en handelsman op Deli.* Uitgeversmaatschappij Geert Groote, Deventer.

Kano, H. (2008). *Indonesian Exports, Peasant Agriculture and the World Economy, 1850–2000: Economic structures in a Southeast Asian state.* NUS Press.

Kehding. (1930). *Aangeboden Door de N. V. Handelsvereeniging V. H. F. Kehding. Ter Gelegenheid Van Haar 50-Jarig Bestaan 1880–1930.* Medan October 18. Overdruk Uit Weekblad Sumatra.

Kho, A. K. (1947). *Pendjara Fasis. Atau Dari Pendjara ke Pendjara.* Toko Buku Djaman. Medan.

Khoo, S. N. (1993). *Streets of Georgetown.* Areca Books. Penang.

Kipp, R. S. (1990). *The Early Years of a Dutch Colonial Mission: the Karo field.* University of Michigan Press.

Koo, W., & Taves, I. (1975). *No Feast Lasts Forever.* Times Book Company, Hong Kong.

Kousbroek, R. (1992). *Het Oostindisch Kampsyndroom.* Meulenhoff. Amsterdam.

Kowner, R. (2011). An Obscure History. *Inside Indonesia.* https://www.insideindonesia.org/an-obscure-history

Kühr, E. (1921). Tjong A Fie. *Nederlandsch-Indië Oud & Nieuw*.

Labrousse, P. (2009). Brau de Saint-Pol Lias à Sumatra (1876–1881). Utopies coloniales et figures de l'explorateur. *Archipel, 77*(1), 83–116.

Langereis, G. D. (1917). Schetsen over Sumatra's Oostkust en het keven aldaar. *Indie* 1e Jaargang 32: 500–505; 33: 523–527.

Langereis, G. D. (1918). Sumatra's Oostkust in Beeld en Woord. *Indie* 2e Jaargang 1: 5–7; 2: 21–28.

Langereis, G. D. (1918). Sumatra's Oostkust. Schetsen over de aldaar wonende menschenrassen, hunne eigenaardigheden en gebruiken. De Chineezen. *Indie* 2e Jaargang 37: 581–586; 38: 596–602.

Langereis, G. D. (1919). Sumatra's Oostkust. Schetsen over de aldaar wonende menschenrassen, hunne eigenaardigheden en gebruiken. Klingaleezen en Bengaleezen. *Indie* 2e Jaargang 45: 709–712.

Li, S. (1984). Important businessmen, The Chang brothers. In *Huaqiao cansang lu* (pp. 183–202). Guangdong Remin Chubanshe.

Lin Renhuan. (1987). Mianlan zuizao de Huaqiao xuexiao – yi dun ben xuexiao. (The earliest overseas Chinese school in Medan—Dun Ben School). *Fujian Wenshi Ziliao (Fujian Literature and History), 16*, 146–152.

Lindeboom, L. (1993). *Oude K.P.M. – Schepen van 'Tempo Doelo' Deel 1*. Van Soeren & Co.'s Gravenhage.

Loderichs, M. A., Buiskool, D. A., et al. (1997). *Medan, beeld van een stad*. Asia Major. Purmerend.

Lohanda, M. (1996). *The Kapitan Cina of Batavia 1837–1942*. Djambatan, Jakarta.

Lorck, W. (1912). *Isles of the East: An Illustrated Guide: Australia, New Guinea, Java, Sumatra*. Royal Packet Steam Navigation Co. (K.P.M.), Amsterdam.

Louys, J. (2024). Quaternary Palaeontological and Archaeological Research in Sumatra. In J. Louys, P. C. H. Albers, & A. A. E. van der Geer (Eds.), *Quaternary Palaeontology and Archaeology of Sumatra*. ANU Press.

Lustrum-uitgave der Anti-woeker vereeniging te Medan 1936. *Lustrum-uitgave der Anti-woeker vereeniging te Medan, 17-6-1931–17-6-1936*. Varekamp. Medan.

Mani, A. (2006). Indians in North Sumatra. In K. S. Sandhu & A. Mani (Eds.), *Indian Communities in Southeast Asia*. ISEAS Publishing, Singapore.

Maurik van, J. (1897). *Indrukken van een 'Totok'*. Van Holkema & Warendorf, Amsterdam. https://www.dbnl.org/tekst/maur005indr01_01/maur005indr01_01_0020.php

McKinnon, E. E. (1984). *Kota Cina: Its Context and Meaning in the Trade of Southeast Asia in the Twelfth to Fourteenth Centuries*. PhD Thesis. Cornell University.

McKinnon, E. E. (1991). The Hoabinhian in the Wampu/Lau Biang Valley of Northeast Sumatra: An update. *Bulletin of the Indo-Pacific Prehistory Association, 10*, 132–142.

McKinnon, E. E., & Bartels, D. (2011). Rock-cut Chambers on the East Coast of Sumatra: A Translation and Review of G.L. Tichelman's Felsengänge an Sumatras Ostküste, with Additions and Amendments, Nalanda-Sriwijaya Centre Working Paper No 5, August.

Meer van der, Mohr, J.C. (1940, August). Uit Het Grijze Verleden Van Deli. *De Tropische Natuur, 29*, 125–136.

Meijer, H. (1987). *De Deli Spoorweg Maatschappij.* Walburg Pers, Zutphen.

Meyer, A. (1945). Heinrich Surbeck 1876–1945. *Sonderdruck aus den Mitteilungen der Naturforschenden Gesellschaft Schaffhausen, XX* (9), 259–263, Jahrgang, Seiten.

Milner, A. C., McKinnon, E., & Sinar, T. L. (1978). A Note on Aru and Kota Cina. *Indonesia, 26*, 1–42.

Missie Kapucijnen. (1917). *Gedenkboek van den 12 1/2-Jarigen Missiearbeid der Paters Minderbroeders-Capucijnen in Nederlandsch Oost-Indië.* Druk van C. N. Teulinos.

Mrázek, R. (2018). Sjahrir: Politics and exile in Indonesia. No. 14. Cornell University Press.

Nasution Khoo, S. (2006). *More than Merchants. A History of the German-speaking Community in Penang, 1800s–1940s.* Areca Books.

Nasution Khoo, S. (2007). *Streets of George Town, Penang.* Janus Print & Resources, Penang.

Naudin ten Cate, A. W. (1905). *Deli in Woord en Beeld.* J.H. De Bussy.

Nield, R. (2015). *China's Foreign Places: The Foreign Presence in China in the Treaty Port Era, 1840–1943.* Hong Kong University Press.

Officieele Pasarmalam en Centrale Pasar Gids. (1933). *Officieële gids ter gelegenheid van de te openen centrale pasar en pasar malam op 24 Februari tot en met 4 Maart 1933.* Deli Courant, Medan.

Overzicht van de Inlandsche en Maleisisch-Chineesche pers, 1925, 1936, no. 13

Paine, S. C. M. (2010). Japanese Puppet-State Building in Manchukuo. In *Nation Building, State Building, and Economic Development* (pp. 66–82). Routledge.

Pallavi Aiyar. (2022, September 08). *Medan: A Chequered History of Hinduism, Islam, Colonialism and Tobacco.* https://pallaviaiyar.substack.com/p/medan-a-chequered-history-of-hinduism

Passchier, C. (1993). Medan, gesticht door planters en handelslui. *Spiegel Historiael, maandblad voor geschiedenis en archeologie*, July/August, 314.

Pelzer, K. (1978). *Planters and Peasants: Colonial Policy and the Agrarian Struggle in East Sumatra 1863–1947.* Springer's Gravenhage.

Pemerintah Daerah Sumatera Utara. (1976). *Sumatera Utara Membangun.* P.T. Percetakan Offset Pertama Sakti, Medan.

Perret, D. (2009). Ethnicity and Colonization in Northeast Sumatra: Bataks and Malays. In *From Distant Tales: Archaeology and Ethnohistory in the Highlands of Sumatra* (pp. 143–168). Cambridge Scholars Publishing.

Du Perron, E. (1946). *Indies Memorandum*. De Bezige Bij, Amsterdam.

Petersen, H. T. (1948). *Tropical Adventure. Sumatra, Land of Loveliness and Stern Destiny*. J. Rolls Book Col. Ltd., London.

Poley, J. P. (2013). *Eroica The Quest for Oil in Indonesia (1850–1898)*. Springer, Dordrecht.

Poortenaar, J. (1925). Poortenaar-van Vladeracken, Geertruida. *Een kunstreis in de tropen*. Thieme, Zutphen.

Pugh, P. (1990). *Great Enterprise: A History of Harrisons & Crosfield*. Harrisons & Crosfield, London.

Rao, G. (2011). *Kai fan chui fen yao qianqiu. Yinni Zhang Rongxuan xian xian shishi yibai zhounian jinian wenji*. The Sun Moon & Star Publishers, Hong Kong.

Rapport omtrent den toestand der pasars te Medan. eerste gedeelte, 1927.

Regerings-almanak voor Nederlandsch-Indië 1894, 1899, 1927

Reid, A. (1995). *Witnesses to Sumatra: A Traveller's Anthology*. Oxford University Press.

Reid, A. (2014). *The Blood of the People Revolution and the End of Traditional Rule in Northern Sumatra*. NUS Press.

Rens, D. (1936). *1886–1936 N.V. Maatschappij tot voorzetting der zaken voorheen Fuchs en Rens*. H.J.W. Becht.

Rivai, M., Damanik, E., & Harahap, A.. (2021). Tamils Identity in Early Twentieth Century Medan. In *Proceedings of the 3rd International Conference on Innovation in Education, Science and Culture, ICIESC 2021*, 31 August 2021, Medan.

Said, M. (1976). *Sejarah Pers di Sumatera Utara, dengan masyarakat yang dicerminkannya, 1885–Maret-1942*. Penerbit Waspada, Medan.

Salomons, A. (1933). *Het Huis in de Hitte: Drie jaar Deli*. Querido, Amsterdam.

Schadee, W. H. M. (1918). *Geschiedenis van Sumatra's Oostkust, 2 delen*. Oostkust van Sumatra Instituut.

Schuh, G. (1943). *Eilanden der Goden: Java, Sumatra, Bali*. Elsevier, Amsterdam.

Schweizer, K. (2019). *Aus der Lindauer Kolonialgeschichte. Als Sumatra-Kulis nicht nur den Liindauer Hermann Näher reich mactten*. www.edition-inseltor-lindau.de

Senembah Maatschappij 1889–1914, Amsterdam 1914.

Senembah Maatschappij 1889–1939, Amsterdam 1939.

Shurtleff, W., & Aoyagi, A. (2015). *History of Soybeans and Soyfoods in the Netherlands, Belgium and Luxembourg (1647–2015): Extensively Annotated Bibliography and Sourcebook*. Soyinfo Center.

Sinar Luckman, T. (1996). *The History of Medan in the Olden Times*. Lembaga Penelitian dan Pengembangan Seni Budaya Melayu, Medan.

Singaram, P. (1985). *Puyalile Oru Thoni* (A Boat in the Storm) 2nd Edition. (in Tamil). https://www.chennailibrary.com/singaram/puyalileoruthoni/puyalileoruthoni.html

Singaram, P. (2019). *Beyond the Sea* (R. Karthigesu, Trans.). Areca Books, Penang.

Stenberg, J., & Minasny, B. (2022). Coolie Legend on the Deli Plantation: Tale, Text, and Temple of the Five Ancestors. *Bijdragen tot de taal-, land-en volkenkunde, 178*(2022), 159–191.

Stoler, A. L. (1985). *Capitalism and Confrontation in Sumatra's Plantation Belt, 1870–1979.* Yale University Press.

De Sumatra Post. (1924). De Sumatra Post 1898–1923. Varekamp & Co., Medan.

Székely, L. (1984). *Tropic Fever: The Adventures of a Planter in Sumatra.* With an introduction by Anthony Reid. Oxford University Press, Singapore (First edition 1937).

Szekely, L. (1995). De carrière van Chaw A. Hjong. *Indische Letteren, 10*, 207. https://www.dbnl.org/tekst/_ind004199501_01/_ind004199501_01_0026.php

Székely Lulofs, M. (1932). *Rubber* Querido, Amsterdam.

Székely Lulofs, M. (1946). *De Andere Wereld.* Elsevier, Amsterdam.

Termorshuizen, G. (2011). *Realisten en reactionairen. Een geschiedenis van de Indisch-Nederlandse pers 1905–1942. Met medewerking van Anneke Scholte.* Nijgh & Van Ditmar/Amsterdam. KITLV Uitgeverij Leiden.

Tets van, G. F. (1920). *Indische Reisindrukken* de Haan, Zeist.

The Singapore and Straits Directory. (1918). *The Singapore and Straits Directory.* 39th Annual Publication. Singapore, Fraser & Neave, Limited.

The Stock Exchange Year-book. (1916). *The Stock Exchange Year-book.* Skinner, Thomas UK.

Thee, K.-w. (1977). *Plantation Agriculture and Export Growth: An Economic History of East Sumatra, 1863–1942.* National Institute of Economic and Social Research (LEKNAS-LIPI).

Tsai, Y.-l., & Kammen, D. (2012). Anti-communist Violence and the Ethnic Chinese in Medan, North Sumatra. In D. Kammen & K. McGregor (Eds.), *The Contours of Mass Violence in Indonesia, 1965–68.* National University of Singapore.

United States Bureau of Foreign Commerce. (1899). *Highways of Commerce: The Ocean Lines, Railways, Canals, and Other Trade Routes of Foreign Countries.* Washington D.C.

United States Office of Strategic Services. (1945). *Programs of Japan in Sumatra.* Research and Analysis Branch. Washington D.C.

Vandenbosch, A. (1930). A problem in Java: the Chinese in the Dutch East Indies. *Pacific Affairs, 3*(11), 1001–1017.

Vandenbosch, A. (1935). Where the Dutch Fear Japan. *Current History, 41*(4), 424–428.

Vandenbosch, A. (1940). Netherlands India and Japan. *Pacific Affairs, 13*(3), 253–262.

Veersema, H. (1939). *Gids voor de Oostkust van Sumatra (Deli)*. C.V. Kohler & Co.

Verslag Betreffende de Gemeente Medan Over het Jaar 1921.

Verslag Betreffende de Gemeente Medan Over het Jaar 1923.

Vleming, J. (1925). *Het Chineesche Zakenleven in Nederlandsch Indië.* Landsdrukkerij, Weltevreden.

Volker, T. (1928). *Van Oerbosch tot Cultuurgebied: Een schets van de beteekenis van de tabak, de andere cultures en de industrie ter Oostkust van Sumatra*. Uitgave van de Deli Planters Vereeniging, Medan.

Waard de, J. (1934, July 15). De Oostkust van Sumatra. *Tijdschrift voor economische geographie*, 221.

War Trade Board of the USA. (1917). *Trading with the Enemy: Enemy Trading List.* U.S. Government Printing Office.

Warnk, H. (2011). From romanticism to colonial pragmatics: Malay language and literature studies in Germany 1800–1945. *Journal of the Malaysian Branch of the Royal Asiatic Society, 84*(2), 67–94.

Warnk, H. (2012). Büffel, Bier und Kuckucksuhren - Die Wormser Brüder Hüttenbach in Südostasien. *Der Wormsgau, 30*, 181–198.

Warnk, H. (2015). Coolie Talk: Malaiisch-Lehrbücher für europäische Plantagenpflanzer in Niederländisch-Indien 1880–1940. In *Koloniallinguistik* (pp. 91–106). De Gruyter, Berlin.

Warren, J. F. (2003). *Rickshaw Coolie: A People's History of Singapore, 1880–1940.* NUS Press.

Westenenk, L. C. (1922). De Chetti. *Koloniale Studiën, 6*, 1–17.

Wiselius, J. A. B. (1884). De emigratie van Britsch -Indische koeli's naar Overzeesche gewesten. In verband met eene eventuëele emigratie van Hindu's naar Oost – Sumatra. IV. De eventueele emigratie naar Oost-Sumatra. *Tijdschrift voor Nederlandsch Indië, 1884*, 356–370.

Wit, A. (1914). *De. Natuur en menschen in Indië*. Nederlandsche Bibliotheek.

Wright, A. (Ed.). (1908). *Twentieth Century Impressions of Hongkong, Shanghai, and Other Treaty Ports of China: Their History, People, Commerce, Industries, and Resources* (Vol. 1). Lloyds Greater Britain Publishing Company.

Wright, A., & Cartwright, H. A. (Eds.). (1908). *Twentieth Century Impressions of British Malaya: Its History, People, Commerce, Industries and Resources.* Lloyd's Greater Britain Publishing Company.

Wright, A., & Cartwright, H. A. (Eds.). (1909). *Twentieth Century Impressions of Netherlands India: Its History, People, Commerce, Industries and Resources.* Lloyd's Greater Britain Publishing Company.

Xiao, W., & Ganzhong, R. (Eds.). (2021). *Haijiao Feihong: Wanqing Qiaoling Zhang Rongxuan Zoudu Shuxin Ji* (Collected Memorials and Letters of Zhang

Rongxuan, An Overseas Chinese Leader in the late Qing). The Great China Cultural Publishers.

Yau, C.-o. (2021). The Dao in the Southern Seas: The diffusion of the Lüzu cult from Meizhou to Bangkok. In *Daoism in Modern China* (pp. 120–158). Routledge.

Yen, C.-H. (1984). Chang Yu-Nan and the Chaochow Railway (1904–1908): A Case Study of Overseas Chinese Involvement in China's Modern Enterprise. *Modern Asian Studies, 18*(1), 119–135.

Yizhibi. (2015). Mianlan Liu Yayu qu lishi yange yi zhibi. In *Seratus Tahun Pancaroba Etnis Tionghoa Medan* (pp. 106–109). Assosiasi Sejarah Etnis Tionghoa.

Yizhibi. (2015). Mianlan Sujialamei qu de kuoda he fazhan. In *Seratus Tahun Pancaroba Etnis Tionghoa Medan* (pp. 99–101). Assosiasi Sejarah Etnis Tionghoa.

Zangger, A. (2011). *Koloniale Schweize.* Transcript Verslag.

Zangger, A., et al. (2020). *Ferne Welten – fremde Schätze.* Museum Heiden.

Newspapers and Periodicals

Dutch Newspapers and Peridicals

Deli Courant (DC), De Sumatra Post (SP), Het Nieuwsblad voor Sumatra (HnVS).

Algemeen Handelsblad voor Nederlandsch-Indië, Bataviaasch Nieuwsblad, Bataviaasch Handelsblad, De Groene Amsterdammer, De Indische Courant, De Indische Gids, De Indische Mercuur, De Java-Post, Java-bode: nieuws, handels- en advertentieblad voor Nederlandsch-Indie, De Locomotief, Het Nieuws van den dag voor Nederlandsch-Indië, De Preangerbode, Soematra Courant, Sumatra, Soerabaijasch Handelsblad, Indisch tijdschrift van het recht; orgaan der Nederlandsch-Indische Juristen-Vereeniging, Indische Letteren.

De Avondpost, Dagblad van Zuidholland en 's Gravenhage, Haagsche courant,

Leeuwarder courant: hoofdblad van Friesland, Nieuwe Courant, Nieuwsblad van het Zuiden, NRC Handelsblad, Het Nationale Dagblad: voor het Nederlandsche Volk, Het Nieuwsblad voor den Boekhandel, Nieuwe Haarlemsche Courant, Nederlandsche Staatscourant, Opregte Haarlemsche Courant, Rotterdamsch Nieuwsblad, De Telegraaf, Trouw, Utrechtsche courant, Het vaderland, De Volkskrant, Zutphensche courant.

Amigoe di Curacao, Eigen Haard, Het Koloniaal Weekblad, Internationaal, Staatsblad van Nederlandsch Indië 1884–1888, Nieuwsblad voor den bookhandel, Nieuw Israëlietisch Weekblad, Weekblad voor privaatrecht, notaris-ambt en registratie

Austrian Newspaper

Neues Wiener Tagblatt

German Newspaper

Frankfurter Zeitung

Swiss Newspaper

Neue Zürcher Zeitung
Zuger Volksblatt

English Newspapers and Periodicals

Malaya Tribune, Morning Tribune, Pinang Gazette and Straits Chronicle, The Singapore Free Press and Mercantile Advertiser, Straits Times Overland Journal, The Straits Echo, The Straits Mail, The Straits Times, Straits Times Weekly, Sunday Tribune

Syonan Shimbun

The Selangor Journal

The China Critic, The Hong Kong Daily Press Office, South China Morning Post (SCMP)

The Far Eastern Review, The China Critic, Investors Chronicle and Money Market Review

The Age, Border Morning Mail, The Brisbane Courier, The Courier Mail, The Daily Telegraph (Sydney), Kalgoorlie Miner, Newcastle Morning Herald and Miners' Advocate, The Sun

The Tennessean, The War Cry, Fortnightly Review, Inside Indonesia, Investors Chronicle and Money Market Review

Chinese Periodical

Su Hwa Trade Journal

Malay and Indonesian Newspapers

Andalas, Han Po, Pertja Timoer, Sinar Deli, Sin Po, Tjin Po, Kita Sumatora Sinbun
Kompas, Harian Indonesia

Websites

http://disbudpar.sumutprov.go.id/objek_wisata/museum-situs-kota-cina/
https://de.wikipedia.org/wiki/Karl_F%C3%BCrchtegott_Grob
https://de.wikipedia.org/wiki/Ludwig_Michalski
https://en.wikipedia.org/wiki/Guan_Yu
https://en.wikipedia.org/wiki/History_of_the_Indonesian_rupiah
https://en.wikipedia.org/wiki/July_1941
https://en.wikipedia.org/wiki/Hirohara_Shrine
https://en.wikipedia.org/wiki/Maidan
https://en.wikipedia.org/wiki/Nuruddin_ar-Raniri
https://en.wikipedia.org/wiki/Sri_Mariamman_Temple,_Medan
https://fr.wikipedia.org/wiki/Xavier_Brau_de_Saint_Pol_Lias
https://id.wikipedia.org/wiki/Gereja_Santo_Antonius_dari_Padua_Medan
https://fk.usu.ac.id/index.php/id/profil/sejarah
https://fh.usu.ac.id/index.php/id/front/1-sejarah
https://kknews.cc/history/e8m484n.html
https://plants.jstor.org/stable/10.5555/al.ap.person.bm000325489
https://politicalgraveyard.com/geo/ZZ/ID-consuls.html
https://skd-online-collection.skd.museum/Home/Index?page=1&pId=12831079
https://www.annedeguigne.fr/fr/evenements/2015-centenaire-de-la-mort-du-capitaine-de-guigne/171-notice-biographique-jacques-de-guigne-1883-1915.html
https://www.bavarikon.de/object/bav:HKO-NDB-00000000SFZ32501
https://www.e-auw.com.hk/entrepreneurial/a-tribute-to-my-father.html
https://www.groene.nl/artikel/what-motivates-geert-wilders
https://www.joodsamsterdam.nl/jacques-deen/
https://www.nobelprize.org/prizes/physics/1913/onnes/biographical/
https://www.thepaper.cn/newsDetail_forward_9477671
https://www.tiktok.com/@lauahyok
https://ektinteractive.com/history-of-oil/
https://flyingundertheradar.blog/2024/09/18/33-chinese-new-year-and-the-house-of-orange-dutch-east-indies-jan-31-feb-2-1938/
https://niadilova.wordpress.com/
http://plantagegeld.nl/
https://jaybeesnotebook.blogspot.com/2012/06/tagore-at-medan-poetphilosopher.html
https://blog.nationalmuseum.ch/2017/05/ein-appenzeller-in-der-fremde/
https://shakunkimatrai.com/chapter-12/
https://www.swiss-spectator.ch/nederlands-de-sumatra-zwitsers/
https://theindoproject.org/a-festive-massacre/
https://www.chennailibrary.com/singaram/puyalileoruthoni/puyalileoruthoni.html

Index[1]

[1] Note: Page numbers followed by 'n' refer to notes.

B. Minasny, D. A. Buiskool, *Stories from Medan, Volume 1*, https://doi.org/10.1007/978-981-95-7707-1

Kolibri 360 GmbH
Ferdinand-Jühlke-Straße 7
99095 Erfurt, Deutschland
produktsicherheit@kolibri360.de